BUSINESS
COMMUNICATIONS

BUSINESS
COMMUNICATIONS

Michael E. Adelstein
Professor of English
University of Kentucky

W. Keats Sparrow
Special Assistant to the Vice Chancellor
of Academic Affairs
East Carolina University

Business Books from
HBJ MEDIA SYSTEMS CORPORATION
A Subsidiary of Harcourt Brace Jovanovich, Inc.

Requests for permission to make copies of any part of the work
should be mailed to: Permissions, Harcourt Brace Jovanovich,
Publishers, 757 Third Avenue, New York, NY 10017.

ISBN: 0-15-505612-3

Library of Congress Catalog Card Number: 82-83693

Printed in the United States of America

05-05612 / 10 9 8 7 6 5 4 3 2 1

to Jay and Janet and to Elizabeth

Contents

PART III COMMUNICATING AND EMPLOYMENT

PART IV COMMUNICATING BY MEMOS AND REPORTS

PART V   ORAL COMMUNICATIONS

APPENDIXES

Preface

Everywhere—in business, industry, government, and the professions—the complaint is the same: many employees cannot communicate effectively, either in writing or in speaking. *Business Communications* is specifically designed to deal with this problem. Consequently, we have introduced several features that our readers—post-secondary students and professionals—can profit from and enjoy.

The approach of *Business Communications* is distinct from other books in its field. Instead of assuming that our readers already write and speak proficiently and need only a cursory review of communication skills, we explain and demonstrate how to improve their skills. Our chapters are organized to focus on the *craft* of writing and speaking. We begin by analyzing the *strategy* of a particular communication situation and then point out the *techniques* useful in applying this strategy. The result is a text that treats business communication as an integrated process. This process enables readers to improve their writing and speaking skills.

Business Communications also teaches students exactly what they need to know to function in a business setting. To achieve this objective, we surveyed nearly 600 business communications instructors throughout the United States. We have also drawn upon our own years of experience as professors, consultants, writers, editors, and administrators. The result is a book that deals with the many stylistic changes in business communications and focuses on what is current and sensible. Our examples and exercises have been taken from life, dealing with familiar college and business situations that both undergraduates and professionals will understand and find challenging and relevant. Throughout, the book serves as a practical guide that emphasizes *what works*.

Part I begins with a general introduction showing the value of learning effective business communications and the importance of understanding the communication process. In discussing communication theory, we minimize technology, emphasize application, and point out the crucial need for audience analysis. Communicating by letters is the subject of Part II. Here, readers learn what factors are important and relevant to specific types of communications. For instance, we stress the need to build goodwill in information letters, to select lively verbs in persuasive letters, and to emphasize key points in a series of collection letters.

Part III gives specific advice on selecting and searching for a job and participating in information and career interviews. In addition, all types of employment communications—the résumé, application letter, and post-interview letters—are covered.

Part IV discusses and documents the formats and methods for writing memos and short and long reports. And in Oral Communications, Part V, we cover ways to make presentations, and plan and conduct meetings and interviews. Of added interest is the subject of listening, an important skill in developing good communications.

The extensive appendixes highlighted in *Business Communications* provide useful reference information. Among them are:

- a glossary of business terminology
- common abbreviations used in addresses
- word processing procedures
- a section on grammar, mechanics, punctuation, and style
- preparation of visual aids

These materials should be helpful in class and at the office. Our readers would be well advised to keep the book for future use at home or at work as a handy reference tool.

Business Communications has also been designed for instruction. Each chapter opens with learning objectives and closes with numerous discussion questions, in-class exercises, and writing assignments. Unlike texts that take many weeks to introduce business communications, the book enables instructors to have their students writing actual communications shortly after the course begins.

In addition, the *Instructor's Manual* includes ample teaching resources ranging from course outlines and guides for teaching each chapter and its exercises to test questions and professional development suggestions. And the optional student *Study Guide* provides a convenient self-study approach for each of the twelve chapters.

So many people have contributed to *Business Communications* that acknowledging them individually would be difficult. Among those who have contributed most significantly are Drema Howard of the University of Kentucky, Paula Lewis Ludlow of Communispond, Inc., Elizabeth Sparrow and Bertie E. Fearing of East Carolina University, John S. Patterson of James Sprunt Technical College, Kaye White Gladson of Pitt Community College, and Lee Roger Taylor of Western Wyoming College. Their guidance has been invaluable. In addition, Gwendolyn Watson of the University of North Carolina at Greensboro, Vanessa Dean Arnold of the University of Mississippi, Mary Ellen Campbell of the University of Montana, and Marie Flatley of San Diego State University have read the manuscript carefully and have made numerous helpful suggestions. To these colleagues, to the people of Harcourt Brace Jovanovich, Inc., who have worked devotedly with us on this project, and to the many others who have helped us, we give hearty thanks.

Michael E. Adelstein
Lexington, Kentucky

W. Keats Sparrow
Greenville, North Carolina

Part I
COMMUNICATING IN BUSINESS

# The Nature of Business Communications

OBJECTIVES

After reading this chapter, you should be able to:

- Explain the importance of communicating effectively in business
- State why business communication should be learned in college
- Discredit five commonly accepted myths about writing
- List ten objectives of this course
- Describe the five-step writing process
- Identify four distinctive characteristics of business writing

PLAN

Communicate or perish.

BELL TELEPHONE MAGAZINE

The Importance of Business Communications

College Business Major: "Don't see why I have to take this course!"
Recent College Graduate: "I should have worked harder in that business writing course. I never thought it'd be so important."
Older College Graduate: "If it wasn't for my writing and speaking, I'd be someone important in the company by now. I'm going to make sure that my son and daughter learn to communicate well at college."

Why the different attitudes? Many students believe that only their technical courses will be valuable in getting jobs, promotions, and high salaries. But people in the business world know that writing and speaking effectively are equally important. This point was demonstrated some years ago by a study of two thousand executives from all levels of management, different industries, and various regions of the country, who selected the ability to communicate as the most significant factor influencing promotion (see table 1–1).

More recent emphasis on the importance of communication skills is provided by a 1979 *Fortune* survey of recruiters who hire the leading MBAs from the most prestigious universities in the country. These representatives express one wish: that business students would learn how to write and speak more effectively.[1]

Business Communications Defined

Communicating effectively is important not only in business, but also in education, health, government, and the professions. So the term *business communications* may be misleading, since it applies not only to people involved in buying and selling products and services, but also to those working in schools, universities, social agencies, hospitals, the armed services, and state and federal government.

Men and women in these organizations are engaged in business communications when they deal with such practical matters as job descriptions, employee benefits, conferences, recommendations, proposals, announcements, and requisitions. These writing responsibilities take specific forms. Some examples are the annual report of the Heart Fund, a notice to parents from the PTA, a solicitation to citizens from the Rape Crisis Center, a memo to nurses from the hospital director, a progress report about campus construction from the business administrator to university trustees, a panel discussion about community services for senior citizens, or a monthly

TABLE 1-1. Economic Development Value Cluster. Qualities Important for Promotion

Items	Consensus Rating*	*Percent Who Gave Consensus Rating*		
		Ideally	Actually In Own Organization	Actually In Business Generally
Ability to communicate	+	98.7%	91.4%	94.7%
Making sound decisions	+	98.4	90.9	93.1
Responsibility, conscientiousness	+	98.0	91.9	91.2
Getting things done with and through people	+	97.9	87.9	91.5
Ambition, drive	+	97.4	91.0	93.5
Capacity for hard work	+	97.3	90.0	91.2
Maturity, mental and emotional	+	97.3	89.9	89.5
Potential for growth	+	96.9	88.0	87.7
Self-confidence	+	96.8	91.6	92.3
Flexibility, resilience	+	96.0	85.4	83.1
College education	+	94.4	82.5	93.4
Good appearance	+	92.1	85.4	92.3
Seeing work as part of firm's objectives	+	92.2	81.7	79.6
Idea man, innovator	+	90.2	72.7	72.7
Courage in risk-taking	+	89.6	63.8	60.5
Technical skills based on experience	+	88.9	84.6	86.4
Graduate work in business administration	+	80.0	50.0	75.0
Superaggressiveness	−	75.3	61.4	47.9
Good bluffer	−	74.8	58.5	49.6
Economic development cluster scores		92.2%	81.0%	82.3%

* Rating given by largest number of respondents under "Ideally": + = "helpful," 0 = "irrelevant," − = "harmful."

SOURCE: Reprinted by permission of the *Harvard Business Review.* An exhibit from "What Helps or Harms Promotability" by Garda W. Bowman (January/February 1964). Copyright © 1964 by the President and Fellows of Harvard College; all rights reserved.

recruiting report from a regional office to the Pentagon.

As you can see, many people in profit and nonprofit organizations are engaged in business communications. They are involved in planning, organizing, supervising, coordinating, instructing, informing, and selling. Each of these activities may require some technical skill or knowledge, such as an accountant's being able to explain the advantage of setting up a trust. But each depends on the effective communication of ideas from one person to another.

As a result, most of the working day (and sometimes the night) is devoted to business speaking and writing. According to Donna Stine and Donald Skarzenski, in their study of about 100 businesses with 100 or more employees, about 76 percent of the working day is involved in business communication.[2] No wonder employees want to improve their speaking and writing skills!

A School-Learned Skill

But it's probably too late for these college graduates to increase their competence significantly. Although some large companies do sponsor short in-house communication training courses, most count on their employees' having learned how to write and speak effectively in college. Except for employer-sponsored courses, there will be few opportunities for you to improve your communication skills after college. Why? There will be no one to teach you, no one to supervise your work and correct your errors, no one to point out your strengths and weaknesses. As Peter Drucker, author of numerous books on management, has pointed out, "Schools teach the one thing that is perhaps most valuable for the future employee to know. But very few students bother to learn it. This one basic skill is the ability to organize and express ideas in writing and speaking."[3]

Business Communication Objectives

So here's a golden opportunity for you to prepare for your career. In this course you will learn to:

- realize the importance of effective communication practices
- understand the communication process
- write effective business letters, memos, and reports
- analyze and evaluate logically the writing and speaking of others
- improve business problem-solving skills
- learn about many office procedures, techniques, and forms
- conduct a job search thoroughly, handle interviews confidently, and write application letters and résumés effectively
- gain confidence in writing and speaking
- speak more skillfully to individuals, small groups, and large audiences
- run small group meetings more efficiently

If you master these objectives, you will stand out in comparison to most entry-level employees, who are generally deficient in communication skills.[4] Thus, you should do well in your career. In some instances, of course, your communication skills may

Figure 1–1.   Good Writing Pays Off—for Someone Else.

"Hey, congrats! That speech you wrote for J.P. was so good he
got a bonus for it."

help others, as figure 1–1 indicates. But in the long run, they will help you significantly in *your* work.

A Personal and Social Asset

Also, you will profit in other ways. As a responsible, college-educated adult, you will play many roles in your community. In all of these, the ability to speak and write effectively will serve you well. As a resident of a community, you may work with a charity, join a civic organization, or participate in a neighborhood homeowners' association. As a member of a political party, you may become active in local, state, or national campaigns. As a parent, you may become involved in PTA, scouting, and Little League work. And as a social person, you may join a golf, tennis, bridge, bowling, or dance group. All these organizations usually elect officers, write newsletters, hold meetings, raise money, and engage in correspondence. The role you play in these groups and the success you attain will depend greatly upon your ability to inform and influence people in writing and speaking.

WRITING

Although communicating effectively involves both speaking and writing well, in this textbook we are mainly concerned with writing. Mastering the ability to speak well is also important, as we will discuss in chapters 11 and 12, but the ability to write well is more complex to learn and more difficult to perfect. We all talk more than we write; so we are more experienced and usually more proficient at speaking. We employ gestures, facial expressions, and vocal inflections to convey our spoken messages, so most of us communicate easily when speaking. And we receive immediate feedback from our listeners, so we can clarify or modify our spoken statements to make them clearer or more persuasive. For these reasons, most of us would rather talk than write.

The Significance of Writing

Nevertheless, business today is requiring more and more written communication.[5] Transactions of any importance must be reported on paper. Even oral agreements made in person or by phone are usually confirmed in writing to avoid misunderstandings. The spoken word vanishes in air unless recorded, but the written word stands as a permanent record of precisely what was communicated on a specific date. In business, industry, government, and the professions, the paperwork today is overwhelming; everything of significance must be written. And the increased use of information-processing technology makes good writing more important than ever.[6]

Student Writing Must Improve

Another reason for focusing on written communication is that not only do most students lack confidence in their writing ability, but most supervisors, managers, administrators, and executives blame the colleges for failing to teach students to write well.

We hear this complaint everywhere. Sometimes, at social gatherings or other meetings, we admit to teaching business communication. Then comes the deluge:

"Why can't accounting graduates write well? We teach them the accounting procedures, but we can't do anything about their writing," says the head of a local firm.

The personnel manager of a large corporation states, "We'd give almost anything for an economist who can write clearly and competently."

A department store executive comments, "The college graduates selected for our training programs write so poorly that we have to let many of them go."

"So you teach business communication!" exclaims a leading businessman. "Well, how about showing those MBAs how to write readable letters, memos, and reports? Can't something be done?"

Yes, something can be done. But first, many students should change their attitudes about five myths.

FIVE MYTHS ABOUT WRITING

Of course, not all students believe in the following five myths about writing. And, naturally, writing problems stem from other sources. But a change in attitude about these myths can change a student's writing performance for the better.

Myth #1: Writing Is Unnecessary at Work

Successful managers are usually portrayed as active people, pacing their thick carpets, pounding their massive desks, shouting orders at their employees, dashing frantically for planes, phoning from luxurious cars, and signing multi-million-dollar contracts. Neither television nor the movies show these leaders opening their attaché cases at home or in their offices, sitting down to write, struggling over an opening sentence or paragraph, and working for hours on a memo, report, or proposal. The media also fail to show the time and energy devoted daily to writing.

A recent survey of 120 Iowa businesses with more than 100 employees revealed that, on the average, workers spend 28 percent of their time on the job in written communication.[7] This result does not surprise us, because we are always meeting graduates who ask, "Why didn't someone tell us we'd be doing so much writing at work? If we'd only known, we'd have worked much harder in our writing courses and taken more of them."

Myth #2: Writing Is Easy

Writing seems simple. It should be easy to transfer ideas into words on a page. After all, thousands of people do this every day in letters, newspapers, magazines, and books. But as we try to select words and phrases, and struggle to arrange them into sentences and paragraphs, being careful at the same time to follow the appropriate writing conventions (spelling, punctuation, grammar, and so on), we perceive how difficult it is to convey an idea clearly and effectively in writing. The reason is simple: writing involves planning, organizing, selecting, analyzing, and evaluating—all aspects of the most complex human endeavor, thinking. Consequently, to write well is no easy matter; it requires hard work.

College students are willing to work hard to achieve other objectives. They devote hundreds, if not thousands, of tedious hours to improving their skills at sports like basketball, golf, or tennis, or at other activities like piano playing, guitar playing, or arts and crafts. But students often fail to realize that learning to write well involves an even greater commitment of time and energy because of its complexity. Interestingly, the learning process is similar, consisting of instruction, practice, and supervision. Instruction is provided by teachers and textbooks such as this one. Practice may be self-motivated or school-imposed. But it is crucial. Here is what Al Hampel, a top executive of Benton and Bowles, whose advertising business grosses about a half-billion dollars a year, tells his copywriters:

> You learn to write by writing. You write dozens, even hundreds, of headlines for each ad. You write, rewrite, and again, rewrite the body copy. . . . Hard work? That's the point. If you lack the self-discipline to push yourself, forget advertising.[8]

And, we might add, without this self-discipline, you can forget about learning to write effectively.

In addition to instruction and practice, there is a third learning component—supervision. This is provided by teachers, who, like athletic coaches, point out weaknesses and show how to correct them.

For most people, writing is not fun. It demands the same kind of commitment, concentration, and painstaking precision needed to cost out a product, design a computer program, or develop a production schedule. But like success with these tasks, good writing brings a glow of satisfaction and a joy of accomplishment.

Myth #3: Writing Requires Special Talent

Many students believe that writers are born, not made. Perhaps so. Perhaps only a few people have the imagination, sensitivity, insight, and aptitude to become fine essayists, poets, dramatists, or novelists. But nearly any high school graduate can learn to express ideas clearly and convincingly.

Attaining this skill may come harder to some than to others, just as some people take longer than others in learning how to drive a car. Naturally, writing demands more intellectual ability than driving. But, with determination, competent instruction, frequent practice, and proper supervision, college students can become proficient in writing.

The beauty and grace of literary prose may indeed be beyond the grasp of many people, but the clarity and accuracy of practical business prose is within their reach. Yet many students give up, believing they need special talent. What they really need is the commitment to learning how to write well.

Myth #4: Writing Requires Inspiration

Many students contend they have to be inspired to write well. John Kenneth Galbraith, economist, statesman, and author, calls this belief "a total illusion." He explains:

> . . . the danger in the illusion is that you will wait for those moments [of inspiration]. Such is the horror of having to face the typewriter that you will spend all your time waiting. I am persuaded that most writers, like most shoemakers, are about as good one day as the next . . . hangovers apart.[9]

Inspiration for writing, if it ever comes, will probably come less frequently at work than at school. Usually teachers assign several topics, hoping to provide their students with at least one interesting subject. But at work, people have no choice, sometimes even having to write about subjects they may know and care little about. Moreover, the writing often must be done under pressure of time—asked for today, wanted yesterday. In fact, one study reported that people in business write under pressure in 43 percent of the situations.[10] Under such conditions, few can dally, so you'd be wise to trust in perspiration, not inspiration.

Myth #5: Writing Consists Only of the Act of Writing

Because they fail to view writing as a process involving several stages, many students write poorly. They merely sit at a desk or flop on a bed, laboriously apply pen, pencil, or typewriter to blank paper, struggle through to the end, copy the finished product neatly, and submit it. Good writing requires much more.

For anything other than brief, simple business communications, you should follow this five-step process, varying our suggested time percentages according to the deadline, subject, audience, and situation:

1. Exploring—20%
2. Planning—10%
3. Writing—30%
4. Rewriting—35%
5. Proofreading—5%

To write effectively, you should concentrate on each stage in turn. If you sit down to write immediately, you will have to think simultaneously of ideas and the way they are arranged and expressed, as well as spelling, punctuation, and usage. Instead, by focusing on one stage of the process at a time, you can specialize in each, and devote yourself completely to the problem each presents.

Of course, these time suggestions and specialization stages may be modified according to your situation and inclination. Naturally, if you have a short deadline, you need to plunge into writing without taking much time to explore and plan. In other instances, you may continue exploring while you write a first draft, searching for additional examples or facts and figures to bolster your points. Or, like some writers, you may wish to revise as you write, changing words, recasting sentences, checking on spelling, punctuation, and similar matters. You need not feel compelled to follow the five stages exactly in the sequence suggested and in the time allocations indicated. Consider them as guidelines to follow or modify as you wish in view of a particular writing situation. But realize what is involved in each stage in the writing process.

STAGE ONE: EXPLORING When you receive a writing assignment, resist the temptation to forget about it until you sit down to write. Instead, spend some time exploring for ideas. Worry about the subject in free moments—as you take a shower, lie in bed, walk to class, ride the bus. Concentrate on searching for ideas. When you get one, jot it down—otherwise, you may forget it.

One obvious way to explore for ideas is to read about the subject. If there is nothing in print—or even if there is—discuss the topic with friends. Doing so will clarify your own thoughts and expose you to questions your readers might ask.

And talk to people who are knowledgeable about the subject. For example, for a report about a proposed student-operated bookstore, interview the manager of a campus bookstore, a college textbook salesperson, or the college business manager.

By exploring the subject in your own mind, at the library, and with others, you should develop some sound ideas.

STAGE TWO: PLANNING   Planning enables you to organize your ideas logically. In this stage, you should examine the points you want to make, eliminate the irrelevant ones, arrange the others in the most effective order, and decide on examples, facts, and reasons to support them. Whether you develop a formal outline for a lengthy report or jot down some notes on a scrap of paper is up to you. But the more you work on perfecting your plan, the easier and better the writing should be.

STAGE THREE: WRITING   When you know what you want to say and have planned how to say it, you are ready to write. You need only dash down your thoughts, using pen, pencil, or typewriter, whichever you prefer. Let your mind flow along the outline. Don't interrupt the flow of ideas to check spelling, worry about punctuation, or search for exact words. If new thoughts pop into your mind, as they often do, check them with your outline, and work them into your paper if and where they are relevant. Keep going until you reach the end. And don't worry if you write slowly; many people do. Few writers dash along without stopping.

STAGE FOUR: REWRITING   The secret of good writing is good rewriting. Only a gifted few can express themselves clearly and effectively in a first draft. James Michener, the well-known novelist, considers himself to be not a good writer, but an excellent rewriter, stating, "I never even write an important letter in the first draft."[11]

In contrast, few students revise their work carefully. They fail to understand the importance of this process or realize how to proceed. Also important is their attitude.

Our natural tendency is to feel exuberant upon finishing a first draft. Why fuss with it? Why not just write or type it up and forget about it? You could certainly do that—just as football players could take on an opposing team without practicing all week. But they probably wouldn't play well. Your first draft is like a practice that allows you to note weaknesses, to correct them, to tinker, to polish, to touch up, to perfect—in short, to write well.

Of course, occasionally you have to go with a first draft and cannot rewrite. But if you have a little time, reread your work slowly and carefully, searching for ways to improve every word, sentence, and paragraph. If there's no deadline pressure, the best way to revise is to get away from what you've written for a day or two. Then you'll be able to look at it objectively, with fresh eyes and an alert mind, almost as if someone else had submitted it to you. You'll be able to read it, not as an author proud of what you've just written, but as a critic aware of faults and weaknesses.

In that role you must attack your first draft harshly, examining it closely, scrutinizing it thoroughly. To help you, we suggest a two-step process. First, focus on main concerns. Is the information complete and clear? Would more details be helpful? Is the tone too formal or too informal? Should the material be arranged differently? Then deal with minor concerns. Select more effective words, sharpen sentences, check punctuation and spelling, and watch for unacceptable grammatical usage. Such a two-step approach would have helped the writer of "Expense and Time Reporting Procedures" (see figure 1–2).

Figure 1–2.   Just a Few Minor Revisions.

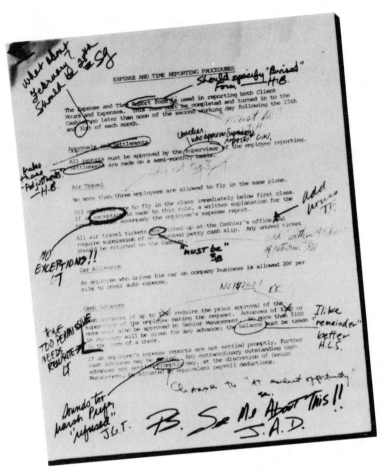

(SOURCE: Reprinted by permission of Xerox Corporation.)

When you work on complex or important communications, you should revise your work in several drafts. Peter Drucker usually writes five or six.[12] John Kenneth Galbraith can sometimes get by with four, reserving the last one for inserting "that note of spontaneity"[13] that makes his writing lively and vigorous.

In this, our fifth draft, we hope we have alerted you to the importance of rewriting and pointed out how you can revise your own work. Whenever possible, take the time to rework your writing, knowing that good writing is the product of good rewriting. And if you have the opportunity, let some other people see an early draft to learn their reactions before revising.

STAGE FIVE: PROOFREADING   Exploring, planning, writing, and rewriting are not enough. Proofreading, the final task, demands less time than the others but is as important. If, through a typist's oversight, words are missing, repeated, or misspelled, letters jumbled, and numbers muddled, readers may discard your communication. Poor proofreading of an application letter, for instance, can cost you the job.

To proofread well, decrease your normal reading speed, stare at each word, and concentrate on what's on the page. It's easy to imagine what's there instead of noting what's actually written. (If you don't believe this, see figure 1–3.) In particular, check the beginning and end of lines and the bottom and top of consecutive pages for omissions or repetitions, and scrutinize all proper names and numbers for typographical errors.

Figure 1–3.   *A Simple Proofreading Exercise. Simple?**

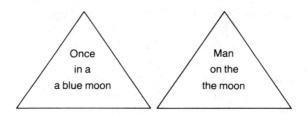

* Did you catch the "in a a blue moon" and "on the the moon"?

Remember: whether you type the communication or merely sign it, you are responsible. Always take the time to proofread painstakingly so a few careless errors will not spoil the effort you have put into exploring, planning, writing, and rewriting.

THE DISTINCTIVE CHARACTERISTICS OF BUSINESS WRITING

Some of these myths—writing is easy, writing demands special talent, writing requires inspiration, writing consists only of the act of writing—should be discarded by all writers, not only those in business. In fact, all writers struggle with word choice, sentence construction, organization, clarity, and grammatical appropriateness. But business writers must also be concerned with other matters: purpose, reader adaptation, personality, economy, and the forms of business communication.

Purpose

The reasons for writing are many. But generally the novelist writes to portray life; the poet, to present experience; the columnist, to entertain readers; the politician, to win votes; the television writer, to attract viewers. To some extent, all are interested in amusing, delighting, pleasing, or indulging readers.

Business writers also aim to please, but they are primarily concerned with informing and persuading readers. The sales manager informs the sales staff about the latest product line, the bank official informs customers about a new checking plan, the personnel manager informs employees about a health insurance change, the supervisor informs management about a production snag, the social worker informs a state agency about a client's status, and the motel manager informs inquirers about a special weekend package plan.

In these and numerous other situations, business writers strive not to entertain readers but to provide clear, accurate information about a person, product, service, or idea.

In addition, business writers usually try to persuade readers either to accept opinions or recommendations, or at least to think favorably of the writers and their companies. For instance, the sales manager wants not only to inform the sales representatives about the new product line, but also to persuade them it is attractive, well made, priced right, and better than anything comparable on the market. The bank official wants not only to inform customers about the new checking plan, but also to let them know the bank is efficient and concerned about its customers.

Sometimes persuasion plays a subtler role, serving only to create goodwill for the writer and the company. When the personnel manager informs employees about a health insurance change, for example, little persuasion is needed. Nevertheless, the manager would want to convince them that the department will handle their records efficiently and answer their questions willingly.

In some sense, nearly every business communication is persuasive, providing an opportunity to gain goodwill for a company, improve the relationship between writer and reader, and create a favorable impression of the writer.

Reader Adaptation

Up to this point in your life, your writing may have consisted mainly of assignments for teachers. But in the business world, writing requires communicating with various people: factory workers, top management, customers, suppliers, shareholders, custodians, clerks. So you must direct your message to the interests, intelligence, and needs of readers, tailoring it to their measurements.

For instance, information about a new policy for patient care would be explained in one way to patients and in another to doctors and nurses. An insurance letter to senior citizens would be unlike one to college seniors. A financial report to security analysts would differ from one to employees.

In these and other business writing assignments, you must ask yourself questions about your readers. Who are they (age, education, economic level, social class, special interests)? What do they already know about the subject? What do they need to know? How will they react to what you've written?

The answers to these and similar questions about readers (see table 1–2) will allow you to adapt your message to them. So you can realize that business writing involves more than writing about a subject. It requires writing in a particular way on a particular occasion about a particular subject to inform and persuade a particular reader or group of readers. That's adaptation.

TABLE 1–2. Reader-Adaptation Checklist.

A. Reader's position vis-a-vis writer

Boss _____ Subordinate _____ Peer, partner, coworker _____
   Client or customer _____ Supplier _____ Consultant _____ General public ____
Interested member of another organization or cause _____ Competitor _____
Length of relationship, if any
   New _____ Less than two years _____ More than two years _____

B. Reader's preparation for the communication

Requested it _____ Expecting it because of prior communications or normal
   routine _____ Not expecting it _____
Knowledge of subject
   Thorough _____ Limited _____ None _____ Unknown _____
Vocabulary level in subject area
   High _____ Medium _____ Low _____ Unknown _____
Open-mindedness on topic
   Willing to change _____ Slightly resistant to change _____ Committed not to
   change _____ Unknown _____

C. Reader's attitude toward writer

Friendly _____ Hostile _____ Neutral _____ Unknown _____
If known, is attitude firm _____, superficial _____, or _____ variable?

D. Reader's concern with subject

Very interested _____ Mildly interested _____ Neutral or indifferent _____
   Unknown _____

E. Reader's probable feelings about proposal findings, or viewpoint of communication

Agreement _____ Disagreement _____ Neutral _____ Unknown _____
If disagreement, is reader likely to feel personally threatened (e.g., loss of job, status,
   or income) _____, or opposed only on grounds of convenience, technique,
   conflicting policies, and so on _____?

F. Reader's biases, if known

Likes _____ or dislikes _____ flamboyance, cuteness.
Prefers conciseness and meticulous attention to detail _____
Likes _____ or dislikes _____ "hard sell" tactics
Is very particular about letterhead, format, type size, binding, spacing, chart
   arrangements, and/or related aspects _____ Others (specify) _____

SOURCE: David W. Ewing, *Writing for Results*. Copyright © 1979. Reprinted by permission of John Wiley
and Sons, Inc., pp. 177–78.

Personality

The personality of your writing has probably seldom been mentioned to you. In fact, as a result of being instructed to avoid using *I*, you may have developed an impersonal style, one that may be characterized as factual, objective, neutral, colorless. In scientific, technical, and newspaper writing, these qualities are usually desirable. But in business writing, particularly in correspondence, and to some extent in memos and reports, your personality should be evident.

What is personality in writing? It is the voice of the writer, namely the writer's natural style, sound, or character. And it is also the tone of that voice, the attitude of the person writing. These qualities—voice and tone—constitute personality.

In business correspondence, for instance, you should sound courteous, friendly, warm, lively, and sincere. Instead, many business writers seem stuffy, cold, formal, stilted, and affected. They fail to realize the importance of personality in business communication, where *what* is said is often not as significant as *how* it is said. If your writing is fresh and natural, you have a better chance of selling yourself and your ideas.

Economy

In business, time is money. If executives, managers, supervisors, and others spend extra time reading wordy communications, the cost can run into thousands of dollars. If customers, suppliers, and clients become irritated while wading through unnecessarily lengthy letters, instructions, notices, or statements, they may take their business elsewhere. We are not advocating that all communications be brief. Nor do we suggest eliminating pertinent information or appropriate courtesies. By *economical writing*, we mean writing that contains no waste. All fat has been stripped away. What remains is lean, tough, tight, muscular.

Forms of Business Communication

At school, you have written themes and term papers. At work, you will write letters, memos, and reports, and perhaps instructions, proposals, evaluations, job descriptions, press releases, notices, speeches, and articles. In this textbook, we will deal mainly with the first three—letters, memos, and reports—because these are the forms you will be required to use most frequently. And if you can master them, you should have few problems adapting to the other types of business communications.

Later in this book, we will examine the formats of letters, memos, and reports. Until then, let us state that they should trouble you little once you have gotten the knack of them. Switching from writing themes to writing business forms is probably no more difficult than playing doubles after being accustomed to singles, or driving a car with an automatic transmission after being used to a stick shift.

The PLAN OF THIS TEXTBOOK

We will proceed from this first chapter in Part I—"Communicating in Business"—to the second chapter, "The Communication Process," which deals with communication theory and its application, semantics, and nonverbal communication.

Then in Part II—"Communicating by Letters"—we will discuss the strategy and technique of writing informative, persuasive, and claim, refusal, and collection letters in chapters 3, 4, and 5 respectively. In the strategy section of these chapters, we consider the most effective rhetorical ways to adapt the message to readers and to organize the ideas in order to obtain the desired action or reaction. The section on technique focuses on ways to use words, sentences, and other matters of style to write clear, crisp, and correct business letters.

Part III—"Communicating and Employment"—consists of a chapter on the job search and a chapter on job communications. These chapters will help you to decide on a career, find prospective employers, write letters of application and résumés, prepare for interviews, and send appropriate responses.

Part IV—"Communicating by Memos and Reports"—includes a chapter on the memo, a chapter on the short report, and a chapter on the long report. Like the chapters in Part II, these are divided into discussions of strategy and technique.

The last section, Part V—"Oral Communications"—is made up of a chapter on oral presentation and one on interviews and meetings. These chapters will help you to speak before others, conduct an interview, read a paper, run a meeting, and listen effectively.

A special feature at the end of the book is a section of reference appendixes containing helpful information about postal abbreviations, mailing instructions, dictation, library research, business terms, letter forms, visual aids, copier guidelines, documentation, word processing, capitalization, punctuation, numbers, and grammar.

All sections of this book are designed to help you improve your ability to communicate effectively in business. But studying this book is only part of your obligation. You must also practice writing and speaking—the more practice the better—and profit from the advice and criticism of your instructor. The more proficient you become in business communications, the better the chances of your finding a job and succeeding in it, as well as in numerous other relationships with people. To communicate well is to do well in the business of business and in the business of life.

SUMMARY

Although people at work know the importance of speaking and writing effectively, many students fail to realize the value of these skills. Not only in business, but in practically any field of student interest—health, education, government, or the professions—the ability to communicate well is significant in obtaining a job, getting a promotion, and reaching top managerial and executive ranks.

Communication skills can seldom be learned or mastered at work. Instead, they should be perfected in college, particularly in business communication courses, where teachers can provide the necessary instruction, practice, and evaluation. These courses may help students not only in their careers, but in their personal and social relationships as well.

Although this textbook deals with oral communication, it concentrates on written communication, because writing is a more difficult and complex skill and because students are less experienced and proficient at it. Moreover, business leaders are demanding that colleges teach students to write well.

Among the reasons students do not write well is their belief in five myths. They should discard their ideas that writing is unnecessary at work, is easy, requires special talent, needs inspiration, and entails only the act of writing. On the contrary, they should realize that writing is frequently required in business, necessitates hard work, demands only normal ability, depends on getting started, and involves a five-step process consisting of exploring, planning, writing, rewriting, and proofreading.

While these statements apply to all writing, business writing is characterized by certain specific qualities. Its purpose is not to amuse or delight but to inform and persuade. It should be adapted to the needs, interests, and personal characteristics of its readers. It should reflect the personality of the writer rather than sound as if it were composed by a computer. It should be economical. And it should follow the conventions required by certain forms, such as the letter, memo, and report.

After a chapter on communication theory and language, we will move to a discussion of business letters and the strategy and technique to be used in writing them. Next is a section on the job search, application letter, résumé, and interview. The fourth section deals with the memo, short report, and long report. The last section is devoted to oral communication—individual and group. The book concludes with appendixes of useful reference information.

EXERCISES

Discussion Questions

1. What does the campus grapevine say about this business communication course? Is it hard? Easy? Challenging? Interesting?
2. What have business people said to you about the importance of speaking and writing well?
3. Before reading this chapter, what were your views about the importance of writing in the business world? Are they different now? In what way? Why?
4. What ratings in table 1–1 surprised you? Why?
5. In what fields do you think business communication skills would be most useful?
6. Peter Drucker says that very few students bother to learn how to speak and write effectively. Do you agree? Why?
7. Cite the various leadership roles that are available in your community outside of work. Discuss specifically how the ability to speak and write effectively would be helpful in these positions.

8. Do you generally find it easier to speak than to write? Name some situations in which you would prefer writing.
9. Which of the five myths did you believe formerly? Are your views different now? Why?
10. Compare your writing process with the one recommended in this chapter. How do you allocate your time? Do you believe that some of your writing problems stem from your inability to devote sufficient time to one or more of the five steps?
11. In what sense is the purpose of every business communication persuasive? Can you think of any exceptions?
12. Is adaptation a new concept to you? To what extent did you adapt your writing in school to the views of your instructor?
13. Why should most business communications have a friendly tone?
14. Since business writing should be economical, does it follow that all communications should be limited to one page?
15. What purpose does this textbook serve in the process of your learning to communicate in business effectively? What other components are there in this learning process?

In-Class Applications

1. Make out a chart ranking the abilities important for success in college. With other members of the class, work out a composite chart. Then discuss how your rankings differ from those of your classmates. Where did you place the ability to communicate? Why?
2. After scheduling a meeting with a college administrator or businessperson, present that individual with a scrambled list of the items in table 1–1. Compare the rankings with those obtained by other class members.
3. Interview a local businessperson about the importance of speaking and writing well. Ask permission to tape the comments or write them down. In class, compare your results with those of your classmates.
4. Proofread the following passages, pointing out and correcting the errors:
   a. The business-forms industry is growing by leaps and bounds because of population increeses and the expansion of record keeping. The more human beings in our counrty, the more need their is for for certificates of birth and death; socail security cards; licenses for driving and marrying; and forms for state, local, and national taxs. In business, countless reccords are needed in selling, accounting, purchaseing, receiveing, and shipping. A businesman recently said recently, "Instead of counting sheep jumping over fences at nihgt, I think about forms being compleeted, filed, singed, and maled For these reesons the futur of the busines-forms industry is is especally bright.
   b. It is aparent from the puhlished figures that the conpany enjoys a strong finanancial condition. Last year, deprecaition exceeded $16,250,00 and earnings after dividend payments were over $20 millon, while capital spending was abut $40 million million. This year we anticpate that both depreciation and redained earnings were higher and capitol itums are espected to total about $27 to $28

million—this will add tonet working capitol, which last year was about $177 million. Next year we believe that per share earnings will will encrease to about $4.20 conservatorily and deprecation may reach or at at least approach $18 million while capital items are expecded to be a bout the same as this year.

5. Along with members of your class, obtain copies of either your college or local newspaper. Then select one or several pages. See if you can find any printing errors.

Writing Assignments

1. Write a paper elaborating on any question in the discussion section.
2. Write an article entitled "Advice for Freshmen" to be used in an unofficial student pamphlet distributed in the fall to all new students. In it, describe the freshman English course and explain the importance of working hard in it. Use a light, informal, interesting style.
3. Write a letter to your instructor (don't worry about its form), stating your career interest and explaining your reasons for it.
4. Select one of the following statements as the basis for a paper about your attitude toward work after graduation:

> I want work that is socially useful.
> I want work that is well compensated.
> I want work that is interesting and challenging.
> I want work that will not consume my entire life.
> I want to shape the nature and direction of my work.
> I want to work in attractive surroundings.
> I want to work with interesting people.
> I want to work with my hands.

NOTES

[1] Walter Kiechell, III, "Harvard Business School Restudies Itself," *Fortune*, June 18, 1979, p. 53. Other recent studies also stress the importance of communication skills. As Joseph M. Williams states in *Style: Ten Lessons in Clarity and Grace* (New York: Scott, Foresman, 1981, p. x), "In every survey that asks business people what subjects they wish they had studied more carefully, their first or second answer is always communication." For example, a 1980 survey of 524 college graduates of the 1960s and 1970s rated by their employers as "very good" or "excellent" recommended English and Business Administration as the most useful study areas for their work (College Placement Council, *College and Other Stepping Stones*, 1980). And a sequential random sample of 4,370 business college graduates at Arizona State University disclosed that 95 percent of the respondents felt that the ability to communicate orally and in writing was an important factor for success in their jobs (Martha H. Rader and Alan P. Wunsch, "A Survey of Communication Practices of Business Graduates by Job Category and Undergraduate Major," *Journal of Business Communication*, 17 [Summer 1980], 40). Also pertinent is a survey by H. C. Edgeworth of 90 of 128 former MBAs who ranked in the upper

20 percent of their class at Florida State University. They selected communication over accounting, finance, economics, and other subjects as the academic area that was most beneficial to their business careers ("Business Communication and Colleges of Business," *ABCA Bulletin*, 17 [Sept. 1978]: 35).

[2] Donald Skarzenski and Donna Stine, "Motivating Business Communication Students: An Introductory Handout," The *ABCA Bulletin*, 42, no. 1 (March 1979), p. 28.

[3] Peter Drucker, "How To Be an Employee," *Fortune*, May 1952, p. 47.

[4] "The Mystery of the Business Graduate Who Can't Write," *Nation's Business*, February 1977, p. 60.

[5] David W. Ewing, *Writing for Results*, 2nd ed. (New York: John Wiley, 1979), pp. 4–6.

[6] William E. Blundell, "Confused, Overstuffed Corporate Writing Often Costs Firms Much Time—and Money," *Wall Street Journal*, August 28, 1980, p. 17.

[7] Donna Stine and Donald Skarzenski, "Priorities for the Business Communication Classroom: A Survey of Business and Academe," *The Journal of Business Communication*, 16, no. 3 (Spring 1979), p. 25.

[8] *Wall Street Journal*, May 19, 1978, p. 26.

[9] "Writing, Typing, and Economic$," *The Atlantic Monthly*, May 1978, p. 103.

[10] Stine and Skarzenski, "Priorities," p. 23.

[11] Lee Linder, "Interview with James Michener," *Herald-Leader* (Lexington, Ky.), April 22, 1979, p. G 1.

[12] Larry Van Dyne, "Interview with Peter Drucker," *The Chronicle of Higher Education*, March 19, 1979, p. R–4.

[13] Galbraith, p. 103.

2 The Communication Process

OBJECTIVES

After reading this chapter, you should be able to:

- Explain the difference between speaking and writing in school and communicating at work
- List the three basic parts of a communication model
- Define the terms *sender, receiver, encode, decode, channel, feedback, noise, environment* and explain their roles in the communication process
- Explain five ways in which the knowledge of a communication model is helpful in communicating
- Describe horizontal, upward, and downward communication
- Explain four key concepts of semantics
- Identify three ways in which nonverbal elements affect the communication of written messages and seven ways in which they affect the communication of oral messages

PLAN

*Think like a wise man but
communicate in the language of the
people.*

WILLIAM BUTLER YEATS

THE PRICE OF FAULTY COMMUNICATION

Forward, the Light Brigade!
Was there a man dismayed?
Not though the soldiers knew
   Someone had blundered:
Theirs not to make reply,
Theirs not to reason why,
Theirs but to do and die:
Into the Valley of Death
   Rode the six hundred.

Alfred Lord Tennyson

Tennyson's famous "Charge of the Light Brigade" commemorates the blind loyalty
of the gallant British cavalry who rode to slaughter during the Crimean War because
of a communication failure between two high-ranking officers. Lord Raglan ordered
the brigade "to advance rapidly to the front and try to prevent the enemy carrying
away the guns." Lord Lucan, commander of the Cavalry Division, thought that
"to the front" meant down the North Valley instead of to the Causeway Heights.
Moreover, he interpreted "the guns" as being the Russians' own artillery instead of
the British pieces lost by the Turks. The result: a suicidal attack by 673 men of whom
only 195 returned.[1]

Almost as well known as this charge of the Light Brigade are numerous stories
in the business world of how communication failures have caused the loss of time,
energy, money, and goodwill. Problems develop daily in writing and speaking to the
public, customers, suppliers, factory workers, salespeople, secretaries, managers, and
executives. Many of these difficulties might be avoided if writers and speakers had
a better understanding of the communication process.

We shall examine this process to help you understand its complexity and to enable
you to improve your communication skills.

THE PROCESS OF COMMUNICATION

In one sense, you have been communicating all your life by talking to others. And
you have also been involved in this process when you prepared a letter or theme for

someone else. But you may not have been involved in communicating in the sense of sending a message to other people so that they understand and believe it, and act as you wish.

To illustrate, compare writing in school, a form of academic game, with writing at work, a form of communication in the sense of sending a message. In school, students write to display their skill and knowledge just as they do in playing soccer, basketball, or baseball. Generally, they are interested in the score or grade.

At work, on the other hand, people write to inform or persuade others, usually about procedures, products, or services, but sometimes only to create goodwill. And at work, they are interested in having readers understand, remember, and react to the message as they, the writers, wish. As you can realize, students are rated on their ability to use language skillfully; people at work, on their ability to use it effectively.

The following classic story illustrates the difference between the two styles of writing:

> A New York plumber wrote the Bureau of Standards at Washington that he found hydrochloric acid fine for cleaning drains, and was it harmless? Washington replied: "The efficacy of hydrochloric acid is indisputable, but the chlorine residue is incompatible with metallic permanence."
>
> The plumber wrote back that he was mighty glad the Bureau agreed with him. The Bureau replied with a note of alarm: "We cannot assume responsibility for the production of toxic and noxious residues with hydrochloric acid, and suggest that you use an alternate procedure." The plumber was happy to learn that the Bureau still agreed with him.
>
> Whereupon Washington exploded: "Don't use hydrochloric acid; it eats hell out of the pipes!"[2]

The point of the story is clear: the reader is the key in the writing done at work. In school, the questions about your writing usually involve how correctly and intelligently you have written. At work, the questions deal with effectiveness. Did the customer buy the item? Did the supplier offer better credit terms? Did the client sign the contract? Did the company place the order? In other words, did the writer get the desired results? That's the bottom line—the results.

So, at work, writing is communication. At school, writing is usually a form of self-expression, allowing you to record your feelings, opinions, and experiences. At school, the focus is generally on you—how you feel, what you think, what has happened to you, and how well you can write about it. Of course, you also write in school to show what you know (exams) or what you have researched (term papers). But these exercises are also writer-centered because their purpose is to evaluate your ability in order to give you a grade.

Writing at work, on the other hand, focuses on the reader. Writers draft their letters, memos, and reports so that readers will understand them easily and react to them favorably. To do this, you will have to think not only of what to write, but of how the reader will react. The pay-off is the outcome: success or failure. Remember: it is not how well you write but how effectively.

THEORY OF COMMUNICATION

By learning some of the basic concepts of communication theory, you can better understand what is involved in the communication process. And you can perceive the difficulties you must overcome to communicate well.

The Communication Model

The theory is traditionally represented in the form of a diagram called a model. A mathematician, Claude Shannon, and his friend, Warren Weaver, were interested in electronic communication and developed the first model in 1947.[3] Subsequent models, refinements of the original, have been primarily concerned with human communication.[4]

In figure 2–1 we show a simplified version of a model dealing with the one-way transmission (sender-to-receiver only) of a message. It consists of three basic parts: the *sender*, the *channel* or medium for sending the message, and the *receiver*.[5]

Figure 2–1. *A One-Way Communication Model.*

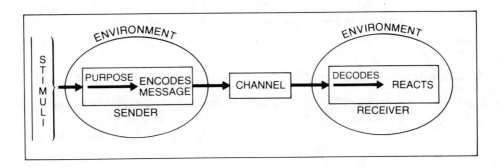

As a result of some stimulus received through the senses, the *sender* realizes a need or purpose for sending a message. This purpose usually is to inform, persuade, or amuse, although some communications result from a desire to impress others, to clarify ideas, or to be sociable (as, for example, when we talk to others about the weather). Naturally, communications may be motivated by several of these reasons. To accomplish some purpose, the sender encodes or translates ideas into symbols— words, pictures, or numbers—with the receiver in mind.

This spoken or written message is transmitted to the receiver by some *channel*. Private channels consist of letters, telephone calls, and personal meetings. Public channels include newspapers, magazines, radio, television, and public addresses. Often, the sender must select not only a general channel but a specific one—for example, one of three local TV stations to advertise a new restaurant.

By listening or reading, the *receiver* decodes the message, translating the sender's ideas and then reacting to them by some change in attitude, belief, relationship, or action. And so the process of one-way communication is complete.

If the receiver provides *feedback* to the message by responding, the process is reversed. The message is the stimulus, the receiver is the sender, a different message is encoded and sent through a channel, and the former sender decodes it and reacts. And so back and forth continues the communication, as in a long telephone call, a lengthy conversation, or a drawn-out correspondence.

Two terms in the model still need to be explained: *noise* and *environment*. Any interference between the encoding and decoding of the message is known as *noise*, although sometimes other terms such as *static* or *interference* are used. The noise may be technical, involving the channel, or semantic, involving the words used to convey the ideas. Because some noise is present in human communication—in the channel or in the sending and receiving of the message—the ideal of perfect communication, as represented in the following formula, is seldom achieved.

$$\frac{RR \text{ (receiver's response)}}{SP \text{ (sender's purpose)}} = 1$$

Environment refers to the internal or external influences that may affect the sender or receiver of a message. Internal factors include moods, feelings, physical conditions, and the like. External factors include social, cultural, economic, religious, and political influences. When doing business with another country, China for example, one would be wise to learn about its business and social customs.

Communication in Operation

The description of this model of the communication process may sound bewildering, but an example will help you to realize how simple it is.

Let's assume you notice an ad (*stimulus*) in your college newspaper for students to work next summer as camp counselors. Needing to earn money for tuition and books (*purpose*), you decide to apply. To do so, you have to write a letter of application (*encode a message*) to the camp director at a post office box number. In writing, you keep this receiver in mind, trying to shape your message so that the director will react favorably. You must make numerous decisions. Should you mention your former paper route? Your working in a fast food restaurant for a month? Your neighborhood babysitting jobs? There are also matters of form. Should you type or handwrite the message? On what kind of paper? And then there are more complicated decisions about words, sentences, grammar, spelling, and style.

When you have encoded the message, you must choose the *channel*. You have already made one decision: to write rather than telephone or see someone. But should you rush with the letter yourself to the newspaper office, send it by regular mail, or register it in order to attract attention?

After getting and reading (*decoding*) your letter, the camp director will react by granting an interview or not, or by requesting additional information. The decision will be conveyed to you by mail or phone, providing you with *feedback* to your letter.

Your success or failure will be influenced by the *environment*. Just as many of your decisions about the application letter were influenced by your education, so the director is similarly conditioned. In addition, the director may react in many personal ways, such as disliking your name or liking your hobby. The impact of environment on communication is enormous.

The application process is a relatively simple example of the communication model. Much more complex would be a description of how it applies to a telephone conversation or a group discussion. But the basic communication process is similar.

APPLICATION OF COMMUNICATION THEORY

What's the point of learning about this model of the communication process?

The answer is that the model provides a conceptual framework for all that follows in this book. Your awareness of the factors involved in communication will assist you in making the numerous decisions involved in specific writing and speaking situations.

The model should also make you conscious of certain communication factors that you may not previously have considered carefully:

1. The importance of the receiver
2. The need to consider the purpose
3. The complexity of encoding
4. The advantages and disadvantages of various channels
5. The problem of the environment
6. The fact that communicating requires more than the ability to speak or write well

Let's look briefly at each of these points.

The Importance of the Receiver

In discussing earlier the difference between the writing done in school and in business, we touched on the importance of the reader. But we cannot emphasize too strongly that the receiver is the most important element in the communication process. If the receiver misunderstands a sentence, misinterprets it, or must struggle to comprehend it, then the sender has failed to communicate effectively. In a sense, the sender is like a quarterback throwing a football. It matters little whether the passer stays in the pocket or scrambles, gets rid of the ball while set or on the run, flips a hard or a soft pass. What is crucial is that the receiver catch the ball. Similarly, the receiver must catch your message. If not, your communication is worthless. It is as simple—and as frightening—as that.

The Need to Consider the Purpose

As the communication model reveals, the sender's purpose is always encoded into the message. If the sender does not clearly understand his or her purpose, the message may be misinterpreted or ignored. For example, in writing a letter refusing to ship merchandise to a customer because of poor credit, the credit manager must first decide on the purpose of the message: (1) to reject the order completely; (2) to ship part of it, extending credit only on that portion; (3) to deny credit now but allow it at a later date if the customer's rating improves; or (4) to accept the order but only on a C.O.D. basis.

If the purpose of communicating is not clear in the mind of the writer, then it will not be clear in the mind of the reader.

The Complexity of Encoding

The problem of encoding involves the difficulty of selecting words to convey to a reader exactly what is in your mind. The words must mean to the reader what they mean to you, and they must be arranged clearly and appropriately in sentences. If not, note what can happen:

> An increased census in our facilities increased revenues and profits. (*Communication noise:* What is a census?)
>
> One day he found a dollar walking in the grass. (*Communication noise:* Was the person or the dollar walking in the grass?)
>
> The new manager still don't know nothing about her duties in the purchasing department. (*Communication noise:* Faulty subject-verb agreement, double negative.)

The first sentence, taken from the quarterly report of a national nursing home corporation, creates a problem because its president has used the industry's term *census* to mean *occupancy*, referring to patients.[6] Most stockholders, however, think of a census as a population count. The result: confusion.

The problem in the second sentence is evident: the meaning is unclear. The sentence should be rewritten to avoid the ambiguity.

In the third sentence, the idea is communicated. All readers realize that the new assistant manager knows nothing about her duties. But noise is created because readers are not accustomed to seeing double negatives and faulty subject-verb agreement in print. Violating this or any other writing convention in regard to spelling, capitalization, punctuation, or grammar results in noise that distracts readers. Note, for example, the impact of the misspelling in this sentense. It can be as disconcerting as a wailing cat outside at night.

Encoding a message is a complex human endeavor, requiring the careful selection of words and sentence structures as well as an understanding of the receiver. According to Paul R. Timm, professor of management and author of *Managerial Communication*, encoding is such a complicated activity that "(1) we must expect to be misunderstood by at least some of our listeners and readers; (2) we must expect to misunderstand others; (3) we can strive to reduce the degree of such misunderstanding, but we can never totally eliminate it nor anticipate all the outcomes."[7] Because of this difficulty in encoding, most of the material in the following chapters is devoted to this process.

The Advantages and Disadvantages of Various Channels

Three channels are commonly used in business: the face-to-face meeting, the telephone, and the written communication.[8] Each has certain advantages and disadvantages.

Face-to-face meetings offer the personal contact that can best reconcile problems and enhance communication. They also provide immediate feedback by the words, actions, gestures, and facial expressions of the persons involved. But such meetings may be difficult to arrange because of time and place problems. In addition, meetings are time-consuming, usually repetitive, and often too long. And because frequently no record of personal meetings is available, misinterpretations and misunderstandings may develop. The participants may forget what was said or think they heard something that was neither stated nor implied.

Telephone calls have some of the disadvantages of face-to-face meetings, although the conversations are generally shorter. In addition, a telephone call may be inconvenient, interrupting the recipient at a busy time. Yet the telephone provides an easy, relatively inexpensive way for people to communicate and allows for audible feedback. A discerning listener can learn a lot not only from what is said but also from the intonations, pauses, and inflections of the other person on the line.

Written communication provides a permanent record. It allows time for writers to work on a statement until it says precisely what they wish. In a sense, it is also inexpensive and convenient, costing little more than a postage stamp, written whenever the writer is ready, and read whenever the reader wishes. But if the time of the writer and secretary, along with the cost of stationery, office equipment depreciation, electricity, and other expenses are computed, written communication can be expensive.[9] Also, as we have pointed out, since people write more slowly than they talk, they require much time and effort to work on letters, memos, and reports. Finally, feedback in written communication is not immediate and can be nonexistent. This means that writers may be unable to alter or modify a message as they can in meetings or telephone conversations.

These three channels—face-to-face meetings, telephone calls, and written communications—are only general ones. More specific channels are available. For instance, as a personnel manager, you might have a choice of the following ways to notify employees about a new dental care benefit:

Pay envelope insert	Videotape or slide presentation
Bulletin board announcement	Memos
Letters to homes	Word of mouth (grapevine)
Employee publication notice	Individual conferences
Posters	Talk at group meetings
Pamphlets	

Which one you select will depend on many factors. And in some instances, you may decide on two or more channels. Some evidence indicates that a combination of oral and written communication is most effective, leading several companies to adopt the slogan, "Talk it over—jot it down."[10]

The Problem of the Environment

The internal environment—your mood, attitude, feelings—may be beyond your control but should not be outside your consideration. Most of us have our good and bad days. When we are upset, irritated, or discouraged, we should be careful not to take out our annoyance or discontent on someone else. Postponing difficult or delicate business problems until a better time is advisable.

The external environment also affects communication significantly, organizational policy being particularly influential. Generally, people at work are restricted by the operating procedures established by top management. Basic to these procedures are management's fundamental assumptions about the nature of employees. Douglas McGregor has described, for example, how managers are usually motivated in one of two ways: Theory X or Theory Y.[11] A third way is Theory Z.

THEORY X According to this theory, people are inherently lazy, eager to shirk work, anxious to avoid responsibility, possessed of little ambition, desiring security above all, and wanting to be directed. In view of these traits, they are best motivated by fear of punishment. Theory X is usually the guiding philosophy in organizations operated according to the principles of scientific management. Often called the *classical school*, scientific management is characterized by a strong central administration, standardized jobs and equipment, and efficiency studies. Such an environment will have a decided impact on organizational communications.

THEORY Y According to this theory, people consider work to be as natural as play, and maybe just as satisfying. Under proper conditions, they will accept responsibility and want to do challenging work, and they will exercise imagination, creativity, and ingenuity in performing it. As a result, rewards are a stronger motivation than threats. In such an environment, organizational communications would differ from those managed according to Theory X.

THEORY Z Since the publication of McGregor's theories, the worldwide success of Japanese companies has resulted in studies of their management method, which one author has designated as Theory Z.[12] Closer to Theory Y than to X, Theory Z advocates employee trust, loyalty, cooperation, group decision-making, avoidance of face-to-face confrontations, lifetime employment, slow promotion, collective responsibility, and absence of specialization.

What impact do these theories have on communication? Here's how they might influence the approach used in writing a memo to employees about proper dress:

Theory X Memo

Some of our employees who meet the public are dressing in absurd taste. If these individuals do not wear standard, conservative attire, we shall have to discharge them.

Theory Y Memo

Because we regard public opinion as important to our success, we believe that the appearance of our employees should create a favorable impression. Dressing in good taste is one way to do this. Lately, however, some employees have worn unusual or sloppy attire. If you feel that your fellow employees or supervisor might think that certain styles of dress are inappropriate for the office, we ask that you be considerate enough of others and of our company not to wear them to work.

Theory Z Memo

We realize that all employees have individual tastes in clothes and like to wear whatever they choose. However, our company needs to maintain its excellent public image, which in part depends on our employees' creating a favorable impression on people. This impression does not result from the wearing of sloppy or bizarre clothes, which some of our employees may have appeared in recently.

We must work together to decide how to deal with this problem. On the one hand, we should give employees as much freedom as possible to express their own individuality in their dress. But, on the other hand, we must recognize that our customers form their opinion of us in part from our clothes.

Your supervisors will discuss this problem with you at your weekly group meeting in order to obtain comments and recommendations.

As you can see, company policy or philosophy plays a dominant role in the way memos are phrased.

COMMUNICATION FLOW Another environmental factor affecting communication is its flow: horizontal, upward, or downward. These designations refer to the direction of information: *horizontal* from someone in one department to a peer in another, *up* from subordinates to superiors, or *down* from superiors to subordinates.

Horizontal Communications Of the three, horizontal (or lateral) communication is usually the least difficult. Except when people in one field explain technical matters to those in another, communications flow clearly. But this technical difficulty is not a slight one. For example, a writer in personnel will often not realize that other employees are unfamiliar with specialized terminology—*vested interest* as it applies to pension plans, for example. Unless people in one department translate such specialized words and concepts into language that nonspecialists in other departments can decode, confusion can result.

Upward Communications Communications that flow upward furnish information and feedback to management, give employees a sense of participation, and sometimes provide profitable suggestions or ideas. Often special channels such as suggestion boxes, gripe forms, and attitude surveys are used to transmit information from subordinates to supervisors.[13] However, one communication problem arises from the reluctance of subordinates to transmit bad news.[14] Few are willing to admit to their failures, confess to their shortcomings, report their mistakes. Instead, they sugar-coat messages to superiors, seldom lying perhaps but often portraying a situation in the best possible light. The result is that upward communications are often written in an environment that prevents management from receiving clear and accurate information except when expressed in numbers—for example, items sold, units produced, or inventory stocked.

Downward Communications Subordinates generally are interested in three types of information from superiors: (1) work-related directions, requirements, benefits, goals, policies, procedures; (2) personal evaluation; and (3) organization news, such as company's financial status, goals, projections, and new products.

Downward communications often fail in organizations because, as Peter Drucker points out, organizations usually are management-oriented.[15] Instead, he contends that managers must get involved with their subordinates to understand what they want and need to hear, what they are interested in, and what they will respond to. In other words, until the manager better understands the economic, social, and cultural environment of employees, communication will not be effective. Management must learn that downward communication will work only after upward communication is well established, and after the attitudes, values, wishes, and aspirations of employees are understood.

Can these environmental obstacles in horizontal, upward, and downward communications be overcome? Certainly. But their existence emphasizes how a knowledge of the communication process aids in communicating. If writers are aware of the difficulties in a communication situation, then they are better prepared to deal with them and to improve their chances of encoding messages more effectively.

There Is More to Communicating Than Writing or Speaking Well

The purpose of explaining communication theory and of discussing communication problems is to show you the complexity of the process and to disclose why there are so many communication problems. It also reinforces the necessity for what we referred to in chapter 1 as reader adaptation. Because the receiver is the most important element in the communication process, you must prepare the message with that person in mind. When you write, you write for a reader. When you speak, you speak to a listener. Your job in communicating is to transmit the meaning in your mind to the mind of the receiver. To do so, you need to know not only how to write or speak effectively but how to perceive and experience the attitudes, feelings, needs, interests, and values of your readers or listeners. And you also need to consider what they already know about the subject, how they will react to it, and why they will react that way. In addition, you need to reflect on their reaction toward you. What do they know about you? How will they feel about you? What do you have in common with them? What role (friend, expert, superior, inferior, and so on) should you assume with them? In other words, you need to develop *empathy* with the receivers of your message. This form of identification with others requires your seeing the world through their eyes and walking in their shoes.

As a result, you would sell an encyclopedia to the mother of a young child in one way and to a college student in another. You would talk about investments with widows differently than you would talk about them with young couples. That is why communicating with one person involves formulating a style and strategy that should be changed in communicating with another. It is not enough, therefore, that you write or speak clearly and correctly. As Robert N. McMurry points out, "There is much more to communication . . . If the communication is not understood, believed, and regarded as having a positive value for its recipients, it will fail in its mission."[16]

One way to avoid such failure is to acquire an understanding of how people use language, specifically, how they express their meaning in words. Consequently, you should know some of the basic concepts of *semantics*, the science of meaning. Remember that the reason for encoding a message is to achieve a goal by expressing ideas in words. So one of your jobs is to find words to convey your ideas. But how do words express meanings? And what do words mean? And can meaning be conveyed in other ways?

Before we proceed to semantics, let us review the communication process briefly. In this chapter we pointed out the difference between writing in school for a grade and writing at work for a business purpose. The communication model demonstrated this process by showing how the sender encodes a message for some purpose and transmits it through a channel to a receiver, who decodes and reacts to it. If this reaction is transmitted to the sender, it is called *feedback*. Another special term, *noise*, refers to anything interfering with the message.

An understanding of the communication process enables you to realize the importance of the receiver, the need to consider the purpose of the communication, the complexity of encoding, the advantages and disadvantages of various channels, the problem of the environment, and the fact that communicating requires more than writing or speaking well.

This brings us to a discussion of semantics in order to understand how we can best select words to convey the meaning in our mind to the mind of a reader or listener.

Semantics

Although relatively new, semantics is a highly active field, as evidenced by the numerous books and articles about the meaning of words.[17] For your practical purpose, we have condensed and simplified this material to the four principles listed on the following page.

1. A word is only a symbol.
2. A word has no fixed or universal meaning.
3. A word's meaning is in the mind of its user.
4. A word's meaning may be derived from its context.

A Word Is Only a Symbol

That a word is a symbol is obvious. The word *money* is not money, a *kiss* is not a kiss, and a *sigh* is not a sigh. Words are merely marks on paper with no inherent meaning. Even an onomatopoetic word like *bow-wow*, which seems to mimic the bark of a dog, is merely a symbol. Otherwise, German dogs would not go *wau-wau*, French dogs *gnaf-gnaf*, Japanese dogs *wung-wung*, or Spanish dogs *guau*.

What we must realize is that a word is a symbol like a flag. And just as a flag has different meanings for different people—those born in the country it represents and those born elsewhere—so a word has different meanings. To many people, the words *tax shelter* suggest a method the wealthy can use to evade paying high income taxes. Yet if these people have mortgages on their homes, they often fail to consider the interest they write off on the mortgage as a form of tax shelter. Like any symbol, the words *tax shelter* and others have no inherent meaning; they represent different things to different people.

A Word Has No Fixed or Universal Meaning

If a word is only a symbol with no inherent meaning, then can a word mean anything the encoder chooses? Theoretically, it can. But for practical purposes, both an encoder and a decoder would have to understand this private meaning. For example, some people refer to cocaine as *dust*; others use the word *dust* to mean money. Similarly, other common words acquire private meanings among various groups such as teenagers, rock musicians, truck drivers, and soldiers. This private language, known as slang, exemplifies the fact that words can mean anything their users wish. Which is just what Humpty Dumpty told Alice, "When I use a word . . . it means just what I choose it to mean—neither more nor less."

Although a word can mean anything the users wish in a private situation or within a special group, it does have a public meaning that is generally accepted. Yet even so, the meaning may not be universal, as this example illustrates:

Dear Friend:

This is a perfect time to buy convertibles. Because there's an oversupply on the market, prices are low, values high. If you're at all interested in convertibles, today is the time to act. Why not give me a call now?

Is the writer selling cars? Sofa beds? Or securities such as convertible stocks or bonds? It could be any of them. With no additional information about the writer or the company, you can't tell.

The point of this contrived example is obvious: *convertible*, like all words, is merely a symbol for something. And, as the example illustrates, the symbol has no universal meaning.

COMMUNICATING IN BUSINESS

Nor is any meaning fixed. A study of the history of our language reveals numerous changes. The word *gay*, formerly used to mean *lively*, now means *homosexual* to most people. In the sixteenth century, *buxom* was a term for a healthy woman, *girls* for young people of either sex, *silly* for feeble, *sly* for skillful, and *presently* for immediately.

A Word's Meaning Is in the Mind of Its User

Customer: May I try on the dress in the window?

Manager: Young lady, do you want to get arrested for indecent exposure?

Humor is usually based on such double meanings. You laugh because you are pleasantly surprised when you discover that the meaning in your mind is not the same as the meaning in the other person's mind. Test this concept of the double meaning on the next joke you hear.

Sometimes students ask their friends to recommend a good course or a good movie, only to regret later that they relied on the advice. The disappointment may be due to differences in judgment, but often it results from a semantic misunderstanding. To one student, a good course is an easy one, requiring little work for high grades. To another, a good course is a challenging one, stimulating a great deal of thought and effort, and producing new knowledge or insights about important concepts. To one student, a good movie is light, pleasant, and entertaining; to another, it is serious, provocative, and realistic. In each of these situations the confusion stems from different meanings of the word *good*.

Similarly, arguments may be heard daily about whether a teacher is liberal, a college regulation fair, a politician honest, or a certain car economical. In each instance we should examine what the speakers mean by *liberal*, *fair*, *honest*, and *economical*. We will usually discover that they are referring to different concepts although they use the same words.

Meaning, therefore, does not reside in words but in minds.

DICTIONARY DEFINITION   But what about the dictionary? Doesn't it explain what words mean?

True, the dictionary provides information about what many people mean when they use specific words. But this meaning may not be useful in a particular instance. For example, you learn that you will be charged 14 percent interest on an $1,800 loan for a car. What will you have to pay? If you look up *interest* in the dictionary, you will find about ten different definitions. In this situation, only one applies: it refers to interest as "the charge for a financial loan." But, so what? This definition doesn't help you. Specifically, it fails to point out the difference between an annual, add-on, or discount rate of interest. And this difference may cost you plenty. With *interest*, *mutual fund*, *term insurance*, *stagflation*, and numerous other words, you had best not rely on the dictionary. Rather, you should find out what meaning the user has in mind.

CONNOTATION   Dictionary definitions are also limited because they usually provide only the denotation or formal meaning of a word. As just illustrated, the denotation can be obscure or of little practical help. But dictionary definitions also omit the connotation of a word: the feelings, emotions, and associations it arouses.

The importance of a word's connotation is best illustrated by synonyms. Both *cop* and *policeman* designate the same individual, but the shorter term labels the man giving out tickets, while the longer one applies to the man helping people out of difficulty. Similarly, Russians engage in *spying*, Americans in *espionage*. In politics, our party has a *leader*, their party a *boss*; we *plan*, they *scheme*; we have an *organization*, they a *machine*; we *persuade* people, they engage in *arm-twisting*; we *pass* motions, they *steam-roll* them through.

Because of connotations, words seldom have precise synonyms. For example, shades of meaning distinguish each of the following: *skinny, underweight, scrawny, slim, slight, svelte, pinched, underfed, bony,* and *spindly*. The word *thin* is probably interchangeable with any of these, but lacks their special nuances.

EUPHEMISMS The importance of connotation can also be demonstrated in our reliance on euphemisms. These words are pleasant substitutes for blunt terms that might be painful, disagreeable, offensive, or demeaning. Many euphemisms reveal the tolerance, sympathy, and understanding of their users. To refer to a *drunk* as an *alcoholic*, to a *cripple* as a *handicapped person*, and to *old people* as *senior citizens* is to be kind. Such simple word substitutions can dignify these people instead of degrading them.

Yet we should not allow euphemisms to deceive us about the truth. People called *public-relations persons, account executives, funeral directors,* and *custodians* are not more important than when they were known as *press agents, stockbrokers, undertakers,* and *janitors*. A person is not any less *dead* for being *deceased*, or more fortunate for being *furloughed* instead of *laid off*.

The problem that euphemisms raise is not only that of deceit but of creating a climate for affected language. Often refined ways of talking impede communication. Sexual discussions, for example, might be more informative if taboo words were permitted. Euphemisms, therefore, may confuse and deceive; or they may please and flatter. Use them when tact dictates and conscience does not reproach.

What is important to you in this discussion about euphemisms and about denotation and connotation is that the meaning of words is elusive. Dictionaries may be generally helpful, but in any specific situation, the meaning of a word resides in the mind of its user. That is why, in a strictly accurate sense, messages do not contain meanings. Meanings are encoded into symbols that are transmitted through channels. But the meanings exist in the minds of the sender and the receiver.

As a writer, therefore, you must be a mind reader. While encoding your message, you must be able to read the mind of the decoder in order to avoid or explain words that might be misunderstood. Remember that words may have one meaning to you, another or even none to your reader. It's a matter of common sense. But there we go: *common sense* does not mean what you might think. It is anything but common.

A Word's Meaning Is Derived From Its Context

If words are only symbols whose meanings are in the minds of their users, how can we ever understand one another? A word's context usually helps. Here's an example:

He received a pass.

Pass in this sentence might denote a grade, a football, a permit, a weekend leave, the right to proceed to first base, a thrust in fencing, a refusal to bid in bridge, or an approving eye from a girl. The context—the preceding or following sentences—will usually indicate the precise meaning.

As a matter of fact, dictionary meanings are derived from context. Lexicographers (dictionary writers or compilers) note new words or new meanings for old words on 3- by 5-inch slips of paper. When these citations are collected in sufficient number from a variety of sources (newspapers, magazines, books), a new entry appears in the next edition of the dictionary.

For example, in the mid-seventies when the oil crisis first began to look permanent and serious, the word *gas guzzler* (and such family members as *guzzlers* and *gas-guzzling*) began to appear in print.[18] Researchers noted the word in several places, one being a 1977 *New Yorker* cartoon: [Car salesman to prospective buyer] "This may be your last chance to acquire a superpowered, oversized, hyperpolluting gas-guzzler. Don't blow it." Numerous later occurrences of the word showed that it was becoming part of our language.

Sometimes, instead of coining a new term, people will add a new meaning to an old one. For instance, *creative* signifying "inventive or imaginative" has been around for quite a while. But lexicographers detected that it was being used in this slightly different sense: "Inventive or imaginative, especially for the purpose of conveying a false impression or perpetrating a fraud."[19] At first, when the word was used this way it appeared in quotation marks, as this example from a 1974 *New York Times* article shows: "The IRS . . . will take strong measures against 'creative' tax devices . . . ." In a few years, the word appeared in this sense in such phrases as *creative accountant*, *creative accounting*, and *creative bookkeeping* without any quotation marks—as illustrated by this sentence from a 1977 *Esquire* article: "Once or twice his highly creative annual accounting was issued without benefit of an auditor's attestation."

As you can see, lexicographers do not coin new words or create meanings. They report how language is being used, no matter how illogically or inconsistently. *Topless waitress* (see figure 2–2) does not mean what it says, *in-law* is not the opposite of *outlaw*, and *retire* has nothing to do with *tire*. Then there are words like *unloosen*, *invaluable*, and *inflammable* that should mean the opposite of what they do.

Related to these illogical words are those with contrary meanings. We can hold *fast* or run *fast*, since *fast* can refer to no movement or to quick movement. Farmers *dust* crops and housewives *dust* furniture, one adding a substance, the other removing one. *Seeded* rye bread has the seeds in; *seeded* raisins have them out. And a *handicap* is usually a disadvantage, but in golf or bowling it is an advantage.

What helps us understand not only these words but all words is their context.

In our brief treatment of semantics, we have explained four key concepts: (1) a word is only a symbol; (2) a word has no fixed or universal meaning; (3) a word's meaning is in the mind of its user; and (4) a word's meaning may be derived from its context. To communicate effectively, in both encoding and decoding, you should keep these concepts in mind.

Figure 2–2. Topless Waitress.

Topless Waitress

(SOURCE: Reprinted by permission of *Verbatim.*)

NONVERBAL COMMUNICATION

The preceding discussion of semantics may suggest that we convey meaning only through words. Not so. Consciously or subconsciously, people use forms of wordless communication in transmitting messages. Both as sender and as receiver, you should become alert to and understand these nonverbal elements of communication.

Nonverbal Communication in Written Messages

In written communication, the message tells nearly all. But nonverbal language plays a role in three respects: time, length, and format.

TIME   What you write is important, but your promptness in replying may help or hinder your message. A quick response indicates your interest; a slow one suggests your lack of interest, regardless of words to the contrary and most excuses. Here's what happens.

People who mail letters to out-of-town addresses often fail to consider that the letters may not be delivered the next day or for several days, because of an intervening weekend or slow mail service. Instead, anxious for a reply, they expect one the following day, or surely in the next two or three. So if a response is not written promptly and mailed immediately, they feel slighted. Also, to them, a few days seem like a week, a week like a month, a month like forever. One device to counteract this problem when you answer letters is to mention that the reply is being made to "your letter, which arrived _____ ."

As you can realize, time in the form of a prompt or tardy response adds a wordless message to the written one.

LENGTH   As we mentioned in the first chapter, business communications should be economical, containing no needless words. But in some situations, a terse letter may suggest a lack of concern or courtesy. Also, as some sales letters reveal, length plays an important role in communication. It is not unusual to receive letters of from four to six pages, extolling *Time, US News*, or a record club. The nonverbal message is that the product is so excellent there is much to say in its favor. Does the length bore or irritate the reader? Evidently not. Instead, the length of the sales message adds a wordless sales message that reinforces the written one.

FORMAT   The format of a written communication also conveys a wordless message. Attractively typed letters on handsome stationery create a favorable appearance just as a well-dressed person does. But in some personal situations, a less formal touch is desirable. Letters of condolence to a personal friend or a business acquaintance should ordinarily be handwritten rather than typed. And so should notes on Christmas and birthday cards, whenever possible. A greeting card with a typed address and only a written signature conveys a nonverbal message that may negate the written one. Just a few words—even a "Dear _____"—are much better.

These are some of the ways that nonverbal elements, such as time, length, and format, can reinforce or detract from the written message.

Nonverbal Communication in Oral Messages

Numerous excellent books have been written about nonverbal language in face-to-face communication.[20] What follows, therefore, is a mere summary of the subject. Our discussion will deal with the sources of the wordless message: voice, hands, body, appearance, time, and space.

VOICE   You're probably familiar with people who say "Thank you" or "I've had a good time" as though they meant it. Others utter the same words but sound as if they didn't. Voice qualities signal the difference. Pitch, volume, rate, rhythm, pauses, and variations in them all affect what we say. Another quality, emphasis, can also change the meaning of a sentence. The same words—"You should phone the customer today"—can be transmitted to send three different messages:

> *You* should phone the customer today.
> You should *phone* the customer today.
> You should phone the customer *today*.

We will discuss the use of voice at greater length in our chapter on oral presentation.

HANDS   One researcher has classified more than one hundred different hand gestures.[21] Some may be used instead of verbal messages: waving to say goodbye, thumbing to ask for a ride, clapping to express approval, pointing to indicate direction or location. Others supplement or reinforce the message: a tight fist to convey anger or joy; a raised finger to enumerate the points in an argument; a pointed index finger to scold, threaten, or accuse. Other hand movements transmit a variety of signals: finger-tapping reveals nervousness or anxiety, a pat on the back or arm signifies affection or friendship.

In these ways, we talk with our hands. No one hears what we say, but many get the message.

BODY Posture conveys various messages. Professors with their feet on the desk, students slouched in their seats, or audiences sitting up and leaning forward are all communicating without words. Rigid postures suggest dislike or insecurity; relaxed ones signal familiarity or security. The ways we stand, sit, or position our bodies all make nonverbal statements.

APPEARANCE Even before we open our mouths, our physical appearance (features, build, clothes, grooming) sends signals to others. We can do little to change our features, but we can shape up and appear attractive. People who are unconventional in dress and grooming strike others as individualists, apt to hold unconventional views. Those who wear conventional clothes and style their hair conservatively often find it easier to communicate and be accepted.

TIME We communicate nonverbally to others by our use of time with them. Latecomers for appointments signal a lack of concern. Early birds send a more favorable wordless message. In addition, the length of time allotted someone says much without words. A thirty-minute interview indicates a greater interest than a ten-minute one.

SPACE The use of space can be a complicated subject, as is illustrated by the research of Edward Hall, who has worked out a scale of distance to show four human relationships: intimate (18 inches or less) for discussing confidential matters; personal (1½ to 4 feet) for conversations with friends; social (4 to 12 feet) for social conversations and for business meetings (7 to 12 feet); and public (farther than 12 feet) for public speeches and similar occasions.[22]

Physical space is also important in other communication situations. If you have ever had a class in a seminar room around a table, or were able to sit in a circle or semicircle in a classroom, you may have realized how the seating arrangement facilitated discussion. When people can look at and talk to one another, they are more apt to participate. In the traditional classroom, on the other hand, students often have to talk to the back of someone's head, an unappealing prospect not conducive to communication.

The decor of business offices—color, light, furniture—and the size and location of the desk and chairs also convey wordless messages.[23] The manager in a huge chair behind a massive desk looking down on an employee sitting opposite sends out nonverbal signals of authority, seeming indifferent to exchanging ideas. The manager sitting at a coffee table next to an employee establishes a friendly rapport, nonverbally communicating a desire to remove the barriers between them and to share ideas.

These are some of the ways that nonverbal communication can speak louder than words. What we say with our voice, hands, body, appearance, time, and space can communicate volumes. So we have to do more than just say what we mean. We have to sound like it, look like it, and act like it.

SUMMARY

In this chapter, we pointed out how the business communication process differs from writing and speaking in school both in purpose and in emphasis. In school, you speak and write to a teacher in order to receive a grade by demonstrating your ability. At work, you speak and write to people to build goodwill or sell a product or service by informing and persuading them. In school, your ability and ideas are central. At work, your readers or listeners are foremost: effective communication depends on their reacting as you wish to your message.

To help you understand the process of communication better, we illustrated communication theory with a model that consisted of a *sender*, a *channel*, and a *receiver*. We showed how the process begins with a stimulus that causes a sender to encode a message for some purpose and transmit it through some channel to a receiver, who decodes and reacts to it. If the receiver responds by returning a message to the sender, this action is called *feedback*. The term *noise* is used to refer to any interference between the message sent and the one received. Both sender and receiver are influenced by numerous internal and external forces called *environment*.

Next we examined how the communication model illustrates the importance of the receiver, the need to consider purpose, the complexity of encoding, the advantages and disadvantages of various channels, the problem of environment, and the fact that communication requires more than the ability to write or speak well. In connection with our discussion of the business environment, we pointed out how management theories such as X, Y, and Z might cause variations in a written message.

Because communication concerns the transmission of ideas in words, we felt it would help you to have some understanding of semantics, the science of the meaning of words. We discussed four concepts in some detail: a word is only a symbol, a word has no fixed or universal meaning, a word's meaning is in the mind of its user, and a word's meaning is derived from its context.

In exploring these ideas, we examined the role of the dictionary, the connotation and denotation of words, and the use of euphemisms.

Meaning is not transmitted by words alone but also by certain nonverbal signs. In writing, these consist of time, length, and format. In speaking, they include the voice, hands, face, body, appearance, time, and space. The wordless messages conveyed by these nonverbal factors may add to or detract from the verbal communication.

This chapter about communication provides a conceptual basis for everything we will discuss in the remainder of this book.

EXERCISES

Discussion Questions

1. In what respect is writing at school a form of game? In what respect is it not?
2. Why is perfect communication seldom achieved?
3. To what extent is the receiver responsible for communication?
4. In what way does faulty grammar affect communication?
5. What are some of the specific channels used by college officials to communicate to students?
6. Illustrate the working of the communication model with a cheer at a football game, a tally at a supermarket check-out counter, or a policeman's signaling the driver of a car before him to pull over.
7. What kinds of feedback do you usually receive on an examination?
8. In a large auditorium, what forms of noise usually interfere with a professor's lecture? What does each mean?
9. In your opinion, is the trend in large corporations today toward managing according to Theory X, Y, or Z?
10. In what ways does your instructor's ability to communicate well in class depend on more than good speaking skills?
11. Why are downward communications dependent on well-established upward communications?
12. What would be the best channel to use for the following:
    a. Asking an instructor to reconsider a grade.
    b. Inviting a professor to talk to a student organization.
    c. Obtaining answers to a four-page questionnaire from an instructor.
    d. Learning whether an instructor will hold class on an exceptionally bad wintry day.
13. Why study semantics?
14. Explain why the dictionary is or is not an authority on the meaning of words.
15. What semantic concept explains the fact that a pancake is called a *griddlecake*, a *flapjack*, a *slapjack*, or a *fritter* in various parts of the country?
16. What is logical or illogical about the following words: *American, drip-dry hanger, pierced earrings*.
17. What do you make semantically of the use of *guy* to refer to a female?
18. Analyze the following by pointing out the double meanings:
    a. *English teacher:* There are two words I will not allow you to use in your papers. They are swell and lousy.
    (*Pause.*)
    Student: But, Professor!
    English teacher: Yes?
    Student: What are the two words?

    b. *Mother:* Son, get up. You're late for school.
    Son: I'm not going.
    Mother: Why?

Son: For two reasons: the kids don't like me and the teachers hate me.
Mother: I've got two reasons why you should go: you're fifty and you're the principal.

19. Do you know any hand movements that convey messages without words other than those mentioned in the text?
20. What nonverbal signals do students transmit to instructors to indicate that the class period is ending?
21. The dictionary lists two meanings for *biweekly*: twice a week and every two weeks. Explain why this is so.
22. Writers, editors, and others have been unable to find an appropriate word to designate the person of the opposite sex whom an individual is living with but is not married to. What is the matter with the following: friend, fiancé(e), lover, companion, suitor, roommate, partner?
23. Discuss (1) the meanings of *thought better* in the following sentences and (2) the semantic principle involved:

    After taking her course, I thought better of her.
    After planning to buy the shirt, I thought better of it.

24. Explain semantically how it is possible to (1) play a guitar by ear; (2) write a long brief; (3) be under the weather; and (4) go to pot.
25. Select one word from each of the following pairs that you believe would be more effective for a speech by management to plant employees, and explain your choice:

    corporation/company   strike/work stoppage
    profits/earnings   personnel/fellow workers
    free enterprise/capitalism   guidelines/restrictions

In-Class Applications

Write out brief answers to the following questions.

1. Explain the meaning of *man* in the following sentences and point out the ones that are sexist:

    a. The Little League team is a *man* short.
    b. Stop sucking your thumb, take your teddy bear, and be a *man*.
    c. Will one of you girls please *man* the tiller.
    d. *Man*, what a catch! (What does *catch* mean?)
    e. This dorm food is fit for neither *man* nor beast.
    f. One girl was screaming, "Get your paws offa my *man*!"
    g. They're switching to a *man*-to-man defense.
    h. Number 43 is your *man*.
    i. If you're not careful, he'll take your *man* with his queen.
    j. To a *man*, they stood up.
    k. He was his own *man*.

2. How many meanings of the word *got* can you find in the following paragraph?

> As soon as I got your call, I got into my car and got to the airport in about half an hour. I immediately got a ticket, got on the plane, and got a good seat near the window. After the plane got up in the air, I got my dinner from the stewardess, but I got upset when I got soaked from her spilling the coffee over me. When we landed, I got a new shirt, fearing that I might have got a cold by continuing to wear the wet one. Then I got a cab for the office where I got word that no one had got a hotel room for me. Therefore, I got one for myself. After I had got my message across to the district manager, I got out of having dinner with my friends by letting them know that I had got a headache. I got to the hotel, got dinner served in my room, and got to sleep before midnight. After I got up the next morning, I got dressed, got a plane home, and got back before the afternoon shift got to work. I hope that I got some results for you.

3. Explain the meaning of the word *nice* in the following sentences:

   a. It was a *nice* day.
   b. He was in a *nice* business.
   c. He was a *nice* person.
   d. The lecture was *nice*.
   e. It's a *nice* day—for fishing!
   f. They throw a *nice* party.
   g. She is a *nice* girl.
   h. She is naughty but *nice*.
   i. It's one of those *nice* accounts.
   j. He gets *nice* prices for his merchandise.
   k. During the annual sale, the store offers some *nice* bargains.
   l. She is a *nice* customer.

4. In the following sentences, interpret the meaning of the verb *mean*:

   a. By neutrality we really *mean* nonbelligerence.
   b. That guy *means* trouble.
   c. He doesn't *mean* you, he *means* the manager.
   d. That painting *means* nothing to me.
   e. Smoke *means* fire.
   f. I *mean* what I say.
   g. I know what I *mean* but I can't say it.
   h. Is my *meaning* clear?
   i. What do you *mean*?

5. Explain the meaning of the italicized words in the following sentences and justify your answer:

   a. Although he was required to pay *adult* prices at the local theaters, he was admitted only to regular movies and not to *adult* ones.
   b. The manager finished his *toast* and then stood up to offer a *toast* to the new president.

c. As he sat thinking about his next move, he glanced around at the *full house* in the casino and then looked again at the *full house* in his hand.

d. In the association, he was recognized as a *banker's banker*.

Writing Assignments

1. Assume that a controversy exists on your campus about whether first-year students should be called *freshmen* or *first-year students*. Write a semantically based argument favoring one or the other.

2. An automobile company has written you for help in selecting the name of its new two-passenger electric car that can go 48 miles an hour and run for ten hours on an overnight battery charge. Write a letter suggesting a name and explaining why it would be appropriate.

3. Assume that students at your college are inadequately informed about campus regulations, academic policies, and new developments. Write a letter to the president of the college, suggesting new channels that might be used to improve communication.

4. Sexual harassment on the job in business, industry, and government is becoming an increasing concern, as it is on college campuses. For a student-faculty committee formed to study this problem at your college, write a definition of this term that would include examples of the prohibited conduct.

5. Explain how you would adapt Theory X, Y, or Z to some leadership role, such as coaching an athletic team, directing a scout troop, or serving as a camp counselor. Discuss what basic assumptions you would make about those subordinate to you and what you would do to motivate them effectively.

6. Write a paper about the nonverbal behavior of one of your instructors.

NOTES

[1] A. J. Barker, *The Vainglorious War, 1854–56* (London: Weidenfeld and Nicolson, 1970), pp. 161–74.

[2] Stuart Chase, *Power of Words* (New York: Harcourt Brace & World, 1953), p. 259.

[3] Claude L. Shannon and Warren Weaver, *The Mathematical Model of Communication* (Urbana, Ill.: Univ. of Illinois Press, 1949), p. 98.

[4] For example: Wilbur Schramm, "How Communication Works," *The Process and Effects of Mass Communication* (Urbana, Ill.: Univ. of Illinois Press, 1955), pp. 4–8; Colin Cherry, "Communication Theory—and Human Behavior," *Studies in Communication* (London: Martin, Secker, and Warburg, 1955); Bruce H. Westley and Malcolm S. MacLean, "A Conceptual Model for Communications Research," *Audio-Visual Communication Review*, 3 (Winter, 1955), pp. 4–7; and Lee Thayer, *Communication and Communication Systems* (Homewood, Ill.: Richard D. Irwin, 1968).

[5] This model is indebted to suggestions in E. Reber Casstevens, "An Approach to Communication Model Building," *The Journal of Business Communication*, 16, no. 3 (Spring 1979), pp. 31–41.

[6] National Medical Enterprises, July 1980.

[7] Paul R. Trim, *Managerial Communication* (Englewood Cliffs, N.J.: Prentice-Hall, 1980), p. 14.

[8] Adapted from Auren Uris, *The Executive Deskbook* (New York: Van Nostrand Reinhold, 1970), p. 28.

[9] According to the Dartnell Institute of Business Research, the cost of a secretary-dictated letter in 1980 was $6.63.

[10] S. Bernard Rosenblatt, T. Richard Cheatham, and James T. Watt, *Communication in Business* (Englewood Cliffs, N.J.: Prentice-Hall, 1977), p. 102.

[11] Douglas McGregor, *The Human Side of Enterprise* (New York: McGraw-Hill, 1960).

[12] William G. Ouchi, *Theory Z* (Reading, Mass.: Addison-Wesley, 1981); see especially pages 71–94. Another excellent book on the same subject is Richard Tanner Pascale and Anthony G. Athos, *The Art of Japanese Management* (New York: Simon and Schuster, 1981).

[13] Cal W. Downs, David M. Berg, and Wil A. Linkugel, *The Organizational Communicator* (New York: Harper and Row, 1977), p. 28.

[14] Robert N. McMurry, "Clear Communications for Chief Executives," *Harvard Business Review*, 43 (March–April, 1965), pp. 131–32.

[15] Peter F. Drucker, *Management: Tasks, Responsibilities, Practices* (New York: Harper and Row, 1973), pp. 481–93. Cf. R. W. Driver, "Issues in Upward Communication," *Supervisory Communication*, 25 (February 1980), pp. 10–13.

[16] McMurry, p. 132.

[17] For an excellent introduction to semantics and a fine bibliography on the subject, see S. I. Hayakawa, *Language in Thought and Action*, 4th ed. (New York: Harcourt Brace Jovanovich, 1978).

[18] Willis Russell and Mary Gray Porter, "Among the New Words," *American Speech*, 54, no. 1 (Spring 1979), p. 41.

[19] Russell and Porter, *American Speech*, 56, no. 7 (Summer 1981), p. 113.

[20] To mention only a few: Ray L. Birdwhistell, *Kinesics and Context* (Philadelphia: Univ. of Pennsylvania, 1970); Mark L. Knapp, *Nonverbal Communication in Human Interaction* (New York: Holt, Rinehart and Winston, 1972); and Shirley Weitz, ed., *Nonverbal Communications: Readings With Commentary* (New York: Oxford Univ. Press, 1974). For an annotated bibliography of nonverbal communication related to business, see Robert W. Rasberry, "A Collection of Nonverbal Communication Research," *The Journal of Business Communication*, 16 (Summer 1979), pp. 21–29.

[21] Paul Ekman, "Differential Communication of Affect by Head and Body Cues," *Journal of Personality and Social Psychology*, 17 (1971), pp. 726–35.

[22] *The Hidden Dimension* (Garden City, N.Y.: Doubleday, 1966), pp. 113–29.

[23] For a more detailed discussion of office furnishings with numerous photographic examples, see Michael B. McCasky, "Hidden Messages Managers Send," *Harvard Business Review*, 57 (November–December 1979), pp. 135–48.

Part II

COMMUNICATING BY LETTERS

3 Information Letters

OBJECTIVES

After reading this chapter, you should be able to:

- Explain why creating goodwill is important in information letters
- Describe the organizational strategies of request letters (both expected and unexpected), replies, order letters, and acknowledgments
- Point out what information may be requested from people seeking credit, and what information must be provided to them if they are denied credit
- Discuss the strategy of recommendation letters and the ethical problems that sometimes arise in writing them
- Explain two principles that should be followed in selecting words for business letters
- Point out how to check for subject-verb agreement in three troublesome sentence constructions
- Explain how to end business letters effectively

PLAN

Strategy
Information
Goodwill
Communication Situation
    Requests
    Replies
    Orders
    Acknowledgments
    Credit
    Recommendations
Technique
Words
    Natural Words
    Specific Words
Sentences
    Subject-Verb Agreement
Stylistic Considerations
    Courtesy
    Beginnings
    Endings
Summary

*Knowledge is of two kinds. We
know a subject ourselves, or we
know where we can find information
about it.*

SAMUEL JOHNSON

STRATEGY

"Could you please tell me what stores in my city carry the jacket you advertised in the February *Playboy*?"

"I'd appreciate information about your accommodations and special rates."

"Please inform me how to change the beneficiary in my life insurance policy."

"I need a bobbin winder for my model 7046A sewing machine. Do you still carry them?"

Inquiries such as these are constantly written in the working world to obtain information about products, services, personnel, operations, plans, finances, and countless other matters. They may come from customers, prospective employees, government officials, stockholders, suppliers, and members of the general public. Regardless of who writes them and to whom they are written, both the request and the reply should contain the appropriate information and build goodwill.

INFORMATION

When requesting information, your letter should specify exactly what you want to know and what you consider the important details to be. When you answer a letter requesting information, your reply should be complete, accurate, and specific. These suggestions seem obvious enough, but often writers fail to consider their readers' requirements. For example, the preceding inquiry about a jacket advertised in *Playboy* could easily be incomplete. What if several jackets were advertised on a particular page in that issue? Or, what if several jackets were advertised on different pages? As you can realize, the writer would be wise to provide all the pertinent information—page number, description, model number, and price if available. The description should be specific (not "a windbreaker" but "an updated and adapted World War II bomber jacket") and the details about it should be accurate (#8412R, price $75).

Complete, specific, and accurate information is obviously as necessary in the reply as in the request. For example, in answering the inquiry about the bobbin winder for the sewing machine, you would be helpful to include not only its price but shipping information about date, charges, and method of delivery. In other words, you should provide whatever information a reader might reasonably want to know even though not specifically requested. Being complete, therefore, means more than

49

merely answering a reader's question ("Yes, we do carry bobbin winders for model 7046A"). And being accurate and specific means stating all the pertinent information correctly and in detail.

As a writer of a request or a reply, therefore, you should ask yourself three questions in reviewing your letter:

Is the information complete?
Is it specific?
Is it accurate?

In addition, you should be concerned about building goodwill.

GOODWILL

People's opinions about a company, state agency, public utility, bank, or university are often formed from letters. Thus a careless, indifferent request or reply suggests a careless, indifferent organization. A careful, courteous request or reply suggests a careful, courteous one. Which of the two organizations would you prefer to do business with?

Information letters, therefore, should do more than provide facts and figures. They should try to build goodwill. Just as you would be friendly to another person in a store, office, or factory, so you should be friendly in letters to create goodwill.

Goodwill is desirable for three reasons. First of all, it may directly pay off, helping you obtain your request or, in a reply, resulting in some benefit. In addition, goodwill may indirectly prove beneficial, creating a favorable image of you and your organization that may be rewarding at some future time. Finally, being friendly and courteous in building goodwill brings a sense of self-satisfaction from knowing that you have been pleasant to others and have treated them as you would have them treat you.

COMMUNICATION SITUATION

We have dwelt on the necessity of stating all pertinent information and creating goodwill because information letters provide excellent opportunities for establishing good business relationships. In view of the previous chapter about the communication process, you should realize the importance of clarifying your purpose in order to encode a message properly for your receiver. By understanding that you want to build goodwill as well as to convey information, you can design your letters more effectively. And realizing that the information should be complete, specific, and accurate can help you to project yourself in the reader's place to consider what that person needs to know.

In all information letters, your purpose and the needs of your readers will depend on the communication situation. We cannot discuss all the circumstances in which information is requested or provided, but we can deal with such common ones as requests, replies, orders, order acknowledgments, credit letters, and recommendations.

Requests

Request letters seek to obtain products, people, or services, or information about them. They include questions about or applications for accommodations, catalogs, prices, appointments, parts, forms, tickets, and scholarships. Although requests differ in many ways, they can be classified in two general categories according to the anticipated reaction of the reader. In numerous situations, the reader expects to receive inquiries. These we will refer to as *requests-expected*. In others, the requests are *unexpected*, which is how we will designate them.

When you write to a motel for a reservation, to a store for its advertised catalog, or to a college for an application, you expect that your request will be answered. So in numerous business situations, you can reasonably depend on receiving a reply because it will be in the best interest of the recipient to respond. The motel, the store, and the college, for example, will reply because they hope to attract travelers, customers, and students. A television station, a chamber of commerce, and a museum will also ordinarily respond to requests although they themselves may not expect to profit directly. But they hope to create goodwill, thereby benefiting indirectly.

REQUESTS-EXPECTED   When a reply can reasonably be expected, the request letter should take the following form:

1. Request
2. Details about request if necessary
3. Explanation of reason for request if necessary
4. If needed, deadline for reply
5. Friendly close

The letter should begin with a request telling the reader what is wanted. This beginning is helpful for two reasons: it immediately satisfies the reader's curiosity; and if the letter has been sent to a large company, it saves time by indicating to whom the letter should be routed for an answer.

The opening request may take two forms, a statement or a question:

Statement: I would appreciate a copy of your annual report as offered in *Forbes*.

Question: Will you please send me a copy of your annual report as offered in *Forbes*. (No question mark is used here because compliance with the request is expected. If compliance is uncertain, a question mark may be used.)

Both are acceptable. Some people favor the opening question form because it is attention-getting; others dislike its abruptness.

Occasionally, the request cannot be adequately expressed in one sentence. If so, the necessary details should follow in another paragraph:

```
I would appreciate information about and rates for holding
the regional meeting of the American Business Communi-
cation Association in your hotel on Friday and Saturday,
April 3-4, 19--.
```

> We will need about sixty rooms to accommodate out-of-town
> members for these days. In addition, we would like to use
> a large meeting room for 150 people both evenings and four
> small rooms for 25 people each during the days. We would
> also be interested in holding a banquet for about 100 peo-
> ple in a private dining room on Saturday night.

The third part of the letter might consist of an explanation if one is necessary or helpful. In the previous example about the meeting, none is needed. But in writing for a copy of an annual report, it might be helpful to add an explanation:

> Since I am interested in a career in the fast-food res-
> taurant business, I would like to learn as much as possible
> about McDonald's.

If you need a reply by a certain date, a request to that effect would constitute the fourth part of the letter:

> I would appreciate hearing from you before February 14.

The letter should then close with a courteous ending, which we will discuss later in this chapter.

The previously outlined five-step approach may not always be necessary. Occasionally, a one-sentence statement will suffice:

> Please send me your price list for the leasing of IBM GSD
> computers as advertised in The Wall Street Journal.

> Will you have your sales representative contact me about
> my carrying some of the sweaters advertised in the Novem-
> ber issue of Redbook?

REQUESTS-UNEXPECTED   Even when an inquiry is neither solicited nor anticipated, most people and businesses will reply if the time, trouble, and cost are not excessive. But you should not take their response for granted. You should make your request as clear, courteous, and convenient to answer as possible. The unexpected request follows this pattern:

1. Request
2. Details about request when helpful
3. Reason for the request
4. Possible benefit for the reader
5. Close: courteous but not presumptuous

The following example shows how digressing from this order can result in an unsatisfactory letter. Here a bank is asking its customers to complete a short questionnaire:

Dear Customer:

    First National is attempting to provide its customers
with the best banking possible. We are constantly trying
to improve our services.

    As a result, we are interested in knowing how our cus-
tomers feel about banking at our branch offices. We would
like to serve our customers as efficiently in these branches
as we do in the main office downtown.

    For that reason we are sending you the enclosed ques-
tionnaire. Will you please complete it and return it to
us.

    Thank you in advance for helping us.

Sincerely,

The main problem here is obvious: the purpose of the letter is not revealed until
the third paragraph. In addition, the writer fails to point out the benefit for the
customer, yet assumes he or she will respond. Some readers, resentful of being taken
for granted, might just decide not to reply.
    The following version of the letter should be more successful:

Dear Customer:

    Will you please take a few minutes to complete the en-
closed brief questionnaire so that we at First National
can improve our service to you.

    We would like to help you as much as possible, particu-
larly at your branch office. In order to do so, we need
your opinion about the services there.

    If you will fill out the enclosed questionnaire and re-
turn it in the envelope provided, we will use the information to improve our branch office service for you.

    We would greatly appreciate your help with our survey.

Sincerely,

Note these points:

1. The revised version gets to the point quickly.
2. It indicates how the reader will benefit.
3. It facilitates the reader's reply by providing a stamped addressed envelope.
4. It expresses appreciation but does not take the reader's reply for granted.

Two footnotes: first, a stamped envelope is often more effective than a printed business-reply one. People feel compelled to respond when they see a stamp, perhaps because they dislike wasting it. Second, although you should provide a return-addressed envelope when writing to an individual or a small company, you need not enclose one to most large organizations; they normally prefer to use their own.

Replies

Depending on certain environmental factors in the communication process, replies may be regular, form, or quick, as we shall explain. The letter of reply generally follows this pattern:

1. Opener: appreciation, answer, reference
2. Explanation or discussion; if applicable, sales or goodwill message
3. Friendly close

REGULAR REPLIES A difference of opinion exists about the beginning of a regular reply letter, which is one written specifically to an individual reader. Some writers believe in thanking the inquirer immediately, others favor answering the request first, and still others suggest one or the other along with a reference to the date of the inquirer's letter. Our recommendation is that you consider the reader's concern and decide accordingly.

If the inquiry is a routine one—perhaps a customer's asking why a store no longer carries a certain line of sweaters—the letter should begin courteously:

> Thank you for writing to inquire why we are no longer car-
> rying the Woolwarm brand of sweaters.

This opening announces the subject of the letter and sets a pleasant mood. An immediate response to the inquiry seems abrupt and is unnecessary:

> Because the Woolwarm sweaters did not wash and wear as well
> as others, we have discontinued carrying them. Instead,
> we now stock the popular Ski Valley sweaters, which . . .

Nor is there any necessity to repeat the date of the reader's letter:

> In response to your letter of November 21, we are glad to
> have this opportunity to inform you why we are no longer
> carrying the Woolwarm sweaters.

In replying to someone handling a voluminous correspondence in a large company, however, a date or subject reference may be necessary. Ways to handle these references will be discussed at the end of this chapter.

In a different situation, when the inquirer may be somewhat breathlessly awaiting your reply, you should answer promptly and come straight to the point:

```
Your application should arrive by Friday, March 15--giving
you ample time to return it before the April 1 deadline.
```

The decision about whether to open with an appreciative statement, a reference to the inquiry, or an immediate answer depends, as you can see, on your analyzing your reader. This brings us back to a key point in the previous chapter about the communication process. Writing well is not enough. You must also consider the receiver of your message, trying to figure out first what strategy will most effectively convey your message to that person. Then you can decide how to begin your reply.

The body of the letter presents the reply itself, containing any helpful explanation or discussion, and if appropriate, a sales or goodwill message. If a brochure or other material is to be enclosed, some reference should be made to it (see the second paragraph of the letter in figure 3–1). Or, if the inquirer has requested material— a catalog, for example—that you are sending by less expensive and hence slower mail, some statement like the following should be made:

```
We are sending our university catalog to you by third class
mail today. You should receive it within the next two
weeks.
```

Be careful not to underestimate the delivery date. When people are waiting for something, days seem like weeks. If the material does not arrive on time, you may annoy or lose customers.

The letter should end with a friendly close, welcoming further questions if applicable or thanking the inquirer again.

FORM REPLIES   Some businesses and organizations receive numerous inquiries. For example, the admissions offices of many colleges operate like huge mail-order businesses, sending out thousands of responses to inquiries about admissions, programs, fees, catalogs, scholarships, and dorms. Instead of writing an original letter each time, the office uses printed forms, automatic typewriters, or other word processing equipment. The letter to a transfer student in figure 3–2, for example, requires only that a secretary type the inside address and the name of the student and person signing the letter. In the sample business form reply (see figure 3–3), the letter is previously prepared and the typist adds only the name and address of the inquirer and the stores where the company's products are carried. You are probably familiar with clever personalized form letters such as those used by the *Reader's Digest*, *Publisher's Clearing House*, and record and book clubs. The object of all these letters is to economize by using a standard form but at the same time to individualize the letter by inserting names and other details so that it does not sound like a form reply. As you can imagine, it's much easier described than done.

Figure 3–1.   Letter Enclosing Literature.

Harper's Ferry, West Virginia 25425   Telephone (304) 555–1110

April 19, 19--

Mr. Michael T. Williams
23 Chester Avenue
Timonium, Maryland 21093

Dear Mr. Williams:

Thank you for your recent request for literature about The Jefferson
Hotel.

Although we feel it is virtually impossible to capture in a brochure
the hospitable atmosphere and the natural beauty found at The Jefferson,
we hope the enclosed literature will serve to familiarize you with our
facilities and recreational activities.

During the summer months, all dates close rapidly. We suggest that
as soon as your plans for a visit are complete, you contact the Reservation
Department to ascertain availability of space during your preferred dates.

The majority of our rooms have baths with doors wide enough to
accommodate persons with wheelchairs. When making reservations, please
indicate that Mrs. Williams uses a wheelchair and, if at all possible,
convenient accommodations will be assigned accordingly.

Each season of the year has its own particular charm, and a vacation
at The Jefferson truly makes a memorable holiday. We look forward to
serving you soon, and should you desire additional information, please
feel free to contact me. I will be happy to assist you with making
reservations as well.

Sincerely,

Mrs. Brenda Hawthorne

Mrs. Brenda Hawthorne
Reservationist

BH/tf

Enclosures

COMMUNICATING BY LETTERS

Figure 3–2.   Form Reply to a College Student.

HAMDEN COLLEGE
Office of Admissions

Card 3322

Dear:

    Thank you for your recent letter requesting information about transferring to Hamden College.

    Enclosed with this letter is a copy of the HC Preview and an application for admission. Please read the preview carefully before completing the application. It will answer most questions about transferring to Hamden College. If you should have additional questions, however, please feel free to contact this office.

    Thank you for your interest in Hamden College.

Yours truly,

:mtp

Enclosure

QUICK REPLIES   A less expensive, less formal, and less attractive but more practical way to handle certain inquiries is to jot a note on the request and return it, making a copy for the files if necessary. Sometimes a printed gummed sticker, available at many office supply stores, is glued on the letter, saying something like:

QUICK REPLY
To give you the
fastest possible response,
we have written in
the margins of your letter.
We believe you would prefer
speed to formality.

Figure 3–3. Form Reply to a Customer.

MAYFAIR SHOES

August 11, 19--

Ms. Carol Falcone
1883 Manassas Drive
Alliance, Nebraska 69301

Dear Ms. Falcone:

Thank you for writing to Mayfair and inquiring about our shoes. Please
find below a list of retailers where Mayfair shoes are available.

Gerard Shoes	Midland Shopping Center
Tash Shoes	Box Butte Mall
Wennekers	Main Street

We are unable to supply specific style and size information for the
stores listed above. If the style or size you are looking for is not
available at any of the locations above, please contact our Mail Order
Department which is located in New York for ordering information.

For your convenience we have added your name to our permanent catalog
mailing list. We will be sending you our newest catalog as soon as it
becomes available.

Thank you again for your interest in Mayfair shoes. If you should have
any further questions, please feel free to call or write us.

Sincerely,

Suzanne Mendez

Suzanne Mendez
Customer Service

Sales Offices ■ Four East 55th Street, New York, New York 10022 ■ Phone 212–555–3212

Corporate Offices ■ Market Street, P.O. Box 497, Brattleboro, Vermont 05301 ■ Phone 802–555–8732

Such replies are sometimes used by manufacturers who advertise in national magazines. If you were to write to one, asking where a particular jacket could be purchased in your home community, you might receive your own letter back with the scribbled name of the store at the bottom. A copy of a request may be sent to the local store to allow for a possible follow-up or to show how the manufacturer's advertising helps to promote the product locally.

Whichever technique you decide to use—a regular, form, or quick reply—will depend on money, time, relationship with the inquirer, and nature of the inquiry. For example, if you managed a small wholesale business that operated on a narrow profit margin, you probably could not afford to write personal letters but would depend on form letters or quick replies to retail customers. But if you managed a large business operation, or one that sold items at a high price and with a big markup, you might be able to afford sending personal letters or ones typed on an automatic typewriter or other word processing equipment. Business circumstances will suggest which channel is the most economical, but you will also have to consider which one is the most effective.

Orders

Recently, as a result of the use of the Wide Area Telephone Service (WATS) lines, which are toll-free to the user, many customers or companies find it more convenient and satisfying to phone orders than to write them. One distinct advantage is that buyers can usually learn immediately whether items are in stock and when they can be shipped. In business, therefore, the telephone is replacing the letter as a channel of communication.

But often WATS lines are not available, or buyers must have written copies of their orders for inventory or budgeting control. In these instances, order forms are frequently used—either those of the buyer's own company or those of suppliers. As illustrated in figure 3–4, these forms contain numerous columns and spaces designated for all the necessary information.

In some business situations, you may have neither WATS lines nor order forms. What then? The order letter is not difficult to write, but it must contain all the necessary details about the desired items. This information usually includes the following:

1. Description of item (name, catalog or model number)
2. Quantity, color, size, or other specifications
3. Price (both of the individual item and the total ordered; include shipping charges, taxes)
4. Shipment (parcel post, UPS, freight, air freight)
5. Payment terms (cash; COD; 2/10, n/30 or however customary)
6. Delivery date and place
7. Order date; order number (optional)
8. FOB information where applicable

Figure 3–4. Manufacturer's Order Form.

PHILMAR TEXTILES, INC.

1691 Howard Street • Omaha, Nebraska 68102 • Area Code (402) 555–7388

CREDIT			

DATE	DEPT. NO.	CUSTOMER ORDER NO	SHIPPING DATE	H.F.C. ☐ CONFIRMED ☐	SALESMAN	AD. MAT NO ☐ SLICK ☐ MAT ☐

SHIP TO

PUT-UP   D & R ☐   ON TUBES ☐

PRE-RETAIL   YES ☐   NO ☐

NEW ORDER ☐   RE-ORDER ☐

SHIP VIA   BUYER'S NAME

TERMS

Style No.	Quantity	DESCRIPTION	PRICE	TOTAL

ALL EXCHANGES BY AUTHORIZATION ONLY — AND PREPAID

The letter itself follows this form:

1. Definite order statement (Please send me, Please ship me, I would appreciate your sending me)
2. Order (usually quantity on left, description in center, cost of the individual item next, and then total price on right)
3. Additional information (shipment, payment, delivery date, etc.)
4. Courtesy close (optional)

This example illustrates the form used for a letter placing an order:

Please ship me the following office supplies:

Qty.	Stock No.	Description	Cost	Total
5	PP5	Flex-form portfolio-BK	$11.50	$57.50
9	CKF	Century key-file	5.50	49.50
3	WF	Wall file	19.45	58.35
300	JP12-#1	Jiffy padded bags 8½ x 12	.19	57.00
		TOTAL		$222.35

Ship on my order 3148 by UPS according to your regular credit terms (n/30) so that the items will arrive no later than December 10.

Acknowledgments

Like orders, acknowledgments vary. They may consist of a few words over the phone, a form postcard, a duplicate invoice, or a letter. If the order will be shipped immediately or almost so, no confirmation may be needed. But if the order is an initial one, an unusually large one, a special one, or one whose shipment will be delayed or denied, then a letter is generally written.

INITIAL ORDER   The initial order may be acknowledged by a personalized form letter or by one written especially for the buyer. Some disagreement exists, as it does regarding replies, about whether the first sentence should express appreciation or state delivery information. Once again, we suggest analyzing the reader. If delivery is routine, then you should begin with an appreciative "thank you." If delivery is crucial, refer to it immediately, stating not just when the items were shipped, but when the buyer will receive them. (But don't make unrealistic promises about their being delivered early.) Here's how the first sentence might be written:

Your order dated July 5 was shipped yesterday by Consolidated Freight and should arrive in your store by July 12 for your sale.

Figure 3–5. Initial Order Acknowledgment.

THE WALL STREET JOURNAL · 200 BURNETT ROAD, CHICOPEE, MA 01021

Dear Subscriber:

Thank you for your payment for your Wall Street Journal subscription. Your subscription has been entered; service is to begin immediately.

Starting with your very first issue, you'll be getting solid business information. Every business day, in each issue of the Journal, you'll get facts useful to you in shaping and sharpening your business decisions and judgments.

You will also discover that the Journal is much more than a newspaper. It's the world's most complete business-information service provided to you economically and practically in the form of a newspaper.

You will find much of the business news is reported in the Journal first --- days and often weeks before it appears in national magazines and local newspapers. And most often, you'll be reading stories that are Journal exclusives.

Many of our readers ask how we are able to achieve day-of-issue delivery of the Journal throughout the country. One answer: twelve printing plants spread across the United States.

And to speed material to various plants, we make extensive use of satellite transmission--a process pioneered by the Journal.

These and other technological advances enable us to provide more than four-million readers with complete, up-to-the-minute news every business day.

As you become a regular reader, we are confident you'll find the Journal indispensable as a source of useful business information that can affect you, your company, your income, your future.

Your name and address, as shown, is how your Journal is being addressed. Is it accurate? If any changes or corrections are necessary, please indicate them in the space below and return in the enclosed envelope.

And again -- thank you.

(SOURCE: Reprinted by permission of *The Wall Street Journal.*)

COMMUNICATING BY LETTERS

Usually, the acknowledgment follows this form:

1. Appreciation or delivery statement, in whichever order is appropriate
2. Sales message about your product, service, or ways to help customer promote or sell it
3. Check on accuracy of order (optional)
4. Close: restatement of appreciation or reference to future business, relationship, or profits

Note how *The Wall Street Journal* acknowledgment (see figure 3–5) follows this pattern. The first paragraph contains both the appreciation and delivery statements. The next seven paragraphs present a sales message, emphasizing the importance and timeliness of the *Journal*. The next to last paragraph contains a question about the accuracy of the subscriber's name and address and a check on the order. And the letter ends with another statement of appreciation.

LARGE ORDER The purpose of acknowledging an unusually large order is to verify it, to indicate your appreciation for receiving it, and to demonstrate your gratitude by taking the time and trouble to mention specific sales features, display information, advertising assistance, or anything else that would help in promoting or selling the product. The letter, which follows the same general pattern as the previous one, might look something like this:

Dear Mr. Griffith:

Thank you for your order of eight dozen children's basketball stands, which should arrive within four days.

You have purchased a fast-selling children's item that we are having difficulty keeping in stock. Please note that this is no toy, but a sturdily constructed item with a steel rim, a heavy duty cotton net, hardboard backboards and platform, and wooden upright. Moreover, it is practical. As the child grows, the goal may be raised by 12–42 inches, making it a challenge for anyone from (as we like to say) 4 to 40!

Many merchants display this basketball stand by setting up demonstration models in their stores, usually against a back wall where a wild shot will do little damage. Both children and parents enjoy trying their skill with the vinyl ball. After they've sunk a shot or two, they're usually hooked. And in an area such as yours where basketball is king, you should do especially well.

If you would be interested in cooperative newspaper advertising, we will pay for one-third the cost as long as our trade name is mentioned. For your reimbursement, we will need only three copies of the ad and one of the invoice for it.

If you determine that you would like additional basketball stands, please let us know as soon as possible because this is a popular item.

Thank you again, Mr. Griffith, for your fine order.

> Sincerely,
>
>
>
> Joseph Hall
> Sales Manager

SPECIAL ORDER   The letter about a special order—one that calls for something unusual or custom-made—is normally written to check on measurements, colors, or other specifications. Its objective is to make certain that the order is correct; if not, the seller may have to absorb a loss. Such a letter might appear merely to acknowledge the order:

> Thank you for your October 11 order for 80 dozen dresses from our regular line.
>
> In response to your special request, we will be glad to make up an additional 6 dozen of style #16666 in junior sizes, 2 dozen each in blue, green, and brown. Please realize that because this order is being made up to your specific requirements, it cannot be canceled or any of the dresses returned.
>
> We will ship your entire order in three weeks to reach you by December 1 so that you can depend on the dresses for your Christmas promotion.
>
> Our dresses have been popular in leading department stores throughout the country. We know you will be delighted with them. And your special order in junior sizes, we are sure, will also do well for you.

As you can see, the acknowledgment not only expresses appreciation, provides shipping information, and adds a sales message, but also verifies the special order.

DELAYED OR DENIED ORDER   Most difficult of all acknowledgment letters to write is the one about being unable to fill the order or to ship it on time. Sometimes an item is no longer carried; sometimes it is temporarily out of stock. In either instance, you should tell what you can do instead of wailing about what you cannot.

Recommend a possible substitute, or if out of stock, offer to ship as soon as the stock is replenished. Here's how you might handle it:

> Thank you for your May 6 order for several styles of men's swimming trunks, which we are preparing to ship
>
> We are temporarily out of the hip-hugger trunks. Therefore, we would like to know whether you would be willing to accept June 15 delivery of these trunks or to substitute our popular boxer trunks (see catalog page 137, style 41J44), which can be sent to you immediately.
>
> Please let me know your wishes--to substitute the boxer trunks or to send the hip-huggers for June 15 delivery --either by mailing the enclosed card or by phoning our toll-free WATS line (800-642-8267).

Note that another option—to cancel the hip-huggers—is not mentioned.

Credit

Plastic money—bank and other credit cards—is largely responsible for turning us into a "buy now, pay later" society. It is not uncommon today for wallets and pocketbooks to contain stacks of credit cards for use in stores, restaurants, gas stations, hotels, and even doctors' and dentists' offices. In fact, some people carry around almost more cards than cash. The resulting revolution in credit has produced new laws, new ways of doing business, and new communications about credit.

The 1975 Equal Credit Opportunity Act was designed in part to protect women from credit discrimination.[1] Formerly, women were often automatically refused credit despite being employed or having other income, or they were extended credit only jointly with their husbands. Now women cannot be denied credit because of their sex or because of the possibility they may get married or leave a job to start a family or to return to housework. They must be evaluated for credit on the same basis that men are. And if they are receiving alimony or child support, this money can be considered as part of their income.

The result of this change has been to increase the number of people receiving credit, the applications processed, and the letters written. Formerly, credit bureaus maintained one file for a family. Now they may have three: one each for the husband, the wife, and the family or joint account. Approximately 2,500 bureaus store about 150 million credit reports in computer banks each year.[2]

These reports normally contain only factual information: name, age, address, social security number, present and past employment data (position held, length, salary), and credit history (past loans and repayment schedule). On the basis of this information, banks, stores, and finance companies decide whether to extend credit. Note that the lender makes the evaluation, not the credit bureau.

Sometimes credit is denied because of erroneous information. To correct such misinformation, the Fair Credit Reporting Act of 1970 entitles consumers to review the information in their credit files upon written request.[3] When credit has been denied, there is no charge for this inspection; otherwise, there is a nominal fee. If the information is found to be incorrect or unverified, it must be removed and corrected with all people previously notified.

What happens when you want to open a charge account in a local store? If the store is a small one, it will probably accept bank credit cards, such as Visa or Mastercard, instead of issuing its own. Depending on its average sales figure and its volume of sales, the store then pays a fee of 1½ percent to 6 percent of your bill to the bank handling the billing and extending the loan. In return for this fee, the bank provides cash to the store almost immediately, even though you may not have received a bill or paid it.

If the store is a large one with its own credit card and billing service, it will ask you to complete an application form. Then it will request a report from the local credit bureau to evaluate what are known as the four C's of credit: Capacity (ability to pay the loan), Character (your trustworthiness), Capital (your financial assets—car, furniture, bank account, for example), and Conditions (economic conditions, such as tight money).

Anxious for business, some stores may extend credit to people who will be denied it by others. Credit managers base these decisions on store policy and on their evaluation of the credit report.

But this is only part of the credit picture. Just as consumers buy on credit, so do businesses. Your local stores purchase their merchandise and supplies through catalogs, from sales representatives, or by attending trade shows or visiting company offices in major cities. When a company receives an order from a new account, it follows the same process as that outlined previously. Normally, either Dun and Bradstreet or the National Association of Credit Management will provide a credit report based on the store's audited financial statements, the promptness of its payments, and other pertinent information. Then the company will decide whether to extend credit or not.

All this credit activity by both consumers and businesses generates a large volume of correspondence. Thus you will frequently encounter certain regular credit situations: these include soliciting credit, requesting credit information, acknowledging a credit application, and granting credit.

SOLICITING CREDIT Stores distribute credit applications to shoppers and to people requesting them. In addition, many retailers actively seek to open credit accounts for newcomers to their communities by obtaining information about them from banks; from telephone, water, or electric companies; or from other sources. These stores then send a welcome letter with an attached or enclosed credit application form as illustrated in figure 3–6. Usually, the letters follow this pattern:

1. Welcome or invitation, or both
2. Statement about advantages of using charge account and shopping at the store
3. Reference to application form
4. Courtesy close

Figure 3–6. Solicitation Credit Letter.

Stewart's
Jenkintown, Pennsylvania 19046

Mrs. M. Unger
583 Halstead Avenue
Jenkintown, PA 19046

February 22, 19--

Dear Mrs. Unger:

We are pleased to extend this cordial invitation to join the Stewart's
family of charge customers.

As a charge customer, you will receive all the Stewart's fashion catalogs
as well as our exciting Christmas book. In addition, you will receive
advance notice of special events; you can shop by mail or phone from the
comfort of your home, and you can say "charge it" at any of our fine stores.

You will be delighted with the unique and individual Stewart's approach
to fashions for women, men, and children as well as for the home. We
endeavor to match the excellent quality of our merchandise with a staff
of people who will give you the kind of concerned and helpful service
you like to receive.

Let us show you how much EXTRA convenience can be yours when you shop with
a Stewart's charge card.

If you do not have an account, please take a moment to complete the form
below and return it to us in the postage-paid envelope.

All of us at Stewart's look forward to the opportunity to serve you.

Sincerely,

N. Geiger

N. Geiger
Credit Sales Manager

You may omit spouse info if not applying for a joint account
       Joint Acct (   )   Individual Acct (   )

NAME Mrs. M. Unger   0679D4 E
ADDR 583 Halstead Ave.
      Jenkintown, PA 19046   SOC SEC NO ....
FORMER   HOME
ADDRESS ....PHONE ....
                               HOW
EMPLMT ....POS ....LONG ....

SPOUSE'S NAME ....
                                          HOW
SPOUSE'S EMPLMT ....POS.........LONG ....

OTHER CHG ACCTS ....

BANK ............................CHKG.........SVGS........

DATE ....SIGNATURE ....

REQUESTING CREDIT INFORMATION   Credit information about most individuals is normally handled by credit bureaus. But sometimes companies write to the references supplied on the application form. A letter such as the following is mailed:

```
Dear Credit Manager:

We would appreciate information about the Schumacher Com-
pany, which has applied for credit with us.

Because it has listed your company as a reference, we would
like you to complete the form below and return it to us in
the enclosed stamped envelope. The information provided
will be kept confidential.

If we can ever assist you with any credit applications,
please let us know.

                              Sincerely,



                              William Terry
                              Sales Manager

— — — — — — — — — — — — — — — — — — — — — — — —

1. When did you do business with this company?
2. What were the terms?
3. What was the maximum credit extended?
4. What amount is currently owed?
5. What was the date of the last purchase?
6. On the average, in how many days were accounts paid?
7. Were any accounts given to collection agencies?
```

ACKNOWLEDGING A CREDIT APPLICATION   Upon receipt of an order from a new account, a business must deal with a specific problem: the merchandise ordered cannot be shipped until credit has been approved. Sometimes credit approval may entail only a slight delay in filling the order. Sometimes it may necessitate a request for references or more recent information than is available from the credit report. A letter requesting such references or information normally follows this pattern:

1. Statement of appreciation for the order
2. Request for references or for completion of an enclosed application form
3. Statement that order will be shipped as soon as credit is approved
4. Assurance that credit process is routine and that information will be kept confidential
5. Anticipation of pleasant business relationship

GRANTING CREDIT   The letter granting credit presents good news to the reader. So writing it is relatively simple. Usually, it consists of the following:

1. Approval of credit
2. Information about shipment of order
3. Explanation of credit terms
4. Sales message
5. Anticipation of pleasant business relationship

Here's how such a letter looks:

> We are glad to approve your application for credit and to add your company to the many we serve.
>
> Your March 21 order has been shipped by UPS and should arrive by Tuesday, April 2.
>
> As you may know, our terms are 2/10, n/30. If you should ever wish to order C.O.D., you may deduct the 2 percent from the invoice.
>
> We know you'll find our fluorescent lamps to be economical and efficient. By replacing a 400—watt mercury lamp with our 360—watt one, you'll get 85 percent more light while saving 40 watts. And other fluorescent lamps will provide you with similar economies. That adds up to more light for less money by using less energy.
>
> We look forward to serving your lighting needs in the future.

Naturally, sometimes credit must be denied. But because that situation calls for an unpleasant letter, we will discuss it in chapter 5.

Recommendations

Sooner or later, you may be requested to write letters of recommendation for associates, employees, friends, and acquaintances. The normal writing problems are increased by an ethical one. How truthful should you be?

The difficulty is compounded by the fact that you usually want to help the person requesting the recommendation, who is counting on you to write a favorable evaluation. Of course, in a few situations, you may be tempted to write a glowing recommendation to get rid of a troublesome or inefficient employee.

But the ethics of business demand honesty. Your integrity as well as your organization's is at stake. You are obligated to mention the individual's strengths and weaknesses, omitting nothing that would significantly affect job performance. And you must be completely honest, even though the person for whom you write the recommendation is legally entitled to see it unless a waiver is signed. The recommendation should include the items listed on the following page.

1. Purpose of letter
2. Qualifications of writer to evaluate individual
3. Evaluation (positive, mixed, negative) with examples or details
4. Summary close

The opening statement informs the reader immediately about the subject of the letter. If it is written in response to an inquiry, that fact should be mentioned in passing or in a subject line.

Writers may next explain their relationship with the recommended person, showing in what capacity and to what extent they know that person. This information is important because it reveals the basis of the evaluation being provided.

The statements should be as factual as possible and should focus on those abilities that would interest the reader. For example, a young woman's skill at tennis might be important if she were applying for a position as a recreation director, but it would be unimportant if she were a candidate for an accountant's job.

The recommendation should close with a summary statement and might include a courtesy sentence expressing willingness to furnish additional information if requested.

The letter of recommendation in figure 3–7 follows this general outline. It also illustrates an important point about the use of negative information in the third paragraph. Because most recommendations are favorable, any detrimental information may receive an unintended emphasis. So, on the one hand, you are obliged to report any pertinent negative characteristics, but, on the other hand, you must be careful not to give them undue weight. For instance, you should not end a letter with mention of an unfavorable trait unless it is a significant one.

TECHNIQUE

Up to this point, we have been concerned with the strategy of information letters. Now we shall turn our attention to certain matters of technique involving words, sentences, and stylistic considerations. In most instances, what we will discuss here can be applied not only to information letters but to other forms of business writing as well.

WORDS

Much of your writing's effectiveness depends on your selection of words. Often they make the difference between a dull letter and a lively one. Because so much business writing is boringly stilted and annoyingly vague, you should select words that are natural and specific.

Natural Words

Many college students believe that business writing requires a special vocabulary. In particular, they feel that letters should include certain formula words and phrases ("I have yours of May 15th at hand"). True, many of these terms and expressions were in style years ago when people, manners, and language were more formal than

Figure 3–7. Letter of Recommendation.

KENTON UNIVERSITY

Northridge, Ohio 45414

COLLEGE OF ARTS AND SCIENCES   March 12 19--
DEPARTMENT OF ENGLISH

Dr. Jeffrey Ronald
Director, Clarksville Community College
Louisville, Kentucky 40201

Dear Dr. Ronald:

    Jean Swift of your English Department has asked me to write a letter
of recommendation for her because she is being considered for promotion.

    Jean was a student in my eighteenth-century English literature
class in 19-- and has served as a graduate teaching assistant and
part-time lecturer in this department for several years. I believe that
I know her well and am competent to attest to her qualifications.

    As a student, Jean was well prepared, interested in the literature,
and active in class discussions, offering several insightful and penetrat-
ing comments. Her papers and examinations were well written, but except
for an excellent term report on "Narrative Techniques in Rasselas," they
warranted B grades due to a slight lack of substance. As an instructor,
Jean was even better. She is excited about teaching, enthusiastic about
her students, and professional in her commitment. Ranking in the top 15%
on student evaluations, she was among the most popular and respected
members of our freshman English staff.

    I was particularly pleased this fall when Jean stepped into the
teaching of English 203, our business writing course, and did so well with
it. This is a difficult assignment because it requires the teaching of
writing at an advanced level with no time available for literature. Jean
handled her work well, made the course interesting and informative for
students, and proved that she is an effective teacher of writing not only
at the freshman but also at the sophomore and upper levels.

    I wish to recommend Jean Swift highly. She is a fine, intelligent
person with a sense of humor, wit, and charm. And she is an excellent
teacher, one who should be a valuable addition to any college or community
college staff. I strongly support her promotion.

                Sincerely,

                Christopher Johns

                Christopher Johns
                Director, Freshman English

they are today. But in the modern working world, this language is as out of place as an evening gown or a tux at the office. Exactly what language do we mean? Take a look at the contrast between a simple letter written by a boy at summer camp to his parents and the version that he might write years later from work:

Dear Mom and Dad,

Thanks for sending me <u>Sports Illustrated</u> and writing. I'm having a great time at camp. The boys in the cabin are real swell guys and the counselor, Bob Bean, is a neat fellow. Yesterday we decided to hike to Bald Mountain. But it rained so we went swimming instead. Today we have a ball game with another camp. I need some more money because I bought ice cream cones for Billy and Dick.

Love,

Jay

* * *

Dear Mother and Father:

Replying to yours of July 29, which I have at hand, may I commence by extending my appreciation for the July 22 edition of <u>Sports Illustrated</u> that I am in receipt of at the present time. I wish to advise you that the companions in my domicile are agreeable and satisfactory. I am also in a position to inform you that our advisor, Mr. Robert Bean, is a gentleman of irreproachable integrity.

Allow me to provide you with the information that here yesterday, July 31, it was decided by a committee in our organization to participate in an expedition to that earthy terrain designated Bald Mountain. It is with regret that I report that the elements prevented the undersigned and his associates from culminating our objective, which was the attainment of the summit of the aforementioned location. In view of the fact that our expedition was canceled because of inclement conditions, we engaged in some natatory activities. At the time of this writing, August 1, we are committed to a baseball encounter with another organization. In accordance with the fact that I expended a considerable amount of money to provide William and Richard with refreshments, I hereby request funds to reimburse me for this outlay. I wish to express in advance my appreciation for your consideration of this matter.

If any additional information is desired by you, please
do not hesitate to let me know at your earliest possible
convenience.

                              Very truly yours,

                              Jayson A. Hackett

What's happened? What's caused deadly language such as this to clutter up business letters? Three factors are probably responsible: (1) the desire to impress, (2) laziness, and (3) ignorance of the communication process.

Of these, the desire to impress is the deadliest. Graduates fresh from college are particularly susceptible to this disease. They love to sound important, to appear businesslike, to display their learning. Consequently, they avoid familiar words, using *initiate* for *begin*, *endeavor* for *try*, and *activate* for *start*. But experienced writers at work know they should express, not impress. They use natural, familiar words.

Laziness is another reason for formal language. Business files are loaded with old letters providing ready-made words, phrases, and even sentences that can be used over and over again despite the fact that they are obviously obsolete. Lazy writers rely on such old-timers as "We beg to acknowledge receipt of yours of April 1," "In compliance with your request of February 14," or "We trust that this action merits your approval." This language belongs in the files collecting dust instead of in current letters designed to win favorable action or build goodwill.

Figure 3–8. Making It Perfectly Clear.

The Federal Register's
horrible example of bureaucratese:

"We respectfully petition, request, and entreat that due and adequate provision be made, this day and the date hereinafter subscribed, for the satisfying of these petitioners' nutritional requirements and for the organizing of such methods of allocation and distribution as may be deemed necessary and proper to assure the reception by and for said petitioners of such quantities of baked cereal products as shall, in the judgment of the aforesaid petitioners, constitute a sufficient supply thereof."

—*Federal government English*

Translation: "Give us this day our daily bread."

—*King James English*

(SOURCE: Reprinted from the May 9, 1977 issue of *Business Week* by special permission, © 1977 by McGraw-Hill, Inc., New York, NY 10020. All rights reserved.)

But perhaps the basic reason for unnatural and unfamiliar language is that writers fail to remember the purpose of communication. When readers decode a message, they react to both what is said and how it is said. Obsolete and stilted language creates noise that distracts readers, interfering with their reception of the message. Natural and familiar language communicates more effectively, as you can see in figure 3–8. Writers who have had communication courses understand the importance of using everyday words and phrases. But many business people who have not had these courses clutter their sentences with language seldom heard in classrooms or boardrooms.

In our years of receiving and reviewing numerous business letters, we've tagged hundreds of these monstrosities. Below, we've compiled a list of twenty-five horrors:

The Monsters	Their Natural Subs
acquaint you with	inform or tell you about
afford an opportunity	allow
as per your request	as you requested
at the present writing	now
at this point in time	now
at your earliest convenience	as soon as is convenient
commence	begin
conclude	end
in receipt of	have received
in lieu of	instead of
input	opinion, information, advice
kindly advise	please let us know
obligation	debt
prior to	before
pursuant to	according to
receipt is hereby acknowledged	we have received
render assistance	help
subsequent to	after
terminate	end
the undersigned	I
to be cognizant of	to know
transmit	send
up to this writing	up to now
we are not in a position to	we are unable to
will you be kind enough to	please

Review the list occasionally during this semester; later, when you are writing at work, you should also take a look at it from time to time.

Remember the importance of sounding natural in your writing. A well-written communication should be conversational, creating the impression that the writer is talking to the reader. Obviously, the conversation should not be on the level of the locker room (male or female). Write as if you were talking to an instructor, a friendly clergyman, or a family doctor; be natural, polite, courteous, and cordial.

The best test is to listen to what you have written and try to visualize the image you've created. Does the writer seem pleasant, friendly, sincere, cheerful? Or stuffy, pretentious, formal, affected? Would you like to meet the writer for a coke or beer? When you write, try to remember these questions about the voice, or personality, of your writing. Try to charm your readers into wanting to know you.

Specific Words

In our haste to write, we often settle for the first word or phrase that pops into our minds. Usually, these are vague and abstract general terms, sounding adequate but signifying little. Although sometimes unavoidable, abstractions should normally be replaced by more concrete, specific expressions, as in these examples:

> *General:* You will receive the supplies soon.
>
> *Specific:* You will receive the supplies by Wednesday, March 4.

> *General:* The company usually paid its bills on time.
>
> *Specific:* During the past three years, Consolidated, Inc., has paid its bills within the 30–day period except during May, July, and August 1980 when payments were 25 days, 14 days, and 9 days late.

These examples illustrate how general statements can be made specific. But there are few helpful tips. You will have to examine your own sentences for yourself. You should be alert for *thing* and its family (*anything, something, everything, nothing*), as you can see for yourself:

> Last week we ordered some things from you but omitted one thing from our list. Now we would like to know whether we could add this thing, or anything else, to our order. If you can do something about it, please write something to that effect. Then everything will be all right because we can authorize you to send us this thing. But if you can't do anything, please forget the whole thing.

Note how the abstract language can be confusing. In the last sentence, has the writer cancelled the original order or just the additional one?

Using concrete, specific words requires making a judgment about the needs of the reader. For example, *several thousand dollars* is more specific than *a lot of money* but less so than $3,456. You will have to decide which to use. But you should realize that, in most situations, the more specific word or expression is desirable because it conveys more information. Observe how progressively more satisfactory the following responses become to the query, "What do you do?"

> I teach.
> I teach at the University.
> I teach English at the University.
> I teach writing at the University.
> I teach business writing at the University.

I teach business writing to sophomores, juniors, and seniors in the College of Business Administration at the University of Connecticut.

I teach sophomores, juniors, and seniors in the College of Business Administration at the University of Connecticut how to write more effective letters, reports, and memos.

Sometimes, for one reason or another, you may not want to be specific. For example, you might want to evade giving a definite price or delivery date. If you wish to be general, fine. Otherwise, try to write in concrete, specific language that allows readers to see, hear, feel, touch, smell, count, or understand clearly what you mean. If not, you may lose or confuse them.

Sentences

Sentences in business writing should be clear, correct, lively, economical, and convincing. These are difficult objectives to attain because writers are usually preoccupied with formulating thoughts. So a first draft is often written in the casual language of speech. But our conversation is often cluttered with incomplete and informally constructed sentences because we do not have the time to consider all the syntactical problems.

A first draft may be written in this highly informal language with incomplete sentences, repetitions, faulty references, grammatical lapses, and limited vocabulary. The second draft then provides you with an opportunity to review the sentences with a microscope, trying to pick out all the blemishes in order to make the final draft conform to what is expected in the written language.

This revising process is important in business writing, which is typically quite conservative, following language conventions that are as formal and correct as the clothes worn in most offices. One particular written construction that troubles many people is subject-verb agreement.

Subject-Verb Agreement

In the regular course of events, subject-verb agreement is simple. Few people would write, "The workers has just entered the factory" or "The secretary have started typing the envelopes." Such constructions are easy because (1) the subject and verb are close together, (2) they appear in normal order (first subject, then verb), and (3) the subject is obviously singular or plural. But when any of these three conditions—proximity, sequence, or number—does not exist, beware.

1. When subject and verb are separated:

   a. The boxes on the cutting table in the back room (is, are) ready for shipping.
   b. The cost of sending parcel post packages (is, are) going to be increased.

The problem is created by the noun (*room, packages*) immediately preceding the verb. When it differs in number (singular, plural) from the subject, as both do in the preceding examples, we can easily go astray. A diagram of this tricky construction reveals its difficulty:

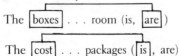

The boxes . . . room (is, are)

The cost . . . packages (is, are)

In writing, the subject (*boxes, cost*) requires verbs that agree with it. In speech and perhaps in a first draft, many people will be influenced by the immediately preceding noun. But if you focus on what you are writing about (*boxes, cost*), you should at least avoid the trap in revising.

2. When the verb precedes the subject:

    a. Enclosed in the envelope (is, are) a copy of the report and a letter from the director.
    b. There (has, have) been many waivers extended to students working away from home during the summer.

Except in these examples and in a few other instances, the subject precedes the verb, signaling whether it should be singular or plural. But when the subject does not lead the way, we cannot rely on our ear to guide us. In talking, it is too taxing to analyze the irregular pattern quickly, so many speakers err. But in writing and revising, there is time to reflect on the problem of agreement. Hence you should be able to select the plurals *are* and *have* in the previous examples. But if you were stumped or had difficulty, mentally invert the verb-subject word order like this:

    A copy . . . and a letter *are* enclosed. . . .

    Many waivers *have* been extended to students. . . .

The main problem is recognizing the inverted order. Once you are aware that it is present in a sentence and realize that you need to analyze the sentence instead of relying on your ear, you should have little difficulty.

3. When the subject is not clearly singular or plural:

    a. The committee (is, are) pleased to know that you will apply for the position.
    b. Everybody in the warehouse (is, are) working on the order.
    c. Neither the secretary nor the clerk (has, have) seen your application.

The three illustrative sentences pose three different problems. The first is that of collective nouns (*board, group, family, committee*), which refer to several people but normally take singular verbs (The committee is. . . .). If you feel uneasy in using the singular with such collective nouns, consider the option of revising your sentence to read: *The members* of the committee *are*. . . .

The second problem is caused by *everybody*, an indefinite pronoun that seems like a plural word. But, like other indefinite pronouns (*each, neither, everyone, anyone*), it takes a singular verb. So even though there might be hundreds of people in the warehouse, when the subject of the sentence is *everybody*, the verb should be *is working* (Everybody in the warehouse is working. . . .).

Subjects joined by *either-or* or *neither-nor* take a singular or plural verb, depending on the subject closer to the verb. Try to remember these examples:

    Neither the supervisors nor the manager *has* lost the traveler's checks.

    Neither the manager nor the supervisors *have* lost the traveler's checks.

Beware of the three constructions—collective nouns, indefinite pronouns, and *either-or/neither-nor*—because the subject is not logically singular or plural. The first two take singular verbs; in the last, the verb agrees with the subject closer to it. Simple? No. But we hope it's simplified.

Stylistic Considerations

Certain writing techniques belong neither to the classification of words nor to that of sentences. These we have designated as "stylistic considerations," because they affect the general style of your writing. In this chapter, we will examine courtesy, beginnings, and endings.

Courtesy

Courtesy is so obviously important in gaining goodwill in business writing that it should not need mention. But because some inexperienced business writers slight or ignore it, a few words may be helpful.

Certainly, no writers are intentionally discourteous except when angry—a state of mind to avoid when writing business letters. But even when not angry, we are frequently tactless, unfriendly, irritating, or insulting to readers because we fail to realize how they will react to our words or tone. In person, we might smilingly say something without offending, but the same assertion in print might be upsetting. As speakers, moreover, we obtain immediate feedback, noting the reactions of listeners. If they frown, grimace, or scowl, we can compensate for whatever may have angered them. Without any such feedback in writing, we must take extra pains to be courteous.

To do so, reread your first draft, asking, "Will it make friends?" Don't be satisfied with merely avoiding anything offensive; strive to convey warmth and goodwill. Rely on certain attractive words: "Please," "Thank you," "I appreciate," and "I was glad." Avoid words with unfavorable connotations, like these in the following sentences:

> Because you failed to include $1.00, we cannot send you the catalog. (*Failed* is a finger-pointing word.)
>
> We insist upon a prompt answer to our letter. (*Insist* is a table–pounding word.)
>
> You must be mistaken about the price; our records disclose that it was $4.95 a dozen. (*Mistaken* is a slap–in–the–face word.)

How much simpler and easier it would be to write:

> Because $1.00 was not included, we cannot send you the catalog.
>
> We would appreciate your answering this letter promptly.
>
> As there is some misunderstanding about the price, would you please check your records to see whether they show it to be $4.95 a dozen.

Courtesy costs nothing extra. Just try the key question, "Will it make friends?"

Beginnings

Beginnings function like first impressions, creating an image that may promote or prohibit the forming of good relationships. To get off to a positive start, use courteous words, be friendly, provide the desired information quickly, and be brief. How brief? We'd suggest a maximum of three sentences. No one likes to wade through a lengthier introduction. And no one enjoys being confronted with clinkers like the following:

I am in receipt of your letter of November 12. . . .

The purpose of this letter is to inform you. . . .

Referring to your letter of June 13. . . .

Two effective openers are "Thank you" and "you."

Thank you for your complimentary letter about our recent television program on black doctors.

You will be glad to know that we do have a replacement part for your lawn mower.

Probably the main weakness in beginnings stems from a writer's failure to organize and formulate ideas. Thus there is the temptation to stall while thinking about what to say. This indecision results in such openings as the following:

```
Dear Mrs. Beasley:

We desire herewith to acknowledge receipt of your letter
of December 3, 19--, in which you inquired about the pro-
visions of a life insurance policy purchased by your hus-
band, Robert L. Beasley, from our agent, Mr. Robert B.
Cornish, in Richmond, Kentucky, on May 3, 19--. This pol-
icy, number 367-69-204, was written while your husband
was a student at the University of Kentucky.
```

At this point, Mrs. Beasley might well be climbing the wall. Because she has gotten this reply, she knows her letter was received. She also knows her husband's name and, in addition, cares little about when, where, and by whom the policy was written. What she wants to learn is whether her husband can borrow money on the policy and, if so, how much and at what rate of interest. She would be better served by this beginning:

```
Your husband may borrow up to $2,700 at the annual rate of
8½ percent a year on the unpaid balance of the loan.
```

Any information needed by the company for filing may be placed under the date or typed separately on the company's copy.

In company-to-company correspondence, or in a reply to someone in a large organization who is probably engaged in extensive correspondence, a date or subject reference, or both, is helpful and appreciated. This information may be handled in various ways: (1) buried in the first sentence; (2) stated in a subject line; or (3) indicated in a reference line printed or typed beneath the date or inside address. Here are some examples:

1. First sentence

The samples ordered on March 28 will arrive by Tuesday.

I will be glad to furnish information about our deferred compensation plan for executives as requested in your January 11 letter.

2. Subject line (see also figure 3–9)

Mr. William Mays
Stankee and Thomson Management Associates
15 Worth Street
Dallas, TX 19870

Dear Mr. Mays:

Subject: Deferred Compensation Plan for Executives

We will be glad to share with you the details. . . .

Figure 3–9. Subject Line After Inside Address.

THE BANK OF BOSTON

With offices at 90 Washington Street, Boston, MA
Please address all correspondence to The Bank of Boston
P.O. Box 11, 002, Fenway Street Station Boston, MA 02115

Ms. Carol Pelligrino   May 23, 19--
32 Parkvale Street
Allston, MA 02134

Dear Ms. Pelligrino:

Subject: Municipal Investment Trust Fund

COMMUNICATING BY LETTERS

3. Reference line

```
11 January 1981

Your file: 99678

Mr. William Mays
Stankee and Thomson Management Associates

(etc.)
```

Because persuasive letters present a unique problem requiring special beginnings to attract reader attention, we shall discuss them separately in chapter 4.

Endings

Depending on their purpose, writers should end business letters by rousing readers to action, expressing appreciation, or conveying goodwill. Here are some examples of each:

Action

As soon as you return the enclosed card to us, we'll rush the IRA information to you.

Why not send us your check today so that we can ship your order immediately?

Please sign the enclosed form and specify the amount you wish to borrow on your life insurance. Then mail it in the business reply envelope we have provided for your convenience.

Appreciation

Thank you again for sending the financial information.

We appreciate your paying your bills promptly during the past year.

We are grateful for your sending Mr. Daniels to explain how to use the word processor more effectively.

Goodwill

If you would like additional information about our convention facilities, please let us know.

We hope that this is the beginning of a long and mutually rewarding business relationship.

We wish you great success in your new business venture.

Action, appreciation, and goodwill endings are to be encouraged. To be discouraged are such weak endings as the participial, the presumptuous, or the perfunctory. Let's consider how each of these fails to do the job. The participial looks like this:

Hoping to hear from you,

Trusting you are satisfied with our offer,

Looking forward to seeing you next month,

All these are incomplete, ineffective, and trite. Besides, they are relics, dating back to the eighteenth century. You must avoid such archaic endings; otherwise you might be forced to continue in appropriate fashion:

Hoping to hear from you soon, I remain
Your humble and obedient servant,

James Boswell, Esq.

You should also avoid the presumptuous ending. Nothing may irritate readers as much as to be thanked in advance for something they may not choose to do or cannot do. Yet how can you express your gratitude beforehand without seeming cocky and overconfident? The following two devices illustrate some possibilities:

1. The conditional *would*

I would appreciate your completing the questionnaire.

2. The conditional *if*

We would be grateful if you would send us this information.

Naturally, if you can reasonably expect the reader to comply with a request, you need not worry about being presumptuous.

The third ending to avoid is the perfunctory one, which takes this form:

Please let us know if we can help you in any other way.

Thank you for your trouble with this matter.

If you have any other questions, kindly let us know.

The trouble with these endings is that they are hackneyed, coming from the files rather than from the heart. Also, they may be used thoughtlessly. For example, a university ended its letter denying admission to a high school applicant with the old standby, "Please let us know if we can help you in any other way." Having been rejected, the student needed no help. The perfunctory ending was insincere and irritating.

You may occasionally use these endings, but do so carefully and try to touch them up with a few details, a slight rewording, or a personal note. Here's how the three previous ones might be reworded:

If you have any other questions about the seminar, the speakers, or the financial arrangements, please let us know. (*details*)

Thank you for taking such good care of our special order. (*slight rewording*)

If the enclosed pamphlet does not answer all your questions, Mr. Bartell, please let us know. (*personal note*)

The reader's name may be used effectively with some endings, but be cautious about inserting it when it might seem tacky or insincere. Perhaps you have had this feeling when receiving a personalized computer letter with your name typed in several obviously blank spaces, as if the letter had been individually sent to you alone and had not gone out to thousands of others whose names were similarly inserted.

SUMMARY

This chapter has dealt with the strategy and technique of information letters. We have described and discussed the organizational patterns for requests, replies, orders, order acknowledgments, credit letters, and recommendations.

In writing requests, you should state your purpose immediately; then provide details, furnish a reason if it would be helpful, and end courteously. When a request might be considered unexpected, you should offer a reader benefit if possible.

Replies may begin with an appreciation statement, an answer to the request, a reference to it, or a combination of these. Your decision depends on your reader and the situation. An explanation or discussion of the request may follow, and the letter should end with a courteous close.

Orders may be phoned, written on order forms, or sent in a letter. If you use the last method, be certain to include all the necessary information: complete description, quantity desired, price, shipment information, payment terms, delivery date, and anything else necessary for filing or payment purposes.

Order acknowledgments typically consist of a phone call, form postcard, or duplicate invoice. But with initial, unusually large, or special orders, or those whose shipment will be completely or partially delayed, a letter is usually written. It should contain a statement of appreciation and delivery information (in whichever order is most useful and effective), a sales message, and a goodwill close. The acknowledgment of a special order should itemize the specific articles desired and mention any restrictions on the order.

Because people are buying on credit to a greater extent, the volume of correspondence about credit solicitations, requests for credit information, credit application acknowledgments, and letters granting credit has increased tremendously.

Credit solicitations are invitations to people to apply for credit accounts. These letters may begin with an invitation or, if sent to newcomers to a community, a welcoming statement. This opener should be followed by an explanation of the advantages of a charge account at the store, a reference to the enclosed application form, and a friendly close.

Requests for credit information should state the purpose of the letter, explain why it is being sent to the reader, contain a reference to the questions asked later, include a statement assuring confidentiality, mention any possible reader benefit, and end on a goodwill note.

Credit application acknowledgments are usually sent to businesses desiring to open new accounts or placing initial orders. After beginning with a statement of appreciation, you should request references or completion of an enclosed application form, mention that the order will be shipped as soon as credit is approved, and assure the reader about the routine nature of the credit inquiry and the confidentiality of the response. Conclude with a goodwill statement.

Another type of information letter is the recommendation. Usually written to help someone obtain a job or promotion, the recommendation letter should contain an honest evaluation of the person being recommended, with an appraisal of the individual's strengths and weaknesses. After explaining, in an initial sentence or paragraph, why you are writing the letter, you should mention your qualifications to evaluate the individual, discuss the person's abilities—with examples or details—and end with a summary statement.

To help you write better information letters, we discussed certain techniques: how to use natural and specific language, how to make certain that subjects and verbs agree in sentences, how to write courteously, and how to begin and end letters effectively.

Selecting natural words involves relying more on the language you use in talking to others and less on the stilted, artificial language found in some old-fashioned business letters. General and vague language should usually be avoided. It should be replaced by specific and concrete words that enable readers to see, hear, feel, smell, count, or understand precisely what you mean.

Subject-verb agreement ordinarily poses no problem, but when the subject and verb are separated by numerous words, when the verb precedes the subject, and when the subject is not clearly singular or plural, you should be careful to make certain that the verb agrees with the subject and not with some other word.

Your information letters should sound pleasant. Half the battle is being aware of the need to be courteous. The other half involves checking your first draft to see that you have projected a favorable image and have avoided all offensive words.

Also important are beginnings and endings. Opening statements should be relatively brief, sound natural, and get to the point quickly. Two ways to begin letters effectively are by using the words *thank you* and *you*. If a reference to a preceding letter is necessary, it may be subordinated in the opening sentence, stated in a subject line, or indicated in a reference line.

Endings should spur readers to action or leave them with a friendly feeling. A few details, a personal note, or a slight rewording of a formula ending can be helpful. In particular, try to end on a positive, not a perfunctory, note. And try to avoid being presumptuous by assuming that your reader will act as you wish. The use of the conditionals *would* and *if* can help you with this problem. Mentioning the reader's name in closing also adds an effective touch.

If you adopt these suggestions and master their strategies and techniques, you should be able to write effective information letters.

EXERCISES

Discussion Questions

1. How did the letters you received from your college influence your opinion of it?
2. What favorable or unfavorable opinion do you have of some organization or business because of its letter to you?
3. Why is it important for writers to distinguish between expected and unexpected requests?
4. Sears has written you about an error in your company's credit account. In replying, would you mention the date and subject of this letter? Why or why not?
5. What difference have WATS lines made in the placing of business orders? When are they used? When not used?
6. Why are initial, special, and unusually large orders normally acknowledged?
7. If you have discontinued an item that a customer orders, should you write anything in reply besides the fact that you cannot fill the order?
8. From your personal knowledge, do you know whether women are discriminated against in any way when applying for credit today?
9. If a woman gets a divorce, should her credit rating be changed?
10. If you are denied credit in trying to buy a car, is there anything you can do about it?
11. Why do you suppose that some employers no longer request written recommendations, but instead ask for references and telephone them?

In-Class Applications

Write out brief answers to the following questions:

1. To what extent is the following request letter effective? How could you improve it?

   Dear Valued Customer:

   We are pleased to enclose with our compliments a copy of The Old Lady and the Banker.

   This educational book has been published as a means of helping children and young adults comprehend the basic nature and benefits of the banking system to an individual and the community. It is intended as an entertaining example to show the importance of thrift and planning in the building of a sound financial future.

   Please give it your careful consideration, for we would appreciate your reactions to both its contents and manner of presentation. We need your opinions as we are contemplating publishing other similar books regarding financial subjects, such as inflation, trust services, etc.

Thank you very much for your cooperation.

Sincerely,

P.S. If you have some members of the younger generation in your family or nearby, we hope you will report their reactions to us also.

2. In the following letter, list the words or expressions that are not natural. In addition, rewrite the letter to improve it, mainly substituting familiar words for the formal ones:

Receipt is hereby acknowledged of your inquiry of September 21 which I have at hand. With regard to your request for information about jams and jellies, I am happy to acquaint you with the fact that we have a complete stock at the present writing so that we will be in a position to take care of your valued order.

Pursuant to your request, we are enclosing herewith our full color gift catalog. Kindly advise us which gift packages you would like to order. Please realize that we are not in a position to ship on credit so that you must transmit a check or money order with your order.

If you would be so kind to let us know your wishes at your earliest convenience, we will commence to work on your order so that it will be delivered prior to Christmas.

3. What are the strengths and weaknesses of the following letter to the faculty? Rewrite the letter to make it more effective.

Dear Faculty:

The Student Center Board is presently planning new programming for next fall. As the new Contemporary Affairs Committee chairman, I am soliciting advice and suggestions for new programming (speakers, panel discussions, symposiums, etc.), particularly ones concerned with contemporary affairs. Hopefully, I will be able to schedule a series of "theme" programs to correlate not only with each other but with specific interests or educational goals of several university departments. In past years, several Student Center Board committees have worked together to present varied activities and programs on related topics, and U.K. professors have utilized this "theme" programming in relation to their classes. However, we must have your suggestions in at the earliest possible time for optimal programming dates. If you have any suggestions or ideas, please drop me a note or call the SCB office at 258–8867 and leave a message. I will get back in touch with you. To facilitate the printing of an all—campus events calendar, please try and have your comments to me by April 20. With your cooperation and support, the University of Kentucky Student Center Board is looking forward to an exciting year of campus programming.

4. Select the appropriate verb in each of the following sentences:

    a. Everyone in our sales force (was, were) assigned a territory.
    b. There (was, were) a great many engineers looking for openings at other companies.
    c. Neither the manager nor his assistants (has, have) seen the report.
    d. There (does, do) not seem to be any quick solutions to the problem.
    e. A discussion of the advantages and disadvantages of stock option plans (is, are) presented in the June issue.
    f. Lying under many papers in the manager's office (was, were) the report and the approval from the site committee.
    g. None of the applicants (appears, appear) qualified.
    h. Neither the president nor any top officials (was, were) present when the chairman visited the plant.
    i. The staff (is, are) supposed to use the reserved parking places in the B lot.

5. Rewrite the following sentences to make them more specific:

    a. I worked as a waiter last summer.
    b. In my senior year in high school, I was involved in many things.
    c. I plan to major in business.
    d. She is a buyer.
    e. He bought a small car.

6. Rewrite the following sentences to make them more courteous:

    a. Your carelessness has resulted in our shipping you an incomplete order.
    b. If you had read the terms in the catalog, you would have known that the net balance was due in 30 days.
    c. You failed to state the color of the socks on your order.
    d. We cannot understand why you have not sent in your deposit for a dormitory room.
    e. You are mistaken about the date of your check.

7. Rewrite the following beginnings and endings to make them more effective:

    a. I was glad to receive your letter of June 15 asking whether we still carry oil-filled electric radiators and I hasten to reply to your inquiry.

    b. Your letter of January 8 was a pleasure to receive. Your thoughtfulness in enclosing a photograph made your request very clear. We so often receive requests like yours, but they are usually vague and difficult to understand. That is why I am making a point of appreciating your use of a photograph with your request. As to the higher base to replace the LR base of your chair, we do have them in stock and will be glad to ship you one.

    c. Please be advised that your letter has been taken under advisement by our adjustment department. Should an adjustment in your water bill be made, you will be so advised in the near future. We trust you will find this procedure satisfactory.

    d. Close of a letter from a bridal salon that has sold a wedding gown and other bridal accessories to a young woman:
    We at Milady Bridal Salon are happy to have been able to assist you in your wedding plans. We look forward to having the pleasure of serving you again in the near future.

    e. It is our sincere and earnest hope that every detail of your business will be handled to your entire and complete satisfaction and that this will be the commencement of a long and pleasant business relationship.

Writing Assignments

1. Write a letter to the Student Periodical Agency, 1883 Baylis Drive, Ann Arbor, MI 48109, requesting the names and prices of magazines available at special student rates.

2. You are manager of the agency in assignment 1. Reply to the request, enclosing a price list and a stamped, addressed order form.

3. As program director of the Student Center, order the following magazines from the Student Periodical Agency: 2 subscriptions to the *New Yorker* at $15 each; 2 subscriptions to the *Ladies Home Journal* at $8.97 each; 2 subscriptions to *Redbook* at $8.97 each; 1 subscription to *Ms.* at $5.97; 1 subscription to *Psychology Today* at $7.97; 1 subscription to *Business Week* at $15.25; 1 subscription to *Rolling Stone* at $7.98; and 1 subscription to *Sports Illustrated* at $15. Enclose a check and have the magazines sent to you at the Student Center.

4. You notice that *Changing Times* is not on the list of magazines offered at special student rates. Write to the Student Periodical Agency, asking whether it is available at a student discount.

5. As manager of the agency, reply that it is not available. However, you can offer a subscription for the school year (nine months) at $6, a considerable savings over the $1.25-an-issue price.

6. Write a letter to *Changing Times*, Editors Park, MD 20782, asking whether the magazine could be offered to students at special rates for one year. Explain that as manager of the Student Periodical Agency, you have had several requests for subscriptions to it.

7. As public information specialist, you handle correspondence for your college television station that broadcasts local programs and those from the Public Broadcasting System (PBS). Write replies to the following letters:

   a. I have never written a letter such as this before but I suppose there is a first time for everything. I am greatly concerned because of the fact that you have taken my favorite program off the air. It is "Cooking Cajun." I would very much like to have this program back on. ("Cooking Cajun" was not taken off the air. The ten-program series ended. But it will be repeated starting April 8 at a time to be announced later.)

   b. The concert given by Miss Saleminus last night on your station was heavenly. It was truly memorable.

    We certainly need more programs like that instead of the trash we get on so many stations.

   c. I am only 11 years old and I like your programs. I've been watching one program "Once Upon a Classic." On the day of June 16 I liked it very much. It remembered me of some of my old friends that was away from home and acted like Heidi that did have no real family. I like your programs very much.

   d. I really like Laura Weber in your show "Folk Guitar." I was wondering if she gives private lessons and, if so, how much they are. I really would appreciate a reply. Thank you very much. (Laura Weber lives near San Francisco. Her programs were recorded several years ago and are distributed in cassettes to stations by a West Coast company.)

8. a. Because you are writing a term report on acid rain, you would like to obtain a transcript of the MacNeil/Lehrer program on this subject that was broadcast on September 23. Write a letter to the television station in assignment 7.

   b. As public information specialist, inform the writer that transcripts of the MacNeil/Lehrer programs are available for $2 by writing to MacNeil/Lehrer Report, Box 345, New York, NY 10019.

   c. Write a letter to accompany your check for the transcript.

9. As an English professor preparing for the fall semester, you want to know whether the university television station is planning to broadcast *Hamlet*, *King Lear*, and *Antony and Cleopatra*, which you will teach in your course on Shakespearean tragedy. Write a letter of inquiry.

10. As public information specialist, reply to the letter, stating that *Hamlet* with Derek Jacobi will be televised on October 27 at 8 p.m.

11. Write to a company of your choice for an annual report to be used for study in your business writing class.

12. Prepare a form letter for the president of that company for use in replying to the previous letter and others from college students. Plan to send not only the annual report but also the most recent quarterly statement.

13. While visiting a friend in New York City, you enjoyed No-Cal Coffee, a bottled carbonated soft drink. Write to the No-Cal Corporation, College Point, NY 11356, to find out whether it is distributed in or near your home or college community.

14. Assume that you wish to transfer to another college next year. Write to the Director of Admissions for a catalog and an application.

15. As assistant registrar, reply to the letter, enclosing the application but sending the catalog by third class mail.

16. You would like to buy a copy of *Managing in Turbulent Times* by Peter Drucker, but it is not available at your bookstore. Noticing an advertisement for the book in the *New York Times* by Harper and Row, its publisher, you decide to write for it. The book costs $9.95. The publisher's address is 10 East 53rd Street, New York, NY 10022.

17. You are the manager of the Thirstee Towel Company, which specializes in selling towels to motels with their names printed on them. Write the following letters:
    a. Acknowledge an initial order from Mr. Christian of the Pirate Motor Lodge, Jekyll Island, GA 31520. The twenty dozen towels will be shipped in about three weeks.
    b. The order from the Big Chief Motel in Cherokee, NC 28719, calls for fifteen dozen towels of style #1883 in brown. This style is available only in white or blue. Inform the manager, Mr. Oconol, of this fact.

18. As editor of your college newspaper, you have been concerned about the small stipends paid to you and your associate editor. Write a form letter to be sent to editors at comparable institutions, asking them what financial and other benefits they receive. Inform them that if they would be interested in the information you receive, you will send them a copy of your report.

19. Assume that you are going to be married at the end of this semester. Write a form letter that could be sent to hotels and motels, asking about accommodations and any special honeymoon features and rates.

20. As manager of a local department store, write a letter welcoming new graduate students to town and inviting them to open a charge account by completing an attached form.

21. The Highlander Company, 1072 Jacoby Road, Akron, OH 44321, has advertised wood golf tees, imprinted with up to two lines of 22 characters including spaces, per line. They are printed in black or red, available in white, yellow, orange, or assorted colors, packaged ten tees in sealed poly bags, delivered free at $15.50 for 500, $25 for 1,000, and $68 for 3,000. As manager of the University Sporting Goods Company, order 500.

22. One of your friends, who is applying for a job as counselor at Kamp Kohut, Oxford, Maine, has asked you to write a letter of recommendation for him to Mr. Harry Reeder, the camp director, 107 Polito Avenue, Lyndhurst, NJ 07071.

23. Your senior high school English teacher is applying for a position with the Indianapolis, Indiana, school system. He has been asked to provide letters of recommendation from former students, and requests that you write about him to Dr. Alvin Potts, Superintendent of Schools, 3859 DePauw Boulevard, Indianapolis, IN 46268.

24. You have asked a close friend to write a letter of recommendation about you for a position that you want this summer. He claims that he could not write an effective one and suggests that you draft it, give it to him, and he will sign it if nothing is objectionable. Write a letter about yourself for his signature.

NOTES

[1] Associated Credit Bureaus, Inc., *What Is a Credit Bureau?* (Houston: n.p., 1976).

[2] Sylvia Porter, *Money Book* (New York: Avon Books, 1976), p. 85.

[3] Associated Credit Bureaus, Inc., *Consumers, Credit Bureaus and the Fair Credit Reporting Act* (Houston: n.p., 1971).

4 Persuasive Letters

OBJECTIVES

After reading this chapter, you should be able to:

- Explain the advantages that sales letters have over other forms of advertising
- Describe the ICA strategy for the sales letter
- List ten ways to begin sales letters and six ways to end them
- Explain Maslow's theory of human motivation and its pertinence to sales letters
- Discuss the strategy of the solicitation letter
- Describe two ways to induce speakers to accept invitations and ten matters that should be mentioned in them
- Explain how to improve sentences by using verbs more effectively
- Point out three main ways to achieve sentence variety
- Discuss the importance of the *you* attitude

PLAN

Strategy
The Sales Letter
    The Product or Service
    The Audience
    The Letter
The Solicitation Letter
The Invitation Letter
Technique
Words
    Selecting Lively Verbs
    Avoiding Sluggish Verb-Noun
       Combinations
Sentences
    The Active Voice
    Sentence Variety
Style
    Paragraphing
    The *You* Attitude
Summary

Of all the uses of language, persuasion may be the most frequent.

JAMES L. KINNEAVY

STRATEGY

- Don't read further unless you'd like to lose some weight!
- Want to end your money worries?
- Imagine a member of your family having cancer.
- You may have already won a prize in our sweepstake contest.
- We can increase your gas mileage by 17%!
- You won't want to miss this meeting.

You've probably received letters with beginnings like one of the above. If not, you will as soon as direct-mail businesses and other organizations interested in the college market obtain a copy of your school's student directory. And as you grow older, your name will appear on many lists—telephone books; community directories; social, religious, and business rosters; tax rolls. You will then be besieged by letters trying to sell you everything from an abacus to a zither or to motivate you to contribute to worthy causes, ranging from AA (Alcoholics Anonymous) to the YWCA. Why are there so many persuasive letters? What makes selling and soliciting by mail so profitable that it has become a $100 billion-a-year business?[1]

The most important reason may be market selection. A direct-mail advertiser can pinpoint the audience that the sales message should reach. Unlike most other forms of advertising—radio, television, newspaper, magazine—direct mail restricts the target audience to people who are likely to be interested in the product or service. For example, it is possible to rent or buy mailing lists on labels or computer tapes for about $25 to $200 per 1,000 names.[2] These lists contain the names and addresses of almost any type of person—from college students, lawyers, farmers, plumbers, and people earning more than $50,000 to owners of dogs, cats, horses, boats, planes, and balloons. There is even a list of left-handed people.

The names of these individuals are obtained from magazines, student directories, book and record clubs, credit card companies, and other businesses and organizations wishing to profit from selling their lists of customers or members. When these lists are used, practically every sales message reaches its mark. There is little waste.

Another advantage of direct mail is that it does not have to compete for reader attention. Newspapers, magazines, radio, and television bombard people with sales messages, vying for their interest. In contrast, the sales letter is opened in the relative peace and quiet of a home or office, where a person may read it without distraction.

It does not compete with other sales messages, as do newspaper and magazine ads that have to vie with one another, or radio and television spots that follow one another pell-mell.

In addition, the letter is a communication channel that offers almost unlimited opportunities for a sales message. Advertisements in newspapers and magazines are restricted by space. Advertisements on radio and television are limited by time. The sales letter, on the other hand, can run on for many pages and even be accompanied by supplementary brochures, pamphlets, price lists, and foldouts. There are few restrictions on color, size, shape, and format.

Finally, direct mail enables readers to respond easily. Unlike radio and television commercials that require leaving the house to purchase an item, or newspaper coupons that must be cut out and inserted into envelopes needing stamps and addresses, sales letters necessitate little work. Readers merely have to sign their names or initial a card, and either mail it or pop it into an addressed, stamped envelope first. What could be simpler?

For these reasons, then—pinpoint market selection, complete reader attention, few length and format restrictions, and convenience of response—direct mail offers numerous sales advantages. And some of the same strategy used in writing sales letters can be adapted to persuasive letters aimed at raising money, attracting people to meetings, inviting guest speakers, and even electing candidates. (The marketing of a politician is like that of a product, as exemplified by the employment of advertising agencies for both.) The strategy we will discuss in the following section, however, will be restricted to business purposes, although it could equally well be applied to political ones.

You may never have occasion to write a national sales letter like those distributed by *Time*, *The Reader's Digest*, and other mass mailers. Their colorful, expensive promotions are produced by staffs of professionals or by advertising agencies specializing in direct mail. But you may have an opportunity to write your own customers or local prospects about some product or service, or to interest other businesses in some items you market or manufacture. Not only will knowing how to write sales letters assist you in business, but it will pay dividends when making oral sales presentations, when writing other persuasive letters, and when shopping as a consumer.

THE SALES LETTER

Selling by mail involves three components: *what* is sold (product or service), *who* it is sold to (the buyer), and *how* it is sold (the letter). Although we shall focus on the letter, the product or service and the audience are also important.

The Product or Service

You should know everything possible about what you are selling. If it is a product, you should thoroughly understand how it is made and why it is made that way. You should also know how it compares with competing products: in what respects it is superior and inferior. And, of course, you should be familiar with price comparisons. Similarly, you should learn as much as possible about any service you are selling.

The Audience

Knowledge about the potential buyers is also important. How old are they? What income group are they in? How much schooling do they have? What are their interests—sports, movies, television, books, music? Where do they live? What are their values, problems, hopes, aspirations, likes, and dislikes? And so on. In no other form of communication is it so important that you analyze and understand the receivers of your message.

You can realize how sales messages are designed for audiences by studying television commercials. In the afternoon soaps, for example, most are pitched to homemakers, urging them to buy various laundry and food products. Many early evening commercials on family sitcoms coax the young viewing audience to purchase soft drinks. And on weekend sports, the locker room or barroom commercials direct the large male audience to buy certain brands of beer. Scattered throughout these and other commercials are black children, families, athletes, and entertainers, because in the 1970s advertisers decided to go after the black consumer market.

Certainly, you can recognize that you should shape the sales message to the potential buyers. You surely would sell insurance in different ways to college seniors, newlyweds, middle-aged couples with several children, and senior citizens.

You can never know too much about what you are selling and to whom you are selling it.

The Letter

Often the first consideration in sales letters involves not the actual letter but the envelope. Because of the huge amount of direct mail selling, people are overwhelmed with sales letters, often referring to them as "junk mail." Although legally entitled to have their names removed from mailing lists,[3] people seldom bother to do so, preferring to throw away bulk mailings addressed to them or to "occupant." As a result, writers design enticing messages for the envelope (see figure 4–1), have letters hand-addressed and stamped, or camouflage the return address with an individual's name rather than a company's. Depending on your readers and your financial resources, you may or may not wish to employ these strategies on your envelopes. But you should be aware of the importance of motivating readers to open their mail.

The actual letter, like many written communications, has a beginning, a middle, and an end. Each fulfills a different function. The beginning of the letter attempts to *interest* readers. The middle is aimed at *convincing* readers to purchase the product or service by creating a desire for it. And the end of the letter serves to *activate* readers, usually by urging them to act soon and by providing a card or order form. To simplify, we refer to these three parts as the ICA of the sales letter:

> I = Interest
> C = Convince
> A = Activate

Figure 4–1. Enticing Envelopes.

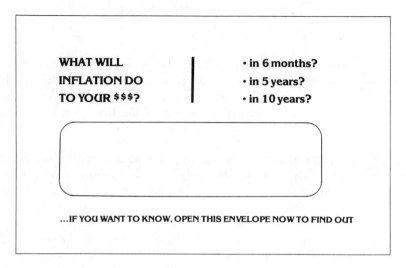

INTEREST   Why should anyone read your sales letter? Usually the envelope reveals that it is a business rather than a personal letter. So why should people spend their valuable time reading a letter that may cost them money? They have other things to do. And other ways to spend their money.

To overcome their probable resistance, you must figure out ways to snare them. Television and magazines can depend upon attention-getting visuals, but seldom will you have the money for them or for such devices as coins, stamps, freebies, or other gadgets. Instead you must devise a catchy or clever opening.

If you haven't hit on such an opening after gazing out the window, staring at the wall, or looking at the ceiling in a futile effort to be creative, run through the following categories for possibilities:

Reader Link
I'm an entrepreneur, too. One day I knew I wanted out. Out of the 9 to 5 world. Out of the same old meetings. Out of offices where people are afraid to take chances.

So I started *Venture*—a big, colorful magazine for men and women who feel the way I do. For people who are determined to succeed—in whatever enterprise they choose.

Whether you already have a business—or are considering going on your own some day—*Venture* offers hard-won advice you can use right now. The kind of thing *I* wish I had when I was starting out!

Venture Magazine

Interesting Facts
According to the latest nationwide accident statistics reported by the National Safety Council, almost 1 out of 10 persons—or about 21,000,000 Americans—will be victims of nonwork-related accidental injuries and will require medical attention this year.

Colonial Penn Life Insurance

Narrative
It's a Sunday afternoon, and you and your family are all enjoying a pleasant drive, when suddenly . . . another driver coming toward you—distracted by the thought of the family dinner party he's hurrying to—suddenly swerves to avoid a dog and hits you head on at 45 miles an hour!

Allstate Insurance

Reference to History, Myth, or Literature
There was an ancient Greek who was so anxious to have people remember him that he set fire to the Temple of Diana just to immortalize his name.

But if *you* want to be remembered, there's no need to go to such extremes—all you have to do is give THE REPORTER this Christmas.

The Reporter

Flattery
I've got a bet on you . . .
The bet? That you're just the type of knowledgeable reader for whom *Newswatch* is written.

Analogy
(See figure 4–2 for the *Wall Street Journal*'s "dewline" analogy.)

The "If-Then" Fish Net
If you'd like to know more about common *illnesses and diseases* . . .

If you wish you knew more about what to do in *medical emergencies* . . .

If you'd value an easy, reliable way to keep up with today's rapid advances in medical *technology* . . .

If you consider it part of your responsibility not only to keep yourself fit, but to see that members of your family stay healthy . . .

. . . then welcome to THE HARVARD MEDICAL SCHOOL HEALTH LETTER, the non-profit newsletter that's all about you.

Harvard Medical School Health Letter

Play on Words
Most of us know how to talk. But few of us know how to speak.

Dorothy Sarnoff, Speech Dynamics, Inc.

Quotation
"It's a funny thing about life," Somerset Maugham once wrote; "if you refuse to accept anything but the best, you very often get it."

Bestletter

Question
Would you spend $12 to be able to see around corners?

That's all it takes to begin a trial subscription to *Barron's*. . . .

Barron's

Figure 4–2.   Example of an Analogy Used to Attract Interest.

THE
WALL STREET
JOURNAL

PUBLISHED BY DOW JONES & CO.,INC. 22 CORTLANDT ST. N.Y.,N.Y. 10007

Announcing a "DEWLINE" for business!

Dear Reader:

Some 20 years ago, air defense planners in the U.S. came up with the concept of the "dewline."

"Dew"—an acronym for distant early warning—was implemented with a "line" of radar stations posted all across Northern Canada.

These radar stations, because of their location, could detect the first signs of an enemy air strike aimed at the U.S., and relay the information instantly to Air Force commanders in America.

The idea, very simply, was to get the news most important to our air defense operations to the "managers" of those operations as fast as possible.

A dewline for business.

If you're like most managers, you may well read the story of the "dewline", and wish you had just such a "dewline"—providing "distant early warnings"—for your own business operations.

Well, that's just the idea behind America's only national business daily.

I'm speaking of The Wall Street Journal.

Sure, you know The Journal. Very possibly you've picked up a copy now and then on the newsstand. And, in all likelihood, you may have a copy of The Journal passed on to you by a business colleague or friend who's a Journal subscriber.

But you can't appreciate how The Wall Street Journal serves as a "dewline" for business unless you receive your own copy of The Journal every business day.

You see, The Journal is the only publication in American busi-

(SOURCE: Reprinted by permission of *The Wall Street Journal.*)

Of all opening devices, probably the easiest but the most dangerous to write is the question, particularly the one allowing a "yes" or "no" answer. For example:

> Are you losing sleep over the crabgrass in your lawn?

If the answer is "no," the reader tosses the letter away. Rather than run that risk, ask open-ended questions or a series:

Open-ended: How is it that some people have a lawn that is weed-free, looks luxurious, and stays green most of the time?

Series: Would you like your lawn to be the envy of your neighbors? Would you like to see it lush and healthy from spring to fall? To get rid of crabgrass and other weeds? To eliminate grubs and other damaging insects?

Effective questions not only attract reader attention but involve people in the sales situation. Note how effectively the three questions in the Bethany Life Insurance Company letter (see figure 4–3) prepare the way for mention of the company's savings plan. But if questions are written thoughtlessly they can be losers. You get the point, don't you?

CONVINCE   The second part of the sales letter should be directed at convincing readers that they need the product or service. But first, you must link this part with the opener. Here's how <u>not</u> to do it:

> James Thurber once remarked, "He who hesitates is sometimes saved."
>
> We're having our yearly anniversary sale in carpets this month. You'll want to take advantage of our low prices by . . . .

Note that the opening quotation is not connected with what follows. Instead, the writer should have cemented the parts together, perhaps like this:

> James Thurber once remarked, "He who hesitates is sometimes saved."
>
> That's why we hope you'll hesitate before buying carpets elsewhere this month until you see what you can save by shopping our anniversary sale.

Here the repetition of *hesitate* and *save* establishes the link. Elsewhere the answer to an opening question, reference to a statement, or comment on a narrative, fact, or analogy will provide a suitable transition.

Your next job is to convince readers that you can solve their problem. Essentially, the sales letter is a problem-solving communication. You are offering your product or service as a solution to your readers' problem, which they may or may not recognize. Sometimes it is apparent to them: acne, excess weight, low grades, or loneliness. Sometimes it is dormant: the possibility of fire, theft, or an expensive illness. Sometimes it takes the form of an unrealized dream: a trip, jewelry, or a sports car. No problem, no sale. If students do not know how to type, or if they own and are satisfied with their typewriters, you have little hope of selling them one. But

Figure 4–3.   Persuasive Letter.

BETHANY SAVINGS & LOAN ASSOCIATION

Florida Central Building   Tallahassee, Florida 32302   (904) 555–5561

Dear Sir or Madam:

I have no way of knowing whether my services or my company's services will be of benefit to you, but I would like you to think about three questions that are of extreme importance to you and your family:

1. Are you, like most people with whom I talk, interested in saving money?

2. Do you, as is the case with most people, find it difficult to save under the common savings methods?

3. Take the number of years you've been working times your average salary. What percentage of that income have you saved so far? How much will you save in the future?

I would like to talk with you about my company's special savings plan that will set aside money for you for future use.

It is a semi-compulsory, guaranteed plan of providing for your own income at retirement.

To receive full information about our exciting plan, and also an attractive Papermate pen, please send the enclosed card with your telephone number as soon as possible. There is no postage required and no obligation on your part.

Sincerely yours,

Enclosure

most people have problems. Analyze what they are and direct your efforts at showing how your product or service will solve them.

For example, most people have a problem with money—making it, keeping it, saving it. Anything that promises to help with a money problem—less expensive car insurance, higher interest rates on bank accounts, ways to lower income taxes— requires little effort in creating desire. What must be done is to convince readers that they will save money, that the plan is safe, and that you and your company are reputable.

What about other human desires? In *Motivation and Personality*,[4] Abraham H. Maslow classified human wants into the following hierarchy of five categories, ranging from the most basic to the most altruistic:

In addition to classifying human needs into five categories—physical, safety, social, esteem, and self-actualization—and ranking them according to their importance to people (as indicated by the numbers on the left in figure 4–4), Maslow presented another concept. He stated that people must satisfy a lower level of need before becoming concerned with a higher one. As the playwright Bertolt Brecht put it, "First comes the belly, then morality."

What has Maslow's theory to do with persuasive letters? It may help you to determine and classify your reader's needs. Here is a list of some general human desires, with Maslow's categories indicated in parentheses:

> To attract the opposite sex (3)
> To be popular (3)
> To have enough to eat (1)
> To be in style (3)
> To protect family (2)
> To gain knowledge (5)
> To be independent (5)
> To escape pain (2)
> To feel good about oneself (5)
> To be clean (1 or 2)
> To be admired (4)
> To own lovely possessions (4 or 5)

The lower the need on Maslow's scale, the stronger its appeal. In selling cigarettes, for example, an advertisement for a brand with low tar and nicotine should do better by stressing its relative health benefit (2) than by emphasizing its use to gain love or social approval (3). Of course, all appeals should be mentioned, but one should be emphasized—the lowest. This logical approach may not always work, as vain efforts to sell cars for their safety features have demonstrated. But Maslow's theory can guide you in deciding how to motivate readers.

The main appeal should be expressed in the form of a solution or benefit for readers. If you are offering a new vitamin compound, for example, you are solving the problem most older people have about feeling tired, being unable to enjoy life fully, perhaps being deficient in health. So you are selling not merely a product but a benefit, a solution to a problem, a promise of good health, vitality, energy, and the possibilities for more fun, greater popularity.

Figure 4–4. Maslow's Hierarchy of Needs.

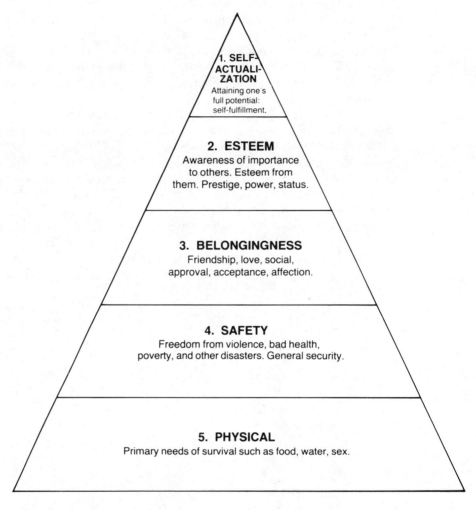

1. SELF-
ACTUALI-
ZATION
Attaining one's
full potential:
self-fulfillment.

2. ESTEEM
Awareness of importance
to others. Esteem from
them. Prestige, power, status.

3. BELONGINGNESS
Friendship, love, social,
approval, acceptance, affection.

4. SAFETY
Freedom from violence, bad health,
poverty, and other disasters. General security.

5. PHYSICAL
Primary needs of survival such as food, water, sex.

Finally, to convince readers, you must offer evidence. In other words, after creating a desire for a product or service, you must show that yours is the best on the market or, at least, excellent and reputable. You may, for example, persuade people to buy an exercise bicycle to lose weight and stay in shape, but you also need to convince them that your bike is well-built, sturdy, reasonably priced, and durable.

How to convince readers? You offer all the evidence you can muster: *facts, figures, testimonials, examples, reasons,* and *details* are some ways. For example, the specifications and other details about the construction of the exercise bicycle would be persuasive, and so would testimonials from people who have used it successfully. If you're selling automobile insurance, you can convince readers by citing facts about your policy, figures about its cost, and reasons why your company's service is better than your competitor's. Or, if you're selling a campus humor magazine, examples of the articles you've featured or plan to carry can be persuasive.

If you're worried about the length of this evidence, don't be. When you have a lot to say about a product, follow the advice of David Ogilvy, one of the great figures in advertising: "The more you tell, the more you sell." He claims that it is only "a myth" that people won't read long copy.[5]

To check this point, you might look at some of the letters that you or your classmates receive. Many will run from four to six pages, presenting reasons or examples of how a product or service will benefit you. You might view these long sales messages as a shotgun blast aimed to hit readers with at least one point.

For instance, we have received a large four-page mailer asking us to subscribe to the *Harvard Medical School Health Letter*. It promises to deal with back problems, glaucoma, alcoholism, high blood pressure, acne, and cancer. It will also provide information about which diets are worthwhile, what exercise people should perform at various ages, and what they should know about new medications and surgical techniques, X-ray hazards, insomnia, first aid, and self-examinations. The sales letter aims at practically every health concern so that no reader's problem will be overlooked.

Besides the shotgun approach, two other strategies are frequently used to convince readers: enclosures and free trial offers. Quite often a brochure, pamphlet, foldout, or sample is sent along with the letter. The more information provided, the better. Naturally, some people do not read the specifications, examples, and details, but they derive a sense of security and comfort just from the presence of this information. It indicates that the writer has massive evidence to support the claims about the product or service. But not every letter should be long.

Particularly if the enclosures are lengthy, the letter should be short. The Harry and David letter (see figure 4–5), a one-pager, accompanied a mouth-watering brochure featuring colored pictures of their gift packages. The letter sells readers on the "incredibly flavorful fruit and wild berries" of Oregon, the care taken to "hand-select" the fruit at precisely the right time, the attention given to cooking in the "small, home-style" kitchen and bakery, the ease of ordering, and the money-back guarantee. The brochure shows the gift packages, lists the prices, and provides an order form. The combination—sales letter and brochure—is hard to beat.

Also successful is the free trial offer of a product for a limited time. Customers agree, for example, to try a magazine subscription for several weeks or months without charge or to examine a book for seven or ten days without paying for it first. At the end of the trial period, they must cancel the subscription, return the book, or pay. Because such free trial offers are expensive for businesses, they extend them only to prime consumers. These people will not usually accept an offer unless they are definitely interested in the product. And when they receive it, they normally feel obligated to buy it unless the product is decidedly inferior, misrepresented, or useless. Sometimes, they find it less of a nuisance to pay the bill than to repackage the item or write a letter canceling a subscription. Or they lose track of time, realizing too late that the trial period is over.

Figure 4–5. A Sales Letter-Brochure Combination.

6

Harry and David®
at Bear Creek Orchards, Medford, Oregon 97501

What's the most valuable gift in the world?

It's something that makes folks stop and smile in remembrance, long after the occasion passes. And it's something that tells folks just how special you think they are. Our customers tell us that those are the kind of gifts they find in our Christmas Book -- and here's why.

Back in the days of the Oregon Trail, the pioneers who came to our beautiful Pacific Northwest found it mighty rough going. But no matter how hard the winters or how difficult the land breaking, there was one priceless treasure in abundance -- incredibly flavorful fruit and wild berries. The simple preserves, cakes and fresh fruit enjoyed by the Oregon pioneers were something city dwellers could only dream of.

> We still take the time and trouble -- like those pioneers -- to search for fully ripe berries and to nurture our fruit trees until they're heavy with the most flavorful, delectable peaches, pears and apples in the world. Our kitchen and bakery are small, home-style. We cook in small batches, so none of the wonderful flavor escapes. And we hand-select every single piece of fruit in our fresh fruit gifts.

These are gifts of pure goodness -- different and long-remembered by the lucky folks on your Christmas list. Gifts that are priceless for the friendly feelings they spread to those around you...priceless because they come straight from nature with just a little help from Harry and me.

> And you do yourself a favor, too, when you send these fine gifts. It's so easy to order -- no holiday crowds to fight, no parking problems, no long lines. And our gifts represent real down-to-earth values. Our prices include everything -- all the extras you usually pay for in stores, such as expert packing, fancy gift boxes AND delivery charges.

ONE OTHER THING...our guarantee means exactly what it says. Harry and I promise your complete satisfaction in every respect, or your money back. Your gifts must be perfect -- your friends and family must be delighted.

That's a promise,

David

©1978, Harry and David

COMMUNICATING BY LETTERS

There is nothing unethical about free trial offers. Readers accept them with full prior knowledge of all the conditions so they are clearly forewarned about the price and time period. But we do disapprove of the sending of odd-shaped products in cartons that customers must rip apart to open, making it impossible to return the products in the same package and difficult to find another.

We also disapprove of another occasional practice: failure to state the price. But because paying money, no matter how little or reasonable, is usually unpleasant, the cost should be mentioned only at the end of the letter after the reader has been fully persuaded of the virtues of the product or service. Of course, when price is a main feature, as in a special sale or introductory offer, it should be headlined. Otherwise, leave it until the end of the letter and state it as painlessly as possible. To do so, mention a savings comparison, break the price down to the cost per day or unit, or show how little it would amount to on some easy payment plan. In addition, if you can allow readers to use their credit cards, you will increase sales, perhaps as much as 20 to 40 percent on expensive items.[6] Here's how some writers have handled price:

> You'll get 26 valuable issues for the low basic price of just $29.95—that's just $1.15 an issue, and a significant savings off the $2.50 cover price.

> Your coverage will cost you only $120 a year. That's only 33¢ a day to protect you and your family.

Some sales letters make no mention of price, leaving this painful subject for the return order card or an enclosed brochure.

ACTIVATE   If you've done your job well, your readers should be persuaded by the end of your letter. So it's vital to get them to act immediately instead of letting them wait to forget your message or have its effect wear off. If a customer walks out of a store saying, "I'll think about it," chances are the sale is lost. If a reader puts your letter aside, ditto. That's why you must spur readers to act. You can offer them a simple, convenient way to buy by providing a card to sign and a postage-paid, addressed envelope to return it in, or a toll-free 800 number to call. Some companies make buying easy by enclosing a thin pencil (no need to hunt for one!) or bypassing the signature, requesting instead some effortless act—for example, putting a provided gummed label or coin-like token (see figure 4–6) in a designated space. The point of all these gimmicks is clear: the easier it is for readers to act, the more likely it is that they will do so.

The professionals use several rhetorical devices to create the feeling that the reader must act *now*:

> *Special Offer*
> Simply O.K. the enclosed reply card and drop it in the mail—we'll do the rest.
> But remember, please, this is a *special* offer made only for quick acceptance, so be sure to send the card *right away!*

Figure 4–6.   A Reply-Inducing Gimmick.

(SOURCE: Courtesy of *Writer's Digest Magazine.*)

Decide Now, "Yes" or "No"

We hope you'll let us know within the next ten days whether you want our service or not. Simply check the "yes" or "no" box on the enclosed card, and return it in the envelope provided.

We look forward to hearing from you and hope you'll be joining the many others who have profited from our financial service.

Limited Supply

Because we have only a limited supply of books, please send us your order today so you'll be certain to get this handsome classic for your library.

The Sooner, the Better

Let me suggest that you act now while this offer is on your mind. The very next issue might contain the answer to a problem you are facing today.

The Bonus (sometimes stated in a postcript)

Completing and signing the application and returning it in the postage-paid envelope within ten days will enable you to receive a bonus gift. We'll send you a heavy-duty, handsome garment bag for travel or home use. But you must mail your membership card within ten days. Why not mail it now?

The Circle (return to opening idea)

Opener: Would you give $12 to see into the future?

Ending: Put your subscription form in the mail right away. And get set to see into the future—to know what could happen in business and finance in the weeks and months ahead, and probably will.

Regardless of how you end your letter, remember that endings should:

- Be short
- Urge readers to reply immediately or shortly
- Make it simple and convenient to reply

Few sales letters end with the ending. Most writers add a postscript, which H. Gordon Lewis states "is more important than any part of the letter except the first sentence," because everyone reads the "p.s."[7] Unlike its cousin in the personal letter, the postscript in direct mail sales adds not an afterthought or something omitted but a final persuader, a clincher. Here is what such postscripts look like:

Don't forget that the price of this financial service is completely tax-deductible!

A new benefit has just been added to our policies. By sending in the reply card now, you will be entitled to . . . .

RECEIVE TWO VALUABLE BONUS GIFTS—ABSOLUTELY FREE!
If we receive the enclosed certificate within 10 days, we'll immediately send you these two gifts . . . .

This offer is backed by our full guarantee.

If you're not satisfied, return the bags and dispenser for a full refund, including shipping charges.

A new device to persuade readers, which might be called the rejection note, is a note-size, folded piece of paper with a simulated handwritten message scrawled on the cover (see figure 4–7) saying something intriguing, like "Please read this only

Figure 4–7. A Rejection Note.

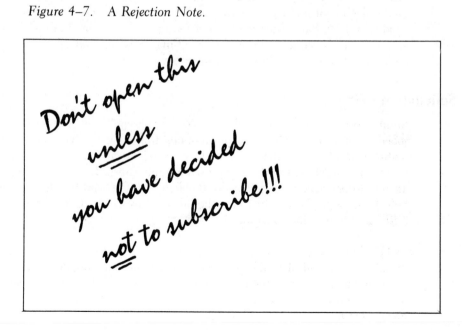

if you have decided NOT to accept our offer." Inside is another sales message, which may begin in this manner:

Honestly, I'm puzzled. I can't understand how you could pass up such a fine offer.

What follows is another attempt to sell readers. If at first you think you won't succeed, enclose a rejection note.

While it is interesting to observe the current use of attention-getting statements on envelopes, fancy enclosures, and rejection notes, these extras are too expensive for most small businesses. Still, sales letters can be highly effective without them, especially if writers know the product or service, the readers, and the strategy of the letter.

But they also must use a good mailing list. As we mentioned previously, national lists are available from numerous sources. Local lists usually may be obtained from community mailing services or from local utilities, directories, clubs, or organizations. Also, companies may compile their own lists from customers, sales representatives' reports, or people who answer ads or inquire about products. What is important about a list is that its names and addresses are accurate and up-to-date and that the individuals listed are potential buyers of the product or service you are selling. It makes little sense, for example, to send letters about a diaper service to childless couples.

But even well-written sales letters sent to prime prospects cannot work miracles. Competition is fierce for the consumer dollar. Even when such variables as the product, price, mailing list, timing, and economic conditions are highly favorable, sales letters seldom pull a response of more than 20 percent and usually generate less than 5 percent. For example, only 1 to 2 percent of the people solicited for mail-order life insurance actually buy a policy, which the companies regard as a good return.[8] What is important is not the response but the profit and the exposure of a company's name. And as the direct-mail business indicates, the bottom line looks attractive to many businesses these days.

The Solicitation Letter

Similar to sales letters are the letters sent by charitable, religious, educational, and social organizations soliciting contributions from readers. You may find yourself writing one of these letters as a student, trying to raise money for a campus Red Cross drive, a scholarship fund, or a community cause. In all instances, you should attempt to persuade readers that the problem is serious and that their donations can help to solve it. To do this, you should reply using an *ICA—Interest, Convince, Activate—*strategy for your sales letters.

INTEREST   Once again, it is imperative to interest readers immediately. But here the attempt should also induce readers to identify emotionally with the particular cause and to believe that their contributions can make a difference. Opening devices that accomplish this include shocking statements, heart-rending questions, and pathetic examples. Note the following:

COMMUNICATING BY LETTERS

Shocking Statement

The threat of severe malnutrition or even starvation faces 400 to 500 million children in poorer countries.

United States Committee for UNICEF

Heart-Rending Questions

What do poor villagers do when they see absolutely no hope of ever growing enough food for their children? What do they do when they see no way to provide water that's safe to drink? No way for children to attend school regularly? No way for the youngsters to have time for normal play?

Save the Children

Pathetic Example

The sad story of a mother stricken with cancer in figure 4–8 illustrates the use of this device.

Some of the other devices used in sales letters—reader links and quotations, for example—may be employed here. Regardless of the strategy, the reader's interest should be attracted immediately.

When letters are written to former contributors, the salutation often refers to this relationship ("Dear Contributor" or "Dear Supporting Member" instead of the customary "Dear Friend"). And the opening sentences usually include a statement of gratitude for past help and a description of the progress being made. The letter in figure 4–9 from the Epilepsy Foundation of America follows that strategy: it expresses appreciation, states how contributions have been used, and provides excerpts from the letters of people who have been helped.

Sending variant letters to two mailing lists, former contributors and non-contributors, is costly but can pay off in more and larger donations. It is the old story of the communication being encoded for a particular receiver. In addition, in local campaigns, a personal touch may often be added by having solicitors jot brief postscripts on letters going to contributors they know.

CONVINCE The purpose of this part of the letter is to convince readers how alarming the problem is and how important it is for them to respond. Typically, facts, figures, testimonials, case histories, and explanations are used to demonstrate the seriousness of the cause or the worthwhile work of the organization. The following portion of a U.S. Committee for UNICEF letter illustrates this point:

In parts of Africa, almost every child under 5 suffers from some protein malnutrition. More than half of all childhood deaths in Latin America are related to malnutrition. And in India, 75% of preschool children are suffering from moderate to severe malnutrition.

With your help, UNICEF can offer practical assistance to the countries most seriously affected. It can help governments establish nutrition programs, train parents and community leaders to increase local food production, and support emergency child-feeding projects.

Reprinted with permission of United States Committee for UNICEF

Figure 4–8.   A Pathetic Example Opener.

Cancer Care, Inc.
AND THE NATIONAL CANCER FOUNDATION

Spring 19--

Mr. Franklin R. Avery
12 West Slope Drive
Sunriver, Oregon 97701

Dear Mr. Avery:

"There isn't one thing I wouldn't do for her," he said, "but
this terrible thing...how can I help her now?!"

I won't beat around the bush with you. Those are the words a
dying woman's husband said to a counselor at Cancer Care.

The man and his wife are in their early forties. Their
daughter is a senior in high school.

A year ago, the mother developed cancer. Now it is past hope
of cure...it is a matter of months.

Trying to help her get well, her husband has spent all the
money he had and gone deep into debt.

He is so frightened of life without her! And his overwhelming
fear has spilled over into his work, so his job is in jeopardy.

Their daughter hadn't been able to face what was happening to
her mother...couldn't talk about it with her dad (or he with
her).

The thing we all fear has happened to this little family...the
unexpected tragedy waiting around the curve of the path, just
when things looked bright.

A year before, a happy, prosperous family. Now, a house of
whispering, shouting strangers.

I'm just very thankful that people at Cancer Care have been
able to help.

Our help began when her doctor contacted us and got the man
to come over and talk with a counselor here.

Figure 4–9. Solicitation to Former Donor.

1828 L Street, N.W. • Washington, D.C. 20036

APPRECIATION?   RESPECT?

YOU HAVE OURS.

FROM ALL OF US engaged in the battle
against Epilepsy <u>you</u> have our thanks
for your help in <u>the</u> fight.

YOUR CONTRIBUTION-

Has bought needed <u>diagnostic equipment</u>.

Has financed needed <u>research</u>.

Has helped <u>educate people and change</u>
<u>attitudes about epilepsy</u>.

<u>Most of All</u> you have helped <u>PEOPLE</u> who
need help.

You never get to hear the thanks of the people your dollars have
helped and the people your continuing contributions of $5, $10,
$15 will help. We Do! And we would like to share it with you,
because the thanks are really for you.

Here is the ESSENCE of just a few of the many letters we receive-

   • <u>A young mother from Brooklyn, New York</u>

       How many times I have had a seizure and people who
     I thought were my friends would just walk away...We
     have four children and the only thing they ask their
     father...<u>Will MOMMY ever get well</u>? I thank God that
     there is a Foundation for people who have Epilepsy.
     Please continue the good work.

(SOURCE: Reprinted by permission of The Epilepsy Foundation of America.)

The letter to former contributors takes a slightly different tack in the "convince" stage. Its readers already believe in the cause. What the writer must do instead is to show that donations are still urgently needed because, although much has been done, much still remains.

ACTIVATE   The letter should end like a sales letter, with a simple, convenient way for readers to act. This close often is combined with a plea for help and a mention that the contribution is tax-deductible. Here's what we mean:

> To bring food, medicine, and hope to these suffering people, please mail your tax-deductible donation to us today in the enclosed postage-paid envelope.

The tax-deduction statement may appear in a postscript, in a line at the bottom of the page, or with other material on the inside flap of the reply envelope. Where it appears may not be as important as that it appears conspicuously.

The Invitation Letter

Invitations fall into two categories: (1) to members of the audience; and (2) to speakers or other participants. In both instances, some form of persuasion is usually needed to induce people to leave the comfort and convenience of their homes. Most would rather stay there, watching television, playing cards, drinking beer, catching up with housework, reading, or puttering. So writers must bear in mind the unspoken question, "What's in it for me?"

AUDIENCE INVITATIONS   Two main appeals can be directed to the potential audience—members of an organization or club, for example. Usually the program will appeal to the basic motivations mentioned earlier—physical, safety, social, esteem, and self-actualization needs. In some way, the speaker or panel will help the audience to solve a problem, such as reducing high energy bills, coping with stress, understanding tax changes, or writing better business letters. So in these and other situations, the writer should emphasize how readers will benefit by attending.

The other appeal can be to reader loyalty. Sparse audiences reflect badly on the sponsoring organization. As president of the student body, if you invite your college president to speak, you would hope for a large turnout to demonstrate that your organization is alive, active, and concerned. So after announcing the facts about the meeting (time, date, place, subject), you might appeal to member loyalty in this manner:

> We hope everyone will attend this meeting to show President Hudson that students are concerned about the possible increase in tuition. Also, we want her to realize that we are seriously committed to solving campus problems, well aware of the issues, and anxious to work as a group to help the administration deal with the political realities. By attending the meeting, you will show President Hudson that she can count on us.

Be certain the invitation letter contains all the necessary information mentioned previously, as well as the price and reservation details for dinner meetings. When readers should act, urge them to do so in the last sentence:

> Won't you please phone Ed Martin (257-1488) today or tomorrow to let him know you'll attend our annual banquet.

SPEAKER-PARTICIPANT INVITATIONS An invitation to speak or participate in a program should praise the person and point out how attendance will be to his or her advantage. The praise should be subtle and sincere, explaining why you selected the individual. The advantage may be more difficult to unearth. Normally, the payment of an ample fee would be sufficient inducement. But usually, only an honorarium or token fee is available; often, nothing. In that case, the speaker may be attracted by the promise of a challenging occasion or some future benefit. Here's a possibility:

> Your incisive statements about gold, which were reported in our local paper, have been discussed at length in our investment class and, afterwards, by many members of our Student Investment Club.
>
> In view of our interest in investments, club members would like to obtain more information about the subject from an expert like you. Specifically, we hope you will be able to address us about the possibility of a return to a world gold standard.
>
> We would appreciate your speaking for about thirty minutes on this subject at our next meeting, at 7 p.m. on Tuesday, November 21, in 205 Student Union Building. Afterwards we usually have a half hour discussion and then refreshments. You may anticipate an audience of about fifty, mainly juniors and seniors, who will soon be active in the business world, many of them locally. It would be beneficial for them to know you in case they want to consult with you or refer clients to you.
>
> Please plan to attend. Our members are enthusiastic about meeting you and providing you with an enjoyable and stimulating evening. I'd appreciate your writing or phoning me at 266-0330 as soon as you conveniently can.

Besides the obvious details about time, date, and place, it is courteous and helpful to inform the speaker or program participant about the following other matters (some of which were mentioned in the previous example).

- the importance of the occasion
- the number of people expected
- the nature of the audience
- the guest's particular part in the program
- the names and backgrounds of other participants
- the general subject of the talk
- its approximate length
- an invitation to a spouse, if applicable
- financial payment if it can be given (stipend, honorarium, or reimbursement of expenses)

An extra inducement to out-of-town guests is an offer to attend to all local arrangements: hotel accommodations, transportation to and from the airport, cocktails, dinner, and so forth.

Note that the invitation followed the ICA formula (Interest, Convince, Activate) with an attention-getting opener, a convincing middle, and an action close that requested an answer. As you can see, the tone is less forceful than the sales letter's, but the strategy is similar.

The main difficulty in writing letters of invitation lies in including all the details, while making the letter sound warm, friendly, and pleasant. Naturally, letters to formal affairs require a formal style, but otherwise invitations should be informal, friendly, never stuffy.

TECHNIQUE

Persuasive letters are among the more difficult business letters to write. Requiring imagination and creativity, they must sparkle and captivate. Writers should appear to be enthusiastic yet sincere, persuasive yet logical, forceful yet reasonable. Readers should be attracted, absorbed, convinced. It's a tall order, calling for effective use of persuasive writing techniques: selecting lively words, particularly verbs; crafting vigorous sentences; and using a compelling style. Here's what we mean.

WORDS

All words in a sentence are important, but verbs are generally most important. The verb functions like the quarterback of the sentence, directing the play of ideas. It signals the action by prescribing what the subject does. Then, like the quarterback, whose leadership largely determines the success of a play, the verb determines the success of a sentence. Note how the change in a verb infuses life into each of the following sentences:

When you join, you'll *have* the same benefits as regular members.
When you join, you'll *enjoy* the same benefits as regular members.

Each piece is *put* into a custom shipping box.
Each piece is *cradled* in a custom shipping box.

This equipment will *free* you from heavy work.
This equipment will *unshackle* you from heavy work.

COMMUNICATING BY LETTERS

You can select lively verbs by choosing fresh instead of stale ones and by avoiding sluggish verb-noun combinations.

Selecting Lively Verbs

Stale verbs are like workhorses exhausted from heavy loads. Fresh verbs are like stallions—bursting with life, ready to gallop, scamper, or romp gracefully and spiritedly.

We cannot kill off the workhorses, but we can rely more on the stallions. The following simplified example will illustrate the point:

The customer hit the salesman.

Here the plain, bland *hit* conveys merely the vague picture of an action. No other verb except *struck* would mean as little in this context. Although some newspaper reporters might prefer *hit* for its editorial vagueness, most writers would select a more descriptive and vibrant verb:

The customer slapped the salesman.

Here the verb is sharper and stronger. Now the sentence comes alive with meaning. A light blow has been struck. Undoubtedly with an opened hand. No serious harm has resulted. Look again:

The customer tapped the salesman.
The customer punched the salesman.
The customer pounded the salesman.
The customer beat the salesman.
The customer smashed the salesman.
The customer clobbered the salesman.
The customer whacked the salesman.
The customer pummeled the salesman.
The customer whipped the salesman.

Here the picture changes as the verb changes. The force and duration of the action have increased, weapons such as a stick or belt are sometimes implied, severe damage may have been incurred; a police investigation may be initiated. All these verbs describe the same action expressed by the anemic *hit*, but each conveys a different picture.

Certain verbs play a major role in weakening sentences. Your attention in particular is called to the following ten:

to be [am, are, is, was, were]	to hold
to do	to make
to get	to put
to give	to take
to have	to talk

Overused and misused throughout the years, each of these verbs has acquired various meanings—from at least fifteen to over a hundred. Hence, they clutter our speech and sneak constantly into our prose. The main culprits, *be* and *have*, must serve frequently as auxiliaries; for example: He *had* phoned the manager. But when used as ordinary verbs, they often can be replaced:

The result of our special *was* a 15 percent sales increase in August.

Becomes:

Our special resulted in a 15 percent sales increase in August.

The revised sentence is not only more concise but more vigorous because the action is expressed directly. The verb *resulted*, although itself subject to overuse, is stronger than the anemic *was*.

Avoiding Sluggish Verb-Noun Combinations

Another bad habit to watch out for—besides using stale verbs—is coupling them with nouns expressing action. The resulting sentence is as handicapped as a basketball team with its high-scoring, giant center benched on fouls. Although the coach may have no capable substitute, the writer can replace the weak verb-noun combination with an effective verb, as these examples illustrate:

Weak: The course *will be of benefit* to him in his accounting work.
Vigorous: The course *will benefit* him in his accounting work.

Weak: He *has strong feelings* about the need to reduce all summer merchandise after July 4.
Vigorous: He *felt strongly* that all summer merchandise should be reduced after July 4.

In the weak examples, the stale verbs (*to be, to have*) are linked with nouns to express the action, resulting in a feeble combination. When the noun is transformed into a verb (*benefit, convinced*), the sentence is revitalized.

Frequently *-ion* nouns and others with common suffix endings (*-ence, -ance, -ity, -ment, -ent, -ant*) are coupled with overused verbs, as the following list indicates:

Weak	Vigorous
to make an appearance at	to appear at
to have perseverance in	to persevere in
to make reference to	to refer to
to be in conformity with	to conform to
to give a subsidy to	to subsidize
to be excellent at	to excel at
to make an acknowledgment of	to acknowledge
to carry out experiments	to experiment
to make a summary of	to summarize

Spotting sluggish verb-noun combinations generally requires staying alert for debilitating verbs or for nouns with common suffixes. But some combinations furnish no such clues:

Weak: The customers *wrote answers* to the questions but failed *to provide any comments* in the allotted space on the questionnaire.

Vigorous: The employees *answered* the questions but failed *to comment* in the allotted space on the questionnaire.

Of course, such combinations should not be revised when converting them would affect the meaning. Note:

He has an interest in the company.

He is interested in the company.

The first sentence indicates that the person owns part of the company, while the second asserts merely that he has displayed some curiosity about it.

Sentences

Relying on lively words, particularly verbs, is not enough. Sentences themselves should generate interest, providing life and strength to persuasive letters. Here are two ways to attain these qualities: (1) use the active voice; and (2) vary sentences in length, type, and openers.

The Active Voice

We talk and think and probably dream in the active voice. But in writing, we often transform ourselves into formal, affected people by communicating in the passive, like this:

A huge selection of charts and charting formats is offered to you by this encyclopedia.

Note how the passive presents ideas backward. Instead of the usual "who–does–what" sentence order, we have an inverted "what–is done–by whom." See for yourself:

Active: This encyclopedia offers you a huge selection. . . .

Passive: A huge selection . . . is offered . . . by this encyclopedia.

The active voice is more direct, more natural, more economical, and more logical than the passive. The result: it is vital in vigorous writing. Learn to recognize the active voice and learn the few occasions when the passive is preferable. But remember that, in persuasive letters, the active voice packs a punch, vitalizing your sentences, giving them impact, immediacy, energy, and strength. In contrast, the passive is considered by most people to be ponderous and sluggish, wordy and awkward, like this sentence. The moral: accentuate the active, eliminate the passive.

Sentence Variety

Variety is the spice of life and of good writing. Uniformity, whether in music, art, home decorating, or dress, creates monotony. A crafty pitcher mixes up his slider, screwball, and fastcurve. A clever quarterback varies his end sweeps, line bucks, reverses, and pass patterns. Similarly, effective writers use both long and short sentences; simple, compound, and complex sentences; interrogative, imperative, and exclamatory sentences; and a variety of sentence openers. They know that monotony is certain to bore readers.

SENTENCE LENGTH   The easiest way to achieve variety is to change sentence length frequently. While preparing a first draft or revision, writers should heed how long their sentences are running. If they tend to be about the same length, writers should avoid the monotonous rhythm by breaking up, combining, or extending them. Some writers can recognize their mistakes better by reading their papers aloud; most spot them by reading silently.

In a paragraph comprised mainly of medium (12–20 words) and long (21–40 words) sentences, the midget sentence (3–8 words) is a particularly effective device to stress a statement or to catch the reader's attention. It can be dynamic. But it must be employed sparingly and cautiously, or else its effectiveness will be weakened. Writers don't count words while composing a sentence. But they are subconsciously aware of sentence length, just as you are almost instinctively aware of when to apply the brakes on your car. In writing, you should at first pay deliberate attention to sentence length, but soon it will become second nature to you. For the present, when revising your papers, observe particularly whether you have avoided a series of either short and choppy or long and rambling sentences.

SENTENCE TYPE   Variety in sentence structure may be achieved in two ways: by grammatical pattern (simple, compound, complex, and fragments) and by rhetorical form (declarative, interrogative, imperative, and exclamatory). For your convenience, these terms are explained in Appendix J.

Grammatical Pattern   Inexperienced writers depend too much on simple and compound sentences. These sentences may be used to advantage—indeed, each has its virtues—but frequently they are used haphazardly and carelessly.

The simple sentence. Simple sentences tend to be succinct and emphatic; they isolate single ideas and clarify convoluted thoughts. Numerous consecutive simple sentences, however, suggest failure to subordinate or coordinate ideas, thereby placing this responsibility on the reader. To require this effort is to write ineptly.

But simple sentences can prove advantageous in some contexts. Advertisements and other copy calling for fast-paced prose should consist mainly of simple sentences.

They are concise. They strike the reader directly. Like short jabs, their impact is jolting. They are crisp and clear. Nothing interferes with their message. Nothing slows readers. Their eyes race down the page. Suddenly, when a complex sentence breaks the rush of simple sentences, readers are forced to slow down, to pause and perhaps to ponder the implications of what they have read.

The previously mentioned midget sentence illustrates another skillful use of the simple sentence. Dropped into the midst of long, complicated constructions, the midget rings out its message loud and clear. Generally, it should be reserved for special occasions: a key idea, a closing statement, or a transition.

The compound sentence. Compound sentences contain distinct ideas that are loosely related but of equal value. For example:

> The bank president prepared the statement and the directors signed it.

As expressed, some vague relationship is suggested between what the president and directors have done. But all we know is that their action occurred and in the stated time sequence.

We frequently employ the compound-sentence pattern in conversation because *and* is the first connective that pops into our mind to link ideas:

> I walked to school with Billy and we saw a snake in the grass. We chased it to my house but it got away. We looked for it and then my mother came out and told us to go to school. We ran all the way. The bell sounded and we walked in the front door. The teacher made us stay after class and that's why I'm late.

Hence the strength and weakness of simple *and* compound sentences. They suggest the carefree informality and flow of conversation. But in doing so, they may over-simplify and distort the relationship between ideas. Sometimes, however, the resulting vagueness and indefiniteness is desirable. Note the advantages of the compound in the previous example: *The bank president prepared the statement and the directors signed it.*

- Both the president and directors are of equal importance.
- No causal relationship is suggested: the directors may or may not have signed it because the president prepared it.
- No specific temporal relationship is suggested: they may or may not have signed it *as, while, when, after* he prepared it.
- No contrast is suggested: they may or may not have signed it despite the president's having prepared it.

As you can observe, a compound sentence provides writers with an effective means of packaging ideas when they wish to obscure the relationship between them. It is also useful occasionally for variety, or to convey a colloquial tone. Otherwise, avoid compound sentences. If you habitually use *and* in your work, examine every instance for possible revision. By eliminating compound sentences, except when they serve as previously indicated, you will strengthen your writing.

The complex sentence. Complex sentences are valuable because they signal precise relationships. They do not occur frequently in speaking, because few of us have the mental agility to formulate, articulate, and structure our thoughts simultaneously. But in writing, we have the time to perform each one of these intricate mental exercises. We can be alert, therefore, for opportunities to use the most sophisticated and valuable verbal pattern—the complex sentence. Because it subordinates one or more minor ideas to a major one, and depicts the exact relationship between them, the complex sentence appears often in mature prose. Observe its versatility and clarity:

> Because the bank president prepared the papers, the directors signed them. (*causal*)
>
> When the bank president had prepared the papers, the directors signed them. (*temporal*)
>
> Although the bank president prepared the papers, the directors signed them. (*concessional*)
>
> If the bank president had prepared the papers, the directors would have signed them. (*conditional*)
>
> The directors signed the papers, which were prepared by the bank president. (*emphasizes directors; subordinates president*)
>
> The bank president prepared the papers, which were signed by the directors. (*emphasizes president; subordinates directors*)

Much of the complex sentence's effectiveness stems from the power of the subordinating conjunction. Observe how it functions as a signal:

> After she proposed the merger . . . .

At this point, the reader knows that what follows in thought also follows in time, that what follows is more important than what has been stated, and that the relationship is chronological, not causal. By means of these signals, therefore, complex sentences convey meanings, indicate emphases, and express relationships in a lucid, compact form. That is why skillful writers frequently use complex sentences.

The sentence fragment. The difference between fragments in business and industrial writing and in freshman composition is that the latter usually occur through carelessness, while the former are deliberate. Sentence fragments in elliptical situations achieve the informality and spontaneity of conversation without disrupting coherence or obscuring clarity. Note the following examples of effective fragments in persuasive letters:

> Does this mean that all food processors are inefficient? Certainly not.
>
> The magazine contains something interesting for all members of the family. For Dad, business news, handyman tips, ways to save money. For Mom, fashion items, news about timesaving devices, housekeeping devices, vacation plans. For the kids, sports articles, features on hobbies, science experiments, and comics.

Sentence fragments in the wrong context can embarrass a writer. But used carefully to complete the meaning of a previous statement or question, or to avoid repeating sentence elements that are clearly understood, fragments can add vigor to persuasive letters. Indeed, yes.

Rhetorical Form   To a limited extent, variety may also be achieved by rhetorical forms—interrogative, imperative, and exclamatory sentences. The sentences we have discussed so far in this chapter have all been declarative statements, as are nearly all our utterances. Therefore, nothing more will be added about them.

The interrogative sentence. Occasionally, questions can effectively vary the rhythm of a paper because of their inverted word order, unusual mark of punctuation (?), and involvement of the reader. Were you aware of a barrier between reader and writer? Do you realize how a question practically reaches out from the page, grabs you, and forces you to react? Like the pointed finger of the old recruiting posters, the question breaks through your equanimity. Don't you see? You can no longer be detached, remote, or aloof. You are coaxed or tricked into involvement.

Especially effective is the question in the middle of a paper or paragraph. Why not reach out to your readers just as you might if you were conversing with them? Your directness, naturalness, and apparent awareness of them will prove appealing.

Now that you know more about the function, importance, and position of interrogative sentences, do you realize that they can serve as transitional devices? In addition, short questions provide a dramatic way of gaining attention or highlighting a point. Will you remember to use them?

The imperative sentence. Imperatives offer another option for achieving variety that business writers can use especially for commands, requests, or instructions. The following examples show how imperatives and questions may be written in patterns ranging from the polite to the strident:

1. Please try to get the report finished by May 3.
2. Will you please try to get the report finished by May 3?
3. Would you be willing to accept May 3 as a deadline?
4. Let's say that the report will be due on May 3.
5. Suppose you shoot for a May 3 deadline.
6. You will complete the report by May 3.
7. Do get the report in by May 3.
8. Don't get the report in later than May 3.
9. Get the report in by May 3!
10. Don't get the report in later than May 3!

Notice the softening effects of *please* in sentences one and two, *willing* in three, and the question mark in two and three. Also observe the emphatic roles of *do* and *don't* in sentences seven and eight, and the harshness of the exclamation marks in sentences nine and ten.

The exclamatory sentence. Exclamatory sentences are compelling when used as imperatives; elsewhere, exclamation marks strengthen the emotional force of the sentence. For writers wishing to generate excitement about a product, service, or company, a vigorous impact can be created by an occasional exclamatory sentence! But beware! Too many exclamations can spoil the sales pitch!

SENTENCE OPENERS   Writers may also achieve variety by mixing sentence openers. If you remember your first-grade primer, it probably read something like this:

> See Dick and Jane. Dick is going to the store. Jane is going to the store. Dick sees the store. Jane sees the store. Dick goes in the store. Jane goes in the store. They are going to buy some food. It is a food store.

Not a far cry from primer writing is the following:

> The six British proof coins are set in an attractive case decorated with an official British Royal Mint medallion. This set is an important addition to any collection. It is an ideal way of starting one. The set is also an excellent way to start friends and relatives collecting.

Monotony in these examples is caused not only by similar sentence patterns (simple declarative) and stale verbs (*is*, *has*), but by the regular use of the subject in the initial position. This opener stems from our speech habits. If you listen to people talk, you will discover that most of their sentences begin with the subject, followed by the verb and the object.

In writing, we have time to think about positioning various sentence elements; we have the opportunity to shift them around for variety or emphasis. Look at the many ways that a single thought may be expressed by changing the word order in the sentence opener:

1. The subject should not always be used in beginning a sentence. (*standard subject opener*)
2. In beginning a sentence, the subject should not always be used. (*prepositional opener*)
3. Not always should the subject be used in beginning a sentence. (*adverbial opener*)
4. When you begin a sentence, do not always use the subject. (*adverbial clause opener*)
5. Beginning a sentence always with the subject is not advisable. (*gerund opener, noun clause as subject*)
6. To begin a sentence always with the subject is not advisable. (*infinitive phrase as subject*)
7. That a sentence should always begin with the subject is erroneous. (*dependent noun clause as subject*)
8. There should not always be a subject at the beginning of a sentence. (*expletive opener*)
9. Do not always begin a sentence with a subject. (*verb opener, imperative*)
10. Do you know that you should not always begin a sentence with the subject? (*verb opener, interrogative*)

COMMUNICATING BY LETTERS

While you might recognize many of these sentence openers, you probably have seldom used more than three or four of them. For instance, have you ever opened a sentence with the infinitive? To do so gives your sentences a nice change of pace. Or, how often has your lead-off word been an *–ing* verbal?

> Drawing on its vast experience, the Mint has established the highest standards of coin production.

> Collecting British proof sets is an ideal hobby and sound investment.

And what about starting a sentence with an *and*? Once upon a time a coordinating conjunction at the head of a sentence was frowned upon. But tastes have changed. You will find that many professional writers start off with *and, but,* and *so* instead of such cumbersome substitutes as *moreover, in addition, however, nevertheless,* and *therefore.* Which is as it should be. One word of warning, though: in formal communications, these initial coordinating conjunctions should be used sparingly.

Alert readers may have spied in the last paragraph a sentence starting with *which.* Here is another possibility for rare occasions. Similarly, an occasional inverted sentence (one with rearranged subject, verb, object, or beginning adverbial modifier) may spice up a passage and emphasize a point. *The Wall Street Journal,* whose prose is often as liberal as its economics are conservative, provides this example:

> Cheap it won't be however.

But misadvised you should not be. Save your inverted sentences for special situations.

STYLE

What is most important in the style of persuasive letters is that it reveal a concern for readers and their problems. By being aware of their point of view, you show you are concerned about them, interested in them, and willing to help them. Seems obvious, doesn't it? But it isn't because this *you* attitude is often ignored by many writers.

Also ignored, but not by professionals, is that persuasive letters must be interesting. Obviously, we've been concerned with this subject in our discussion of lively verbs and sentence variety. Now we'd like to mention the importance of attractive paragraphing to create eye appeal.

Paragraphing

Persuasive letter writers have learned from their advertising brethren that white space increases attractiveness. The more white or unused space on the printed page, the more inviting an ad. And so with sales and solicitation letters.

If you have any doubts, just flip through some of the examples in this chapter. The *Wall Street Journal* letter is chock-full of one-sentence paragraphs, the Harry and David letter uses indented paragraphs to provide appeal, and the Cancer Care letter alternates two- and three-line paragraphs. So forget most of what you learned previously about proper paragraphing in writing sales and solicitation letters. Instead, worry about their visual impact. Remember: by keeping paragraphs short, you attract readers and keep them reading.

The *You* Attitude

The problem we have in accepting the reader's point of view is that we are absorbed in our own. We're basically self-centered, interested in our ideas, achievements, qualifications, feelings. As a result, we're apt to write a simple statement like the following:

> We're proud to announce the opening of our new branch bank in the Stoney Brook area and to offer our fine banking services to the community. Our drive-in windows will be open weekdays from 8 a.m. to 6 p.m. Our offices will be open from 9 a.m. to 3 p.m. Mondays through Thursdays, and from 9 a.m. to 6 p.m. on Fridays. Our manager, Mr. Chase, and our employees will be glad to welcome all customers.

Change the *we* attitude to the *you* attitude and you have:

> You are invited to enjoy the services of our new branch bank now conveniently open for you in the Stoney Brook area. You may use our drive-in windows from 8 a.m. to 6 p.m. on weekdays. Or, if you wish, you may transact business in the offices from 9 a.m. to 3 p.m. Mondays through Thursdays, and from 9 a.m. to 6 p.m. on Fridays. You will find our manager, Mr. Chase, and all our employees anxious to please you.

The difference in wording between these short examples is slight but, in impact, significant. The first statement employs the *we* approach, portraying the writer and the bank as self-centered and proud of themselves and their service. The second employs the *you* approach, portraying the writer and the bank as considerate of readers, concerned about their needs, and interested in them. Because of our dislike of braggarts and our preference for people concerned about us, we naturally react more favorably toward the second statement.

To say that business writers should use *you* frequently would be an oversimplification. What is important is that the writer think in terms of readers and their needs, and write in terms of their interests and desires. Readers are not primarily concerned about the writer or the company; they are not basically interested in its problems, difficulties, or predicaments. Like all human beings, they want to be flattered a little, courted a little, liked a little, and noticed a little. When a sign in a nearby shopping center announces that "Sears will open a new store here to serve you," they feel good. When it states "Sears is proud to open a new store here," they feel nothing. The *you* approach makes the difference.

Some final words: the *you* approach should not be thought of as a gimmick guaranteeing success with readers. It is not a device; writers should not perfunctorily sprinkle *you*'s throughout their sentences. It is essentially an attitude, a way of thinking that focuses the attention of writers on their readers. The *you* approach results in the use of *you* and *your*, but these words are relatively unimportant in themselves.

What is important is the feeling they generate in the writer. And in persuasive writing, that feeling should not be one of indifference. It should be one of vital interest and concern for readers and their problems. That means writing with their viewpoint in mind. Or, in a nutshell, using the *you* attitude.

SUMMARY

This chapter has focused on three types of persuasive letters: sales letters, solicitation letters, and invitations.

Sales letters are effective in selling services or products because they can be mailed to lists of carefully selected readers, they do not compete with other advertisements or commercials for reader attention, they are not significantly limited in length or format, and they enable readers to respond quickly and conveniently.

Writers of sales letters should know their product or service, understand the nature of the prospective buyers, and be familiar with the strategy of sales letters. Essentially, these letters are directed at problem solving, that is, satisfying the need of readers with the offered product or service.

Writers may use an attention-catching message on the envelope to induce readers to open it. The letter itself should follow the ICA format: Interest, Convince, Activate. Numerous types of beginnings are available to interest readers: facts, narratives, reader links, flattery, and questions, among others. Questions may be open-ended and more than one may be used.

To convince readers, it is important to create a desire for the product or service and then demonstrate that it will satisfy reader expectations. Maslow's theories about human motivation are helpful in analyzing reader needs. And facts, reasons, testimonials, examples, and details are valuable in demonstrating the quality of the product or service, and the company offering it. The use of abundant evidence, enclosures, and free trial offers also helps to convince readers. Price must be mentioned, but it should appear near the end and be stated in the least painful way, for example, on a per-day or per-unit basis. Mention should also be made about easy payment plans and credit-card use.

The ending of the letter should activate readers by urging them to decide immediately and by making it convenient for them to act, perhaps by having them sign and return a postage-paid card.

The solicitation letter also follows the ICA format, although its tone is usually less emphatic than the sales letter's. The interest-generating introduction may take two forms: an expression of appreciation to former contributors or an attention-getting opener to others. Convincing readers involves describing the problem and showing how the writer's organization can alleviate it with additional donations. The activate step consists of an appeal for help, mention of the tax-deductible nature of the contribution, and a request that the reader act immediately in whatever convenient way has been provided.

Invitations may be extended to members of an audience or to speakers and participants. To attract an audience, a writer should appeal to whatever basic needs (see Maslow) the program would satisfy and to whatever loyalty members have to the sponsoring organization. To attract speakers and participants, a writer should praise them by explaining why they were selected and should also point out what benefits they will derive by accepting. Depending on the situation, speakers should be informed about the date, time, and place of the meeting, the general topic and length of their talk, other participants, the number and nature of people attending, and arrangements for the speaker's expenses, time, lodging, and transportation.

The technique of writing persuasive letters involves selecting lively verbs and eliminating sluggish verb-noun combinations. The active voice and sentence variety— in length, type, openers, and rhetorical form—also enliven and strengthen prose. Other valuable techniques include the use of short or indented paragraphs to make the page more appealing to readers. Finally, there is the crucial *you* attitude, which consists of writing with the reader's viewpoint, interest, and concerns in mind.

EXERCISES
Discussion Questions

1. What sales letters do you receive in the mail? How do you think your name was obtained? Do you open and read all the letters? Why or why not? How effective are they?
2. What products or services are best suited for selling by mail? Which are not?
3. Why should you learn about sales letters if you are not going into a sales career?
4. From your previous summer or part-time work experience, cite an example illustrating the importance of knowing your product or service thoroughly, or understanding the nature of the buyer.
5. What are your feelings about "junk" mail? Does it perform a valuable service in providing information to the public or is it a nuisance that should not be entitled to a low mailing rate?
6. Should a question be used at the beginning of a sales letter? Discuss the advantages and disadvantages, and how to use this service effectively.
7. Provide an example to show why a sales letter is considered to be a problem-solving communication. Bring a letter to class or recall one you have received or seen.
8. In what way does Maslow's motivation theory help the writer of a sales letter?
9. Discuss the advantages and disadvantages of the shotgun approach, the use of enclosures, and the free trial offer.
10. You are writing students on your campus about a new college humor magazine priced by subscription at $6 a school year for six copies, and at $1.50 per copy on the newsstand. What is the best way to state the price? Where should it appear in the letter? How would you try to convince students to subscribe?
11. Why would it be advantageous to have two mailing lists for solicitation letters?
12. You are writing members of your high school class, inviting them to attend a reunion dinner at which the principal, coach, or a favorite teacher will talk. How can you appeal to your classmates to attend?
13. Why appeal to speakers? Aren't they sufficiently flattered by the invitation? Don't they enjoy being honored in this way?
14. Why provide information to speakers in the invitation? Why not wait to see whether they will accept?

15. How can you tell a fresh verb from a stale one? Might a verb be fresh in one context and stale in another? Explain.
16. Why might a newspaper reporter prefer *hit* to *pounded* in the example used about the customer's striking the salesman?
17. What are the advantages and disadvantages of simple sentences? Compound sentences? Complex sentences?
18. What impact does a sentence fragment have on the reader? Explain.
19. Analyze the paragraphing in one of the sample letters in this chapter. Point out how it differs from normal paragraphing by referring to specific examples.
20. Does the *you* attitude consist only of using *you* instead of *we/our?*

In-Class Applications

1. Eliminate the sluggish verb-noun combinations wherever possible:
   a. That example was a fine illustration of the waste in local government.
   b. Classes must be taken in courses that are in close relation to the work that you are engaged in the performance of with the company.
   c. The personnel director is to make a selection this week of a person to fill the position for which there is a vacancy.
   d. The department head will then place his signature on the voucher, thereby giving you a certification of it.
   e. He gave a refund of half the amount to the customer.
   f. The incentive program helped the company to have an increase in sales.
   g. He came to the conclusion that the community will derive a benefit from the fact that a national magazine will have a feature on the college next month.
   h. She gave preference to sales representatives who made an inquiry about her children.
   i. He conducted an investigation of the delay in the shipping department.
   j. His letter was supposed to be an explanation of the policy.
   k. He is the winner of the trophy given as an award to the most improved company bowler.
   l. The company would put its prices even lower but fair trade regulations forbid doing so.
   m. We have made a study of the problem and arrived at the conclusion that new packaging, direct-mail advertising, and increasing the sales force will double the volume of business in two years.
   n. Her speech at the employee's banquet was a direct answer to complaints about fringe benefits.
   o. His recommendations to increase productivity were in sharp contrast with those submitted by outside management.
   p. His assignment was to make a study of employee morale and to give recommendations to adopt or reject the proposed house organ.
   q. Of the 80 people sending in replies, 67 made an indication that customers have a preference for stores giving trading stamps.
   r. I believe that these courses will give us the opportunity to find an attractive series of sales positions.

2. Improve the following compound sentences and justify your changes:
   a. The company will not sell zone franchises but will award franchises on an individual basis and in some locations, multiple units will be available to qualified investors.
   b. Drainage alone has not proved to be sufficient to control skidding and it necessitates, therefore, the need for additional control measures.
   c. The part is so complicated in shape that it is impossible to find these stresses mathematically and other methods have to be used.
   d. A charge account will enable you to phone our personal shopper and place your order.
   e. This operation permits the performance study of the construction equipment and any deficiency can be controlled immediately.
   f. Dr. McGowan and his assistant are glad to give any student personal help and they are available from 3 to 5 o'clock every afternoon.
   g. The controller is the chief accounting officer of a private business and his job is to manage the work of the accounting staff.
   h. Most modern accounting firms have computers that take care of the routine work, and the accountants can devote their time to analyzing and evaluating business operations.
   i. John received his high school education at one of the best Philadelphia schools and he graduated with honors.
   j. Production of the camera has been curtailed by the strike and we cannot promise delivery within two months.

3. Analyze the point of view in the following paragraphs. Where appropriate, indicate how to improve it:
   a. It is with great pride that we announce the opening of our new store in the Brookside Shopping Center. It will be the largest of our four stores and we are certain that it will be greatly appreciated. It gives us great pleasure to extend an invitation to the people of this fine community.
   b. The college and pro teams are getting ready for the opening kick-off and we're getting ready to describe all the colorful action. We'll have complete scores of all the games, stories about the major clashes, interviews with leading coaches and players, and previews of next week's contests. Our numerous color photographs will provide vivid pictures of the most memorable and exciting scenes. We are going to cover this football season better than we have done any in the past.

4. Improve the following sentences by changing the verb from the passive to the active:
   a. If further information about this offer is needed, you can get in touch with me at your convenience.
   b. Your participating in our panel discussion would be greatly appreciated by us.
   c. It is hoped by the directors that your support will be given to this worthwhile project.
   d. An appraisal for tax deduction purposes can be supplied by us upon a request being received from you.

Writing Assignments

1. You are the manager of a student enterprise that has arranged a special plan for students to dine with friends at six of the better restaurants in town. By purchasing a $10 membership card, students would be entitled to a free dinner at each restaurant. The only restrictions are that the free dinners must be the less expensive of the two and that the cards are valid for only a year. Write a letter to all students informing them of the plan.

2. You are the sales manager of a student enterprise planning birthday celebrations for students at college. Write a form letter to parents, asking them to remember their son's or daughter's birthday by arranging to have a cake properly inscribed and decorated with candles delivered on the appropriate day. You will also plan a surprise party in the student's honor. Cost: $3.50 for a large cake; $6 for an extra large one.

3. Several women have decided to establish a Super Woman Service on campus. Hearing that you're taking a course in business writing, they've asked you to write a catchy and informative letter for distribution to all dorm students. The women offer a wide range of services including tutoring, running errands, giving haircuts, making wake-up calls, planning parties, and tuning up cars. Rates are $4.00 an hour plus expenses.

4. Your student enterprise, Cocktail Party Associates, offers a complete catering service for informal get-togethers. You furnish the desired number of uniformed help, the needed supplies (glasses, linens, punch bowl, dishes, etc.), and hors d'oeuvres. The price depends upon the number of students needed, the hours, and the food. Write a letter to all faculty and staff members encouraging them to try your service.

5. You are manager of a student business that solicits parents every year just before finals to send their son or daughter a *Survival Kit* to provide special nourishment for the stresses and strains of the examinations. The kit contains such items as cookies, brownies, pretzels, potato chips, crackers and cheese, nuts, and gum. Write a letter for mailing to all parents, suggesting that they purchase such a kit to be delivered to their student at the beginning of finals. Parents may attach a card to the order form at the bottom of the page. The price is $10.00 and the deadline for ordering is two weeks before the first examination.

6. You have obtained a mailing list of all high school students planning to attend college next year. Write a letter to be mailed in July, offering them your book, *How to Succeed in College*, for $3.75, which is 75¢ less than the price that it sells for in campus bookstores. Your book sold 12,000 copies last year, drew numerous letters of praise and appreciation from readers (you may make up quotations from them if you wish), and was favorably reviewed in *Redbook*, *Rolling Stone*, *Esquire*, and *Playboy* (you may also make up quotations from them).

7. As manager of the Student Periodical Agency, which handles subscriptions to all popular magazines, many of them at special student discounts, write a letter to all campus organizations and residence halls, informing them of your service and enclosing a brochure listing 64 magazines at student discounts of from 25–50

percent. Your agency is student-owned and operated, has a local office, and has serviced students and faculty members for three years. You may obtain magazine prices from notices posted on your campus bulletin boards or use these examples (all for one year): *Time*, $18 (reg. $31); *Newsweek*, $16.25 (reg. $32); *Psychology Today*, $6.99 (reg. $12); *Ms.*, $5.97 (reg. $10); *TV Guide*, $16 (reg. $20); *Rolling Stone*, $9 (reg. $18). These are the lowest authorized prices; the magazines cannot be sold for less. Another advantage of your service is that it is local: if there are any problems with the subscriptions, customers can phone you.

8. As manager of the Student Periodical Agency, draft a letter to the faculty informing them that, as educators, they are entitled to special rates on the 64 publications listed on an enclosed brochure. Probably, many faculty members subscribe to these magazines, unaware that they can obtain them at these reduced rates. In addition to seeking new business from them, you would like to take care of all their magazine business, including renewals of magazines not available at special rates and any gift subscriptions they may give at Christmas or other times. You handle all nonscholarly periodicals published in the United States.

9. As manager of the Student Periodical Agency, write a letter for November mailing to all students and faculty members who have ordered subscriptions through your agency. Try to interest them in giving magazines as Christmas gifts, particularly to other students and faculty members who are eligible for the special rates. Refer to an enclosed brochure and mention that a handsome card will be sent to the recipient announcing your gift.

10. As manager of the Student Periodical Agency, draft a form letter to be sent to subscribers about eight weeks before their subscription's end. Your problem is that the publisher begins at about that time to seek renewals from these subscribers, sending out computerized letters about every two weeks. You receive a commission only if you obtain the renewal. Try to persuade subscribers to renew through your student agency.

11. Write a letter for the A–1 Cleaners, urging out-of-town students to store their winter clothes with your company during the summer months. You pick up and deliver, charge only the regular cleaning costs, require only I.D. card identification and a $2 deposit that may be applied to the bill, which is due in the fall when the students want their clothes.

12. As president of the student body, you've just received a letter from Nancy Liederman, coach of the women's basketball team. She is recruiting Lisa Towns, the leading woman basketball player in Kentucky, who is interested in your college. Lisa is a 6'3" center, who averaged 37 points a game, and is being recruited by ten other schools but has an aunt living in the community and has indicated a definite interest in your school. Try to persuade her to accept the athletic scholarship being offered by Coach Liederman.

13. You are in charge of your high school class' five-year reunion, the first one it is celebrating. You are planning a dinner at a local hotel with a popular teacher, coach, or administrator as the featured speaker. Write a letter asking one of these individuals to talk. Assuming that that person has agreed, also write a letter to all your former classmates, inviting them to attend. Make up whatever time, date, location, price, and other details you wish.

14. Your Student Association has depleted the funds it had available in its Student Emergency Loan Fund. This was used to extend interest-free loans up to $50 to students for a month or two in order to help them pay for tuition, books, food, or rent. Usually these loans are repaid, but some students have left school, unable to pay their bills. Write a letter to all faculty members, asking them to contribute to this fund.
15. You are working for the vice president of student affairs, who is chairperson of the campus United Way drive. She has asked you to draft a letter for her to solicit contributions from the faculty, administrators, staff members, and other employees. You should be able to obtain information about the local United Way. If not, assume that it provides support for 23 human service agencies in your community, whose names and work are described in an enclosed pamphlet. Contributions support such local services as disaster relief, medical research, day care, Big Brother-Big Sister, Red Cross, Salvation Army, Urban League, and programs for youth and the mentally retarded.

NOTES

[1] Michael deCourcy Hinds, "The Junk-Mail Business Is Getting Sophisticated," *Courier-Journal* [Louisville, Ky.] June 25, 1981, Sec. C, p. 10.

[2] Hinds. See also "Marketing Via Direct Mail," *Small Business Report*, 6 (February 1981), p. 26.

[3] By requesting a name-removal form from the Direct Mail/Marketing Association, 6 East 43 Street, New York, NY 10017, individuals can have their names removed from 180 lists compiled by brokers, mail-order houses, and computer operations. On the other hand, those wishing to receive more mail about their favorite interests or hobbies can write to the same address for an add-on form.

[4] Abraham M. Maslow, *Motivation and Personality*, 2nd Edition (New York: Harper and Row, 1970), pp. 35–47.

[5] David Ogilvy, *Confessions of an Advertising Man* (New York: Ballantine Books, 1963), p. 95.

[6] H. Gordon Lewis, *How to Make Your Advertising Twice as Effective at Half the Cost* (Chicago: Nelson-Hall, 1979), p. 46.

[7] Lewis, p. 45.

[8] "Is Mail-Order Life Insurance a Bargain?" *Changing Times*, Nov. 1980, p. 44.

# Claim, Refusal, and Collection Letters

OBJECTIVES

After reading this chapter, you should be able to:

- Compose claim letters that bring satisfaction
- Employ a strategy for effective refusals
- Refuse a request, credit, or order without losing goodwill
- Know the customer categories and special circumstances defining a collection situation
- Explain the typical stages in a collection pattern
- Build goodwill through techniques with words, sentences, and style
- Employ passive constructions when appropriate
- Emphasize key points
- Achieve a pleasing tone in your letters

PLAN

*It is easier to catch flies with honey
than with vinegar.*

ENGLISH PROVERB

STRATEGY

Though some letters have to communicate unwelcome news to readers, these letters can do the job pleasantly and courteously. Unless they are handled with tact and consideration for the reader, claim letters, request refusals, collection letters, and the like could cause unhappiness or disappointment—and thus lose sales, damage the public image of your organization, or even make enemies. But if handled thoughtfully, they can do the job while keeping the reader's goodwill.

This chapter teaches you how to communicate unpleasant news while keeping the goodwill of your reader. First, it introduces you to strategies for claims, general refusals, and several special types of letters with messages that could result in unhappiness. Then it explains techniques for using words, sentences, and tone that will help you write unpleasant messages without alienating customers. Your sensitivity in composing the types of letters described here is a diplomatic skill essential to all executives.

CLAIM LETTERS

Because we are all subject to human error, we must expect others to make mistakes: incorrect charges on invoices, incomplete shipments, inaccurately priced tickets, inexact specifications, inadequate instructions, unsatisfactory service, faulty merchandise, and the like. To correct such mistakes, it is often necessary to write claim letters asking satisfaction for the grievance.

These letters can easily create unpleasant situations. The people who receive them might view the claims as unjustified. Or they might have concerns about bad publicity, damage to their reputations, the fairness of the requested adjustment, or the cost of adjustment. As figure 5–1 suggests, no one enjoys receiving complaints. So the claim letter requires special sensitivity and diplomacy if it is to prevent a hostile reaction and encourage a satisfactory adjustment.

By calling attention politely and calmly to whatever is wrong, you increase the chances of having your grievance handled promptly and satisfactorily. But by sounding off, you will irritate the reader and appear irrational; as a result, you probably will have your adjustment request turned down. Anger, scorn, ridicule, name-calling, threats, and derision are counterproductive. You must indicate that you are a fair

Figure 5–1. *No One Likes Complaints.*

"Of course, my door is always open, Adams! But it's for fresh air—not complaints."

(Source: From *The Wall Street Journal*, Permission—Cartoon Features Syndicate.)

and reasonable person if you expect to be treated like one. Thus, you should not write while angry or upset. The claim letter should soberly:

- Explain the situation that has prompted you to write.
- Describe, if appropriate, the loss or inconvenience.
- Appeal to the reader's sense of fairness to right the wrong.
- Indicate a satisfactory adjustment, specifying exactly what you consider to be reasonable and appropriate.

The claim letter in figure 5–2 illustrates the calm, reasonable tone that brings results. Note how the writer even flatters Zak's by mentioning that this is the first problem in ten years.

From several personal experiences, we have learned that a company will usually deal equitably and even generously with a polite and reasonable claim. However, if your claim letter does not bring satisfaction, you may wish to seek advice or support from one of the consumer protection agencies whose addresses are given in Appendix I.

THE REFUSAL PATTERN

How do you react when you open a letter, glance at the letterhead, and then read "I regret to inform you that . . . ," "It is my sad duty to report that . . . ," or "I am sorry to say that . . ."? If you are like most readers, your reaction is to become hostile toward the person or organization writing to you. In fact, since you can anticipate the bad news, you may toss the letter aside.

COMMUNICATING BY LETTERS

Figure 5–2.   Claim Letter.

Men's Department
Zak's
32 Seventh Avenue
New York, N.Y. 10001

Dear Sir or Madam:

RE: Zak's Account No. 403-296-6887

All three long-sleeved wool shirts (15½ x 32) I ordered from you were moth damaged when they arrived yesterday, thus causing the first problem I've had in almost ten years of shopping with Zak's.

Please send me instructions for obtaining replacement shirts or a refund ($132.00) under the terms of your customer satisfaction guarantee. And will Zak's cover the postage if I need to return the three damaged shirts?

Yours truly,

R. C. Walker

To prevent such hostile reactions, you will need to be more diplomatic than the author of the following letter:

Dear Ms. Monroe:

I hate to have to tell you this, but in reviewing applications for our Coastal Plains District Sales Supervisor position we have decided to eliminate from consideration anyone who does not have several years of full-time sales experience. Of course, since you do not have any full-time experience, we have had to cut you from our list.

Good luck in finding the job you want.

Sincerely,

W. B. Fitzsimmons
Personnel Manager

CLAIM, REFUSAL, AND COLLECTION LETTERS

The blunt opener, the unkind refusal, the insincere closing, the curt tone—all of these stir ill will in the reader and make an enemy for the company.

The writer of the preceding refusal letter has actually followed the strategy for delivering pleasant messages. In delivering pleasant messages, you quickly tell your readers what they want to hear—the good news. The resulting goodwill favorably disposes the readers to any details that follow in the letter and, at the same time, wins friends for you and your company. However, as several writers have recently noted, in delivering bad news you should be less direct and more tactful than in delivering good news.[1]

In reporting disappointing news, you should generally follow a *four R's* strategy: first you establish grounds for communicating with the reader (*relate*); next you offer an explanation (*reason*); then you bury the bad news in a succinct paragraph (*refuse*); and finally you console the reader (*reconcile*).

In outline form, here are the four steps:

- **Relate:** Open with a pleasant buffer introduction establishing rapport with your reader but avoiding any implication that a refusal will follow.
- **Reason:** Review the positive reasons for your refusal (for example, "in order to keep your costs down") to put the reader in an agreeable frame of mind and to lead up to the disappointing message which follows.
- **Refuse:** State the refusal, taking pains to be as inoffensive as possible by:
   —being brief (but not curt),
   —embedding the unpleasant news in a further explanation of the reasons for it,
   —avoiding negatives ("cannot," "will not," "you fail to") and apologies ("regret," "sorry"),
   —using, if necessary, positive or restrictive terms ("only," "exclusively," "solely") to couch the disappointing message,
   —making the refusal impersonal by avoiding the use of "you,"
   —implying rather than stating the bad news, but
   —ensuring that the reader will not misunderstand the news.
- **Reconcile:** Conclude by consoling the reader and bolstering goodwill.

As the letter in figure 5–3 illustrates, writers often devote one paragraph to each of the four major steps.

Is a letter following this refusal strategy brief? No. But a shorter letter could hardly have softened the disappointment as well. Time-consuming to write? Yes. But, as was the case with the letter in figure 5–3, a refusal letter can sometimes be a basic form letter that you personalize for many different recipients. The resulting goodwill makes the four R's strategy well worth the time and effort.[2]

THE REFUSAL SITUATION

Although the general refusal pattern applies to many disagreeable business messages, specific patterns exist for a number of them. Typical of these specific patterns are those for request refusals, credit refusals, and order refusals. Mastering these patterns will help in writing these disagreeable messages.

COMMUNICATING BY LETTERS

Figure 5–3. Four-Step Refusal Letter.

‖ ‖ DATA-TECH, INC. ‖ ‖

PERSONNEL OFFICE

March 4, 19--

Ms. Hattie E. Monroe
2019 Pinecrest Road
Alton, NH 03809

Dear Ms. Monroe:

    I have reviewed your application with Frances Montagu, Vice President of our Marketing Division, and we are both impressed by your fine academic and extracurricular record and by your part-time work the past two years at Fine Feathers, Ltd. ⟧—relate

    As our advertisement stated, the Eastern District Sales Supervisor's opening requires a bachelor's degree such as the one you will complete this spring. The ad also noted that preference would be given to college or university graduates with extensive experience in sales. ⟧—reason

    We believe this sales experience mentioned in the ad to be most advantageous for all new sales supervisors. So the applicant pool from which we will select our Eastern District supervisor has been narrowed to include only those who have worked several years as full-time sales representatives. ⟧—refuse

    Someone with your fine record and strong motivation will one day make a valuable addition to a sales division, and I hope you will soon find an opening. ⟧—reconcile

Sincerely,

WB Fitzsimmons

W.B. Fitzsimmons
Personnel Director

WBF:pw

125 Loblolly Boulevard   Portsmouth, New Hampshire 03801   603–555–4700

Request Refusals

A letter agreeing to a claim is, of course, easy to write. It simply grants the adjustment, expresses regret, explains the cause, assures the recipient that the error will not occur again, and ends courteously. Consenting to the request creates so much goodwill that even an incomplete or poor letter can hardly do much damage and a good one can win friends and customers.

But in those situations in which the claimant is to blame or partly so, a letter may refuse the adjustment or offer only a partial one. Such a letter requires care, tact, and consideration. Even then, it may not satisfy the reader, but at least you will have handled the difficult situation in the best possible manner.

If you have determined with certainty that you are not at fault for the problem, your request refusal should follow this plan:

- Begin with a statement of appreciation for the reader's letter.
- Agree with the reader about some aspect of the situation.
- Explain in detail your investigation of the request.
- Politely refuse the adjustment.
- Build goodwill by granting any possible concession or by appealing to the reader's sense of fairness.

Note that the letter in figure 5–4 refuses the adjustment request for a new coffee maker. But because the writer takes pains to be considerate, the reader is not alienated. In fact, the helpful tone encourages the reader to continue as a customer.

Credit Refusals

As you may recall from chapter 3, credit ratings are based on the four C's of credit: *character*—the applicant's record for honest dealings; *capacity*—the applicant's ability to earn enough to make the payments; *capital*—the applicant's assets (for example, savings and real estate); and *conditions*—the general economic outlook, the local financial conditions, and the applicant's expendable income projections. Obviously, when credit is refused on any or all of these grounds, people can easily be offended.

Thus, when people with poor credit ratings send in charge orders, you should not refuse credit in such a way as to lose them as customers. Instead, you should try to do business on a cash basis and to create a friendly relationship so that if their credit ratings improve, they will order from you in the future.

Of course, often the temptation in writing a credit refusal is to assume the applicant is a poor risk and not to bother being tactful. As a result, you might easily be curt and offensive: "regret to inform you that . . . ," "our policy at this time is not to extend credit . . . ," "poor credit rating . . . ," "unsatisfactory references . . . ," "deny your request . . . ," and the like. The problem is that such a letter accomplishes the wrong purpose: while refusing credit, it antagonizes the applicant and drives away a prospective customer.

An effective credit refusal letter has a constructive purpose—getting the applicant's business on a cash basis. To do this, writers of credit refusal letters usually follow the steps listed at the top of page 140.

Figure 5–4. Request Refusal Letter.

Discount Appliance Shop

593 ELKTON BOULEVARD   ORANGE, NEW JERSEY 07052   (201) 555-2347

September 2, 19--

Dr. E.S. Morea
1591 Dobbins Road
Hasbrouck Heights, NJ 07604

Dear Dr. Morea:

Thank you for informing us about your defective Mr. Java coffee maker and ⎤—*appreciation*
returning it promptly.

We agree with you that a new coffee maker should not stop working after five ⎤
months. Therefore, immediately upon receiving it, our expert appliance re- ⎬—*agreement*
pair technician examined it carefully. She noted that the electric unit was ⎦
corroded as a result of its immersion in water. Because the instructions
accompanying the coffee maker recommend that it be cleaned without getting water ⎤ *detailed*
on the electrical unit, the damage has occurred either through oversight ⎬ *explana-*
or accident. Since the manufacturer's guarantee does not apply under such ⎦ *tion*
conditions, we cannot exchange your coffee maker for a new one.

However, we can make your Mr. Java like new for you by replacing the damaged ⎤
electrical unit with a good one. In doing so, we will pay all the labor and ⎬—*refusal*
overhead charges; we ask only that you reimburse us $8.65 for the wholesale ⎦
cost of the unit.

Please let us get to work quickly. Merely phone 555-6711 to give us ⎤
your permission to install the new unit. Then we will expedite the ⎬—*build goodwill*
repair job and return your Mr. Java to your home in a few days. ⎦

Sincerely,

Lee Wong

Lee Wong
Manager

- Open with a friendly tone.
- Tactfully refuse credit.
- Offer incentives for cash buying.
- Stress the benefits of buying the writer's products.
- Urge the reader to place a cash order.

Observe how the letter in figure 5–5 refuses a large credit order. Note, too, that the letter explains the reason for the refusal while keeping the reader's goodwill and encouraging a cash order.

Of course, following these suggestions will not ensure cash orders from all customers you have to refuse credit to. But used effectively, this constructive approach can at least prevent you from thoughtlessly driving away potential customers.

Order Refusals

Often, customer orders have to be refused because the merchandise is out of stock or no longer handled, because the order provides inadequate information, because the person ordering does not qualify (perhaps is not a resident of your sales district or is not an authorized dealer), or because substitute merchandise may better serve the customer. Again, the problem is to show how the refusal can benefit the reader.

Some of these situations can be handled with little difficulty. For example, rather than flatly refusing an order because it cannot be shipped right away, you can send a notice that "the merchandise you ordered will be shipped in three weeks." Or in the case of a long delay, you can specify the date the goods will be available and ask for authorization to ship at that time.

If your company sells neither the merchandise ordered nor a suitable alternative, you might send a letter telling where the items can be bought—while taking the opportunity to promote your own goods:

> Dear Mr. Isaacs:
>
> Wintersport, Inc., Freeport, ME 04033, is the exclusive U.S. dealer for the Norwegian Sweater you ordered. Wintersport accepts orders by mail or phone (555-865-3111).
> For your other outdoor wear, take a look at our "Country Clothes" in the enclosed brochure. These fashions are carefully selected by Fairfax, Ltd., for the discriminating sportsman . . . the man who wants classic good looks in natural fabrics and the traditional manner.
>
> > Cordially,

The courtesy of this letter gains the goodwill of both the reader and the competitor. And its promotional ending may gain a new customer for Fairfax, Ltd.

Greater planning is required for refusals of other orders: those providing inadequate information; those from unqualified persons; and those for which you recommend alternate brands, models, or varieties.

Figure 5–5.   Credit Refusal Letter.

AMERICAN CRAFTSMAN WOOD STOVES

4740 MORRIS STREET   FORT WORTH, TEXAS 76100   817-555-1689

Mr. James Baldree
Alternative Heating Shop
Spooners Creek Marina
Morehead City, NC 27821

Dear Mr. Baldree:

Thank you for your order for twenty American Craftsman Wood Stoves. **]** *friendly tone*

The credit information provided to us by you and your references indicates a strong personal credit record for the two years you have taught at Carteret Community College in Morehead City. However, your new Alternative Heating Shop has not been open long enough to establish a solid commercial credit history. Such histories are necessary for opening all new accounts with American Craftsman. **]** *tactful refusal*

You can still add our fast-selling American Craftsman Stove to your lines before the fall season by sending a cashier's check and taking advantage of our 5 percent cash discount (a savings of $495--the price of one stove--on an order for twenty units). Or you may wish to place half of your order now and order the remainder when your inventory needs re-stocking. This option not only will help your shop build a sound financial reputation for establishing credit but will also assure that your stock always includes our latest technological improvements. **]** *incentive*

Our constant improvement of the operating features and heating efficiency has made the American Craftsman the top-selling wood stove in the South for the past three years. This record, together with our dealer-shared television spots, our manufacturer's five-year warranty, and a 33 percent markup for retailers, have made our stove the "dealer's choice." **]** *benefits*

Just complete and return the enclosed order form with your cashier's check attached. Your order will be delivered within two months--well in advance of the peak sales season this fall.

Sincerely,

Cecil P. Goodson

Cecil P. Goodson
Marketing Division

CPG/ja

Enclosure

ORDERS PROVIDING INADEQUATE INFORMATION   Unfortunately, orders that give inadequate or unclear information are commonplace. The problem in asking for the necessary information (instead of guessing) is that the customer often takes the easy way out and simply cancels the order. Why? Many people dislike completing additional forms or having to wait.

You might counter this reaction with the following strategy:

- Being careful not to stir hopes that the goods are on their way, open by reinforcing the reader's confidence in the ordered items, thus forestalling a cancellation.
- Then, after showing how the customer will benefit by replying, request the necessary information.
- Provide an easy, cost-free way to reply.
- Close with additional reinforcement of the reader's confidence in the merchandise and an assurance of quick shipment.

The letter in figure 5–6 follows this strategy, asking for the necessary information and encouraging the reader to provide that information by completing a convenient card.

The positive tone of a letter asking for additional information depends greatly on its avoidance of unpleasant expressions—"you neglected," "incomplete," "unclear," and the like. A tactful attitude avoids irritating or embarrassing a reader.

ORDERS FROM UNQUALIFIED PERSONS   Orders from unqualified persons may be refused for many reasons. Filling the order might violate franchise or distributorship agreements, territorial restrictions, or state or federal laws. The order might be refused because it is too small or presents shipping difficulties. Whatever the reason, your objectives are to prevent the reader from losing interest in the merchandise and to explain the advantages of obtaining the merchandise from one of your dealers.

You might use these guidelines:

- Open by reassuring the reader that the merchandise is the right choice, thus implying your receipt of the order and forestalling a change of mind.
- Tactfully explain why the merchandise is available only through a dealer, pointing out why the customer benefits by buying from this local or regional firm (checking the goods before buying, immediate delivery, convenient service).
- Give the name and address of the appropriate dealer and urge the customer to buy from that person.
- Close by stressing the benefits of purchasing the merchandise and reinforcing the customer's desire for it.

Notice that by using a "blind copy" notation, as the sample letter does in figure 5–7, you can notify dealers of your referrals and help them serve potential customers.

Figure 5–6. Request for Additional Order Information.

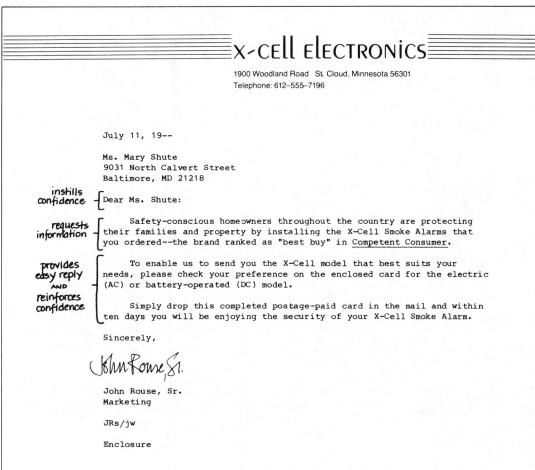

instills
confidence

requests
information

provides
easy reply
AND
reinforces
confidence

X-cEll ElEcTRONICS

1900 Woodland Road St. Cloud, Minnesota 56301
Telephone: 612-555-7196

July 11, 19--

Ms. Mary Shute
9031 North Calvert Street
Baltimore, MD 21218

Dear Ms. Shute:

Safety-conscious homeowners throughout the country are protecting their families and property by installing the X-Cell Smoke Alarms that you ordered--the brand ranked as "best buy" in Competent Consumer.

To enable us to send you the X-Cell model that best suits your needs, please check your preference on the enclosed card for the electric (AC) or battery-operated (DC) model.

Simply drop this completed postage-paid card in the mail and within ten days you will be enjoying the security of your X-Cell Smoke Alarm.

Sincerely,

John Rouse Sr.

John Rouse, Sr.
Marketing

JRs/jw

Enclosure

SUBSTITUTE ORDERS Orders for which you recommend alternate brands, models, varieties, and the like involve an ethical point: you should recommend an alternative to the order item only if it is for the reader's benefit, not just to make a sale.

The strategy for such a letter is as follows:

- Open with an explanation, being careful not to berate the competitive brand or variety.
- Present the alternative, avoiding the negative word "substitute."
- Point out benefits of the alternative for the customer, noting if necessary the higher price.
- Ask for authorization to ship (if necessary, on trial) and provide an easy means for replying.

Figure 5–7. *Reply to Order From an Unqualified Person.*

Wilton Sporting Goods
manufacturers of the world's best

916 Mirabeau Street
New Orleans, Louisiana 70119

April 15, 19--

Mr. Edward Kaminsky
425 East 73rd Street
New York, NY 10021

Dear Mr. Kaminsky:

Because of its advanced design, superior craftsmanship, and excellent
handling, the Wimbledon World Class tennis racket you ordered is already
a favorite of professionals and serious amateurs. Its lightweight alloy
frame can stand up so well to the stress of fast serves and deadly lobs
that our dealers report it is the most durable, trouble-free racket on the
market.

reassures reader of right choice

To provide owners with a wide selection of custom strings and grips and
personalized service, we sell Wimbledons only through authorized dealers.
Our dealer in your area is Rafferty's Sport Shop, 760 Lexington Avenue,
New York City 10017.

explains AND gives address

Rafferty's factory-trained personnel will be pleased to help you select
the Wimbledon with the strings, grip, and grip size that suit you best.
Let them show you how a Wimbledon World Class can give you the winner's
edge on the courts.

closes by stressing virtues of merchandise

Sincerely,

Aaron Goldberg

Aaron Goldberg
Public Relations Office

jdp

(bc Rafferty's Sport Shop)

the blind copy does not appear on the original letter, only on the copy sent to Rafferty's

Figure 5–8. Order Reply Recommending Alternative Selection.

Harry Brent's Kennels

6001 GOLFVIEW DRIVE
BIRMINGHAM, MICHIGAN 48010

Ms. Scarlet Foster
104 Hardee Road
Shellman Bluff, GA 31786

Dear Ms. Foster:

Thank you for your recent order and welcome to the long list of
satisfied dog owners whose carefully selected pups were sired in our
famous Harry Brent Kennels.

The A.K.C. "rough" collie pup (male) you ordered has a long, thick
coat suited to harsh northern winters. In your semi-tropical coastal
area of Georgia, this type of Collie would find the high temperatures
between May and October uncomfortable and perhaps unhealthful.

—explanation

For warmer climates like yours, we recommend, at the same price, a
"smooth" Collie. A "smooth" Collie has a luxurious, thin coat that is
not only warm enough for southern winters but also cooler and healthful
in the extended warm season. This favorite variety of Collie has the
majestic look and pleasant disposition that many of us know from the old
"Lassie" television series. And, of course, all of our pups are hand-picked
from A.K.C. championship lines.

presenting of alter- native AND its benefits

May we send you a choice "smooth" Collie male? Since we now have
several beautiful eight-week-olds in our kennel, yours can be delivered
by air freight as soon as we receive your instructions on the enclosed
quick-reply form.

request for authorization to ship

Yours truly,

Harry Brent
Harry Brent

HB:rh

Enclosure

As you read the example in figure 5–8, notice that the check sent with the original order was not returned. Keeping the check implies the order is "on hold," thus encouraging a favorable reply.

When the alternate brand has a lower price, sending a refund with the letter strengthens your recommendation. When the alternate costs more, you still keep the check and note the higher price in the letter after you have explained the benefits for the customer.

THE COLLECTION PATTERN

Even though businesses check credit ratings carefully, some people do not pay when billed. To collect delinquent accounts, credit departments usually design form letters that are sent out at regular intervals, with shorter intervals between mailings toward the end of the collection process.

This series of letters has two purposes: (1) to collect the overdue accounts, and (2) to keep the goodwill of the customers. Thus, each mailing must be firm but not irksome. Why? Because the continued goodwill of the customers is necessary if you are to have their future business. And, certainly, you would not want to annoy customers and turn them against you when they might have valid reasons for not paying promptly.

Obviously, however, no series of collection letters should go on indefinitely. After a certain point, it may become clear that letters will not work or are not cost effective. Referring the account to a collection agency, repossessing the goods, or filing a lawsuit may then be the logical follow-up to the last stage in the collection pattern.

THE COLLECTION SITUATION

For collection purposes, customers are classified according to their credit histories as *good risks*, *fair risks*, or *poor risks*. Understanding these classes of debtors will help you decide on the kind of appeals you would send, at what intervals to send them, and how long a series to send.

Good risks with overdue accounts are relatively unusual. But occasionally a good customer will misplace a bill or, when out of town or in hard times, default on payments. The early collection letters for this type of person have a gentle, friendly tone and appeal to pride, decency, and self-interest. Hints of betrayed trust and urgent demands are sent only after numerous friendly appeals have failed. Often, the collection letters for good risks are sent monthly for two or three months and twice a month for several months thereafter, resulting in as many as nine letters.

Fair risks include people who have only a few bad marks in their credit histories, usually for late payments. They are often well-intentioned individuals who, perhaps because of disagreement with a creditor, decided to delay payment of a bill. Or they may be poorly organized people who sometimes budget carelessly, or scrooges who simply want to earn interest on their creditors' money. A long series of reminders and inquiries, all appealing to pride and cooperation, thus should precede the more urgent appeals. The collection letters to fair risks often span a period of five or six months, with one letter for each of the first few months and three per month thereafter, totalling as many as eleven or twelve letters.

Poor risks have usually been dunned by creditors so often that they ignore routine notices and gentle reminders. Also, their credit standing is so poor that losing charge privileges makes no difference. Thus, the collection series aims chiefly at collecting the debt. The letters move quickly to forceful appeals referring to repossession, small claims courts, or garnished wages (where legal) to motivate action. Generally, letters in a poor-risk series are mailed two or three per month for just two or three months.

The actual number of mailings and the intervals between appeal stages depend not only on customer classification but also on such circumstances as the type of credit or the amount of the debt. As an example, for agri-business credit you would not send urgent appeals until after harvest. And for a debt of $2,500, you could justify a more extensive collection plan, taking more time to get tough, than for a mere $25. Much depends also on your relationship with the customer and the prospects for collection.

Standard Collection Series

Collection series are prompt, regular, and flexible. They follow various plans, depending on customer classification and other circumstances. But the general plan shown in figure 5–9 gives you a clear view of the six appeal stages typically involved and a rough timetable showing when they might be used. As noted previously, circumstances can cause the intervals between stages to vary. Circumstances may also suggest that during the second and fourth stages of this pattern you send several different reminders and appeals. But you would not ordinarily send more than one inquiry, urgent appeal, or ultimatum, since doing so would suggest you are bluffing.

Figure 5–9. Stages in a Standard Collection Series.

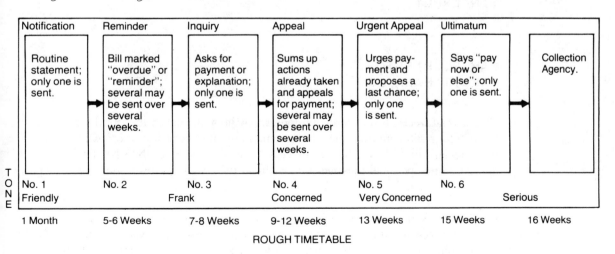

Each of the six stages in the standard collection pattern shown in figure 5–9 is explained in the following pages. The illustrations of stages two through six are based on an actual collection series designed by a Connecticut mail-order firm.[3]

NOTIFICATION   The notification is the routine statement or bill sent to all credit customers. Because this familiar appeal is a form notice, it is inoffensive to the customer and inexpensive for the firm. It clearly states the account name, amount due, due date, credit terms, and address to which payment should be sent. It often includes an addressed reply envelope.

REMINDER   Without offending, the reminder nudges the customer's memory that payment for the bill has not been received, as seen in this example:

```
APRIL 14, 19--

DEAR MR. CARSON:

MAYBE YOU'VE ALREADY MAILED YOUR PAYMENT -- IF
SO, PLEASE ACCEPT MY THANKS.

IF NOT, MR. CARSON, WILL YOU DO ME A SPECIAL
FAVOR AND REVIEW THE AMOUNT DUE ON YOUR ORDER
FOR THE EXECUTIVE'S WORKSHOP.  OUR CHARGES ARE
FOR THE PERIOD BEGINNING THIS PAST FEBRUARY AS
EXPLAINED IN DETAIL ON THE ENCLOSED INVOICE.

THANK YOU FOR YOUR PROMPT ATTENTION.

SINCERELY,



SAM R. PIENTO
CREDIT MANAGER
```

Over several weeks, two or three reminders may be sent, each with a similar message but in a form different from the others: computer-written letters, humorous postcards, the original bill with a rubber-stamped OVERDUE or SECOND NOTICE, and the like. Since personal messages might offend the customer, form notices are often used at this stage.

INQUIRY   When you can no longer assume customer oversight, you move into the next stage—a frank letter asking for either payment or an explanation. As seen in the following example, this letter is designed to force some response from the customer—either to make the payment or to break the silence. But to be effective, the letter should not provide excuses for the customer by asking such leading questions as "Was something wrong with our workshop?" Afterwards, if the customer provides neither the payment nor an explanation, the path is cleared for more forceful steps:

```
MAY 12, 19--

DEAR MR. CARSON:

WHAT WOULD YOU DO?

SUPPOSE YOU HAD TO TAKE SOME ACTION TO COLLECT
A LONG-STANDING DEBT, AND THE ONLY FACTS YOU
HAD WERE:

◊ AN UNPAID BALANCE THAT WAS SEVERAL MONTHS
  OLD
◊ MANY UNANSWERED REQUESTS FOR PAYMENT

IF YOU HAD TO DECIDE KNOWING ONLY THIS, WOULD
YOU CONTINUE TO WRITE LETTERS AND SPEND MORE
MONEY TRYING TO COLLECT?  OR WOULD YOU TURN
THE MATTER OVER TO A COLLECTION AGENCY WITH
INSTRUCTIONS TO TAKE THE NECESSARY STEPS TO
ENFORCE COLLECTION?

IF YOU BASED YOUR DECISION ON THE AVAILABLE
FACTS, YOU WOULD PROBABLY DO AS WE MUST NOW
DO--LET THE COLLECTION AGENCY DEMAND PAYMENT.
BECAUSE CONTINUED INDIFFERENCE CAN BE DAMAGING
TO YOUR CREDIT, COMMON SENSE DICTATES THAT
IMMEDIATE PAYMENT IS THE BEST ANSWER.

YOUR PROMPT RESPONSE WILL MAKE LEGAL ACTION
UNNECESSARY.  SEND YOUR PAYMENT TODAY.

VERY TRULY YOURS,


SAM R. PIENTO
CREDIT MANAGER
```

APPEAL While the earlier stages may be handled routinely, the appeal stage is tailored to have the most impact on the customer. Often the letters in this stage of the collection pattern sum up the actions already taken and appeal to the customer for payment.

Appeals should never be based on the company's need for money. Rather, they should be based on why paying will benefit (or on why *not* paying will harm) the customer.

For example, you can remind the customer of the importance of a good credit rating and continued credit privileges, thus appealing to economic self-interest. Or you can suggest that bad credit can damage the customer's reputation, thus appealing to personal pride.

You can even refer to the customer's satisfaction with the goods or services, thus appealing to a sense of fair play.

An effective approach is to use only one or two of these appeals per letter, as is done in the following appeal letter:

May 24, 19—

Dear Mr. Carson:

I had to make a decision when your order for The Executive's Workshop came to me for approval last February.

My judgement was that your bills were paid promptly and therefore your order was approved for immediate shipment. The balance of $18.21, dating back to February, is itemized on the enclosed bill.

Please restore my confidence in you and preserve your good credit rating by sending your payment at once.

Sincerely,

Sam R. Piento
Credit Manager

The gravity of the situation should be clear in the appeal stage. The letters should have a reasonable tone that does not destroy the customer's goodwill. But they should suggest that the appeal is the last stage before urgent actions are necessary.

URGENT APPEAL To emphasize that the situation is now critical, the urgent appeal letter is often signed by a chief executive instead of by the credit manager. It demands immediate payment and often refers to the unpleasant consequences of further delay, such as losing credit privileges, having the customer's employer contacted, or bearing the burden of court action. Here is an example of an urgent appeal:

June 17, 19--

Dear Mr. Carson:

We want permission to contact your employer . . . to deduct a definite amount from your paycheck each week. Your
balance to date is $18.21.

Or, to prevent this unpleasant action, send your payment
in full at once.

Sincerely,

J. G. Coogler
Vice President

Yet this next-to-last stage in the series continues to reflect concern for the customer's goodwill. After all, even a poor credit risk can be a good cash customer. So the urgent appeal does not usually state a deadline. Instead, as a last resort it sometimes proposes an installment plan—but only if the amount of the bill and past customer relations justify continuing the account. This plan may enable the company to collect its debt, even though late. Perhaps more importantly, it may also enable the company to retain the customer's business.

ULTIMATUM The final letter says, in effect, "Pay now or suffer the conse-quences." It emphasizes, as the following sample does, that payment must be received very soon, often by a specified deadline of one to two weeks, or the company will take strong action. This action, which is either stated or implied, includes referral of the account to a collection agency or to the courts:

August 8, 19--

FROM: Collection Division

Dear Mr. Carson,

You have been given every opportunity to settle your account now long past due.

Failure to pay is a serious violation of a legal obligation. When this happens a creditor has the right to enforce
collection as provided by law. No doubt you are aware of

the possible consequences, such as court appearance, attachment of salary, attorney fees, and interest charges.

You have one week to make payment prior to further action.

Sincerely,

Sam R. Piento
Credit Manager

Remember, however, that the purpose of this final letter is still to collect the bill *and* avoid the trouble and expense of strong action. To do this, it should be firm without angering the customer. If successful, it should even keep the customer's goodwill.

Short Collection Series

For some situations the standard collection series might be inappropriate. For example, using a long series of strong appeals to collect church pledges or membership dues might cause the supporter to resign. And the drawn-out stages of the standard series might not be cost effective for collecting a small account such as a magazine subscription. In these situations you may wish to use a shorter, less urgent series.

NOVELTY LETTERS   To minimize the risk of losing a member of a club or church, some writers send novelty letters to nudge the overdue member into paying. These lighthearted letters are mailed early in a short series.[4]
   Typical of these letters are the following:

- *the string-reminder letter:* "Just a little reminder . . ."
- *the fishhook letter:* "We're fishing for your payment . . ."
- *the safety pin letter:* "For your convenience in pinning your check . . ."
- *the stamp-attached letter:* "For a free reply in the enclosed pre-addressed envelope . . ." (And for stirring guilt if the customer fails to use the stamp for this purpose!)
- *the half-and-half letter:* your appeal on the left; space for the customer's check to be attached on the right.

To letters using these devices may be attached a piece of string, a plastic fishhook, or a safety pin.
   If several novelty letters do not bring payment, you might end the series with a candid but nonthreatening letter spelling out the consequences of nonpayment—lapsed membership or unmet goals. However, rarely would such a series be used to harass a fellow member to the point of losing goodwill. Nor would such a series be suitable for collecting a large bill: the debtor might have problems enough without the writer's trying to make a joke of them.

THREE-LETTER PATTERN   To collect a small account, you may want to limit the series to three letters sent at monthly intervals: a reminder, a stronger reminder, and a final notice. Because of the small amount of money involved, these letters rarely employ urgent appeals or harsh ultimatums that might jeopardize the customer's goodwill. Instead, as the short series in figure 5–10 illustrates, they usually appeal soberly to the customer's wish to continue doing business with your company.

Figure 5–10.   First of a Three-Letter Collection Pattern.

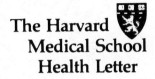

The Harvard
Medical School
Health Letter

Dear Subscriber:

The Harvard Medical School Health Letter is a publication written for the educated layman -- a person like you. Each month it examines timely health issues you want to know more about.

In past months, we've given readers the facts about such various subjects as: this country's number one food additive, sugar...contagious diseases carried by household pets...and a simple test for cancer that everyone over 40 should have.

Information of this sort is not only important, but essential for all of us to know. The Harvard Medical School Health Letter gives you the concise, reliable, and credible information that you can depend on.

As a subscriber, you not only inform yourself, but you may convey this information to friends and relatives as well.

To ensure prompt delivery of future issues, please mail us your payment along with the enclosed invoice today. We've provided a postage-paid envelope for your convenience.

                              Subscription Manager

Figure 5–10 (cont'd.). Second of a Three-Letter Collection Pattern.

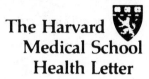

The Harvard
Medical School
Health Letter

Dear Subscriber:

Thank you for your subscription to The Harvard Medical School
Health Letter.

During the coming months--and, we hope, long afterward--the
Health Letter will serve as your pipeline to today's important medical information and opinion. While the Health Letter's expert editors
cannot replace your own doctor, we believe that our unique publication
will help you and the members of your family become better informed
about medicine--the science of your health.

Every month, you will receive your copy of the six-page Harvard
Medical School Health Letter. It presents, in the opinion of 16 participating members of the faculty of Harvard Medical School, an authoritative general review of current medical information...on everything
from the common cold to cancer.

It would help us hold down costs of such vital information if you
would pay the accompanying invoice promptly.

Thank you.

                                    Subscription Manager

P.S. Immediate payment would be greatly appreciated.

Figure 5–10 (cont'd.). *Third of a Three-Letter Collection Pattern.*

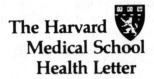

**The Harvard
Medical School
Health Letter**

Dear Subscriber:

Our mailroom has been instructed not to send you the current issue
of the Harvard Medical School Health Letter. This action was taken
regrettably, but we simply could not afford to send you any more
issues without receiving payment.

We are a non-profit publication and carry no advertising whatsoever.
Therefore, we rely solely on our readership to meet our expenses.

If you pay your bill immediately, however, your subscription will be
reactivated and you will receive the current issue promptly.

But you must act today! Please use the enclosed postage-paid envelope
to mail us your payment.

Don't risk missing out on even one issue.

                                   Subscription Manager

     BR:cd

The novelty devices and the three-letter plan illustrate a key point about collecting bills—an imaginative series may be effectively adapted to the collection situation.

TECHNIQUE

Certain writing techniques can enhance the letter strategies explained above. Among these techniques are selecting appropriate words, constructing skillful sentences, and projecting a constructive tone. The remainder of this chapter is devoted to explaining how to attain these skills.

WORDS

To project an effective tone as you write disagreeable letters, you must be especially careful in selecting your words. Often a single word will signal to your reader that your attitude is unpleasant, even though you may not intend it to be.

Inoffensive Wording

Your communications should be inoffensive. They should not be demanding, scolding, critical, overly familiar, or presumptuous. You need not memorize this list of admonitions; you need only listen to your words as they would sound to your readers. The key question is: "Do the words make friends?"

Here are some before-and-after examples:

Demanding:	We insist upon a prompt answer to our letter.
Inoffensive:	We would appreciate your answering this letter promptly.
Scolding:	You should have examined the calculator in the store or returned it within the ten-day refund period.
Inoffensive:	We provided an opportunity for examining the calculator in the store or for returning it within ten days.
Critical:	Perhaps you could afford to run a store that way, but we cannot.
Inoffensive:	We try to be fair and reasonable with all our customers. Naturally, if we granted you this favor, we would have to grant it for others. Such a policy would have to result in higher prices.
Overly Familiar:	I'd be glad to drop by some afternoon, sip a martini with you, and chat about your cable television installation.
Inoffensive:	If you wish, I'd be glad to visit your home to talk about your cable television installation.
Presumptuous:	Thank you in advance for your trouble in this matter.
Inoffensive:	I would be grateful if you could send me the information.

Remember that using offensive language, whether intended or not, can cause you to lose customers. Therefore, you should check to see that the language you have chosen is friendly—a quality that helps to win or retain customers.

Courteous Wording

Courteous wording is so obviously important in writing that it should be unnecessary to mention it. But because courtesy in unpleasant messages requires extra care, a brief reminder may be helpful.

As noted in chapter 4, few people are intentionally discourteous except when they are angry, and this frame of mind is one to avoid when writing. But especially in composing letters with unpleasant messages, you should take pains to be tactful and friendly and to avoid irritating or insulting the reader. Unless you are careful in choosing words with favorable connotations, trouble may result:

> We have received your letter in which you claim that the lamp was damaged in shipment. (*Claim* here is insulting.)
> Because you failed to include an estimate, we cannot award you the contract. (*Failed* is irritating.)

How easy it would have been to write:

> Thank you for taking the trouble of letting us know about your damaged lamp.
> Because an estimate was not included, we cannot award you the contract.

Positive Wording

Which kind of meteorologist would you be? Take your choice:

> It'll be another nice day, although skies will be overcast in the morning.
> It'll be another cloudy day, although the afternoon will be sunny.

Usually the first meteorologist will make the better entrepreneur and the better writer. It is not a matter of overstating or overselling, but of accentuating the positive and minimizing the negative. A half-empty glass can just as well be termed half-full— and there is usually some sort of hopeful or optimistic prospect in any transaction.

Note how the following unpleasant situation has been handled:

Negative: We regret that we cannot ship the entire order by December 1.

Neutral: We regret we cannot ship the order by December 1. Please let us know if you would like it sent later.

Positive: Although we cannot ship the entire order by December 1, we can assure you that one-third of it will be sent then, and the remaining two-thirds by December 10. Consequently, you will have the merchandise available for your Christmas business.

You should examine every situation to make the best of it. There are inherent advantages and disadvantages in most. Your challenge is to choose language that stresses the advantages.

Sentences

The two strategies discussed here—passive constructions and emphatic devices—can improve your skill in writing effective sentences. They are useful in all writing situations, but are especially useful for controlling tone and stressing key points in disagreeable letters.

Using the Passive Voice Only When Appropriate

Most books on writing are full of nonsense about the passive voice. The time has come to recognize it for what it is: a two-edged weapon, injurious when handled by the inept but devastatingly effective when wielded by the skillful. But to be effective, its use must be justified by function, not by custom or chance.

By examining the passive voice, you can see why for years many people have faulted it. Essentially it inverts the grammatical function of words in a sentence. The agent (logical subject) instead of executing the action of the verb as it normally does, now is either omitted or becomes the object of a preposition. For example:

>*Active:* Electric utilities [*agent*] have increased fuel charges.

>*Passive:* Fuel charges have been increased. [*agent missing*] Fuel charges have been increased by electric utilities. [*agent*]

Observe that in the passive version *fuel costs*, the grammatical subject, actually is not increasing anything but instead is being increased. In addition, what would normally be the subject, *electric utilities*, is here cast as the object of the preposition *by*. As you can see, the passive voice reverses the traditional functions of subject and object, of agent and receiver of the action.

Note the difference again in these examples:

>*Active:* The vice president disapproved your job offer.
>*Passive:* Your job offer was disapproved by the vice-president.

>*Active:* The plant manager will fire him.
>*Passive:* He will be fired by the plant manager.

Because the passive voice violates the normal grammatical relations in sentences, it is often unnatural to the ear. In speaking we rely almost exclusively on the active except sometimes in formal discourse. For instance, all of us would say:

>He finished the accounting problem at 2 A.M.

Instead of:

>The accounting problem was finished by him at 2 A.M.

Consequently, because the active voice is generally more natural, direct, and economical, it is usually preferable—as we pointed out previously (see pp. 117–118). Nevertheless, the passive serves effectively in five situations.

1. *When the recipient of the action is more important than the agent*. Often, what is being done is more significant than the person doing it. When this condition exists, the passive is particularly effective because it casts the recipient of the action in the important role of subject. In this passive construction, therefore, the recipient receives the desired emphasis:

> The report was written by the lab technicians, signed by the research directors, and then forwarded to the division head.

Here the matter being discussed, the report, is stressed: it is made the subject of the sentence, although it performs no action and is indeed the object of action by others.

Each situation must be analyzed in context to determine what should receive the emphasis. For example, both of the following sentences are appropriate:

> Business will be radically changed in the next twenty-five years by the computer. (The sentences that follow discuss other ways in which business will be changed.)
> The computer will radically change business in the next twenty-five years. (The sentences that follow discuss how the computer will affect business.)

The point to remember is that the passive should be selected when you decide to stress whatever receives the action.

2. *When naming the agent might be cumbersome or unnecessary*. When naming the agent might be cumbersome or unnecessary, you should use the passive. To illustrate:

> The plane was piloted safely through the storm. (Omit *by the pilot*.)
> Bill Johnson was elected to represent the clerical workers. (Omit *by the clerical workers*.)
> Your order will be shipped Tuesday. (Omit *by the shipping department*.)

3. *When the agent is obvious, unknown, indefinite, or should remain concealed*. More frequent is the use of passive to prevent mention of the logical subject because it is unknown or indefinite, or because the writer prefers not to reveal it. Consequently, whoever executes the action of the verb remains unmentioned; only the recipient is stated. For example:

> Time-sharing systems have been developed that will permit many people to make simultaneous use of a central computer through remote terminals hundreds of miles away. (Unknown)
> Low-cost semiconductors are being used increasingly in appliances and other consumer products. (Indefinite)

In these sentences, although the lead-off nouns are subjects, they are acted upon by forces that are unknown or indefinite and thus must remain unnamed.

In the following sentence, the passive is effectively employed to evade the responsibility for an unpleasant decision:

> The applicant pool from which we will select our sales supervisor has been narrowed to include only those who have worked several years as full-time representatives.

Of course, whether it is ethical or prudent to conceal the logical subject by the passive can be determined only in context.

Sometimes you may need to resort to the passive to avoid cluttering a letter or report with innumerable *I*'s or *we*'s. Yet even in this circumstance, you should make every effort to avoid the passive:

> *Use of* I: I conclude from the marketing survey that an automobile car wash would be unprofitable.
> *Passive:* It was concluded from the marketing survey that an automobile car wash would be unprofitable.
> *Active:* The marketing survey reveals that an automobile car wash would be unprofitable.

As you can see, the passive is effective when you wish to avoid overusing the personal pronouns, as it also is when the subject is unknown, indefinite, or should be concealed.

4. *When issuing orders, instructions, and requests.* To avoid the harshness of the imperative, or the indelicacy of the verb *must*, you may use the passive. The effect gains in tact what it loses in vigor. Note the gradations:

> a. You must not take time off for a coffee break until 10:30.
> b. Do not take time off for a coffee break until 10:30.
> c. Time for a coffee break should not be taken until 10:30.

The first is strong but harsh, the second compelling but severe, while the passive third is firm but mild because it is impersonal.

When you write instructions, use of the passive enables you to avoid constantly repeating *you*, using the imperative, or employing sexist language and such vague subjects as *people*:

> *Before:* You should set the left and right margins by adjusting the two guides above the keyboard. (*Awkward use of* you)
> *After:* The left and right margins should be set by adjusting the two guides over the keyboard. (*Passive construction avoids awkwardness*)
>
> *Before:* Remove the shell from the chamber by pressing the eject button. (*Imperative*)
> *After:* The shell should be removed from the chamber by pressing the eject button. (*Passive construction avoids command*)
>
> *Before:* Before the customer can submit an offer to purchase, *he* must sign the completed document. (*Sexist, implies only male's signatures are valid*)
> *After:* Before an offer to purchase can be submitted, the completed document must be signed. (*Passive construction avoids gender of customers*)
>
> *Before:* People must show their identification cards. (*Vague subject*)
> *After:* Identification cards must be shown. (*Passive construction is stronger here*)

When writing to stockholders about purchasing additional shares, when explaining to mechanics how to install an air conditioner in a car, or when providing planting instructions for gardeners, you too may find the passive appropriate.

To avoid the taint of a command, some requests are softened by the passive:

Harsh: Mail your payment at once.
Softened: You are requested to mail your payment at once.

However, whenever possible, the person making the request should be named, thereby preventing abominations like this:

Before: It will be appreciated if you will mail your payment at once.
After: We would appreciate your mailing the payment at once.

Each request requires individual consideration.

5. *When necessary to avoid confusion or awkwardness.* You will occasionally discover that the passive can help to clarify other sentences. If so, use it. Similarly, the passive may sometimes prevent awkwardness, especially when variety is desirable in long paragraphs expressed only in the active voice. But in all instances, a skillful writer is like an experienced carpenter who understands tools and how they work. There are no rigid rules.

Your knowledge of how the passive functions will help you decide when you can use it effectively. You should be guided by realizing that the active voice is generally preferable because of its naturalness, directness, and conciseness. But in certain contexts, the passive is helpful, practical, efficacious, and downright handy.

Emphasis

Stimulating speakers emphasize key words and ideas by raising their volume, varying their intonation, slowing their rate of speed, changing their facial expressions, and employing gestures. Writers can apply none of these techniques. Yet, as you learned in chapter 4, they can gain emphasis by various other means, such as short, balanced, and periodic sentences. Visual devices, pacing, position, parts of speech, and strong statements can also help you achieve emphasis, as we will show in this section.

VISUAL DEVICES You can visually simulate a speaker's increased volume by employing capitals or underlining. Both techniques, which are confined to informal writing, appear frequently in business letters and advertising. The larger the print, the more the words appear to SHRIEK at you. Underlining also attracts *attention* in much the same way. And don't forget the exclamation point!

Also startling, and therefore effective, is the one-sentence paragraph.

The danger of these devices is that you may become addicted to them. Soon every third or fourth sentence is exclamatory, underlined, capitalized, or printed separately. The resulting visual cacophony spoils your effect. But on some occasions, when used sparingly and cautiously, the mechanical devices can provide a punch that words and sentences alone cannot.

PACING In speaking we tend to slow down and even pause to accentuate key words and significant ideas. Otherwise, we normally chatter merrily along. In writing, we can similarly control speed by forcing readers to pause or stop whenever we wish. A variation in punctuation marks will arrest or slow their progress. Short sentences and paragraphs also force readers to pause. Observe the differences in these two versions of the same material:

1. The profit outlook for the rubber industry seems to be good because high automobile sales are resulting in large purchases of new tires as original equipment, while heavy buying of replacement tires as well as increasing interest in the radial and belted-bias-ply tire are also contributing to the huge demand.
2. The profit outlook for the rubber industry seems to be good. High automobile sales are resulting in large purchases of new tires as original equipment. The buying of replacement tires has also been heavy. In addition, increasing interest in the radial and the belted-bias-ply tire is contributing to the huge demand.

In the second passage the ideas are much clearer after having been broken down. Greater stress has also been placed on the individual reasons for the favorable profit picture.

In the following example, observe how the reader's progress is stopped just before the significant idea. Although *however* might have been inserted elsewhere, it has been placed appropriately to emphasize what follows:

You have only one week, however, before we will turn your account over to a collection agency.

Dashes may also provide the pause that emphasizes:

The problem of providing for recreation is not so much one of available space as it is one of allocation—and location.

In writing, you are conducting your readers on a tour of your ideas. When you arrive at something you want them to observe closely, slow down. Apply the brakes by using the appropriate punctuation marks, short sentences, and short paragraphs.

POSITION Position is not everything in life or writing, but it is important. In reading, although a person's eye takes in several words at once, it is attracted to the sentence's beginning because of the preceding space and capitalization, and to its ending because of the period and the following space. Realizing the importance of these positions, you should place your key ideas there rather than in the middle. Note how the emphasis changes in the following sentences:

The 11 percent average annual increase in gross loans of major commercial banks during the past seven years compares favorably with the rate during the previous decade of 9 percent. (*Emphasis on percent of increase*)

In the past seven years, gross loans of major commercial banks have increased at an average rate of nearly 11 percent annually, a favorable comparison with the 9 percent pace during the previous decade. (*Emphasis on time*)

Although the beginning and ending are approximately equal in importance, the ending has a slight edge because it contains the last words that people read and therefore remember. That is the reason why closing with a preposition should be avoided except when the revised sentence would be awkward. For example:

First draft: Sales reps have additional policies to abide by.
Revised: Sales reps have to abide by additional policies.

But:

First draft: Banks are now offering checking accounts that interest is paid on.
Awkward revision: Banks are now offering checking accounts on which interest is paid.
Better revision: Banks are now offering checking accounts that pay interest.

First and last impressions are important in writing sentences—as they are in life. Pay special attention to them.

PARTS OF SPEECH AND SENTENCE ROLE Words have a pecking order: independent clauses are usually more important than dependent ones, dependent clauses than verbs, verbs than nouns, nouns than adjectives or adverbs, and subjects than objects. The roles of both verbs and subjects have already been discussed (see "Using the Passive," p. 158); let us look now at the other parts of speech.

Suppose in the following sentences that the writer wished to emphasize the qualities needed by a sales supervisor rather than the need for a sales supervisor:

1. Data-Tech, Inc., prefers an experienced, mature, creative sales supervisor.
2. Data-Tech, Inc., prefers a sales supervisor with experience, maturity, and creativity.
3. Data-Tech, Inc., prefers a sales supervisor who is experienced, mature, and creative.

The first sentence is the weakest because, besides placing the necessary qualities in the middle of the sentence, it expresses them as adjectives preceding the noun. Although the second presents the qualities as nouns at the end of the sentence, the third is slightly more emphatic because it unites the qualities in a separate clause at the end of the sentence.

Ordinarily writers have options: If they are skillful, they are aware of their various options and select the one that best suits their needs. If not, they plod along, grabbing whatever crosses their minds.

STRONG STATEMENTS Vigorous writing contains firm, resolute statements. Weak writing contains anemic statements. Although writers must be cautious, they should avoid hedging, which can deaden a sentence. The tendency to qualify every statement is prevalent in disagreeable letters—where tactfulness sometimes leads to beating around the bush—and also common to writers hesitant to express their own opinions. Elsewhere there may be little need to maintain such discretion.

The hedged or qualified statement lacks assurance. Observe how the recommendation in the first sentence here is weakened in the second:

1. We recommend that the company issue 7½ percent convertible subordinated debentures due 19––, convertible into the company stock at $45 a share.
2. We are generally inclined to suggest the recommendation that the company issue 7½ percent convertible subordinated debentures due 19––, convertible into the company's stock at $45 a share.

"Weasel words" like *somewhat, usually, rather, almost,* and *generally* sneak into sentences, sapping their strength. With highly critical audiences, these qualifiers may be essential. But other audiences may need to become aware of the main idea or facts instead of being distracted or confused with minor exceptions or slight qualifications.

Hedging is also dangerous because it is contagious: it leads to the double and triple hedge. Seldom is the timid writer satisfied with a single qualification. For example:

It *appears* that *perhaps* we *may* be able *generally* to adopt your suggestion.

Such sentences are characteristic of people who can't make up their minds, not of successful executives.

Another type of anemic statement is the negative one. It comes in two forms: (1) the pure negative for negation and (2) the un-negative for affirmation. Whenever an idea can be expressed positively, it should be. Notice the problems in the following sentences:

The employees are not enthusiastic about the proposal. (Were they cool, indifferent, hostile, or unimpressed?)
James Cooper is not an exceptional sales manager. (Was he above average, average, or below average?)

Of course, the weak negative might be preferable for reasons of tact, as in the second example. Otherwise, the affirmative should be used because it is clear, concise, and vigorous.

In some instances the negative is not only vague but confusing. Some double negatives fall into this category, particularly those in impersonal constructions:

Confusing: It is not the desire of this company not to allow its young engineers to assume some responsibility.
Positive and clear: It is the desire of this company to allow its young engineers to assume some responsibility.

A single negative can be just as unclear:

The basic price of these machines is not beyond the financial range of 60 percent of the companies interested in them.

Can 60 percent afford them? Or 40 percent? The affirmative statement requires no struggle:

> The basic price of these machines is within the financial range of 60 percent of the companies interested in them.

The double negative occasionally troubles readers, but its main limitation is that it is weak. In some situations, it may convey the cautious effect the writer intends. But more often we want our writing to be vigorous.

Because clarity and vigor are usually desirable, you should rely on strong statements, eliminating as many negatives as possible in either the first or subsequent drafts. The advice is simple to remember: think and write positively.

STYLE

The stylistic element known as *tone* is the personal attitude you convey through your speaking and writing. In conversation, your tone of voice tells the people you are addressing if you are joking or serious, pleasant or unpleasant. When you say, "I've enjoyed talking with you," your hearers know from your inflection whether you mean it.

Causes of a Counterproductive Tone

Although tone is not as apparent in writing as in speaking, your readers usually can sense your attitude. As noted earlier, if your words convey a mood that displeases your readers, you will damage the effectiveness of your communication. Displeasing your reader is especially impractical in writing disagreeable letters.

Several pressures might naturally cause an offensive tone in your writing—dread of having to write a letter or memorandum, irritability from postponing the chore until you can no longer postpone it, a consumer grievance, a computer breakdown, a criticism from a superior, early deadlines at work, a dead car battery, illness, or unpaid bills. How convenient it is to lash out in your writing. So you lay your ire on your reader—and alienate a person whose goodwill bears upon your future.

Such pressures often lead to a counterproductive tone, as found in figure 5–11. The point is that you may very well find yourself writing for the same purpose R.C. Walker had in the letter—to blow off steam, with no regard for consequences.

Boomerang Effect

Before you write just to relieve your frustration, consider the boomerang effect. People ordinarily respond in the tone you use with them; if you are irate, sarcastic, or belligerent, they will generally be so toward you. Thus, you must curb your hostility and the inclination to take your bad humor out on your reader. But developing such a productive attitude does not come easily—it takes a conscientious and deliberate effort.

Figure 5–11. Counterproductive Adjustment Letter.

Men's Department
Zak's
32 Seventh Avenue
New York, N.Y. 10001

November 3, 19__

YOU KLUTZES:

Where do you get the shirts you sell? From World War I army surplus?

I wouldn't be surprised if that's the case. The three I ordered from you that arrived today have so many little holes in them they look as though they've been feeding moths for half a century. Your buyers must be cheapskates who enjoy gouging poor customers like me to get even the last hard-earned buck.

You can bet I'll never buy another #*!X*!* thing from you. I'll go elsewhere to do my shopping next time.

I know where I'd wish you'd go, too.

Disgustedly,

R. C. Walker

A Level-Headed Image

In the first place, you should avoid writing when upset. Wait until your steam has cooled down; sleep on the problem or take out your frustrations on the handball court. Check yourself; try to analyze why you are upset. By the next day, you may have transformed yourself into a calm, level-headed person.

In the second place, you must try to empathize with your readers' emotions and tensions, and compensate accordingly. You must be tolerant of errors, understanding of mishaps, and sympathetic toward the predicaments of others. By trying to see problems from your readers' point of view and by being pleasant, gracious, understanding, and level-headed, you will turn the boomerang effect to your advantage.

By compensating for your normal reaction to a vexing situation, you will create goodwill rather than hostility in your readers.

If you cannot manage such a complete turnabout in your attitude, then you must distinguish between what your emotions tell you to say and what your head tells you to say—and say the latter. In literature a writer often creates a persona or mask whose utterances are those of the writer as a writer instead of the writer as a person. And in politics, office seekers sometimes hire public relations firms to help them create favorable public images.

From time to time you may find it prudent in your writing to do as such writers and politicians do and learn to project an image to your audience that is conducive to your purpose. Certainly you should not deceive, but you need not be tactlessly blunt.

Note that R.C. Walker is probably still disgruntled about his moth-damaged shirts while revising his letter into a more reasonable version (figure 5–2). But the level-headed tone he manages to project encourages his reader to act as he wishes.

SUMMARY

Disagreeable letters do not necessarily have to make enemies, drive away customers, or lose sales for your company. Using a tactful approach as you deliver bad news can help you avoid alienating your readers. In filing a claim, for example, you should call attention politely and calmly to whatever is wrong. And in writing general refusals, you should follow the four R's pattern to prevent hostile reactions—(1) relate, (2) reason, (3) refuse, and (4) reconcile.

Specific patterns apply for handling request refusals, credit refusals, and order refusals, as well as for collecting overdue accounts. All of these are designed for two purposes: (1) to accomplish the task suggested by the titles, and (2) to retain the goodwill of the customer.

Techniques involving words, sentences, and style can help your letters do their work. Inoffensive, courteous, positive language helps them win or retain friends. Using the passive when appropriate and emphasizing important ideas help them communicate effectively. And projecting a calm, friendly tone helps them avoid the boomerang effect of offensiveness.

Disagreeable letters are among the most difficult to write. But knowing the patterns for writing them will ease your task and provide you with diplomatic skills essential for effective writing.

EXERCISES

Discussion Questions

1. What traits do the letters in this chapter have in common? Why do they require you to be especially careful when you write them?
2. How do you react to a letter beginning, "I regret to inform you . . . ."? How do your classmates react? Are your reactions typical?

3. Have you received letters with disappointing messages? What are your feelings toward letter writers who introduce bad news with trite phrases?
4. Explain the problems in composing an effective claim letter. What points ought to be covered in such a letter?
5. As you seek redress for a grievance, how might a consumer protection agency assist you?
6. Name the four steps in the general refusal pattern. Discuss the purpose of each step.
7. Discuss strategies for request refusals that will not alienate readers.
8. How does proper use of the credit refusal pattern bolster customer goodwill?
9. Describe several situations in which orders sometimes have to be refused.
10. What steps are involved in writing a letter to a customer whose order is incomplete?
11. Discuss the guidelines for replying to orders from unqualified persons.
12. What are the guidelines for replying to orders for which you recommend alternate brands?
13. Why are collection patterns necessary in all businesses extending credit? What two purposes do these patterns serve?
14. Into what risk categories can credit customers be placed? Explain the customer characteristics in each category. How do these classifications affect a collection pattern?
15. Describe the six appeal stages of a standard collection pattern. At what stages might you send more than one mailing? Only one mailing?
16. Under what circumstances would a short collection series be appropriate?
17. Discuss your reactions to the offensive wording in the examples cited in this chapter. Why would someone choose such words?
18. Explain five situations in which the passive serves effectively. Provide examples.
19. Name five means for achieving emphasis in writing. Provide examples.
20. Define *tone*. How can you achieve an effective tone in your writing?

In-Class Applications

1. In each of the following pairs of words or phrases, select the one you believe would be more appropriate to include in a disagreeable letter:

   bill/debt   pay up/remit
   lawsuit/legal action   credit customer/debtor
   job seeker/applicant   failed to include/omitted
   earnings/profits   ignored/overlooked

2. Improve the following statements by changing the offensive, discourteous, or negative language:
   a. Instead of hiring you, we are going to hire someone with an M.A. degree.
   b. I trust that you will come by my office.
   c. Send us our money.
   d. I cannot ship the turntable you ordered before December 1.
   e. You have not paid us your debt.

3. Explain why you would or would not change the following passive constructions and, where changes are appropriate, revise accordingly:
   a. If further information about this subject is required, you can get in touch with me at your convenience.
   b. If a company representative could come to my home, some idea of an adjustment that your company would consider fair could then be given to me.
   c. Town housing for students should be approved by the university officials.
   d. When we normally think of wealth, material objects are brought to mind.
   e. The ability to analyze an AC circuit is used time and again by the electrical engineers.
   f. Your first order placed with our company is greatly appreciated.
   g. The Amendment to the Articles of Incorporation was approved by the stockholders at the annual meeting held on May 22, 19--, and became effective June 3, 19--.
   h. Steel can be rolled into thin sheets to make fenders for cars in almost the same manner as dough can be rolled into pie crusts.
   i. The extension agent is informed about recent research in monthly bulletins published by the College of Commerce.
   j. Although compensation increased by 7.4 percent, college and university professors were subjected to a 5.5 percent rate of increase in price level, an inflationary trend related to, and dependent upon, political and military events.
4. Revise each of the following sentences to place greater emphasis on the italicized word or words:
   a. A leading automobile corporation uses one of the smallest econometric studies; a model of annual demand for cars by *George Chow*, a professor at Columbia University.
   b. A steel company gives a boost to *new programs* by a cost-accounting maneuver.
   c. Even though *effective human relations are impossible without compassion and altruism*, some people believe there is no room for these attitudes in business.
   d. Organizations must serve the individual through his *strengths*, regardless of his limitations and weaknesses.
   e. A *small brass cuspidor* was visible in one corner of his office.
   f. You will have to arrive at a *practical and economical* decision.
   g. The fund is growing rapidly not only in *asset value*, but in overall size and area of operations.
   h. The Federal Reserve Fund Board reported that total consumer credit reached a record debt of *almost $550 for every man, woman, and child*, or $100 billion in May, 19--.
5. The following passage was written to stockholders, many of whom are elderly persons. Can you pinpoint its main weakness? Rewrite the passage:

   Counsel for the Company has advised that for Federal income tax purposes, the receipt of the additional shares will not constitute taxable income to the stockholders, that the cost or other basis to the stockholders of the old shares held immediately prior to the stock split will be the tax basis of the total number of shares held immediately after the stock split, and that the holding period for the new shares will include the holding period of the shares being split.

6. Make these sentences more emphatic by eliminating the negative:
   a. She did not condense her article without destroying some important points.
   b. By not paying their bills on time, they do not improve their credit rating.
   c. Contributions to your IRA account cannot be withdrawn with no penalty before you are 59½ years old.
   d. Please do not jeopardize your credit standing by not sending us the $45.56 that you have owed since Christmas.
   e. Some merchants do not consider it unethical to increase prices the week before sales. Then, they do not fail to offer large discounts, which are actually not accurately advertised.
   f. Only a few sentences containing adjectival clauses should not be revised.
7. Revise the following statements to improve their tone:
   a. You are wrong about your bill because our records indicate the plates were $4.95 a dozen.
   b. That's the politician in him.
   c. Your failure to give a turn signal is what caused the cyclist to collide with your car.
   d. I have your letter in which you say you do not owe the shipping charges.
   e. We do not approve of your snooping around our work area.
   f. We have raised our prices to keep them in line with the economy.
   g. Your order has arrived.
   h. To answer your question, absolutely not.
   i. I am sorry that we cannot send you a Zenophon 35 mm lens for three more weeks.
   j. The day is already half gone.

Writing Assignments

1. While you were returning from a business convention, your flight from Biloxi-Gulfport, Mississippi, on Aero Airlines was thirty minutes late in arriving in Atlanta. As a result, you missed your flight on Tidewater Airlines from Atlanta to Norfolk. Your overnight stay in Atlanta cost $95. Write to Aero Airlines headquarters, 110 Williams Street, Eureka, CA 92118, asking for reimbursement.
2. Recently you ordered two sterling silver candelabra from Bachelder's Silver Shop, 935 West Schreyer Place, Orono, ME 04473, and enclosed a cashier's check for the complete amount of the order. On receiving the order, you were disappointed with the appearance of the candelabra, even though they were clearly and accurately represented in the sales brochure from which you made your selection. Write a letter asking to return them for a full refund less shipping costs.
3. Six months ago, you bought an expensive Futura brand watch at a local jeweler's. But it has never kept time properly, and the dealer from whom you bought it has not been able to fix it and has refused to replace it or to give you a refund. Write to the national office of the Futura Watch Company, 2061 Kenyon Road, Urbana, IL 61801, asking for an appropriate adjustment.
4. Recently you were involved in an automobile accident for which you were not responsible. The insurance adjustor does not agree with you that you should be

permitted to have a new fender and bumper installed on the 1965 Mustang convertible you have recently restored to new condition. Instead, he insists that you should have the damaged ones repaired. Write a letter to the district claims supervisor, Mrs. Ivy Hines, presenting your adjustment claim.

5. You had the twenty-four-hour flu last week and missed a major test in one of your classes. You simply stayed in your room until the fever broke and did not go to a doctor. However, at the beginning of the term your professor announced there would be no make-up work in the class without a written excuse from a doctor, lawyer, or other official. You feel this absence policy should not be followed in this instance. To prevent an automatic failing grade on the test, write an appropriate letter to the professor asking for an adjustment.

6. Rewrite the following claim letter to make it more effective:

> I regret having to tell you that I am very disappointed with the skirt you have just altered for my daughter. As you may recall, it was originally sent to me without any alterations. I returned it and received it yesterday but to my dismay the skirt is about two inches too short. As a result, my daughter will be unable to wear it at all.
>
> Although the skirt was shortened according to the sizes on the order, my daughter probably was not measured correctly. I realize now that I probably should have checked the size more carefully, but I felt your salespeople were more experienced.
>
> I would appreciate your suggestions about the skirt.

7. As a recent graduate of your college or university, you have been invited by the president of your fraternity or sorority to give the featured talk at the annual banquet. Draft a letter explaining why you must refuse.

8. For years, as Christmas gifts your company has mailed executive desk calendars to regular customers. Because of rising costs, this year the company discontinued the practice. Several important customers have inquired why they have not received calendars this year. Draft an appropriate reply.

9. A local civic group has extended you an unsolicited written invitation to join. However, because you disagree with a certain part of the organization's stated purpose, you feel you must decline the invitation. Write a letter for this refusal.

10. A university student has written to your company asking for part-time work. Your company often hires students part-time, but at the moment all positions are filled. Write a letter informing the student that no vacancy exists.

11. The every-member canvasser from your church recently sent you a letter asking you to increase your annual pledge, but you have a reason for refusing. Reply by letter.

12. Write a letter refusing the claim in writing assignment 1.

13. Write a letter refusing the claim in writing assignment 2.

14. Write a letter refusing the claim in writing assignment 4.

15. Write a letter refusing the claim in writing assignment 6.

16. As the owner of a wholesale ski equipment firm, you have received a $6,000 order from a new retailer. Since the retailer's credit history does not warrant thousands of dollars of credit, you must refuse to extend credit. Write a letter doing so.

17. Your retail store just received a credit application from a husband and wife who recently moved to your town. But because the couple has a long history of ill

luck, their references do not justify credit for them. Write a letter denying them charge privileges at your store.

18. You have received an initial order for 20 dozen towels from the King Arthur Motel of Greenwood, SC 29646. Because this is a new account, you will have to ship the towels C.O.D. or obtain credit references. Write Mr. Burton, the manager.

19. Assume that you have received credit references from Mr. Burton, investigated, and decided not to grant credit. Write the letter, suggesting C.O.D. terms and promising shipment within three weeks.

20. Mr. Beau Powers, 1385 York Avenue, New York, NY 10017, recently ordered a camel-colored cashmere topcoat from your clothing store, but did not specify the size. Write a letter asking for his coat size.

21. Mrs. Ada Hardison, 7065 Hilltop Drive, Erie, PA 16509, ordered a set of the *Harvard Classics* from Elite Book Publishers. As Elite's marketing director, you must write and tell her that the *Classics* are available only through local book stores. The store closest to her is Goodspeed's Intimate Bookshop, 1111 Peyton Avenue, Erie, PA 16507.

22. Mr. Jim Griffin, 1819 Malabu Drive, Lexington, KY 40502, ordered a pair of Boz 1001 stereo speakers from you, including a check for the speakers and shipping. However, the Boz 1001s have now been replaced by a newer model, the Boz 1002s, which require less wattage for full performance. Write to Mr. Griffin asking if you can send him the 1002s at the same price.

23. As the credit manager of a clothing store named Preppy Duds, prepare a standard collection series suitable for use with your good risk credit customers. Use an appropriate hypothetical date on each mailing.

24. Prepare the series explained in writing assignment 23, but suited for use with poor risks.

25. As chairperson of your church's finance committee, prepare a short collection series for members who have not fulfilled their pledges during the past two quarters.

NOTES

[1] See, for example, the following articles: Vanessa Dean Arnold and Mosetta S. Soskis, "'We Regret to Inform You'—News of Nonappointment," *The ABCA Bulletin*, 40 (June 1977) pp. 37–38; and Kevin J. Harty, "Some Guidelines for Saying 'No,'" *The ABCA Bulletin*, 44 (December 1980) pp. 23–25. Much of the following discussion is based on these articles.

[2] This standard refusal pattern will not work well in every "no" situation; see, for example, Frederick W. Harbaugh, "'No' Letters to Applicants: Let's Tell it Straight," *The ABCA Bulletin*, 40 (September 1977) p. 28. According to Harbaugh, a more direct and candid refusal is preferable to the pattern described here—"not rude bluntness, but straight-to-the-pointness. . . . No one likes to bear bad news, but . . . we are almost always on surer ground when we bear it confidently, concisely, courteously, and unapologetically."

[3] Based on the Bureau of Business Practice, 24C Rope Ferry Road, Waterford, CT 06386.

[4] For a longer analysis of novelty collection letters, see Donald J. Leonard, ed., *Shurter's Communication in Business: Fourth Edition* (New York: McGraw-Hill, 1979), pp. 181–184.

Part III
COMMUNICATING AND EMPLOYMENT

6 The Job Search

OBJECTIVES

After reading this chapter, you should be able to:

• Draw up a comprehensive self-evaluation work sheet
• List several books, magazines, and newspapers that can help in the employment process
• Explain how the college career counseling and placement office can help in the job selection and search
• Describe the function of information interviews
• Point out the advantages and disadvantages of private and public employment agencies
• Explain the importance of the hidden job market

PLAN

Job Selection
Self-Evaluation
  Education
  Experience
  Ability
  Interests
  Analysis
Job Decisions
  Picking a Field
  Choosing a Job
Job Search
When Location Is Important
  Information Interviews
  Job Interviews
  Newspaper Sources
  Private Employment Agencies
  Public Employment Agencies
  Temporary-Help Agencies
When Location Is Unimportant
  Campus Interviews
  Published Announcements
  Personal Contacts
  Other Techniques
Summary

He or she who gets hired is not
necessarily the one who can do that
job best, but the one who knows the
most about getting hired.

RICHARD NELSON BOLLES

JOB SELECTION

What if the rest of your life depended on passing a course?

Naturally, you'd do everything possible to pass it. You'd attend class regularly, take detailed notes, read the assignments twice, consult supplementary sources, work painstakingly on required papers, cram for exams, confer with the professor, and do anything else helpful.

But the question, pardon the pun, is academic. Your life will not hinge on passing a course. Yet, in many respects, it will depend on your choosing a rewarding and satisfying job. After all, that job may well determine what happens to you during the next forty to fifty years. And measured in terms of money, it could mean a million dollars or so may be at stake (based on 40 years at $25,000 average). If that isn't enough, consider that your quality of life—where and how you live—will be affected. So, in a manner of speaking, the rest of your life will depend on your job. And so will the lives of your spouse and children.

What are you doing about a job now? If you're like many students not majoring in hot fields such as engineering and computer science, you're probably postponing a decision until senior panic sets in. If so, don't wait. Start thinking and deciding and working on your job choice now. But you have to know how to go about it. The process consists of two steps:

1. Evaluating yourself
2. Deciding on the best job for you

Then when you're a senior (assuming you're not one now), you'll be ready to begin your actual job search. In this chapter, we'll discuss the job selection and search; in the next, we'll cover job communications (résumés, application letters, interviews, and follow-up letters).

By starting early to plan for your life after college, you'll be ahead of the game. And you'll also have a better chance of landing an interesting, satisfying, and rewarding job instead of having to take whatever you can find.

SELF-EVALUATION

Begin with a marketing analysis of the product you will be selling—yourself. You may know yourself well, but you need to see yourself as future employers will see you. The burning question they want answered is "How can this college graduate help my organization?" To make certain you can answer that question thoroughly, confidently, and positively, you should take stock of your education, experience, ability, and interests.

From this information will come the self-knowledge to give you confidence, assurance, and conviction in seeking a job. And it will also be invaluable in preparing a résumé. Begin by writing these headings on four separate notebook pages: *Education, Experience, Ability,* and *Interests.* On each page, list all the information you can recall. Then analyze this material, perhaps heeding some of the following suggestions.

Education

On the education page, list all high schools and colleges attended, the dates, special courses or programs taken, major and secondary fields of interest, and any other business, vocational, or on-the-job training courses. Jot down all honors won, offices held, extracurricular activities engaged in, and clubs, organizations, and teams belonged to. Then write out the names of courses you liked most, those liked least, and exactly what you liked and disliked about the subject matter.

Experience

On the experience page, list all your jobs, no matter how insignificant—delivering newspapers, cashiering in supermarkets, cutting grass, or working as a lifeguard. Add any volunteer work you have done. For each experience, write the name of the employer, dates when employed, title, and a detailed description. Near the bottom of the page, write an evaluation of each job, stating which you liked, which you disliked, and the specific reasons why.

Ability

For the ability page, you may need some help. Various classifications of skills are available from books in your college library or placement bureau.[1] The most comprehensive and authoritative is the *Directory of Occupational Titles (DOT)*, which divides skills into three basic groups—those used primarily with data, people, or things—and then further subdivides these.[2] Other lists of skills are more general and less systematic, consisting of an alphabetical arrangement or perhaps none at all, like the following:

supervising	meeting the public
coordinating	working in the lab
researching	reading voluminously
selling	budgeting
motivating	creating
managing	counseling
collecting	negotiating
advising	committee work
repairing	typing
organizing	writing

By going through such lists, you will be able to identify and jot down numerous skills that you possess. And if you have had experience in work or extracurricular activities, you can add those traits that characterize your performance, such as some of the following:

promptness	ability to get along well with others
dependability	willingness to work hard
enthusiasm	poise in meeting people
cheerfulness	desire to do well
dedication	resourcefulness
efficiency	initiative

Interests

On the interests page, list your hobbies, your talents, and the activities you enjoy. What can you do better than most people? What do you particularly like? What do people praise you for? For a good time, what would you do? If you had a million dollars (or even a few thousand), what would you do for fun?

Then think about what kind of work would interest you. Indoors or outdoors? Alone or with a group? With your hands, mind, or both? Solving new problems or doing repetitive work? With details or not? Competitive or relatively secure? Confined to one place or moving around? Physically demanding? Mentally stressful?

Another way to pin down your interests is to consider the subjects that attract you to articles, books, television programs, and films. If you enjoy reading about foreign countries or watching programs about them, then list travel as one of your interests. If clothes, new styles, and the designer world have always fascinated you, then list fashion as one of your interests. Try to discover as much as you can about what you particularly like to know, see, and do.

Analysis

Compiling information about your education, experience, ability, and interests should be a continuing process, not one completed in a few hours. Feel free at any time to add or delete pertinent information. When you feel that you have taken thorough stock of yourself, analyze what you have compiled.

Figure 6-1. Work Sheet for Self-Inventory.

Self-Evaluation Work Sheet

One important aspect of choosing a position is understanding yourself. Self-evaluation can help you analyze what is important to you in the kind of work you will do and the kind of organization in which you will work.

The following are some of the things you should consider in your own self-evaluation. Your answers should be honest. They are meant to help you and should not represent a "good" or "bad" value judgment.

1. What are the things you do best? Are they related to people, data, things?

   _____ related to _____
   _____ related to _____
   _____ related to _____

2. Do you express yourself well and easily?

   Orally: Yes _____ No _____ In writing: Yes _____ No _____

3. Do you see yourself as a leader of a group or team? Yes _____ No _____

   Do you see yourself as an active participant of a group or team? Yes _____ No _____

   Do you prefer to work on your own? Yes _____ No _____

   Do you like supervision? Yes _____ No _____

4. Do you work well under pressure? Yes _____ No _____

   Does pressure cause you anxiety; in fact, is it difficult for you to work well under pressure?
   Yes _____ No _____.

5. Do you seek responsibility? Yes _____ No _____

   Do you prefer to follow directions? Yes _____ No _____

6. Do you enjoy new ideas and situations? Yes _____ No _____

   Are you more comfortable with known routines? Yes _____ No _____

7. In your future, which of the following things are most important to you:

   a. Working for a regular salary _____ b. Working for a commission _____

   c. Working for a combination of both _____

8. Do you want to work a regular schedule (e.g., 9 a.m. to 5 p.m.)? Yes _____ No _____

9. Are you willing to travel more than 50 percent of your working time? Yes _____ No _____

10. What kind of environment is important to you?

    a. Do you prefer to work indoors? Yes _____ No _____

    b. Do you prefer to work outdoors? Yes _____ No _____

    c. Do you prefer an urban environment (population over a million)? Yes _____ No _____
       Population between 100,000 to 900,000? Yes _____ No _____

    d. Do you prefer a rural setting? Yes _____ No _____

11. Do you prefer to work for a large organization? Yes _____ No _____

12. Are you free to move? Yes _____ No _____

    Are there important "others" to be considered? Yes _____ No _____

COMMUNICATING AND EMPLOYMENT

To do so, review the information carefully, looking for key points to underline. Some of the questions in the *Self-Evaluation Work Sheet* (see figure 6–1) may help. What you're trying to do is to zero in on the type of work you are best qualified for and interested in.

You might wish to receive professional assistance with this analysis. A trained counselor at your college career planning and placement office may spot qualities you have overlooked. For instance, you may think little about your numerous neighborhood solicitations for cancer, heart, or other fund-raising drives. But your counselor might feel that they reveal initiative, ability to get along with people, and communication skills. Along with other evidence, this information may indicate that you should consider certain fields of work.

If your college does not have a counselor, find out if one is available at the public employment office, or if someone there can refer you to one. Getting professional advice may be well worth paying a fee for because of the importance of your career choice. Sometimes there is an extra charge for tests to determine your interests and abilities. In many instances, this money may be well spent—although the tests often only reinforce what people already know about themselves from their self-evaluation.

As a result of your own analysis or with the help of a counselor, you should arrive at certain conclusions about yourself and your career goals. The trick now is to match those conclusions with the opportunities available and the qualifications needed.

JOB DECISIONS

Job decisions involve choosing a particular field that appears promising and interesting to you, and then selecting a job within that field. For instance, if you want a career in business, you might select from among the following jobs: accountant, auditor, actuary, buyer, marketing analyst, personnel worker, production manager, purchasing agent, sales representative, securities broker, systems analyst, and traffic supervisor.

Picking a Field

Whether or not you have already declared a major at college, you should investigate various fields of work—either to make certain that your choice of major is still a wise one for you or to get more information for deciding on a major. Among the more popular career areas are the following:

advertising	manufacturing
airlines	military service
banking	motion pictures
business	politics
communication	publishing
computer science	radio-TV
education	recreation
energy	retailing
government	utilities
insurance	writing, editing
journalism	

In making your decision, you should consider the availability of job openings and the possibility for advancement opportunities in certain fields. Projections about the future growth of various industries and job opportunities in them are printed in numerous business and government publications. In addition to articles that appear from time to time in the newspapers,[3] *Wall Street Journal, Barron's, Forbes, Fortune, Money,* and *Changing Times,* you should consult such government publications as the most recent *U.S. Industrial Outlook, Occupational Projections and Training Data, Occupational Outlook Handbook for College Graduates,* and the *Occupational Outlook Quarterly.*

In addition, you might wish to talk to local people in your field of interest. If so, let your fingers walk through the Yellow Pages of your telephone directory or, if you are in a small community, one from a nearby medium-sized or large city. A telephone call or, better yet, a short visit with a manager there can be enlightening.

Choosing a Job

There's still the matter of choosing a job within a field. (Of course, in some instances, you may reverse this process: selecting a job first—for example, personnel work—and then deciding in which field you will seek employment.)

To learn about various occupations—including many that you may not have heard of—do some research work. Spend some time with the previously mentioned *DOT,* which describes about 20,000 jobs, covering such matters as their physical demands, working conditions, and training requirements. A smaller version of the *DOT* is the *Occupational Outlook Handbook,* which not only attempts to forecast future employment opportunities in some 850 occupations but describes the nature of the work involved, the working conditions, prospects for advancement, and the like.

These government publications and others like them may be found in your college career and placement office, which is an invaluable source of information and assistance with the entire employment process—from helping you with your self-evaluation to arranging interviews for you. Plan to visit this office soon and talk to the counselors there about their services.

Also, talk to others. Talk to your parents (see figure 6–2), their friends, and your friends' parents about their work. Talk to people on buses, in stores, in lines, on planes, and everywhere else. Talk to your professors, talk to alumni, talk to older students. Job-talk whenever you can, wherever you are, to whomever you find.

All this reading and talking should help you to narrow your decision. Then match your interests and qualifications with the employment opportunities, the educational requirements, and the work conditions and characteristics of a specific job. For example, you might like to be a systems analyst but realize that you would not do well in this highly detailed and precise work. Or you might want to go into accounting, but because of that field's diminishing opportunities in your region, you might decide to turn to a related one, such as actuarial work, credit management, or financial analysis.

In essence, what you're engaged in is the process of marketing yourself. You are acquiring all the available information about the product (yourself), the competition (employment opportunities), and the market (who's hiring whom). Chances are that

Figure 6–2. Parental Employment Advice.

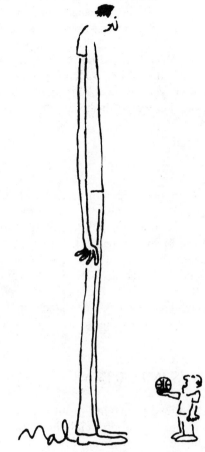

*"Listen, son, with the average salary in the
N.B.A. being $120,000 a year, you are going to
play basketball whether you like it or not!"*

(SOURCE: From *The Wall Street Journal*, Permission—Cartoon Features Syndicate.)

after such a thorough study, you will be able to select a job in a field that will prove interesting, satisfying, and rewarding for you.

This decision may involve no change in your present major, or a slight shift in its focus, perhaps from marketing to personnel relations. Or it may mean a significant change of your major. If so, test your decision by talking to several people doing this type of work. And you might try to find similar work in a part-time job, an internship, or a summer position.[4] For example, if banking is your top choice, look for a summer job at one of your local banks, perhaps filling in for vacationing employees. If government work sounds appealing, contact specific agencies or check with the federal or state employment offices. If retailing seems attractive, inquire at some of the nearby department stores, especially ones that run regular management training programs for college graduates. Sometimes, part-time or summer work not only can help you to decide on a career but can open up a job for you later on.

All of these suggestions will help you in selecting your future life's work. And you'll be far ahead of other students who have not thought seriously or at length about what they want to do. Consequently, you will have a head start on them as you begin your job search in the months preceding graduation.

JOB SEARCH

By the beginning of your senior year, you should have zeroed in on what you want to do, although you may still wish to keep some options open. You may have selected advertising, for example, but be uncertain about whether account management, media analysis, or market research is for you. How do you proceed?

First, decide where you want to go—either to your dream city or anywhere you can get a good job offer. In other words, your first step is to decide which is the most important: the job or the locale. Of course, you can have the best of both options—your ideal job may be available in Dream City. Positions in advertising, for instance, exist in all medium-sized or large cities throughout the country.

WHEN LOCATION IS IMPORTANT

If you're determined to live in Dream City for personal or family reasons, then you ought to concentrate your job search there, an approach advocated by Richard Nelson Bolles (see figure 6–3). Begin by familiarizing yourself with the community, unless you know it well already. Write or visit its chamber of commerce to obtain information about business conditions and companies; subscribe to its major newspaper (if necessary, ask the librarian for its name and address); find out whether recruiters from companies in that city will be interviewing on campus; contact former students (check the alumni office) or other people living there now; read travel guides and articles in the library; and look in its Yellow Pages. Also, search through the geographical listings in the *College Placement Annual*, available in your placement office. This valuable publication, which provides listings every year of over 1,000 employers interested in college graduates, is indexed conveniently according to both occupation and location. So all you have to do is to look up Dream City in the index.

Next, plan to visit your ideal community, perhaps during your Christmas or spring break. If you can't get there, then you must depend on a mail campaign, applying for jobs advertised in the *Dream City Herald* or elsewhere, or mailing letters to every organization that might possibly have an opening for you. (For illustrations of these letters, see chapter 7.)

Figure 6–3.   Job-Hunting When Location Is Important.

JOB MARKETS IN THE UNITED STATES
14,000,000
(that's the total number of non-farm employers)

1 You narrow this down by deciding just what area, city or county you want to work in. This leaves you with however many thousands of job markets there are in that area or city. **2** You narrow this down by identifying your Strongest Skills, on their highest level that you can legitimately claim, and then thru research deciding what field you *want* to work in, above all. This leaves you with all the hundreds of businesses/ community organizations/agencies/schools/hospitals/projects/associations/ foundations/institutions/firms or government agencies there are in that area and in the field you have chosen. **3** You narrow this down by getting acquainted with the economy in the area thru personal interviews with various contacts; and supplementing this with study of journals in your field, in order that you can pinpoint the places that interest you the most. This leaves a manageable number of markets for you to do some study on. **4** You now narrow this down through further personal visits to those 'markets', with this question uppermost in your mind: *can I be happy in this place, and, do they have the kind of problems which my strongest skills can help solve for them?* **5** All of the above is called Informational Interviewing. When your II is completed, you will have a list of the companies or organizations you already visited, which still look interesting to you; and you will now carefully plan how to approach them for a job, in your case — ● *the* job.

(SOURCE: From *What Color Is Your Parachute?* by Richard Nelson Bolles. 1982 Edition. Copyright 1982. Used with permission. Available from Ten Speed Press, Box 7123, Berkeley, CA 94707. $7.95 + $.75 for postage and handling.)

Information Interviews

Your chances are better if you can visit Dream City. Before going, try to arrange some interviews with executives, section or division heads, or managers. Write to these people, telling them when you plan your trip and that you are eager to learn about opportunities in the field and in their organizations. Or, as a second choice, you may phone when you get there, mentioning that you are in the city for just a brief time and would appreciate seeing them for their advice. In these instances, it is important to learn the names of the people you want to meet by consulting directories, phone books, or local people, or by phoning and asking a telephone operator or secretary.

The advantage of information interviews is that they are nonthreatening to employers. Because you are not applying for a position, an employer need not worry about having to refuse you. Besides, the situation is flattering. Most people like to give advice, to play the role of counselor to beginners in their field. From your viewpoint, the advantages are numerous. You have an opportunity to receive valuable information, make an important contact, and present yourself subtly as a possible job applicant. After all, there's nothing to prevent an employer from thinking, "This

Figure 6–4. Sexist Discrimination.

"She'll probably hire him; she likes big dumb blonds."

(SOURCE: From *The Wall Street Journal,* Permission—Cartoon Features Syndicate.)

is a fine young person who looks like the type that could do a good job for us." (For a humorous twist to this statement, see figure 6–4.)

Yet even if the interviews result only in information and contacts, you should be satisfied. Sound advice about the future of the field, companies in it doing well or poorly, new developments, expansion plans, and employment possibilities is all useful and valuable. Also helpful would be the names of people to see, employment agencies to consult, and contacts to phone about finding a job. In addition to questions along these lines, you might ask such personal ones as "How did you get started in this field?" or "What do you especially like about your work?"

Remember that at this point, you are seeking counsel, advice, and suggestions. Of course, if the ideal job should fall in your lap, you wouldn't turn it down. But basically, you are preparing yourself for waging an all-out job offensive after graduation, when you will have more time in Dream City to obtain interviews, respond to newspaper ads, register with private employment agencies, and become familiar with public agencies.

Job Interviews

You can always go to the personnel department of large companies for job interviews. But a better bet, if possible, is to see someone in charge of a department or division who supervises people in your line of work and may know of an opening for you. Openings occur all the time as a result of illnesses, resignations, promotions, and deaths. A department or division head may know better than the people in personnel about an impending change that might provide a spot for you. But even if there aren't any openings, persist in trying to talk to someone in authority about being considered when an opening occurs. Remember that managers are always on the lookout for qualified, energetic, interested, cheerful, and friendly people.

But sometimes doors will remain closed to you unless you can name-drop. That's why your information interviews may be helpful. And that's also why such contacts as friends, relatives, their friends, professors, alumni, and people you talk to about a job can all be valuable. At the mention of a name, closed doors may open, like this:

> "Ms. Gallagher, I'm Betty Host. Ann Green suggested that I contact you to schedule an appointment at your convenience."

> "Well, I'm really not seeing anyone these days, Betty, but if Ann Green told you to get in touch with me, I'll be glad to make some time for you."

Whenever possible, whether you contact people cold or with a name as reference, try to see them in person about a job interview rather than phone them. As you can understand, it's much harder refusing someone standing before you than someone on the other end of the telephone line. But even if you meet with numerous rebuffs, don't give up. Stay in touch with all prospects, sending them short letters to let them know that you are still available and interested. Otherwise, employers may scratch you off their list of candidates, assuming that you have found work elsewhere.

Above all, in seeking interviews, be bold. He or she who hesitates may lose a job. Nothing ventured, no job gained.

Newspaper Sources

Seeing department or division heads who supervise people doing your kind of work is ideal because you will be talking to a person in authority, one who often makes the final hiring decision. Also, you will not be competing with the many other applicants filling out forms in the personnel office or replying to newspaper ads. Yet, if you can't get leads to see people or gain entry to them on your own, you may have to rely on personnel departments or help-wanted ads.

In large community newspapers, help-wanted ads are indexed either under fields (public relations, insurance, and so on), type of work (writer, marketing researcher, etc.), or skills (office-clerical, sales, etc.). You can save yourself time by studying the organization of the help-wanted ads. But don't overlook a miscellaneous section. And remember, entry-level jobs of all kinds are often listed under a "college graduates" heading.

You will also see that three kinds of ads appear: those identifying a company, those providing only a box number, and those identifying an employment agency. The first type is preferable because you can research the company and shape your application accordingly. The box number or *blind ad* is often inserted when management does not want its employees to know that it is hiring.

In follow-up interviews about classified ads, be wary of sales, management trainee, and other offers that require you to pay money for enrolling in short courses, buy products, or pay deposits in some form. These are often come-ons that fail to result in actual jobs.

Don't depend on running your own ads; employers seldom read the classified section. On the other hand, notices of your availability and qualifications in trade and professional journals can be successful. Nearly every field, from aerobic exercising to window washing, has a national organization with a magazine or newsletter.

To the enterprising, newspapers can be helpful in other ways. Stories about local businesspeople, their plans, activities, speeches, and statements furnish leads that may develop into interviews. A talk at the Rotary Club by Jim Snapper, Vice President of Ideal Company, about the use of teleconferences in business, provides an opening to praise his speech, raise some questions, and request an appointment to explore the subject further. Similar opportunities can be realized from newspaper stories about the expansion of plants, creation of new divisions, addition of product lines, award of large contracts, and the like.

Private Employment Agencies

Private employment agencies may be helpful, but you should approach them with caution. Most important, check their reputations by phoning the local Better Business Bureau and by talking to local business people. Try to find out which ones specialize in placing people in your field. Then visit several agencies, comparing their services, reading their contracts carefully, and evaluating their counselors. Be cautious about those boasting of high success rates unless you can check with some of the people they have placed. Because these agencies normally make their money by charging fees based on a percentage of their clients' salaries, counselors often try to persuade clients to accept a job—any job—that is offered. In this way, insecure job hunters

Figure 6–5. A Job Offer?

"WE HAVE SOMETHING WITH TERRIFIC FRINGE BENEFITS. NO SALARY — JUST FRINGE BENEFITS."

(Source: © 1980 by Sidney Harris—*Changing Times*)

are often scared into settling for less attractive positions than they desire, resulting in under-employment and unhappiness. But the agency gets its fee.

Yet many agencies are reliable, having established fine reputations over the years. Often employers do some or all of their hiring through these agencies, which know much about the local job market, companies, employers, and ways to obtain jobs from them.

Some agencies specialize in certain fields. Frequently their ads will point this out—or you could ask during an information interview what employment agencies might be helpful in your job hunt.

But be careful. Make certain you understand the fee arrangement. And don't let yourself be talked into a job that you would not ordinarily be willing to accept or that is not worth the fee that you would have to pay for it. This advice applies even if your employer pays the fee, as happens in some instances. Don't ever let yourself feel so desperate that you would accept any job (see figure 6–5).

Public Employment Agencies

Another avenue to explore in Dream City is the public employment agency, usually a state-run organization funded in part with federal money. Listed in the Yellow Pages or in the state government section of the phone book, the agency may appear under such various headings as "Employment," "Job Services," "Economic Security," or "Manpower Services." If you can't find it, call Directory Assistance (411).

Although public employment agencies list positions mainly in the less skilled and lower-paid levels (domestic, clerical, machine trades, bench work, etc.), they do have some professional, technical, managerial, and sales listings. Best of all, they charge no fee. And your registration with an agency may provide you with valuable counseling information, as well as access to the Job Bank, a computerized service that prints a daily local and statewide list of available jobs.

Also, through your local agency's Interstate Clearance System, your application will be computer-matched with jobs available in over 2,500 offices throughout the country. If you're in luck, you might strike a Dream City position.

Although public employment agencies may be more valuable to graduates of two-year rather than four-year colleges, all job seekers should visit one.

Temporary-Help Agencies

A newcomer to a community may find immediate help from a relative newcomer to the employment market—the temporary-help agency. These organizations provide employees to industry for short periods of time to fill in for vacationing or ill people or to help out during times of heavy workloads. The advantage of investigating a position with such an agency is that it would give you immediate income when you move to Dream City while allowing you to learn a lot both about the business community and about individual businesses. Also, an employer, impressed with your work, might offer you a permanent job. This possibility occurs with some frequency despite a fee that has to be paid to the agency by you or your employer.

Some national temporary-help agencies may have local branches in your community where you can register; your records can then be transferred to the Dream City branch when you move.

WHEN LOCATION IS UNIMPORTANT

If you are generally undecided about location, being flexible and fancy free, you will have more job-hunting possibilities than your Dream City friends. You can best take advantage of these opportunities through campus interviews, published announcements, and personal contacts.

Campus Interviews

Most convenient and inviting of all interview opportunities are those conducted on campus by company recruiters. Arranged by your placement office, these interviews offer you a chance to talk to business representatives who definitely intend to employ a number of college graduates. But don't depend entirely on getting a job in this way. You'll be competing with students both on your own campus and on others. The upshot, as the *College Placement Annual* points out, is that "only a small number of college graduates are hired as a result of campus interviews."[5] But even if you're not hired, you can learn a lot about interviewing and about the job market by meeting with college recruiters.

COMMUNICATING AND EMPLOYMENT

Published Announcements

Every year, as we mentioned previously, the *College Placement Annual* provides listings of over 1,000 employers interested in hiring college graduates. But competition for these openings is intense—about 400,000 students pore over this publication. Less well known are the *Changing Times Job Survey*, which you can order from *Changing Times*,[6] and *Peterson's Annual Guide to Careers and Employment for Engineers, Computer Scientists, and Physical Scientists* (Edison, N.J.: Peterson's Guides).

Although the *Wall Street Journal*, the Sunday *New York Times* Business Section, and the *National Business Employment Weekly* contain pages filled with employment ads, few are for entry-level positions. But it will cost you little more than a postage stamp to write to expanding companies running large notices in these publications for engineers and other specialists. If they're adding to their work force, they may need entry-level employees as well.

You should also look for announcements in publications of professional associations in your field. Usually, your professors can tell you about organizations with newsletters, journals, or bulletins listing job vacancies. In addition, some associations provide job placement services at their annual or regional meetings. Of course, there is usually much competition for these openings, but you should apply for any position you are qualified for.

Personal Contacts

Most important of all may be contacts.[7] Some studies show that as few as one job in five is advertised; the others are filled in the hidden job market by employers who learn through their friends, acquaintances, and employees about an applicant. Large companies have to advertise publicly to avoid discrimination suits, but someone with inside connections often has an advantage. So here's another opportunity to let anyone and everyone know that you are job-hunting. Tell it to the world: professors, family, friends, acquaintances, administrators, and all their friends, plus people you see and meet—your postman, hair stylist, grocer, neighbors, mechanic, bank teller, and various store sales people. Attend meetings, workshops, conferences, conventions, and seminars. All you're looking for is a slight crack in the door: "That reminds me, I heard yesterday that Bill Givens is leaving his job at National Loading. You might try them."

And don't overlook the other applicants you meet in your job hunt. Compare notes. Exchange information about openings and experiences. Stay in touch to bolster one another. It's easy to become discouraged after being rejected. But if you keep looking, and keep talking to people about job openings, you should succeed.

Other Techniques

Naturally, you should pursue any and all the techniques mentioned previously in the Dream City job search: application letters (see chapter 7), information interviews, newspaper sources, and private, public, and temporary-help agencies. Place them on your list of avenues to explore, because one may lead you to the desired job.

But remember: no technique can perform miracles. Yet knowing as much as possible about the employment process and laboring over your job selection and search will give you a decided advantage over many other graduating seniors and will increase your chances for an attractive job. Besides, working hard on preparing for your future will let you know that you have tried your best. You owe it to yourself not to settle for less.

SUMMARY

This chapter has been concerned with the job selection and job search steps of the employment process.

The selection process consists of two steps: evaluating yourself and applying that evaluation in deciding on a particular job. In your self-evaluation, review your education, experience, ability, and interests in order to analyze what career you would be best suited for and would find most appealing. In analyzing this information, you might seek the advice of a professional employment counselor. You might also consult this person about deciding on a field and choosing a job in it, or you could refer to the numerous books, articles, and government publications that provide helpful information.

The job search usually entails a basic decision about whether you want to work in a particular location or not. If you do, then you might visit that place or write to various employers there. A visit—either before or after you graduate—should be used for going to interviews, combing newspaper help-wanted ads, and investigating private, public, and temporary-help agencies. If location is unimportant, you should schedule campus interviews, mail application letters, search published announcements, and make contacts with everyone you know or meet.

Some of these techniques may be more helpful than others, depending on such variables as the job market, your skills, and local factors. But all are worth investigating. Nothing should be left undone because nothing may be more important in your life than deciding on and searching for a job.

EXERCISES

Discussion Questions

1. How can the library be useful in your self-evaluation?
2. In what ways can your career counseling and placement office assist in the job selection and search?
3. Mention three ways a summer job can help you to find employment after graduation.
4. In what ways can you obtain information about your Dream City without living there?
5. How can the *College Placement Annual* help students look for a job?
6. Why is it usually easier to obtain information interviews than job interviews?
7. Discuss the advantages and disadvantages of public and private employment agencies.
8. How might working for a temporary-help agency assist you in your job search?

9. How can your professors help you in your job search?
10. Explain the importance of the hidden job market.

In-Class Applications

1. List your skills on a piece of paper. Then exchange and compare lists with two classmates. Note whether any of the skills on their lists should also appear on your own.
2. Write the answers to the Self-Evaluation Work Sheet in figure 6–1. Exchange answers with a classmate. See whether each of you can determine what type of job the other would like.
3. Obtain information from one printed source about future job opportunities for college graduates. Compare your information with your classmates'.
4. Find out what you can learn in the library about your Dream City. With your classmates, determine the most valuable sources of information.
5. Ask a counselor from your college placement office to talk to your class about its services. Beforehand, plan questions with your classmates based on your knowledge of the employment process.
6. Find out the names of publications in your major field. Report to the class on whether vacancies are announced, and if so, in what job areas, at what salaries, and where.

NOTES

[1] Richard Nelson Bolles, *What Color Is Your Parachute?* (Berkeley: Ten Speed Press, 1981), pp. 188–206. This highly readable, entertaining, best-selling manual may be more suitable for job-hunters other than recent graduates, but it is the best in the field. Also recommended is Richard Lathrop, *Who's Hiring Who* (Berkeley, Calif.: Ten Speed Press, 1977), pp. 27–59.

[2] See the most recent edition, which is published in Washington, D.C. by the Superintendent of Documents. Less complete but helpful and more readable are the annual *Occupational Outlook Handbook* (Washington, D.C.: Department of Labor) and William E. Hopke, ed., *Encyclopedia of Careers and Vocational Guidance*, Fifth Edition (Chicago: J. G. Ferguson, 1981).

[3] Usually, in early December, wire service press releases carry news about the annual *Endicott Report*, a yearly survey conducted by the Placement Center at Northwestern University to determine the needs of major corporations for college graduates.

[4] For summer jobs throughout the country, see the latest edition of Barbara O'Brien, *Summer Employment Directory of the U.S.* (Cincinnati: Writer's Digest Books).

[5] Statement in the 1978 edition, p. 10.

[6] The annual March edition of this publication contains helpful job information and also tells how to obtain its annual job survey, which contains the names and addresses of companies and government agencies with openings.

[7] According to "At Work," *Changing Times*, January 1981, p. 62, a recent study at the University of Michigan found that a majority of workers in a nationally representative sample said they heard about their jobs through friends and relatives.

7 Employment Communications

OBJECTIVES

After reading this chapter, you should be able to:

- List the six parts of the traditional résumé and explain what information should appear in each
- Write an effective traditional or functional résumé
- Describe the three-part strategy of the application letter
- Write an effective application letter
- Explain each of the six parts of the interview process
- Discuss the guidelines for five post-interview letters
- Point out how to avoid problems in pronoun reference, case, and agreement; in parallelism; and in the overuse of the pronoun *I*

PLAN

Strategy
The Résumé
  Heading
  Career Objective
  Education
  Work Experience
  Personal Data
  References
  Format
The Letter of Application
  Interest
  Convince
  Activate
The Interview
  Advance Planning
  Same-Day Preparation
  Opening Procedures
  Main Interview Procedures
  Closing Procedures
  Post-Interview Procedures
Post-Interview Letters
  Letter of Appreciation
  Letter of Inquiry
  Letter of Acceptance
  Letter of Delay
  Letter of Refusal
Technique
Words: Problems with Pronouns
  Pronoun Reference
  Pronoun Case
  Pronoun Agreement
Sentences: Parallelism
Style: Avoiding Overuse of the
    Pronoun *I*
Summary

> *The most qualified people don't always get the job. It goes to the person who presents himself most persuasively in person and on paper.*
>
> JERROLD G. SIMON

STRATEGY

Getting a job depends greatly on communicating skillfully. You may have excellent qualifications—the necessary experience, education, and personal characteristics—but derive little good from them if you can't write an attractive letter of application or résumé or handle yourself well in an interview. So to be a job winner, you should know how to deal with employment communications effectively, especially how to write winning application letters and résumés, and how to participate in winning interviews.

Among these employment communications, the basic one is the résumé, a record of your qualifications that you should enclose in application letters and take with you to interviews. The résumé, often spelled resumé or resume, is sometimes called a data or qualification sheet, a *vita* or *curriculum vitae*, or a personal profile. Because it is such a basic employment document, let's discuss it first and then move to the application letter, interview, and post-interview letters.

THE RÉSUMÉ

The résumé presents your credentials, showing an employer who you are (name and personal data) and what you have done (education and work experience). The information for this fact sheet should come from the self-inventory mentioned in chapter 5. How you select, organize, and display this information is your decision. No standard form exists—people like to arrange their qualifications in ways that will emphasize their particular strong points. However, two general approaches are popular: the traditional (often referred to as the chronological) and the functional. In the traditional résumé, some or all of the following sections are standard: (1) heading; (2) career objective; (3) education; (4) experience; (5) personal; and (6) references.

Heading

The heading of the résumé should contain your proper name (no nickname), address, and phone number. If you plan to move shortly because of graduation, list both current and future addresses, showing when you will be available at the new one.

No other date should appear because you may want to send out résumés for weeks without disclosing how long you've been looking for a job.

Career Objective

Next should appear your career objective, expressed in terms specific enough to show an employer that you should be considered for a particular opening but not so specific that it might disqualify you from similar jobs. Often the objective may be stated in immediate and long-range terms:

<u>Job Objective</u>: Staff cost accountant with the goal of working into a supervisory or management position in the accounting department.

<u>Career Objective</u>

Short range: management trainee   Long range: merchandise manager

Avoid such generalizations as "opportunity with growing company" or "stimulating and creative work." Remember that you are writing to employers with certain slots to fill. They want to know whether your objective matches their need. They are not looking for college graduates willing to do anything.

Education

Unless your job experience is more impressive, present information about your education first. In reverse chronological order (present to past), list all the colleges attended, degree or degrees received or expected, dates, and major and minor fields. You may mention your overall grade point average or your major GPA if helpful. Depending on space and possible interest to employers, you may add information about special courses, research, internships, other academic activities, and the percentage of your expenses earned. If you have paid for most of your education, be sure to say so. You will have something in common with many top business managers.

Work Experience

This section of the résumé should provide information about any full-time, part-time, college-credit, or summer jobs you have had. Work experience of any consequence—whether paid or volunteer—should be listed in reverse chronological order along with the dates of employment, name and address of employer, nature of the business, specific duties performed, and the skills necessary to achieve them. In describing these duties and skills, use past-tense verbs and write-in phrases, omitting the pronoun *I* and other unnecessary words. Some of the following verbs may be helpful:

achieved	organized
created	planned
conducted	presented
coordinated	reported
designed	supervised
developed	trained
directed	wrote
managed	

Here's what an entry might look like:

```
Sales representative, WJOB-TV, 313 S. State Street, Ann
Arbor, MI, 19-- -19--. Sold time for local TV station.
Called on new and old accounts; presented regular, spe-
cial, and package plans; processed orders; checked for
customer satisfaction. Often proposed spots, coordinated
with advertising department, and reviewed billings.
```

Because employers do not expect recent college graduates to have had much experience, they are interested in almost any work you have done. Do not feel sheepish about mentioning unskilled jobs. These may not have contributed much to your practical business experience, but they often show that you are responsible, conscientious, industrious, and enterprising—all important qualities to employers.

Personal Data

Available space plays a determining role in deciding what information to include about your other accomplishments and interests. Among the separate categories might be extracurricular activities, honors, military service, interests, and personal facts. Anything that will look good on your résumé (see figure 7–1) can be included here if it does not fit elsewhere.

If you have been active in college, you might include a section entitled "Extracurricular Activities" to show the offices you have held, sports engaged in, and organizations joined. Add any community work with social, religious, political, charity, or civic groups. Contained here or in a separate section might be honors: scholarships received, honorary organizations elected to, prizes won, or graduation honors attained. If neither your extracurricular activities nor your honors are extensive, you might include them under the "Education" section.

Also included in this portion of the résumé should be a section on military service if it enabled you to develop important skills, demonstrate leadership ability, or show some recognition of merit through promotions or special assignments. Or indicate your military service under "Experience" to show what you were doing during this period.

Another possibility is a section called "Interests" that would give employers an insight about you through the ways you spend your free time. What you collect,

Figure 7–1. Looking Good for a Good-Looking Résumé.

"A word to the wise, Pfaffinger. Do something, anything, that
will look good on your resume."

(SOURCE: Reprinted by permission of Chicago Tribune Syndicate, Inc.)

read, work on, and make all reveal something about your character and personality. This information distinguishes you from other candidates by showing your particular pleasures (wild river rafting, working on old cars, making quilts, playing bridge, collecting depression glassware) and provides a valuable way to break the ice in interviews. So if you mention your interests, be prepared to discuss them.

The "Personal Data" section may also include date and place of birth, marital status, health (anything less than "excellent" may be suspect), height, weight, and willingness to travel and relocate. This last bit of information is important to many employers who need to send representatives on the road frequently or to transfer them to different plants.

The Fair Employment Practice Law prohibits employers from asking for information about age, race, color, religion, or national origin, but if you feel that any of this information would be useful in obtaining a job, you may include it although you are not obliged to do so.

References

Also optional are references. If you have sufficient space in your résumé, you might list them. Usually, at least one reference should be a recent employer to vouch for you as an employee, and another should be a professor to report on you as a student. When furnishing such references, you should provide their names, titles, addresses, and business phone numbers.

When references are not furnished on the résumé, you should indicate that they are available on request or may be obtained from your college placement bureau. Often they are not requested. Since most written recommendations are highly favorable, many employers believe they are of little value. But some employers like to phone references, feeling that this channel of communication can be useful in revealing enthusiasm or lack of it.

Before giving the names of references, you should first ask their permission. Otherwise, they may be annoyed at your presumption. Usually, it's wise to request recommendations from professors shortly after you've had a course with them so that their memory of you is fresh. If you contact them later, leave your résumé to help them with details about you.

At many schools, recommendations are sent to the placement bureau, where they are kept in your file to be mailed to employers upon request. Under such circumstances, you should sign a waiver before requesting a recommendation, stipulating that you will have no access to it. As a result, your references will feel freer to write honestly of your strengths and weaknesses, and employers will place greater trust in the evaluations, knowing they are confidential.

Most references go to some trouble in writing recommendations and would like to know how the applicant fared. Why not drop them a note when you accept an offer?

Format

The traditional format—with sections on career objective, experience, education, honors, interests, personal data, and references—is illustrated in figure 7–2. Note how the address change is presented, details about work experience are provided, specific courses are mentioned, personal information is supplied, and reference requests are anticipated.

The second résumé (see figure 7–3) exemplifies the functional format with skills emphasized. The writer has omitted details about college courses and personal matters in favor of the other information provided. Note how the grade point average and part-time jobs are mentioned.

The third résumé (see figure 7–4) illustrates an informal functional type, whose headings can vary. Note that the writer is applying for a particular job as indicated by the heading, that the position is for the summer of his sophomore year, and that he has included information about hobbies, part-time jobs, and personal details.

You may target a résumé for a specific job, develop different versions for different jobs, or depend on only one for all jobs. If you take either of the last two courses, you need not type the résumés individually but can have them photocopied or reproduced by offset printing, an inexpensive process that increases their attractiveness.

Figure 7–2. Traditional Résumé.

JOSEPH A. SENIOR

<u>Permanent Address</u>
116 12th Street, N.E.
Washington, D.C. 20002
Telephone: 202-555-2828

<u>College Address (until May 2)</u>
317 Parker Road
Cleveland, Ohio 44105
Telephone: 216-555-2204

CAREER
OBJECTIVES
Personnel Manager, specializing in improving
hiring practices, motivating low achievers,
improving employee morale, and reducing turnover.

EXPERIENCE
TRW Corporation, 18997 Euclid Avenue,
Cleveland, Ohio 44109

Summer
19--
Interviewed, tested, and evaluated applicants.
Wrote memos about employee benefits for
personnel department.

Summer
19--
American Express, Paris, France.
Processed checks and provided information to
American tourists.

Summer
19--
Camp Lakeside, Oxford, Maine.
Taught sailing, boating, and swimming.
Organized canoe trips.
Supervised campers.

EDUCATION
B.S. in Psychology, May, 19--, Case Western Reserve
University, Cleveland, Ohio. Completed courses
in Industrial Psychology, Psychology of Industrial
Personnel Procedures, and Psychological Testing,
as well as business courses in Personnel Management,
Employee Relations, and Organizational Behavior.

HONORS
ACTIVITIES
Senator, Student Government (2 years); member,
University Concert Band (3 years); Omicron Delta Kappa
(national honorary).

INTERESTS
Water sports, jogging, chess, crossword puzzles.

PERSONAL
Single 6'1" 193 lbs. Excellent health
Willing to relocate.

REFERENCES
Available upon request from Placement Bureau,
Case Western Reserve University, 27865 Adelbert Avenue
Cleveland, Ohio 44106.

Figure 7–3.   Functional Résumé.

PHYLLIS GREEN
2328 Clays Mill Road
Syracuse, NY 13202
315-555-6700

JOB OBJECTIVE Acceptance into management training program with future
opportunity to become buyer.

EDUCATION

State University of New York at Caldonia
B.S. Business Administration. Included numerous courses in textiles.
May, 19--   GPA 3.15 (A = 4.0)

LEADERSHIP AND ORGANIZATIONAL SKILLS

* As Homecoming Chairperson, planned and supervised activities
  of 65 students, managed a budget of $2,300, and hosted a
  banquet for 250 alumni.

* Directed student summer advisory program for new freshmen.
  Supervised staff of eighteen, wrote advisory booklet,
  scheduled fall events, and provided payroll data.

* Organized Heart Fund Drive with 53 volunteers. Planned canvassing
  assignments, wrote solicitation materials, and supervised
  collection and tallying of donations.

FASHION, DESIGN, AND SALES HONORS

* Winner of Mademoiselle Magazine Summer Internship for submission
  of promotion for man-made fibers.

* Won second place in design at Caldonia Fashion Show of Clothing
  for Older Women. Competed against 24 other entrants.

* Salesperson of the month, McAlpin's Department Store,
  August, 19--.

EXPERIENCE

* Assistant Buyer, Richardson's Department Store, Dewitt Mall,
  DeWitt, NY. May 19-- to date. Trained and supervised sales
  staff, maintained inventory, and assisted in buying of sportswear
  and junior wear.

* Salesperson, McAlpin's Department Store, Turfland Mall,
  Galeville, NY. Summers and part-time, 19-- and 19--.
  Responsible for displays and selling.

* Other part-time and summer experience includes work as a waitress
  and as a secretary.

INTERESTS

Collecting jazz records, gourmet cooking, needlepoint.

REFERENCES

Academic, business, and personal references available upon request.

Figure 7–4. Informal Functional Résumé.

TOM L. CUMMINS

QUALIFICATIONS FOR COUNSELOR
POSITION AT CAMP RIPPLING BROOK

3138 Edgewood Drive, Ann Arbor, Michigan 48103

(313) 555-4422

Experience with Young People

Assistant Scout Master, Troop 543, Ann Arbor, from
September, 19-- to date. Have led overnight
camping trips and hiking trips.

Instructor, Sunday School, Christ Church Episcopal.
Have taught third grade for past two years.

Assistant Coach, Bobcat Little League Baseball Team,
May-August, 19--.

Camp Skills and Interests

Played varsity baseball, Ann Arbor High School, 19--.

Substitute, University of Michigan Baseball Team, 19--.

Organized two canoe trips and three backpacking trips in
Upper Peninsula for University of Michigan Wilderness
Society during two-year period. Handled supplies, finances,
and transportation.

Senior Life Guard certification. Worked at Packard Pool as
lifeguard, May-August 19--.

Related hobbies: golf, tennis, painting, crafts.

Education

Ann Arbor High School, 19-- - 19--.

Completed sophomore year, University of Michigan.
Major: Physical Education-Recreation. Courses include
Fundamentals of Camping, Recreation Planning.

Work Experience

Have held various jobs cutting lawns, working at a gas
station, and shoveling driveways.

Personal Information

Born: May 4, 19--   Health: Excellent
Height: 5' 11"   Weight: 175

References wil be furnished upon request.

Attractiveness counts. The appearance of your résumé is important. Fuss with it to develop the most appealing layout for your credentials. Actually, the résumé is an advertisement for you and, like an advertisement, it should have a lot of white space, wide margins, and attractive headings. Naturally, it should be prepared on good quality 8½″ × 11″ bond paper, typed impeccably (pay to have it done if you can't type well), and proofread meticulously to avoid any misspelling or other blemish.

A counselor or experienced person at a typing service can help by evaluating your résumé, but you should not feel compelled to pay the large fees of a résumé service—the ample instructions in this chapter and, if you desire, in other sources,[1] should suffice. You are certainly now capable of writing an inviting one-page résumé, which is the standard length unless you have had unusual work experience.

THE LETTER OF APPLICATION

When you go job-hunting in person, bring your résumé with you (see figure 7–5); when you apply by mail, send it along with a letter of application. With the letter and résumé, you can apply for jobs all over the country, answer ads in newspapers and other periodicals, and search for better jobs in future years. Your application can go wherever the mailman travels, carried through rain or hail or sleet or snow

Figure 7–5.   A Résumé Request.

"So you want to get into lemonade, huh? Could I take a look at your resume?"

(SOURCE: From *The Wall Street Journal*, Permission—Cartoon Features Syndicate.)

from your desk to an employer's. And all for little more than the price of a stamp!

Think of the résumé as a summary of what you have done, and the application letter as a statement of what you can do. Like a sales letter, it should sell a product—you. And like a sales letter, it should follow the *ICA* (Interest, Convince, Activate) formula. But unlike some sales letters, it should be individually typed, addressed to a specific person (the president, general manager, or personnel director, for example), whose name you should find out, and usually limited to one page. Naturally it should be perfectly typed on attractive 8½″ × 11″ bond paper and be free of spelling errors.

Like résumés, application letters vary according to writers and their qualifications. The model in figure 7–6 presents a sound four-paragraph approach. Here is another, following the ICA formula.

Interest

The first sentence in the application letter is tricky to write. It should be strong, so your letter will stand out from others. But, unless you are applying to a hard-sell company or for a creative position in advertising or some other field, it should not be so explosive that it might damage your chances. Best to play it safe. Here are some techniques to help you:

Name-Dropping
"Professor Starr of our Economics Department suggested that I might be particularly qualified for a position in marketing with your company because of my research with him on pricing policies."
(Whenever you can name-drop, do so at the outset. Get your foot in the door immediately.)

Question
"Are you interested in a recent college graduate with more than the qualifications for the dietitian's position described in the April 17 *Herald*?"
(Of course, you must document the additional qualifications in the body of the letter.)

Summary
"Because of my two summer positions with a local bank, my degree in economics with five courses in banking and finance, and my fluent command of French, I believe that I could be of value to your International Banking Division."
(Note that this letter is being sent "cold," the writer neither responding to an ad nor being referred by someone.)

New Development
"The new Federated Department Store in the Gateway Shopping Center will do well because the growing population in that area needs a progressive, efficient store that carries quality merchandise. In view of my part-time sales positions in several similar stores and my degree in marketing, I feel that I could contribute as an assistant buyer to Federated's success when it opens in September."
(This letter is prompted by the announcement about construction of a new store.)

Figure 7–6. Guidelines for Application Letter.

```
                    221 Poplar Street
                    Missoula, Montana  59801
                    September 18, 19--


                    Mr. John P. Johnson, Vice President
                    Ajax Accounting Company
                    555 Tamarack Drive
                    Billings, Montana  59801

                    Dear Mr. Johnson:

                    First Paragraph.  In your initial paragraph, state the reason for the
                    letter, the specific position or type of work for which you are apply-
                    ing and indicate from which resource (placement center, news media,
                    friend, employment service) you learned of the opening.

                    Second Paragraph.  Indicate why you are interested in the position, the
                    company, its products or services--above all, what you can do for the
                    employer.  If you are a recent graduate, explain how your academic back-
                    ground makes you a qualified candidate for the position.  If you had
                    some practical work experience, point out the specific achievements or
                    unique qualifications.  Try not to repeat the same information the
                    reader will find in the resume.

                    Third Paragraph.  Refer the reader to the enclosed resume or application
                    blank which summarizes your qualifications, training, experiences, or
                    whatever media you may be utilizing to present yourself.

                    Final Paragraph.  In the closing paragraph, indicate your desire for a
                    personal interview and your flexibility as to the time and place.  Re-
                    peat your phone number in the letter and offer any assistance to help
                    in a speedy response.  Finally, close your letter with a statement or
                    question which will encourage a response.  For example, state that you
                    will be in the city where the company is located on a certain date and
                    would like to set up an interview.  Or, state that you will call on a
                    certain date to set up an interview.  Or, ask if the company will be re-
                    cruiting in your area, or if it desires additional information or references.

                    Sincerely yours,

                    Thomas L. Smith
```

"Many businessmen today claim college graduates can't spell and can't write. If you're interested in someone who can do both, as my grades in several writing courses show, then I would appreciate being considered for a position in your public information department."

Convince

After you have attracted interest in the opening paragraph, which usually consists of only a sentence or two, you need to convince the reader of your qualifications by using one or several of the following techniques: stating your qualifications for the job, showing your knowledge of the organization, explaining your interest in working for it, and offering proof of your skills and abilities. Among these statements should be a reference to your enclosed résumé. Realize that the application letter highlights items detailed in the résumé just as the sales letter mentions items described in an enclosed brochure. The sample application letters (see figures 7–7 and 7–8) illustrate how this information can be provided.

Activate

Following the body of the letter (one to three paragraphs), the final section should activate the reader to grant you an interview or to communicate with you about the possibility of one. That is, after all, your purpose—few jobs are offered without an interview. So you should conclude with a request for a meeting, usually one you will phone to arrange, instead of leaving it for the employer to ignore or forget:

```
May I meet with you to indicate specifically how I could
help your company? I'll phone on Wednesday to arrange a
time convenient for you.

I am eager to discuss my ideas about cash and profit fore-
casting with you. Therefore, I shall phone Thursday morn-
ing to determine when we might meet.
```

Writing to someone at a distance indicates that you are willing to travel at your own or the employer's expense. While there is no guarantee of a job, few employers would ask you to incur substantial expenses unless they were seriously interested in you. Here is how you might handle the long-distance situation:

```
If my experience, education, or skills interest you, Mr.
Davis, please write or phone me collect at 202–555–6364.

I am thinking about making a trip west in May. If you are
interested in my qualifications, I would like to meet with
you. In a few days, I shall phone to discuss this
possibility.
```

```
I would like to talk to any of your recruiters or repre-
sentatives about my other ideas and accomplishments. If
one plans to be in the Washington—New York area, I would
appreciate a letter or a collect call to set up a meeting.
```

What is important in an application letter is that it sell you to readers. That's why we treat it like a sales letter. Anyone can write a letter applying for a job. But few people can write letters that interest employers and that motivate them to interview the writer.

To develop such a letter, you may have to go through five or ten drafts. Then you may have to type and retype the ones for mailing, or pay to have them done. And you will have to proofread each final application letter painstakingly to be absolutely positive that no errors—misspellings, typos, or missing or repeated words—eliminate you from consideration. Scary? Somewhat. But, as you know, your life may depend on it.

And your life may depend on your persistence in writing and sending out letters of application. Many will go unanswered; many will draw rejections, often perfunctory form letters. But remember that it takes only one to give you a crack at your dream job. Don't get discouraged. Don't give up. Do persist.

THE INTERVIEW

The purpose of the application letter and résumé is to obtain an interview; the purpose of the interview is to land a job.

Interviews vary greatly. They may be held in college placement offices, company headquarters, hotels, motels, restaurants, or airports. They may be conducted by experienced recruiters, inexperienced executives, groups of people, and even with several other candidates. They may last on campus from about fifteen minutes to about an hour; but off campus, they may take longer, particularly during visits to companies. Regardless of the type of interview, you should prepare for each carefully, no matter how uninterested you are—the job may turn out to be surprisingly attractive.

In preparing for an interview, you must be concerned with six stages: (1) advance planning; (2) same-day preparation; (3) opening procedures; (4) main interview procedures; (5) closing procedures; and (6) post-interview procedures.

Advance Planning

Before the day of the interview, you should prepare yourself: get your records ready, learn all you can about the company and the job, plan answers to standard interview questions, formulate your own questions—even practice for the interview if it's one of your first. Of course, after you've had numerous interviews, you need not spend as much time preparing as you initially do.

Even though you may have sent a résumé to a company, filled out its application forms, and forwarded other papers, you should have copies of all pertinent records in case the interviewer requests them. Plan, therefore, to bring such records as your

Figure 7–7.   Unsolicited Application Letter.

219 Morris Place
Sioux City, IA 51101
March 5, 19--

Mr. R. R. Braun. Director
Employment and Compensation
Maytag Company
Newton, IA 50208

Dear Mr. Braun:

Because of my major in Business Administration, my college
sale experience, and my enthusiasm about your products, I
believe that I could be valuable to you in your Marketing
Division.

This May I will graduate from the University of Iowa, where
I took numerous courses in marketing, management, and
accounting, in addition to a minor in psychology. During
the school year, I operated a magazine agency, which consisted
of advertising, selling, and processing subscriptions at special
rates to about 1,500 students, faculty, and organizations.
Details of my education, experience, and other matters are
presented in the enclosed resume.

I am particularly interested in working for Maytag because
of the excellent reputation of its products, whose
exceptional quality is verified in Consumer Reports. I
believe that Maytag has an especially promising future
with its new line of energy-saving washing machines and
pilotless gas ranges.

Do you have any openings in marketing now? Can you send
me a job description or other information about them? And
would you please let me know how I may apply? I would
appreciate hearing from you.

Sincerely,

Wes I. House

Wes I. House

Figure 7–8. Solicited Application Letter.

3802 E. Lupine Avenue
Phoenix, AZ 85028
March 3, 19--

Director, College Relations Department
Corporate Personnel
D. M. Hurst, Inc.
151 West 34 Street
New York, NY 10001

Dear Director:

I believe that I am exceptionally well qualified for the entry-level position of assistant department manager that you describe in the College Placement Annual 19--. The degree that I will receive from the University of Arizona on May 8 represents four years of preparation for just such a position in women's apparel.

The courses I have taken in merchandising, textiles, and clothing design, plus my work experience as assistant manager of a woman's specialty shop, have given me valuable knowledge about business management and clothes. I have also studied textiles and design in San Francisco as part of my coursework. The training that I received in fabric selection during that period has been a great asset to my understanding of the clothing field.

The enclosed resume contains details of my coursework and work experience. If you wish, I will be glad to furnish references to provide information about my reliability and skill as student, worker, and leader.

I would like to work in your San Francisco store and would be glad to travel there for an interview. Will you please inform me if one can be arranged?

Sincerely,

Ann Butte

Enclosure

résumé, academic transcript, list of references (if not on the résumé), and any samples of your work (drawings, published articles, photographs, seminar papers, etc.). You should carry these in an attaché case, briefcase, portfolio, or large pocketbook.

In addition to obtaining these records, you should research the industry, the organization, the job, and even the interviewer, if possible. One of the most effective ways of impressing interviewers is by showing them that you know about conditions in their industry and about their organization, its plans, projects, and problems. This knowledge indicates your interest, your business-like approach to finding a job, your intelligence, and your maturity. In addition, you flatter interviewers, suggesting the importance of their organizations. As a result, you will at least be one-up on those competitors who have done no research and who ask self-revealing questions like "What products does your company make?" "Where is it located?"

Information about these and such other matters as size, sales, subsidiaries, profits, history, organization, recent developments, competitors, and growth potential of national corporations can be obtained from the following sources:

- *Annual Reports* (Probably the best source of information about large companies, annual reports may be available in libraries or stockbrokers' offices, or may be obtained by writing the company.)
- *Business Periodicals Index* (An index to articles appearing in over 170 business periodicals. Check company and industry, e.g., Anheuser-Busch and brewery or beer.)
- *Dun and Bradstreet* (Numerous books published by Dun and Bradstreet should be helpful in providing factual information and biographical information. Check its *Reference Book of Corporate Management, Million Dollar Directory*, and *Middle Market Directory*.)
- *Everybody's Business* (Subtitled "The irreverent guide to corporate America," this almanac is delightfully entertaining and highly informative.)
- *Fortune Magazine*, May and June issues (The May issue lists the first 500 and the June issue the next 500 largest corporations according to sales. Other data is included.)
- *Forbes Magazine*, May 15 issue (It also lists the largest corporations.)
- *Moody's* (This investor service publishes several bound and loose-leaf volumes that provide helpful information. See *Moody's Advisory Reports, Moody's Investors Advisory Service*, and *Moody's Stock Survey*.)
- *New York Times Index* (This index may provide valuable recent information about a *Times* newspaper story concerning a company.)
- *Standard and Poor's* (Like *Moody's*, this investor service publishes numerous materials about companies for investors. See its *Industry Surveys* and *Listed Stock Reports*.)
- *Value Line Investment Survey* (This investor service provides information similar to that in *Moody's* and *Standard and Poor's*, but it sometimes discusses future prospects to a greater extent.)
- *Wall Street Journal Index* (This index lists summaries and stories about companies reported on in the *Journal*. This is an excellent source for recent information.)

For small local or regional organizations, play detective. Talk to attorneys, accountants, reporters, competitors, suppliers, chamber of commerce and community officials, and ask them for information or for leads.

You should also learn as much as possible about the job you are seeking—especially the responsibilities entailed and the salary expected. The *DOT* or *Occupational Outlook Handbook* will be helpful. Also try to find out from such sources as David Harrop's *Paychecks: Who Makes What?*, John W. Wright's *American Almanac of Jobs and Salaries*, or from placement officials or government printed sources what the standard salary ranges are for your position.

If possible, you should try to get a line on interviewers by questioning placement officials or students who have already had interviews. Off campus, chatting with the secretary might be helpful. If you can establish some mutual interest, such as in skiing or backpacking, the interview may go easier and your chances may be better.

In addition to assembling your own records and researching the job, the company, and the interviewer, you should consider how you would answer certain standard questions and formulate some of your own.

The following are some typical interview questions you may be asked:

Company and Job
Why do you want to work for us?
Why should we employ you?
Why are you interested in this work?
How would you describe the ideal job for you?
What do you want to be doing five years from now? Why?

Education
How did you happen to go to college?
Why did you choose this college and how do you feel about it?
What caused you to choose your major?
What subjects did you like the best? The least?
What school activities did you participate in? Why? Which did you enjoy the most? The least? What did you learn from them?
If you were starting college over again, what would you do differently?
What was your most rewarding college experience?

Personal
What sort of person are you?
What do you consider to be your greatest strengths? Weaknesses?
What personal accomplishments have been most rewarding to you?
What about yourself would you like to improve?
What have you done that shows initiative and willingness to work?
What do you like to do in your spare time?

Some additional questions and an interviewer's purpose in asking them are presented in figure 7–9, a section taken from a company's guide for its interviewers. From reading these questions and the ones presented here, you can realize the importance of planning answers, either in your mind or in writing, so you will not be startled into silence or stunned into stammering out a weak response.

Figure 7–9. Guidelines for Interviewers.

1. WHICH OF YOUR JOBS ON YOUR RÉSUMÉ (or in your current job, or most recent job) DID YOU LIKE BEST? WHY?

2. HOW DID YOU GET YOUR JOBS? (Your objective in asking this question is to determine whether he/she campaigned for them, got them through mommy or daddy, fell into it, or sought it as a goal. And look for whether he/she takes pride in the way he/she got the job. If he/she does, it's a plus. If not, it does not necessarily come out as a minus.)

3. WHY ARE YOU INTERESTED IN A POSITION WITH US? (You want to find out whether he/she is thorough enough to have learned something about us before he/she came.)

4. WHAT ARE YOUR PERSONAL PLANS FOR THE SHORT-RANGE FUTURE? LONG-RANGE FUTURE? (Don't elaborate unless he/she asks for it. See what he/she regards as short and long range. If he/she ASKS what you mean by short range, suggest that one to five years might be called short range, and three or more years might be called long range. Look for a person who has goals and a strong sense of direction.)

5. WHAT KIND OF POSITION WOULD YOU CHOOSE IF YOU HAD THE COMPLETE FREEDOM TO DO SO? (How compatible is that with the job he/she is applying for?)

6. EACH OF US HAS MAJOR ASSETS AND MAJOR LIABILITIES. WE TRY TO BUILD ON THE ASSETS, OF COURSE, SO WHAT DO YOU REGARD AS YOUR MAJOR ASSETS?

7. WHAT ARE YOUR HOBBIES?

8. WHAT WAS YOUR FATHER'S OR MOTHER'S OCCUPATION? (This is an interesting opportunity to watch for his/her reactions to an emotional question. Is he/she happy and proud to tell you about his/her dad, or mom, or reluctant to discuss it. Generally speaking, the more open he/she is in discussing it, the better.)

9. THANK APPLICANT FOR COMING IN FOR THE INTERVIEW AND. . . . HUSH. (Just stop talking, fiddle with your notes, look at the ceiling as if you are thinking, but be quiet for just a moment in a manner to indicate you are indeterminate about the applicant. The objectives: Test applicant's closing power and techniques, applicant's desire for the job, and willingness to commit himself/herself to being successful in it.)

(SOURCE: Reprinted by permission of the University of Kentucky Placement Office.)

In addition, you should formulate some of your own questions. They might include some of the following:

What duties does the job call for? What characteristics does it require?
What training and work can I expect during the first few years?

COMMUNICATING AND EMPLOYMENT

Were college graduates hired last year? What positions are they in now?

Does the company encourage professional growth by paying for membership in professional societies, participation in seminars, or enrollment in graduate courses?

Are there opportunities to change career goals or is someone locked into the track started on?

What plans does the company have in the next ten years?

You should also prepare a sales pitch for yourself, emphasizing three or four main selling points (see your self-inventory) that you want to introduce during every interview. For example, if you've done volunteer work helping senior citizens fill out their income tax forms, plan to mention it during the interview. Or, if you're good at organization, be prepared to tell how you arranged for some special event on campus. Be ready to blow your own horn, quietly but convincingly, and know what tune you want to play.

You can also prepare in advance for interviews by practicing. Trade off interviewer-interviewee roles with a classmate or ask an established business acquaintance to interview you. Or take the advice of Robert O. Snelling, head of Snelling and Snelling, Inc., Employment Services, who suggests going to "as many interviews as you can to broaden your experience in selling yourself. Try going to a second- or third-rate company for practice, before you go to your first choice."[2] Another helpful tip is to videotape a practice interview if your college has the equipment and you have the courage.

Finally, double-check the date, time, and place of the interview. Your best laid plans will go astray if you fail to arrive.

Same-Day Preparation

On the day of the interview, you should focus your attention on three matters: (1) your appearance; (2) punctuality; and (3) the interviewer's name.

You should dress attractively but conservatively—suit, white shirt and tie, tailored dress, or skirted suit—appearing neat and businesslike, much as you might dress if you got a management position with the organization. Strive to be well groomed: hair cut and combed, hands and fingernails clean, make-up minimal, and shoes brushed or polished. Take special care with your appearance—doing so will make you not only look good but feel confident.

After getting ready, plan to arrive for the interview about fifteen minutes ahead of time. If you arrive too early, you'll get nervous and apprehensive; too late, you'll make a bad impression. While you wait, review your records and your sales pitch.

If you did not learn the name of the interviewer previously, obtain it from a secretary or whoever else is available. If it's simple to pronounce, like George Bates, there's no problem. But if it's apt to be difficult, like Jill Goldstein (rhymes with *stein* of beer), find out how to say it correctly. Pronouncing an interviewer's name properly wins points for you; mispronouncing it may lose some.

Opening Procedures

Your initial contact with the interviewer is important because first impressions count heavily. One research study indicates that an interviewer reaches a final decision on the average of four minutes after the interview starts; another study increases the time to seventeen minutes.[3] Regardless, a significant impression influencing the decision is created. So relax as much as possible, greet the interviewer by name, and follow the interviewer's lead, shaking hands firmly if the gesture is made, and sitting down when invited. Wait for the conversation to begin and follow the subject of the opening remarks, matching small talk with small talk and pleasantries with pleasantries. Do not try to direct the conversation or interject your ideas until later.

In some ways, the opening minutes of an interview are similar to the first few rounds of a boxing match with each person trying to size up the other. Recognize this stage for what it is and try to relax as much as possible, finding a comfortable position in your chair and something to do with your hands. Don't smoke, chew gum, or fidget; do smile—it's your best face.

Main Interview Procedures

The interviewer will signal the end of the initial interview stage, usually by leading off with something like, "Tell me about yourself," or "What can you do for my company?" During your responses, you will be evaluated on your appearance, personality, ability to communicate orally, and other qualities as suggested by one company's rating scale (see table 7–1). As shown there, the interviewer is determining whether you are personable and presentable, whether you speak effectively, and whether you have certain qualities, such as poise, confidence, enthusiasm, vitality, maturity, intelligence, leadership ability, dedication, and humor.

In the ensuing conversation, project a positive image of yourself by being friendly, honest, and sincere. As much as possible, follow these suggestions:

1. Avoid harsh criticism of others, whether a previous employer or a professor. You may note a difference of ideas or values but angrily condemning others reveals a surly nature, a temper, and perhaps disloyalty. Speaking well of others makes a more favorable impression.
2. Be optimistic, cheerful, enthusiastic, and hopeful. Interviewers are not looking for doom-and-gloom people. They want employees who are realistic, but who bring new ideas, visions, and dreams into their organizations. To project this image, the career counselor of the Harvard Business School suggests sitting on the edge of your chair and leaning forward.[4]
3. Indicate that you get along well with people, if indeed you do. Mention your interest in others and enjoyment in working with them. Show you are well rounded, participating in sports, activities, organizations.
4. Strike a balance between talking too much and too little. Avoid single-word answers like "yes" or "no." If you are talking too much, ask a few of your previously prepared questions about what the job entails and what kind of person the company wants. If you are not talking enough, ask whether the interviewer would like to hear about your previous work or activities. Realize

TABLE 7–1. An Interviewer's Rating Chart

PERSONAL APPEARANCE	Poor appearance, careless, unkempt 10 20	No evidence of special care of dress or person 30 40	Generally neat and of good appearance 50 60	Evidently very careful of appearance 70 80	Immaculate in dress and person 90 100
PHYSICAL CHARACTER-ISTICS	Sluggish, sleepy 10 20	Lacks vitality; acts listless 30 40	Looks to be in good shape 50 60	Looks energetic and alert 70 80	Seems to be in excellent condition; especially energetic 90 100
VOICE	Unpleasant; irritating 10 20	Hard to hear; speaks indistinctly 30 40	Pleasant; good tone 50 60	Very clear; easy to understand 70 80	Unusually pleasing in quality, strength and clarity 90 100
POISE	Ill at ease; embarrassed 10 20	Somewhat ill at ease 30 40	Shows no unusual lack of poise 50 60	Apparently entirely at ease 70 80	Unusually self-possessed 90 100
ABILITY TO EXPRESS SELF	Confused; illogical 10 20	Somewhat scattered and involved 30 40	Gets ideas across fairly well 50 60	Logical, clear and convincing 70 80	Superior ability to express self 90 100
SELF CONFIDENCE	Timid, Hesitant 10 20	Cocksure, Overbearing 30 40	Reasonable assurance 50 60	Feels very sure of self without cockiness 70 80	Not only sure of self but inspires confidence in ability 90 100
EDUCATION	Lacks fundamental training for the job 10 20	Fair education for the job 30 40	Good educational background for the job 50 60	Good education; is improving it by further study 70 80	Exceptionally well educated for the job 90 100
INTELLIGENCE	Slow 10 20	Has little to offer; rather dull 30 40	Grasps things easily; is a good listener 50 60	Alert; asks intelligent questions 70 80	Exceptionally keen, alert and understanding 90 100
AMBITION	Ambitions not in line with job 10 20	Wants job but not thinking beyond it 30 40	Wants to work; wants to get ahead 50 60	Plenty of drive; has plans for getting ahead 70 80	Excellent motivation; unusually thorough plans for making progress 90 100
PERSONALITY	Not suitable for this job 10 20	Personality questionable for the job 30 40	Personality satisfactory for this job 50 60	Very desirable personality for the job 70 80	Outstanding personality for this job 90 100
	100 200	300 400	500 600	700 800	900 1000

Total Score: _____

(SOURCE: Reprinted by permission of the University of Kentucky Placement Office.)

that you are being evaluated not only as a speaker but also as a listener. So, at times, be all ears and no mouth.

5. If you have a valid reason for a low GPA, mention it. (Perhaps you worked for most of your expenses; or after adjusting in your sophomore year, your grades improved significantly.) If you have no valid excuses, the less said about your grades the better. Instead, stress your willingness to work hard and your determination to succeed.

6. If salary has not been mentioned, you may ask about it near the end of the main interview. While you will usually be offered the going salary, which you should have researched beforehand, realize that more important to you are your future opportunities with the organization—questions about these will make you appear more farsighted to the interviewer. As mentioned previously, you should find out what last year's college graduates are doing now, what challenges they have had, what promotions await them. Some counselors advise ignoring salary until you are offered a job; all agree you might be downgraded for emphasizing salary too much. Interviewers are seeking people who want to work for the challenge, satisfaction, fulfillment, and achievement they get from a job and for the future potential it has for them. Those applicants overly interested in salaries and fringe benefits are apt to be too self-centered, concerned mainly with their own welfare rather than the company's.

7. Realize also that you are being evaluated not only on your statements but on your nonverbal communication. Sometimes what is said is given less weight than what is not said. Good interview communication techniques call for a lively voice, upright posture, steady eye contact, and the avoidance of slang, nervous habits, and vocalized pauses ("uh's," "ah's"). Practice sitting up straight, looking alert and interested, using gestures, smiles, and some body movements, and searching the interviewer's face for clues (interested? bored? displeased?). Remember the discussion of body language, watch for cues, and be aware of signals you are transmitting.

Closing Procedures

At some point, you will sense that the interview is drawing to a close. The interviewer may simply stand up, ask if you have any final questions, or signal the end in some other way. At this point, your objective is fourfold:

1. To summarize how you can serve the company well
2. To express appreciation for the interviewer's time and consideration
3. To indicate interest in the position
4. To find out when you will hear further

For this parting, you might even want to prepare or memorize a few sentences.

Of course, you may be offered or turned down for the job on the spot. If the latter, try politely to learn the reason for your rejection and, if appropriate, ask for information about possible job leads with other organizations. If you are offered the

COMMUNICATING AND EMPLOYMENT

job and so wish, you may ask for time to consider. Explain that you are impressed with the company, but that you would like to reflect on the offer for a while because of the importance of your decision. If you have other key interviews or are awaiting word about other attractive positions, mention this fact. Because employers want you to be fully committed to their organization, few will pressure you into an acceptance. But they will expect to hear from you shortly because they cannot keep positions open for long.

Normally, you will be neither hired nor turned down at the end of the interview. If the company is interested in you, it will want to consider you further and will notify you accordingly. Under any circumstance, you should ask when you can expect to hear about the job.

Post-Interview Procedures

After the interview, write a summary of it as soon as possible. Include all the facts: date, time, and place of the interview, name of the interviewer, salary mentioned, and important statements. Jot down any personal interests or concerns of the interviewer in case you meet again. Also, evaluate the interview, indicating how well or poorly it went, the reasons for this judgment, and ways you could improve in future interviews. Finally, note what you said that seemed favorably received and what seemed unfavorably received.

This summary should help you not only in any further relationships with the interviewer or company but also in your other interviews. For additional help with interviews, consult some books on the subject.[5]

POST-INTERVIEW LETTERS

Depending on what occurs during the interview, you may want to write letters of appreciation, inquiry, acceptance, postponement, or refusal. Although some career counselors feel that appreciation letters are unnecessary, we think they are important.

Letter of Appreciation

This letter is a courteous follow-up effort on your part, thanking the interviewer and acting as a reminder of your interest and qualifications. For example:

> Thank you for the interesting meeting we had last Monday in Alumni Hall. I enjoyed talking to you and learning more about Bankamerica's operations, particularly how it achieves its above-average loan loss record.
>
> After considering what you said about the opportunities available at Bankamerica, I am more interested than ever in working for this leading money center bank. And as I mentioned to you, I believe that my summer experience with our local bank and my concentration in banking and fi-

nance, along with my extracurricular activities as treasurer of two organizations, would all qualify me for your training program.

Since the weather was perfect, you should have enjoyed your long weekend of skiing. I look forward to hearing from you and hope you will have favorable news for me.

Letter of Inquiry

It is frustrating not to hear from a prospective employer when expected. If you have not been notified several days after the promised time or if you have waited a decent interval for an answer to an unsolicited application letter, you may write to inquire. In doing so, state the status and history of your application and explain why you want to hear about your chances. Close with an appreciative note. In general, be firm but diplomatic, hiding any annoyance, such as the following writer does:

I would appreciate hearing from you about my application for a position in market research.

After my interview with Mr. Lawrence Bean, your recruiter, on April 10, he said that you would notify me by May 1. Although it is almost a week after that date, I have not received word.

I regret having to trouble you about my application, but I must make certain commitments by May 20. I would be grateful for any information before then about my employment opportunities with your company.

Letter of Acceptance

In a sense, the acceptance letter is not crucial because it does not matter how you reply; you still have the job. But you should write effectively to reinforce the favorable impression you have created. Normally, you should immediately accept the offer, express appreciation for it, ask any questions you may have, confirm or announce when you will begin, and end by looking forward to starting work. Here's an example:

I am delighted to accept your offer to become assistant purchasing agent for the Baker Company. And I appreciate the confidence you expressed about my ability to contribute to the growth of the firm.

The terms stated in your letter are fine. I do, however, have a question about whom to contact to help my wife find a job. Please let me know the name of this person so she can start her job search soon.

On April 6 we will be moving so that I can begin work on Monday, April 10. I look forward to meeting Mr. Bryant that morning and to working with him.

Please know that I appreciate the opportunity to join the Baker Company and that I shall do my best to demonstrate that your confidence in me is deserved.

Letter of Delay

You may be offered a job but want to delay accepting it because of the possibility of a better position. This is a delicate situation, but if you handle it reasonably and courteously, you should not suffer from requesting a postponement. The trick is to be appreciative, positive, and fair, as this example indicates:

Thank you for offering me the position of sales representative with the Kirsch Company. I appreciate your confidence in my ability to handle this outstanding line.

Although I am keenly interested in working as a sales representative for a leading national company such as Kirsch, I am anticipating a possible offer to become assistant sales manager for a smaller firm. Its president has assured me that I will hear within a week. At that time, I will phone you immediately.

If this arrangement is not satisfactory, please let me know.

Letter of Refusal

If you decide not to accept an offer, you should be courteous and honorable in letting the organization know immediately. In addition, you should try to leave a good impression because you might want to apply for a job there in the future. Here's a sample:

Thank you for offering me a position in the managerial training program of the Hyatt Hotels. I feel honored to have been selected.

Because Hilton International has made me an attractive offer, however, I have decided to accept it. You may recall that one of my interests is traveling.

Thank you again for your interest in me. I wish you success in your exciting expansion plans and hope that we will have the opportunity of meeting again soon.

TECHNIQUE

In writing application and employment-related letters, you should be particularly careful about your words, sentences, and style. While everything previously discussed about these matters certainly pertains to these communications, we will focus here on pronouns, parallelism, and the problem of the overused *I*.

WORDS: PROBLEMS WITH PRONOUNS

Pronouns, which are among the shortest, simplest, and most frequently used words in our language, can create problems unless used carefully. We would like to call your attention to three special situations: pronoun reference, pronoun case, and pronoun agreement.

Pronoun Reference

Pronouns are substitutes for nouns (the woman . . . *she*) and should clearly refer to them. But look what can happen when a writer is sloppy:

Reference unclear: Last summer I worked at the Atlanta airport. As a result of my experience, I decided to make this my career.
Problem: What does *this* refer to?
Improved: Last summer I worked at the Atlanta airport. As a result of my experience, I decided on a career in air freight.

The culprit here is the solitary *this* appearing somewhere in the sentence. When *this* appears alone, check to make certain that the reader will easily understand what it refers to. If not, add a noun. ~~This will be helpful~~. This addition will be helpful.
   Another troublemaker is *which*:

Reference unclear: One of my duties was preparing travel vouchers for the engineering department, which required a thorough knowledge of state travel regulations.
Problem: At first reading, *which* seems to refer to *the engineering department*. Actually, it should refer to *preparing travel vouchers*.
Improved: One of my duties for the engineering department was preparing travel vouchers, a job which required a thorough knowledge of state travel regulations.

The pronoun reference lesson is simple: whenever you use *which, he, she, it, they, them, who, whom,* or *this* by itself, be certain that the word it refers to is obvious.

Pronoun Case

Personal pronouns (those referring to persons) change form according to their role in a sentence. Note the following list:

COMMUNICATING AND EMPLOYMENT

As Subject	As Object	As Possessive
I	me	mine
he	him	his
she	her	hers
we	us	our
they	them	theirs
who	whom	whose
whoever	whomever	whosever

With the possible exception of the *who–whom* family and their *-ever* cousins, these pronouns are all friends of yours, presenting no problems in most sentences. But in three situations, you may have trouble:

1. *The double object*

> The manager left the purchasing to Mr. Pival and (I,me).

Because we usually talk about ourselves and what we're doing, we are inclined to use *I* in most instances except (1) directly after a verb (*He hired me*) or (2) directly after a preposition (*He gave it to me*). But the double object involves a slightly different situation: If you chose *I* in this sentence, or were uncertain, here's a simple trick: remove the other object (Mr. Pival), leaving:

> The manager left the purchasing to _____ (I,me).

Now there's no problem. Although this trick is simple, using it depends on your realization that you cannot rely on your ear. Instead, you must stop, remove the other object, and then make the obvious choice. If you go through this process, the double object construction will not bother you.

2. The *who/whom* problem

Frankly, the easiest way to decide between *who* or *whom* is to substitute *that*. For instance:

> I wrote recommendations for the employees (who,whom) the manager thought were most deserving.

In this and similar situations (as you probably already know), you can duck the problem by using *that*:

> I wrote recommendations for the employees that the manager thought were most deserving.

But sometimes you must take a stand:

> The company has not yet informed me (who,whom) I should see.

By analyzing (taking apart) the sentence, you should be able to see the relationship more clearly:

> The company has not yet informed me / (who,whom) I should see.

Now you can more easily realize that the verb *should see* has a subject (*I*) and acts on the object *whom*.

Once again, you must stop, look, and analyze the construction. Don't guess; don't play it by ear; do take the sentence apart.

3. The *-ing* problem

> I would appreciate (you, your) contacting me as soon as it is convenient.

What we're dealing with here is a somewhat rare species, an *-ing* verbal used as a noun, known to English teachers and a few others as a gerund. Usually, you are not troubled by this construction:

> *Your* informing me next week is fine.
> I could hear *his* loud dictating.

In both these sentences, you would have no difficulty in choosing the possessive form of the personal pronoun before the gerund. For the same reason you should use this form in the demonstration sentence: I would appreciate *your* contacting me as soon as is convenient. But if you would like to place special emphasis on the person performing the action, then you would not use the possessive:

> I would appreciate *you* contacting me.
> (Implied: I would appreciate it if *you* contacted me instead of someone else doing it.)

Unless you wish to convey this special meaning, you should use the possessive.

Pronoun Agreement

Pronouns should be single or plural to agree in number with the words they represent. One problem arises with certain pronouns, called *indefinite*, which generally take singular verbs. So they normally require singular pronouns. Each of these should agree with *its* antecedent. Here the singular *each* takes the singular *its* rather than the plural *their* often used in conversation. But this pronoun convention often results in relying on the sexist *he/his* or the awkward *he or she/his or her*:

> Everyone working in the department reported his sales to me.

To avoid offending anyone, change the subject from singular to plural:

> All employees in the department reported their sales to me.

COMMUNICATING AND EMPLOYMENT

Another pronoun agreement problem arises with collective nouns, those collecting or referring to groups of people in a singular form, such as *company*, *team*, *committee*, and *family:*

The company had not yet announced (its,their) decision.

Even though the company may consist of fifty or one hundred employees, the word itself is singular in the sentence (not *companies*), thereby requiring the singular *its*. Whenever you are troubled by this convention, change the collective noun:

The company officials had not yet announced their decision.

Remember that your writing will be more agreeable to employers and employees if your pronouns agree. Be particularly careful about the indefinites and the collectives.

Sentences: Parallelism

In writing a series of words or phrases, use similar constructions so you express yourself clearly and effectively. This practice is referred to as *parallelism*, probably because the identical elements can be diagrammed in parallel form:

I have operated a card sorter,	I enjoy skiing,
a console keyboard,	hiking,
and a speed printer.	and cooking.

A sentence with a series not expressed in parallel form should be revised if possible:

Unparallel: I supervised seven employees, purchased supplies, and was the person who paid the bills.

Parallel: I supervised seven employees, purchased supplies, and paid the bills.

Parallelism is also usually called for with such double conjunctions as *either/or*, *neither/nor*, and *not only/but also:*

Poor: I will either accept your offer or take the position offered by Imperial.

Improved: I will accept either your offer or Imperial's.

Basically, writing parallel constructions involves two steps. The first is *recognition*—realizing that you are using a series of words and phrases in an unparallel form. The second is *revision*—redoing these words and phrases so they appear in similar grammatical structures. ~~To do so is good writing~~. To do so is to write well.

STYLE: AVOIDING OVERUSE OF THE PRONOUN *I*

The main stylistic problem you may encounter in writing application and other employment letters involves the overuse of the first person *I*. Obviously, in writing about yourself, it is impossible to avoid using the first person. But one *I* leads easily to another, resulting, if you are not careful, in drowning readers, who may not only sink away but think you conceited. So be on your guard against *I*-itis, striking out unnecessary *I*'s, trying to substitute other words or phrases whenever possible, and particularly avoiding successive sentences starting with *I*.

Here, for example, is what a first draft might look like:

```
    In addition, I like the fact that your company works on
flex-time. I enjoyed working at the Greenville plant last
summer. I really liked the four-day, 40-hour workweek
because I could take long weekend trips. I followed a
schedule of working from Mondays through Thursdays. I
arrived at my station at 7 a.m. and I left at 5:30 p.m.,
and I had a half hour for lunch and two 10-minute coffee
breaks. I believe that this schedule resulted in increased
production, lower absenteeism, and higher morale.
```

Working to reduce the *I*'s, you might revise the passage this way:

```
    In addition, your company's flex-time schedule inter-
ests me. Working at the Greenville plant last summer was
enjoyable, especially because of the four-day, 40-hour
workweek that allowed for long weekend trips. On Mondays
through Thursdays, we worked from 7 a.m. to 5:30 p.m. with
half an hour off for lunch and two 10-minute coffee breaks.
This schedule seemed to result in increased production,
lower absenteeism, and higher morale.
```

This *I*-hunt resulted in eliminating all eight *I*'s and the monotony of the *I*'s at the beginning of five successive sentences. Not bad for about ten minutes' work. And what is good about eliminating the *I*'s is that the revised passage reads less awkwardly and more clearly. So eye the *I*'s in your writing and eliminate as many as you reasonably can.

SUMMARY

No matter where you apply for a job, you will probably have to submit a résumé. Your name, address, and telephone number, your career objective, your education, and your work experience should be provided here and, if space permits, personal data and references. Whenever the résumé is mailed, an application letter should accompany it. Like a sales letter, the application letter should follow the ICA (Interest, Convince, Activate) format, first catching the reader's attention, then convincing this person of your ability, and finally arranging for an interview.

You should prepare for the interview by planning for each of its six stages. Several days in advance, you should get your records ready, research the company, plan answers to standard questions, formulate some of your own, and even practice for the interview. On that day, you should concentrate on dressing and grooming yourself well, being on time, and learning the interviewer's name. During the opening stage of the interview, follow the interviewer's lead. Later, in the main stage, plan to assert yourself, to state your qualifications and to ask questions planned beforehand. The interviewer will signal the next stage, the close, which is a time for you to summarize your qualifications, express appreciation, indicate interest, and find out when you will be notified.

After the interview, you should jot down pertinent information about it and evaluate how you did, trying to find ways to improve. This summary may be valuable in future relationships with the interviewer or company, and the evaluation may be helpful in other interviews.

Also part of your post-interview activities may be the writing of letters of appreciation, inquiry, acceptance, delay, or refusal. In the writing of these as well as the application letter, you should be careful about your use of pronouns, seeing whether the nouns they refer to are obvious, checking whether their case conforms to their function in the sentence, and determining whether they agree in number with the words they represent.

And just as these three suggestions about pronouns are stated in similar sentence structures, so you too should use parallelism in your writing whenever expressing a series of words or phrases. This repetition is pleasing, economical, and effective; however, the repetition of the pronoun *I* in employment or other letters may be distracting. So you should be conscious of its possible overuse, and when appropriate, substitute other words or phrases for it.

EXERCISES

Discussion Questions

1. What is the purpose of a résumé? Explain its six main divisions. Why write the résumé before the application letter?
2. How is the application letter like a sales letter? Explain your answer first in terms of the writer and then the reader.
3. Why not learn all about a company from the interviewer?
4. Name six sources of information about large corporations.
5. What should you bring with you to an interview?
6. If you were an interviewer, what questions would you ask?
7. What does an interviewer look for in an interview?
8. In an interview, how should you handle the matter of salary? Your unfavorable opinion of a professor or employer?

9. Why should you take notes after an interview? What should you note?
10. If you're offered a job by one company but expect a better offer from another, what should you do?

In-Class Applications

1. Revise the following sentences to correct any pronoun problems:
   a. Our bank was part of the Federal Reserve System and their fractional reserve requirements were enforced.
   b. Among those attending were my professor, my friend, and me.
   c. Many letters are written every year by students requesting information from a company about an opening which they have listed in the *College Placement Annual*.
   d. I want to thank you for your assistance in helping me to find an excellent job for the summer. This is certainly appreciated by me.
   e. I like the plan that allows each trainee to work for about a month in one department and then write a report of their observations.
   f. It was him who agreed to see the placement official about the interview.
   g. The salesman submitted a report with each one of their orders.
   h. The interview which took place at the airport between Mr. Price and I was informative and enjoyable.
   i. Since everyone is looking for jobs in the *College Placement Annual*, they should realize how difficult it is to find one.
   j. I could not decide who to write to for further information.
   k. Management is supposed to use the parking lot reserved for them.
   l. The office members were not surprised at him resigning soon after the announcement was made.
   m. I will be glad to meet with whomever is in this area.
   n. The agreement was just between the interviewer and I.
   o. At the recommendation of Dr. Jacobson and I, the interview room was renovated.
   p. None of the applicants appears qualified to Tom and myself.

2. When possible, revise the following sentences by using parallel construction:
   a. We found that for boring and repetitive work, background music can effect an increase in productivity, result in a reduction of worker fatigue, and it can lower the rate of accidents.
   b. The biggest time waster of all is unorganized, unplanned, or inconsequential work.
   c. Titles of books and periodicals should be in italics or underlined when typed.
   d. The company is known for its prompt deliveries because it usually ships by express freight or its merchandise is sent via air freight.
   e. Some of the negative factors causing rejection of applicants during interviews were the absence of goals, the fact that they were not poised, and lacked tact.

3. Revise the following statement to reduce the *I*'s:

> In my sales work last summer, I learned several strategies. I found that if I asked for only ten minutes of a buyer's time on the first visit, I could get in to see people whom I would have been turned down by otherwise. I then asked the buyer several short questions and I listened carefully to the answers because I had learned that others would rather talk. Formerly, I had turned buyers off by starting with a sales presentation. I also realized that I might not make a sale in my first visit, but that if I maintained contact with the buyer every month, I would make a sale soon. I succeeded partially because I made a point of presenting new and useful information each time. I think that I could use these techniques effectively in the work that I would like to do for your company.

Writing Assignments

1. Assume you will be graduating this semester. Write an application letter and résumé for one of the following:
   a. A job advertised in a local newspaper. Submit a copy of the ad or one you make up.
   b. A job opening listed in the College Placement Bureau. Submit a copy of the ad or one you make up.
   c. A company recommended to you by a professor, who has worked for it and suggests that you mention her name to Mr. Barker, the president. Make up the name and address of the company.
   d. A Dream City company whose address you obtained from a phone book.
   e. A company advertising for project engineers, district sales managers, and product managers in a half-page ad in the *Wall Street Journal*. It needs these people because of its highly successful division, which is expanding. Make up the name and address of the company.
2. Write an application letter and résumé for an out-of-town job you would like to have this summer. Assume one of the following situations and make up the details.
   a. The job has been advertised in your school newspaper.
   b. The job announcement was posted on a bulletin board.
   c. The job was advertised in a local newspaper.
   d. You heard about the job from a teacher, a friend, or a family friend, who has suggested that you mention his name.
3. Assume that you are graduating this semester. Write an application letter and résumé for one of the following ads in your local newspaper.
   a. Finance Management Careers. We are interested in career-minded, hard-working, ambitious college graduates to train for management positions in our branch offices. Applicants must have previous business experience and enjoy working with people. Please reply to Box 264, city.
   b. Marketing position with national corporation in your city. Need bright, mature person with ability to write and speak well. Must be college graduate with

some courses in business. Will train. Above-average starting income, rapid advancement, and job security. Send résumé to Box 1250.

c. Field Representative. Major California wine company. Preferred qualifications: degree, some selling experience, car, willingness to travel in your state. Must be personable, self-motivated. Base salary plus bonus and profit-sharing. Regional Recruiter, 1000 E. Avon Ave., Evanston, IL 60018.

d. Management Trainee. If you've got your sights on a career in retail management, it's worth your while to look into a career at Eco-Drug. We're the nation's largest and fastest growing retail drug chain, providing a top-notch, step-by-step, hands-on training program, and offering tremendous advancement possibilities to hard-working, conscientious people. If you are a college graduate, aggressive, intelligent, and personable, then apply to Bernie Kruchow, Eco-Drug Company, 400 Main Street, Johnston, PA 15901.

e. Accountant. Young, expanding corporation in the fast-food business is looking for sharp, career-minded recent graduates with bachelor's degrees in accounting. Will be responsible for financial analyses, budgeting, special projects, and review and refinement of monthly statements. If you demand a challenging career with the potential to advance, then Belks is the place for you. Write Donna Masters, Box 277, newspaper, city.

4. Assume you have read that a new company is going to open a large store in your community. You will not graduate for a year or two but would like to work there part-time during the school year and full-time in the summer to gain experience and to pay expenses. You also hope that this job will lead to a full-time position after graduation. Write to the company, making up the necessary details.

5. You have been interviewed for one of the positions described in the preceding four exercises. The interview went well and you were told that you would hear within a week. Although it is now twelve days later, you have not had word. Write a follow-up letter.

6. You have been offered one of the previously mentioned jobs. Write each of the following:

a. A letter accepting the position.

b. A letter declining the position.

c. A letter asking for a ten-day time extension because of a possible offer from another company.

d. A letter asking for additional information about benefits.

NOTES

[1] For an invaluable general aid in job-hunting containing excellent advice and numerous sample résumés, see David Gootnick, *Getting a Better Job* (New York: McGraw-Hill, 1978). More specialized are the following: Donald L. Warrington, *Guide to Effective Résumé Development* (New York: Metropolitan Life Insurance Co., 1978), which is available free of charge in many college placement offices; Adele Lewis, *How to Write Better Résumés* (Woodbury, N.Y.: Barron's Educational Series, Inc., 1977); Stephen D. Lewis, "Are You Teaching a Practical Up-to-Date Résumé," *ABCA Bulletin*, September 1977, pp. 15–17; and Tom Jackson, *The Perfect Résumé* (New York: Doubleday, 1981).

For a valuable survey of the preferences of chief personnel officers in the 500 largest corporations in the United States, see the article of that title by Barron Wells, Nelda Spinks, and Janice Hargrave in *The ABCA Bulletin*, June 1981, pp. 3–7.

[2] Quoted in "Career Questions: Answers From the Experts," *Ford's Insider: Continuing Series of College Newspaper Supplements*, 1980, p. 10.

[3] Both studies are mentioned by Helen Carl in "Nonverbal Communication During the Employment Interview," *The ABCA Bulletin*, December 1980, p. 18.

[4] Malcolm N. Carter, "A Sharpshooter's Guide to the Job Hunt," *Money*, June 1981, p. 46.

[5] For example, see Anthony H. Medley, *Sweaty Palms; The Neglected Art of Being Interviewed* (Belmont, Calif.: Lifetime Learning Publications, 1981); and David Gootnick, *Getting a Better Job* (New York: McGraw-Hill, 1978).

Part IV

COMMUNICATING BY MEMOS AND REPORTS

8 The Memo

OBJECTIVES

After reading this chapter, you should be able to:

- Explain the purposes of memos
- Know the guidelines for writing effective memo messages
- Itemize for clarity, emphasis, and easy reference
- Choose words that clarify your intention
- Construct tighter, stronger sentences
- Know six ways for achieving verbal economy

PLAN

Strategy
Purposes of Memos
   Internal Messages
   Quick Responses
   Company Politics
Memo Form
   Headings
   Special Parts
   The Message
   Itemizing
Technique
Words: Clarity
Sentences: Combining Overlapping
    Elements
Style: Economy
   Wordiness
   Six Tips for Verbal Dieting
Summary

Put it in writing.

TWENTIETH CENTURY
AMERICAN SAYING.

STRATEGY

Scratch a typical tycoon, a magnificent magnate, and below the surface you will probably find that he excels as a memo-writer. That is likely whether he is in business, government, or the military. It's a particularly American trait.

Memos fly through the business world and across the bureaucracies like driven snow. 'Yeh, sure, Fred, I'll be there at noon next Wednesday. But you'd better memo me about it.' Or, 'Right, Mr. Secretary. That is what we ought to do. And I'll see that you get a memo.' Or, 'Get this down straight, sergeant, and file a memo in triplicate.'[1]

This chapter deals first with the versatile and increasingly important form of communication referred to in the article quoted above—the *memorandum*, commonly called the *memo*.[2] Second, it discusses three writing techniques—choosing clear words, combining overlapping sentence elements, and eliminating wordiness—that are especially applicable in writing memos.

Memorandums (or *memoranda*) are simple, efficient means of communicating within a company, corporation, or other organization. They are simple because unlike business letters they usually omit the formality of expensive letterheads, inside addresses, salutations, complimentary closes, and signature blocks. They are efficient because their concise format enables writers to get to the point quickly and readers to comprehend easily.

Since nowadays virtually every American organization lives by the slogan "Put it in writing," countless employees use the memo form to send, read, and reply to in-house messages. As the work force grows, memos are used more and more every year in business, industry, and government. In fact, a recent study indicates that writers already spend more time writing memos than any other form of communication.[3]

Yet people often mistakenly assume that, because memos look simple and are primarily in-house communications, they do not require thoughtful preparation. Too often the consequence is a garbled message that baffles readers or an offensive tone that irritates them. Thus you should exercise as much care in writing memos as you would in writing letters or reports.

As memos are used more frequently, proficiency in writing them is increasingly a criterion for rewarding and promoting employees. Management is always on the lookout for people who express themselves well in writing: effective communicators are scarce and their skill is valuable. Your memos will enable others to evaluate your ideas, to obtain an insight into your personality, and to note your effectiveness. To write good memos is therefore to improve your chances for recognition and advancement.

Purposes of memos

Because memos are so versatile, they are used for a variety of purposes, sometimes even substituting for letters or reports.

Internal Messages

Memos transmit routine internal messages—announcements, requests, policy statements, confirmations, notices, reminders, suggestions, acknowledgments, congratulations, informal invitations (lunch, coffee break), thank-you's, and the like.

Memos are used to follow up telephone calls and key conversations with employees. They communicate news affecting decisions or actions, and they are frequently found clipped to articles or reports that are routed among colleagues.

The memo is increasingly the format for short in-house reports—preliminary reports, progress reports, recommendation reports, or evaluative reports. In such cases, the message of the memo may run to several pages and the conventions of formal reports (headings, visual aids, documentation, appendixes, etc.) may be used.

Quick Responses

Often the memo can be used to obtain a quick written response from an individual or a group. For example, an executive might send the following memo to a secretary:

> Please jot down below the names of the companies that have already entered bids for cleaning our buildings.
>
> 1. _____ 4. _____
> 2. _____ 5. _____
> 3. _____ 6. _____

The secretary would then make a copy of the reply before returning it.

Here's another example of using the memo form to elicit a quick response—this time in setting up a meeting with a number of people:

> We need to meet to discuss our increasing credit losses. Please indicate below your three top preferences (1, 2, 3) and return the form to me:
>
> Tuesday, October 26, 3–5   _____
> Wednesday, October 27, 1–3   _____
> Thursday, October 28, 10–12   _____
> Friday, October 29, 1–3   _____

Remember: the easier it is for others to reply, the sooner and the more likely you will hear from them.

Company Politics

Because memos are used by so many people for so many reasons and sent to so many recipients, they often serve ulterior purposes. One of these purposes is to protect the sender in case something goes wrong. For example, someone leaving on vacation might send the following message to her boss:

> During my two-week vacation, my duties will be covered by the following people:
>
> Joe Green: handling correspondence, phone calls
> Janet Black: checking page proofs
> Connie White: distributing promotional materials
> Linda Brown: distributing sales materials
>
> These individuals have also been notified by memo of their assignments.

Another kind of political purpose is exemplified by the "for the record" memo. Because comments at meetings are often forgotten, someone wishing to provide a basis for a later "I told you so" will write a memo like the following:

> Although I will work hard to see that the proposed new outlet store will be a success, I want you to know that I feel the additional capital expense and the time, trouble, and energy needed to make that operation successful are not worth it.
>
> I think we should continue to work through a jobber, but as you know, most of the others favored an outlet store.

If the outlet store is successful, the writer will say nothing, hoping the boss has forgotten the memo. But if the outlet store fails, there will be a copy of the memo on file to remind the boss if necessary of the writer's earlier misgivings.

Copies of memos have another political use. In the B.C. (Before Copier) days, the nuisance of using carbon paper (particularly in erasing errors) caused writers to send out as few copies as possible. But today when extra copies require only the pressing of a button, writers often send them to anyone interested in the subject—and to anyone else in a position of authority who might be favorably impressed with the writer. For example, a sales representative returning from a meeting where she displayed a new product might send a memo to her regional sales manager about its favorable reception and a copy to the national account supervisor.

More often than not, the promiscuous sending of copies can backfire: many business people complain about being "copied" to death and finding their in-baskets piled high with needless copies of memos.

Sending copies all over the place can create another problem. Usually a message is written to one person with that individual's personality and interest in mind. A copy sent to another person without thought about how that individual may react can have unforeseen results. For example:

> I've scheduled an afternoon meeting at 1:20 with Bill Taylor from our Chicago office. I realize this will shorten your tennis match, but it was the only time Bill could give us.

A copy sent to the marketing manager, primarily to inform her about the meeting, also inadvertently lets her know that your co-worker often returns from lunch later than the one o'clock deadline.

Memo form

Some companies use a three-page memo form with inserted carbons that can be obtained at most office supply stores. The message is typed on three copies: one for the writer's files and two for the recipient. The recipient replies in the space indicated, keeps the copy of the original message and the reply, and returns the third copy.

Figure 8–1.   Printed Memo Form With Check-off List of Actions.

Inter-Office Exchange   Date...................................

Memo to .... from ....

TAKE ACTION INDICATED
NOT LATER THAN

SUBJECT { ....
          ( ) SEE ATTACHED SHEETS

Return to me .... ( )
See me personally .... ( )
Need not be returned .... ( )
Being sent for your
  information .... ( )
Furnish data requested ... ( )
Take action indicated ..... ( )
Take up with .... ( )

Investigate and report to . ( )

Express your judgment ...( )
Set time when we may
  discuss this .... ( )
                        ( )

PUT IT IN WRITING Written messages save time, reduce errors and prevent interruptions

COMMUNICATING BY MEMOS AND REPORTS

This triple pagination may sound involved, but the copies are color coded and instructions are printed just as on Visa and Mastercard slips. These forms are used both within organizations and sometimes also for short external messages when a quick reply is needed. Usually, memo forms are simple (see figure 8–1), often not even containing the action suggestions on the left-hand side of our example.

If no memo form is provided, company letterhead stationery is sometimes used, although the expense may be staggering. Plain paper with "MEMORANDUM" typed near the top of the paper is far less expensive and, except in unusual circumstances, just as acceptable.

Although memos come in many sizes and shapes, they usually have three components: the memo heading, any necessary special parts, and the message. We will first explain the layout—the heading and special parts. Then we will discuss the message.

Headings

Memo headings may be printed or typed across the page in this form:

```
TO:                       DATE:
FROM:                     SUBJECT:
```

Or they may appear in this form:

```
TO:                       DATE:
FROM:
SUBJECT:
```

If the "date" entry is not printed on the form, the date should be typed either four spaces above the "to" or to its right, as shown in figure 8–2. All business communications, no matter how trivial, should be dated. The date is necessary for reference.

Since writing the date wholly in figures (9–11–19––) confuses many readers, the month should always be spelled out:

```
DATE: September 11, 19-- (conventional style)
DATE: 11 September 19-- (military or corporate style)
```

The military or corporate style has the advantage of omitting the comma, saving space, and separating the figures for the day and year.

The memo may be addressed by name to one or more individuals (in the latter case with the order of names determined by rank, importance, or—so as not to offend anyone—alphabetization):

```
TO: Ms. Etta Avent
    Mrs. Martha LaPierre
    Mr. P. James Powers
```

Figure 8–2. Memorandum.

Serendipity Company, Inc.

MEMORANDUM

TO: All Serendipity Company Personnel   July 21, 19--

FROM: Maurice P. Tietlebaum, Payroll Officer

SUBJECT: U.S. Savings Bonds Payroll Deduction Plan

We wish to remind you about participating in the Payroll Savings Plan for the purchase of U.S. Savings Bonds.

This program provides you with a convenient and proven method to save money, thereby investing in the future for yourself and your family.

Note the advantages of this form of savings:

• Your money is readily available when you need it.

• Your return is guaranteed.

• Your bonds are not subject to state or local income or personal property taxes until you redeem them.

You choose the amount you want to save and the size of the bond you want to buy. Then complete an authorization card at the Payroll Department, 1204 Rouse Building.

Once the card is completed and signed, your savings plan becomes automatic, taken care of for you by the Payroll Department through the convenient payroll-deduction method.

The Serendipity Company is pleased to offer this service as another way to assist you in obtaining financial security for yourself and your family.

/jrs

2011 SYLVAN AVENUE • KNOB NOSTER, MISSOURI 65336 • (816) 555–4846

Figure 8–3. Memo With No Subject Line.

MEMORANDUM   WAS

TO: All Staff

FROM: A. L. Harris

DATE: July 18, 19--

I am sure you've read in the paper about the state's substantial short-fall
in revenue and the plan to make that up by cutting as many nonessential
services as necessary to prevent the projected deficit.

Most state agencies will be deeply affected and WAS is no exception. We
will do everything possible to comply with the spirit of this mandate;
while each individual contribution may seem small, in the aggregate they
can be substantial.

Before I tell you what you can do, let me report to you that we may have
already "lost" 1.4 million dollars in capital equipment funds appropriated
to WAS for the biennium.

Here are some things we can all do to help:

1. Credit cards will be used for long-distance phone calls <u>only</u>
    when it is impossible to make the call on the office KATS system
    and it is essential that the call be made at all. Any credit
    card calls made after this date will be questioned.

2. The volume of long-distance calls will be reduced to an absolute
    minimum in both number and length. Even on the KATS system
    every long-distance call is charged to WAS.

3. All travel, in-state and out-of-state, will be reduced to an
    absolute minimum. Every out-of-state travel request will be
    questioned and far more than cursory justification will be
    required. In-state travel should be made as efficient as
    possible in terms of grouping visits.

I would appreciate any suggestions from any of you on how we might effect
substantial savings without reducing our fundamental services, at least
no more than absolutely necessary.

pab

The memo may also be addressed to a group:

TO: Children's Department Sales Staff

Except in informal messages, recipients' names are frequently preceded by courtesy or professional titles (Dr., Mrs., Mr., etc.).

The "from" line provides the name(s) of the person(s) sending the memo. Only if the writer is already known to the recipient is the writer's official title omitted. To personalize or authenticate a memo, writers frequently add their initials or their signatures after their typed names (see figure 8–3).

The "subject" (or *re*, for *regarding*) line helps the writer by limiting the memo to a single important subject, helps the reader by announcing the subject, and helps the file clerk by labeling the subject. The subject should be stated economically, carefully, and specifically. It should not merely describe the subject (a payroll deduction) but should inform the reader about the subject (a U.S. savings bond payroll deduction plan). Once in a while writers prefer to omit the subject line (as seen in figure 8–3).

Special Parts

When necessary, memos include one or more of these stenographic parts: reference initials, enclosure notation, copy notation, subsequent-page caption. These parts, which are discussed in Appendix A ("Letter Parts and Layout Style"), are listed in the order in which they should appear.

The Message

The announcement of your message in the "subject" line leads you to discuss it immediately. This quick introduction of the subject fosters economical coverage of the material and a natural tone.

Some writers are inclined to pad or are indecisive about what to say. So they write elaborate preambles to the main point or they approach the main point gradually, stalling while they formulate their ideas. But such long-winded introductions in memos exasperate readers.

The writer of the Megawatt Audio memo in figure 8–4 reviewed the background for the message even though doing so was unnecessary. The revision in figure 8–5 states the point quickly and then provides a brief explanation that helps readers to understand and remember the new policy. Otherwise, readers might not have the patience to reach the key last sentence or might be confused by the torrent of words.

Getting to the point quickly satisfies readers' curiosity. Keeping them in suspense may cause them to lose interest and toss a memo away before they read it completely.

Often the memo is used for short reports that must be carefully planned to enable readers to retrieve certain portions of the message quickly and conveniently. In such cases, it is helpful to organize the message under headings (discussed further in chapter 10) that label the major divisions and subdivisions.

Figure 8–4.   Long-Winded Introduction.

MEMORANDUM

To: Megawatt Audio Electronics Employees   **Date:** May 5, 19--

From: Fitzhugh Davis, Personnel Director

Subject: Procedures for Medical Care

In the past, Megawatt employees who needed medical care for on-the-job illnesses or injuries arising during the working day have gone in some cases to the Megawatt Infirmary and in other cases to the Pitt County Hospital. Under policies which have prevailed from time to time in the past, both of these procedures for securing medical care have been appropriate.

Due to the large increase in part-time personnel anticipated for the coming year and due to limitations in infirmary staff, it will not be possible for the infirmary to provide medical care for noncritical illnesses and injuries in the future. Therefore, when medical care is needed for illnesses or injuries that do not require immediate attention, you are requested henceforth to go directly to the hospital.

FD:br

Except in a few reports where formality is expected, whether the memo is personal or impersonal depends on the subject and on the relationship of the writer with the recipient or with others who may receive copies. It should always be interesting and, whenever possible, friendly and pleasant—the traits of the memo in figure 8–6. Naturally it cannot be as personal as a letter—the mechanical "to," "from," and "subject" lines alone prevent that—but it should convey the feeling that a human being has written it and not an automatic typewriter. Too many memos sound overly formal and unnatural.

Itemizing

A layout strategy often used for memos and reports is itemizing: the listing of important points for clarity, emphasis, and easy reference. By indenting phrases, sentences, and short paragraphs, and by labeling each item with a number, letter of the alphabet,

Figure 8–5.   Opening With the Main Idea.

MEMORANDUM

To: Megawatt Audio Electronics Employees   **Date:**   May 5, 19--

From: Fitzhugh Davis, Personnel Director

Subject: Revised Procedures for Securing Medical Care

Megawatt employees needing specialized medical care for on-the-job
illnesses or injuries should now go directly to the Megawatt Infirmary.

Those employees needing routine medical care for on-the-job illnesses
or injuries should now go directly to the Pitt County Hospital.

Because an anticipated increase of part-time employees will tax our
limited infirmary staff, we can treat only emergency cases.

FD:br

---

bullet (● an inked-in lower case *o*), or dash, you can represent each important point, stage, or step of a procedure on a different line, thus isolating it from the others.

Compare the following two presentations of the same subject:

Cleaning the Air Filter on Your Briggs & Stratton Lawn Mower Engine

Under normal conditions, clean the air filter and re-oil it every 25 hours. Under extremely dusty conditions, clean it every few hours. To service the filter, you should first remove the screw on top of the filter housing. Next, carefully remove the filter housing, preventing dirt from entering the carburetor. Then remove the foam element from its housing and clean it: do this by washing the element in kerosene or a liquid detergent and water to remove dirt. Dry the element completely by wrapping it in a cloth and squeezing it. Then soak the element with engine oil and remove any

Figure 8–6. Friendly Memorandum.

MEMORANDUM

TO: All Faculty   **DATE:**   April 15, 19--

FROM: Myrna-in-the-Main-Office   *Myrna*

SUBJECT: New Typewriter Policy

We have another new rule, folks, called "SIGN YOUR NAME
WHEN YOU TAKE A TYPEWRITER FROM THE MAIN OFFICE." There is a
sign-out sheet for this very purpose on the desk adjacent to
the mail room. Why? Because the typewriters have been disappearing for too many days at a time, sitting silently in
someone's locked, empty office while others are anxious to
use one. So let's have 'em brought back when you've finished.
Then one and all may type to their heart's desire.

As this memo is being distributed, I know not the where-
abouts of the following two typewriters: (1) manual Royal #2,
and (2) Royal electric. If you're still using it (them), come
in and sign your name. If not, bring it (them) hither! Thanks.

---

excess oil by squeezing the element. Finally, reassemble the housing with the filter inside and fasten the housing to the carburetor.

Cleaning the Air Filter on Your Briggs & Stratton Lawn Mower Engine

Under normal conditions, clean the air filter and re-oil it every 25 hours. Under extremely dusty conditions, clean it every few hours.

To service:
1. Remove the screw on top of the filter housing.
2. Carefully remove the air filter housing, being careful to prevent dirt from entering the carburetor.
3. Remove the foam element from its housing and clean it.
   a. Wash the element in kerosene or a liquid detergent and water to remove dirt.
   b. Dry the element completely by wrapping it in a cloth and squeezing it.

    c. Soak the element in engine oil and remove any excess oil by squeezing the element.

4. Reassemble the housing with the filter inside and fasten the housing to the carburetor.

(SOURCE: *Briggs & Stratton Operating and Maintenance Instructions: Models 92500 to 92598 and 92900 to 92998* [Milwaukee, Wisconsin: Briggs & Stratton Corp., n.d.], p. 3.)

The second version takes readers by the hand and leads them slowly and carefully through each stage of the procedure. It also ensures that they will perform each step in order, completing one before beginning another. Should they have any difficulty, they can easily find where they have gone astray. Naturally, readers may still err, but the writer has done everything possible to prevent them from doing so.

Itemizing is also helpful in writing complicated instructions, directions, or procedure manuals that must follow a precise time sequence, as seen in figure 8–5. Most college students are familiar with instructions arranged in series of neat steps like the following:

1. Pick up the registration forms at your dean's office.
2. Complete these forms.
3. At the time designated for you in the schedule, enter the Coliseum.
4. Turn your personal record form in at table 1.
5. Check the board to see whether all your courses and sections are still open. If not, rearrange your schedule.
6. Proceed to register for each class by going to the department tables located on the north and south concourses.
7. Turn your IBM cards and your schedule card in at table 5.
8. Before Tuesday, September 12, pay your tuition and other fees at the Administration Building.

Another familiar situation is the one in which certain specific information is required before some desired action can be accomplished. For example:

To obtain information about your magazine subscription, please let us know the following:

• Your name and address
• The name of the magazine
• The date you subscribed
• The amount of the enclosed check
• The name and location of the bank on which the check was drawn

In addition to providing clarity, itemizing helps emphasize ideas. Important points may be spotlighted, as they are in figures 8–2 and 8–3.

Note that numbers and letters imply order or rank. When neither order nor rank is intended, bullets or dashes may be more appropriate.

The disadvantage of itemizing is that it consumes a great deal of space. But by providing a list that readers can follow step by step, you significantly increase the

          COMMUNICATING BY MEMOS AND REPORTS

possibility of their acting exactly as desired. Furthermore, readers appreciate a clear presentation.

Like other attention-getting devices, indenting loses its effectiveness when overused. But if reserved for providing instructions or emphasizing important points, it can help the reader grasp ideas quickly and easily.

For that reason, remember that ideas can be presented visually as well as verbally. Your medium is the written word, but often words can be arranged in ways that will clarify complex data or ideas for your reader. Business writing generally, and memo writing particularly, can never be too clear. Whatever strategy you can employ to ease the burden of reading will improve your writing.

TECHNIQUE

Three traits of good business writing are especially desirable in memos: accurate word choice, able sentence construction, and concise expression of ideas. The remainder of this chapter will show you techniques for choosing clear and simple words, for composing effective sentences, and for expressing ideas concisely and economically.

Words: CLARITY

The success of memos and other forms of business communication depends greatly on whether their messages are clear. Choosing words with precise denotations and connotations, and using words that are concrete and specific will help you avoid fogginess—or, as a popular bumper sticker says it, "eschew obfuscation."

Obfuscation—confusion—results when words are used thoughtlessly, particularly in two typical memo situations: (1) the horizontal communication from one department to another in which technical terminology is used; and (2) the downward communication to all employees from a CEO (chief executive officer), or someone similar, in which the vocabulary level is too difficult for some readers.

Here's an illustration of how technical terminology (and sexist language) can be avoided:

> *Original:* Each member may designate one person as principal beneficiary and one person as contingent beneficiary. A member who does not wish to name a person may name his estate as beneficiary of the insurance policy.

> *Clarified:* You may select one person as your principal beneficiary, who will receive the money from the policy when you die. In addition, you should name a contingent beneficiary, who will receive the money if the principal beneficiary is not living. However, if you do not wish to name a person, you may indicate that the insurance should be paid to your estate. Then the money will be given to your heirs according to the instructions in your will.

Note that in the clarified version, technical terms (for example, *principal beneficiary, contingent beneficiary, estate*) are defined or explained so that readers will understand them.

The second confusing situation often occurs when executives are formulating policies for employees, as in the example:

> *Original:* The department seniority of an employee shall be computed from the day, month, and year of his being hired or transferred into a particular department, except when reinstated after a layoff for a lack of work for less than one year, in which case, the employee will receive credit for department seniority accrued prior to the layoff, and he will again start accruing seniority beginning with the date of his reinstatement.

Note that this message is not only difficult to follow but is also sexist:

> *Clearer, non-sexist revision:* The department seniority of employees shall be figured from the day when they are hired or transferred into a department. But if they are laid off for less than a year due to lack of work, this lay-off time will not count toward seniority.

Communication failures caused by thoughtlessness or poor word choice occur in numerous business situations. But if you keep in mind the communication model on page 25 and remember the importance of getting your message through so that it can be decoded accurately by the reader, you should not have too much difficulty in selecting clear words.

Sentences: Combining Overlapping Elements

Just as you can improve your choice of words, you can improve your sentences by combining short, overlapping elements.

Successive short sentences, often having or referring to the same subject or verb, result in wordy writing. When this occurs, you can usually combine the sentences by eliminating the repeated words and making some adjustments. Here's the situation:

> The tractor-trailer rig weighs ten tons. It has a life expectancy of a million miles. It is used for hauling hogsheads of bright leaf and burley tobacco. During its life the rig will haul much tobacco. It will haul enough to fill two or three tobacco warehouses.

Here's an X ray of these sentences:

> The tractor-trailer rig weighs. . . .
> It has. . . .
> It is used. . . .
> The rig will haul. . . .
> It will haul. . . .

Among the numerous ways of combining these sentences to write the passage more economically is the following:

> If it is operated for its full life expectancy of a million miles, the ten-ton tractor-trailer rig will haul enough hogsheads of bright leaf and burley tobacco to fill two or three tobacco warehouses. (Reduced 29 percent)

Let's look at some sentences with the same or a similar verb:

> Short-term interest rates may move higher. But long-term rates are expected to advance little. As for the stock market, it might move slightly lower.

After combining:

> Short-term interest rates may move higher, long-term rates little, and the stock market slightly lower. (Reduced 38 percent)

Another situation calling for sentence-combining occurs when the first words of a short sentence repeat the last words of the preceding one, as in this example:

> The physical therapist did not have the time to see the last private patient. The last private patient had broken her leg in a skiing accident.

The revision:

> The physical therapist did not have the time to see the last private patient, who had broken her leg in a skiing accident. (Reduced 15 percent)

Another way to combine sentences is to use a colon. This punctuation mark eliminates words by signaling readers that what follows will simply explain, amplify, or illustrate what has preceded. Usually the colon makes it possible to avoid the repetitious last-word/first-word sentence situation:

> The new manager introduced a stringent policy. This policy stipulates that buyers must obtain her signature on orders over $500.

Note how the colon eliminates the overlapping elements:

> The new manager introduced a stringent policy: buyers must obtain her signature on orders over $500. (Reduced 20 percent)

If sentence-combining changes a desired emphasis or provides too much information for a reader to digest easily, do not use this technique. But generally, it will not only reduce wordiness but produce tighter, stronger, and more effective sentences.

Style: economy

As we noted earlier in this book, good writing is economical; it avoids waste. Particularly in business and industry, where people have much to read and little time, prose should, in Mark Twain's words, have "a minimum of sound to a maximum of sense." On no account, however, should completeness, clarity, and courtesy be sacrificed for the sake of mere brevity. Your memo, letter, or report should state all that needs to be said. It should be easy to read and simple to understand. And it should convey its ideas with tact and with consideration for the reader's needs. But the communication should not include a single useless word, just as an assembly line should not contain a single useless operation. To write with economy is not to write little, but to waste little.

Wordiness

You may find economy difficult to achieve because of writing habits developed earlier in school. In class an instructor probably asked you to write a 350-word composition about your summer vacation, your best friend, or your ideas about democracy. That night you started to develop your padding skill; by now you probably are a master of the art. Self-taught, often unaware of your increasing proficiency, you have acquired techniques enabling you to crank out 750 or even 1,500 words with little effort, stopping only to tally your words. This approach to writing results in redundancies like the following:

> In discussing this subject, I plan to commence from the very beginning.

Or in using ten words when one—*today*—would do:

> In the modern contemporary world of this present-day age. . . .

The principle to keep in mind may be stated as follows:

> Omit any and all words for which you do not have any use.

No. What we really mean is:

> Omit useless words. (Reduced 69 percent)

The length of a memo, letter, report, or other communication is seldom specified. The busy reader wants only that it be as concise as possible. No matter where you work, you will be more appreciated and respected if you whittle down your writing to just what is necessary. To accomplish this objective, you must remove the fat from your communications.

But cutting your work to the bone is an arduous and painful task. You must take valuable time to organize your ideas and prune away irrelevancies before you begin your draft. Later, you must spend more precious time in revising the draft and eliminating excess words. Because these activities are tedious, padding not only survives but prevails.

Once you realize you are inclined to wordiness, you have already taken the first step toward writing economically. The next step is to view your written work as if it were the first draft of a costly telegram.

Obviously, you cannot use a telegraphic style, or your message might be neither complete nor courteous. And your message may not be clear; as George H. Douglas has pointed out, it may become "too compact, too stuffed full of hard and uninterpreted detail."[4] But certainly you can eliminate unnecessary words. And by saving words you will enrich your writing. Just as an obese person becomes more attractive by losing weight, so your papers will become more effective by losing words. But again remember: completeness, clarity, and courtesy should not be sacrificed to economy.

Six Tips for Verbal Dieting

The following half-dozen tips for verbal dieting suggest specific ways for you to fight wordiness in sentences.

1. REDUCE "WHO," "WHICH," AND "THAT" CLAUSES Many sentences containing adjectival clauses should be revised. Usually the streamlining may be achieved by eliminating *who*, *which*, and *that*. Sometimes the verb of the clause may disappear, too:

Salaries that are paid to representatives comprise 80 percent of the marketing budget.

Changed first to:

Salaries paid to representatives comprise 80 percent of the marketing budget. (Reduced 17 percent)

And finally to:

Representatives' salaries comprise 80 percent of the marketing budget. (Reduced 33 percent)

Sometimes the verb cannot be eliminated but its form may be changed:

The delay that was caused by the missing computer programs resulted in costs rising 3 percent.

Becomes:

The delay caused by the missing computer programs resulted in costs rising 3 percent. (Reduced 14 percent)

Occasionally the changed verb may replace the entire clause:

> Sign the form that is enclosed and return it.

Reduced to:

> Sign and return the enclosed form. (Reduced 33 percent)

In certain instances, the *who*, *which*, or *that* clause will require different treatment. Sometimes a preposition may replace the subject and verb, as in this example:

> An athlete who has had business experience can qualify for the position.

This may be cut to:

> An athlete with business experience can qualify for the position. (Reduced 17 percent)

Similarly, the entire clause may be replaced by an adjective:

> During the sales campaign, which is now in progress, she is working overtime.
> During the current sales campaign, she is working overtime. (Reduced 31 percent)

These ways of streamlining sentences with adjectival clauses need not be memorized. But you should examine carefully all such clauses to eliminate waste. In revising your papers, go on *which* hunts, and look out for *who* and *that*.

2. ELIMINATE INTRODUCTORY CONSTRUCTIONS ("IT IS," "THERE IS," "THERE ARE")
Introductory constructions generally indicate that writers have not carefully formulated what follows. Instead of getting to the point directly, they back up to it by leading off with *it* or *there* and adding some form of the verb *to be*. The remedy is to eliminate the introductory construction:

> There are many theories to explain stock market fluctuations.

Revised:

> Many theories explain stock market fluctuations. (Reduced 33 percent)

Frequently, the opening *it* may be removed by transforming the noun following it into a verb:

> It is the belief of most lawyers that confidence is an important attribute in the courtroom.

Reduced to:

> Most lawyers believe that confidence is an important attribute in the courtroom. (Reduced 26 percent)

Another way of treating the anticipatory subject *it* is to omit entirely the introductory phrase. Such formula openers as *it appears that, it may be stated that,* or *it is likely that* can either be eliminated or changed to *perhaps* or *probably.* Note how much more concise and direct the result is:

It appears that the company policy should be reevaluated.

Revised:

Company policy should probably be reevaluated. (Reduced 33 percent)

Expressions like *it is interesting, it is worthwhile,* or *it is my belief* may be avoided entirely. If your statement is interesting or worthwhile, let your readers conclude as much for themselves. Otherwise you may detract from its effectiveness just as the person prefacing a humorous anecdote with *I've-got-a-funny-story-to-tell* often spoils what follows.

Not all introductory constructions can be removed. Some are necessary for meaning; others help to avoid awkwardness. When they are used to express existence, they should remain:

There are thousands of industrial applications for plastics.

Eliminating *there are* would change the meaning by stressing the ingenuity of industry:

Industry has thousands of applications for plastics.

Some introductory constructions may be helpful in sentences. Among such phrases are *it is important that, it is clear that,* and *it is apparent that,* but even these should be carefully evaluated before being allowed to remain.

Without an introductory construction, the following sentence is awkward:

A long time elapsed before we received his offer to purchase.

But opening with *it was* eliminates the awkwardness:

It was a long time before we received his offer to purchase.

The introductory phrase "it was" is idiomatic and therefore sounds more conversational.

3. REMOVE UNNECESSARY PREPOSITIONS   Prepositions are pesky creatures that pop up everywhere in weak writing, like crabgrass in a thin lawn. The chief culprit is *of,* a seemingly innocuous word that has bloated sentences for years. Notice how it infiltrates simple statements:

The increase of enrollments in colleges of business is of national interest.

Eliminating the *of*'s tightens the sentence:

Increasing enrollment in business colleges is causing national interest. (Reduced 25 percent)

Further reduction can be achieved by cutting out the preposition *in:*

> Increasing business college enrollment is causing national interest. (Reduced 33 percent)

Other commonly overused prepositions are *on, by, to,* and *with.*

Prepositional phrases such as *in connection with, in regard to,* and *with reference to* are particularly deadly. These pompous expressions merely pad sentences. The single preposition *about* makes the sentence more concise and natural, as the following demonstrates:

> He was inquiring with reference to the desalination contract.

Revised:

> He was inquiring about the desalination contract. (Reduced 22 percent)

Some verbose prepositional phrases may be replaced with one-word substitutes, as the following list indicates:

Verbose	Better	Verbose	Better
concerning the matter of	about	in the event of	if
during the course of	during	in the majority	usually
for the purpose of	for, to	of instances	
in all cases	always	in view of	because (since)
in many cases	often	on the occasion of	when, on
in most cases	usually	with a view to	to
in order to	to	with the object of	to

Especially sly are members of the *fact* family: *in view of the fact that, notwithstanding the fact that, despite the fact that, due to the fact that,* and the monstrous *on account of the fact that.* Even such an experienced and skillful writer as E.B. White, in the preface to Strunk's excellent little book, *The Elements of Style,* states that he is batting only .500 on eliminating *the fact that.*[5]

4. CUT OUT DEADWOOD   In a sense, everything that can be eliminated from a sentence—without affecting its meaning—can be classified as deadwood. *Deadwood* as used here refers to empty adjectives and adverbs and also to redundancies. Spotting them is often difficult, but eliminating them is simple: just strike them out.

Our mania for unnecessary adjectives and adverbs stems in great part from the inflated language of advertising. A product will be labeled *the very best* instead of *the best;* its sales will be termed *highly satisfactory* instead of *satisfactory;* and its *future potential* will be characterized as *extremely promising* instead of *promising.* The unwillingness to allow a noun or adjective to stand on its own feet without some crutch adjective or adverb results in such sentences as this:

> Dwindling auto sales produced an unexpected emergency that threatened to create a very serious crisis in an extremely precarious economy.

COMMUNICATING BY MEMOS AND REPORTS

One wonders. Can an emergency be anything but *unexpected*? Can a crisis be anything but *serious*, no less *very serious*? Can *precarious* be intensified by *extremely*, or is the result weakened by the overstatement? Doesn't the following revision state the financial predicament as effectively?

> Dwindling auto sales produced an emergency that threatened to create a crisis in the precarious economy.

Wasting adjectives and adverbs also produces *doublets*. These tautological expressions have moved from religious use (*revered and respected, sin and wickedness*) and legal jargon (*cease and desist, give and convey*) to business writing. The following example shows the doublet disease:

> *Each and every* one of the directors is *anxious and eager* to provide *full and complete* information.

Notice how the deadwood makes the sentence sound insincere.

Redundancies that have become part of everyday speech are difficult to ferret out. Many fall into categories of time, color, number, shape, nature, and personal reference:

> **Time:** In this modern era of today . . .
> **Color:** The car was light blue in color.
> **Number:** The craftsmen in the plant total 29 in number.
> **Shape:** The parking area is oblong in shape.
> **Nature:** Most sales clerks are courteous by nature.
> **Personal:** The supervisor told me his personal ambition.

When people insist on adding needless prepositions to verbs containing prefixes, redundancies result. For example, someone should not *recall back, reduce down, return back, repeat again*, or *refer back*, but merely *recall, reduce, return, repeat*, or *refer*.

Many redundancies elude classification. However, to an alert mind searching diligently to trim overweight sentences, they should be apparent. Note the following sentences:

> Accounting students should not be interested *only* in their technical courses *alone*.

> The college placement director will provide any *possible* assistance *that he can offer*.

> The company offered fringe benefits *such as, for example,* life insurance, hospitalization, stock-option plan, *and so forth*.

Not all redundancies are useless, however. As with the back-up systems that prevent catastrophic breakdowns in manned space capsules, the judicious use of repetition in writing and speaking can sometimes prevent breakdowns in the communication process. For instance, in trying to direct auditors to the accountants' office in room 307, if the auditors were not aware that all rooms numbered 300 were on the third floor, you would prevent confusion by saying "The accountants are *on the third floor in room 307*." Consequently, you may use unnecessary words, but only when they are necessary to help your readers.

Useless redundancies in someone else's writing are often simple to spot; in your own, they are more difficult to detect.

5. SIMPLIFY SENTENCE STRUCTURE: REDUCE DEPENDENT CLAUSES TO PHRASES OR ADVERBS; AND PHRASES TO ADVERBS

Often sentences are needlessly complicated. Simplifying their structure avoids wordiness, eliminates sluggishness, and increases clarity. Dependent clauses in complex sentences can be reduced when they repeat the subject of the main clause:

Complex: While he was inspecting the factory, the fire marshall noticed an exposed wire.
Revised: While inspecting the factory, the fire marshall noticed an exposed wire. (Reduced 18 percent)

Complex: Because the salesman was uncertain of the price, he lost the order.
Revised: Uncertain of the price, the salesman lost the order. (Reduced 25 percent)

A dependent clause expressing purpose can be reduced to an infinitive phrase:

The steel contractor subcontracted part of the construction in order that the building would be completed by Christmas.

Revised:

The steel contractor subcontracted part of the construction to complete the building by Christmas. (Reduced 25 percent)

Occasionally, a dependent clause can be replaced with a single adverb:

As you realize is natural in these situations, production costs have increased since estimates were prepared.

Revised:

Naturally, production costs have increased since estimates were prepared. (Reduced 41 percent)

Prepositional phrases have been discussed already (tip 3) but should also be noted here. Frequently, a prepositional phrase can be replaced by an adverb or an adjective:

Complex: In a hurried manner, he signed the letters.
Revised: Hurriedly, he signed the letters. (Reduced 38 percent)

Complex: For a final point, let me mention the unfavorable balance of trade.
Revised: Finally, let me mention the unfavorable trade balance. (Reduced 33 percent)

In some cases, participial phrases can be replaced with an adjective:

Complex: He has satisfied the regulations set forth by the city.
Revised: He has satisfied city regulations.

Sometimes such a streamlined sentence will jar the reader by its brevity. If so, you may properly leave it wordy to preserve sentence rhythm or to attain the dignity and formality necessary in some contexts.

6. REPLACE *-ION* NOUNS   To a writer who aspires to sound like the chairman of the board, multisyllabic words—particularly those with suffixes such as *-ion*—convey status. To the reader, picturing the writer as a stuffed shirt, they convey pretentiousness. If only, to paraphrase Robert Burns, God had given us the gift to see our prose as others do.

Reading a paragraph clogged with polysyllabic *-ion* nouns is as difficult as driving a car over a road full of ruts. However, few writing blemishes are as easy to find and as simple to remove. The prescribed treatment calls for transforming (not "the transformation of") the *-ion* noun into a verb or verbal:

The committee took into consideration the adoption of the proposal.

Step 1: The committee considered the adoption of the proposal.

Step 2: The committee considered adopting the proposal. (Reduced 40 percent)

Naturally, *-ion* words cannot always be changed. But, whenever possible, replace these polysyllabic monstrosities with simpler, more familiar words. The following list provides some examples:

accusation/charge	commiseration/console
admonition/warning	illumination/light
altercation/dispute	remuneration/pay
imperfection/fault	termination/end
modification/change	perception/view

Other suffixes to avoid are *-ment* (*settlement* for *settle*); *-ance* (*encumbrance* for *encumber*); *-ity* (*conformity* for *conform*); *-ency* (*tendency* for *tend*). Yet none of these appears as frequently as (not "with the *frequency* of") *-ion*, or are as obvious.

SUMMARY

The memorandum is a simple, efficient format for communicating routine internal messages. It opens with a heading (*date, to, from, subject*) and includes any necessary special parts (reference initials, enclosure notation, copy notation, subsequent-page caption). Its message is characterized by a quick introduction, division headings (if appropriate), and a natural tone.

A useful strategy in writing memos is itemizing. Enumerating key points will emphasize them and thereby enable readers to remember them.

In memos and other business communications, taking pains to choose accurate, specific words will help you communicate with greater clarity and sophistication. By combining short, overlapping sentences, you will not only clarify your statements but also make your style more pleasant. By cutting out useless words and statements, you will eliminate waste while rendering your communications easy to read and simple to understand.

"Putting it in writing" causes many executives lots of grief. Mastering the format for memos and developing a knack for saying things emphatically, clearly, accurately, and economically will go a long way towards preventing such suffering.

EXERCISES

Discussion Questions

1. Why are more and more memos being written every year?
2. In what ways are memos different from letters?
3. For what purposes is a memo a suitable form of communication? An unsuitable form of communication?
4. Describe the writing style generally appropriate for the message of a memo.
5. Why do some executives send out unrevised first drafts of memos? What impressions do readers form of such communications?
6. Why are specific words clearer for readers than general ones? Cite examples of abstract words and their more concrete synonyms.
7. As a reader, do you prefer economical writing over wordiness? Discuss why.
8. Is it easy to be concise when you write? Why or why not?
9. What is the difference between being brief and being curt or abrupt?
10. Does brevity take precedence over everything else? Discuss.
11. Jonathan Swift once wrote to a friend that his letter would have been shorter if he had had more time. What did he mean?
12. Why is economical writing generally clearer than long-winded writing?

In-Class Applications

1. From your student government association, fraternity or sorority national headquarters, and other sources, collect several memos and analyze their handling of messages. Point out to your classmates any details you find to be handled especially well or especially poorly. How might the poor examples be improved?
2. Interview an executive in a large organization about the average number of memos he or she writes and receives per week. Prepare your findings for discussion in class.
3. Interview secretaries about the way they handle headings and special stenographic parts in memos. Since there are many different preferences for handling such details as capitalization and placement of items on the page, you will probably

COMMUNICATING BY MEMOS AND REPORTS

find secretaries following a number of typing and layout practices different from the ones explained in this chapter. Note these differences, explain them to your classmates, and lead a discussion about why you would prefer to handle certain details of a memo one way rather than another.

4. Eliminate the wordiness in the following sentences:
   a. Please feel free to call on me personally at any time at your convenience.
   b. Some of the letters merely answered the questions on the questionnaire and let it go at that.
   c. The real danger is that many of the engineers will be released as soon as the government contract expires.
   d. He was not aware of the actual facts in the labor dispute or the final outcome.
   e. As a general rule, the stories about business conventions are grossly exaggerated.
   f. Receiving the parts by Friday is an urgent necessity.
   g. In addition to having the important essentials required by the company, the Owensboro site had five definite advantages.
   h. After due consideration, the manager concluded that evidence of enthusiasm among his sales force was sadly lacking.
   i. Because the daily use of computers is increasing, business administration students are required to learn certain true facts about them.
   j. The economist did not foresee any real improvement of the unfavorable balance of trade for some considerable time.
   k. Among the harmful constituents of smog are benzpyrene, chlorides, arsenic, fluorides, nitrates, sulfates and many others.

5. Compose sentences with each containing a different example of one of the following, and then show how to eliminate the verbosity:

A *which* clause	A *time* redundancy
Unnecessary adverb	Two *of*'s
Two *-ion* words	A *fact* phrase
A *regard* phrase	A *who* clause

6. Condense the following passage by eliminating unnecessary words:

   Individuals who own or use gas appliances of any kind can now unplug them and move them around as easily as a man or woman can move an electrical appliance. The invention that has made it possible to enable gas appliances to be moved about in this fashion is a new "quick-disconnect" coupling. This coupling is designed to replace permanent fittings that are now in use. The coupling consists of a socket that is threaded into the gas pipe, and it also has a nipple that may be screwed on to the hose from a stove, a broiler, a dryer, or some other gas appliance that is similar. The insertion of the nipple in the socket causes the opening of a spring-loaded valve that in turn allows the gas to begin its flow to the appliance. The company manufacturing the coupler is of the opinion that the device will result in the development of new gas appliances, such as small, portable items like barbecues or deep-fat fryers, and other similar things, for the first time. The cost of this new coupling device will be approximately five dollars, or close to that price.

7. Rewrite each of the following sentences, eliminating the wordiness. Be certain to place the most important element in an independent clause:
   a. Students should have enough illumination for note-taking. Thirty foot-candles of illumination should be sufficient.

b. Inflationary pressures will continue for a long time. They may not get out of control but they will continue. Therefore, students planning their future should consider these pressures.

c. The fuel cell is like a battery; it is a simple device. It has two electrodes. These electrodes are separated by an electrolyte.

d. The name of our executive vice president in charge of research is Mr. James Eckstrom. Today and tomorrow he will be in St. Louis.

e. Often you can't get receipts for deductible expenses. The government expects you to have receipts for deductible expenses. However, the government will accept a daily record showing complete information about certain deductible expenses.

f. The most common form of letter received was the block form. There were exceptions but basically the block form was used by a majority of firms.

g. On August 1 my Toyota was serviced at your garage. It was greased and the oil was changed.

h. The field of engineering is a field with vast opportunities.

8. In each problem below, combine the sentences into one. Where applicable, use the italicized sentence as your main clause:

a. The box is tan. It was delivered by UPS. It was delivered to my office. *It contains three textbooks on business writing.*

b. The presidential candidate made four promises. He said he'd stem inflation. He said he'd help the poor, the elderly, and the unemployed. He vowed he'd provide aid for budget-troubled cities. And he promised he'd cut taxes.

c. The medics arrived. They came to the field by helicopter. The helicopter was battered and riddled with holes. They placed the wounded on stretchers. *Then they piled the stretchers in the helicopters and left.*

d. The Excalibur has classic lines. It is responsive. It operates economically, too.

e. Liqueurs are after-dinner drinks. They are often called cordials. Mild ones are around 60 proof, such as Triple Sec. Strong ones are around 100 proof, such as Chartreuse.

9. Try your hand at clarifying the wording of this whopper. Written by an economist for a Chicago company, the passage is used in seminars conducted by the Gunning-Mueller Clear Writing Institute of Santa Barbara, California, as an example of obfuscation:

> The unpredicted recovery of the Gross National Product in the fourth quarter of 19––, which actually overcompensated for losses suffered during the first and second quarters, has coalesced with transformations in fiscal policy implemented in the fall to have a momentous impact on the overall economic scenario for 19––, albeit the GNP figures for the year should nevertheless fall within the parameters of the earlier predictions of our longitudinal study.

Writing Assignments

1. As president of student government, you have organized a Student-Faculty Week during which students would be entertained by faculty members in their homes. Write a memorandum to the faculty requesting them to participate and to specify which evening they would like to have students visit their homes. Student gov-

ernment will provide all transportation and will make other arrangements, including the attempt to assign students according to their interest in the faculty member's academic field.

2. As the manager of a local company, you have just completed a course in business writing. Because you feel that the administrative and clerical personnel would benefit from the course, you have decided that your company will pay half the expense of books and tuition to everyone passing it. Write a memorandum announcing this plan and providing information about registering for an evening course that will be offered shortly.

3. As assistant principal of a large high school, you've been asked to deal with the problem caused by the unexcused absence late in the spring of growing numbers of seniors observing Skip Day. Because the school receives an allocation of $2 per student based upon the daily attendance as of 10 a.m., the absence of 500 seniors represents a serious financial loss. Devise a way of dealing with this problem and write a memorandum to be posted on bulletin boards.

4. As a student member of the Student Affairs Committee of the University Senate at your school, you have been concerned about student problems with vending machines on your campus. Dr. Alice Wing, the chairperson of the committee, has asked you to submit a list of specific student complaints so committee members can study the nature and extent of the problem:
   a. Write a memo to all members of Student Government asking them to submit a statement about specific complaints to you within 30 days. It should mention the type of machine (beverage, food, candy, etc.), along with its location, and the approximate time and date of the problem. Send a copy of the memo to Dr. Wing.
   b. Write a similar memo to student resident advisors in the dorms, asking them to provide you with the same information. Send a copy to Dr. Wing.
   c. Assume you have received the requested information about the vending machines. Send a memo to Dr. Wing, referring to the information on an attached page and urging prompt action by the committee. Send copies to the committee members: Dr. Tom Ecton, Dr. Otis Cooper, and Dr. Jean Wroebel.

5. You are chairperson of a student committee to select the best teacher in your college:
   a. Send a memo to other committee members, asking them to inform you when they can meet for two hours on Mondays, Wednesdays, or Fridays between 1 and 4 p.m.
   b. Send a memo to each, setting up a meeting on Wednesday, October 25, from 1 to 3 p.m. in University Hall. Ask them to prepare to discuss the procedure to be used in selecting a teacher.
   c. Your committee has narrowed down the candidates to three: Dr. Harry Daniel of Accounting, Dr. Harriet Jacobs of Economics, and Dr. William Adler of Business Administration. Write a memo to their respective chairpersons (Dr. Dan Hines of Accounting, Dr. Jay Raymond of Economics, and Dr. Harry Bryant of Business Administration), informing them about the selection of one of their department members and requesting a letter of evaluation and the results for the past five years of student evaluations of the faculty member.

The chairpersons must also obtain a waiver from each of these individuals to have the results made available to your committee. Be certain to state that all this information will be kept confidential.

    d. Send a memo to Dr. Carol Dunsway, President of the University, telling her that Dr. Harriet Jacobs has been named to be the recipient of the best teacher award this year. Express the desire to have President Dunsway attend Student Awards Night to present the award on Thursday, May 4, at 8 p.m. in room 215 of Mendenhall Student Center.

    e. Send a memo to all members of your committee, thanking them for working with you, reminding them to keep the name of the recipient confidential, and saying you look forward to seeing them at Student Awards Night.

6. The placement bureau has a problem because students fail to appear for scheduled interviews or because they cancel an appointment on the day of the interview— too late to set up interviews for other students on a stand-by list. During the past year, there were 189 no-shows and 409 late cancellations. In addition to being unfair to students on stand-by, students who fail to show or who cancel late create an adverse impression of the University. Some recruiters may decide not to return in future years. Others may be so irritated that they will not select any candidates.

    Consequently, Furney James, director of the placement service, has asked you to draft a memo to be sent to all faculty members. It should contain the reasons for a new Placement Service policy and the penalties for offenses. For a first no-show offense, students must see a professional staff member before another interview. For a second offense, the student will not be allowed another interview unless a request for reinstatement is received from the student's department chairperson. For late cancellation offenses, students will be asked to schedule an appointment with a professional staff person when they phone or appear to cancel their first interview. After a second cancellation, students will not be granted another interview until they obtain a request for reinstatement from their department chairperson.

    The memo should contain a request that all faculty members read it to their classes.

7. You are the chairperson of a committee to plan a conference to make students aware of the problems of handicapped students on campus. After finding that committee members can meet on Wednesday afternoons from 3 to 5, you decide to arrange a meeting to discuss the proposal that must be submitted for financial support:

    a. Write a memo to the other committee members, scheduling a meeting and asking them to be prepared to provide a title for the all-day conference, an outline of a program, a designation of a target audience, a budget, suggested speakers, and other ideas.

    b. As chairman you have phoned Dr. Mark Hunter of the Education College and Dr. Ruth Gorden of the Counseling Office to invite them to speak at the conference. Both have accepted. Write them a memo, confirming the phone call; stating the date, time, and place; and asking them to let you know the titles of their speeches, which should take a maximum of twenty minutes.

    c. Write a memo to your committee members, telling them that the proposal has been accepted and that the budget will be $2,000. Mention also that

Hunter and Gorden have agreed to speak. Schedule a meeting for next week to discuss promotion of the conference, arrangements for lunch, and invited guests.

d. The conference has been held and, according to questionnaires completed by the audience, it was successful. Write a memo to your committee, telling them about these results and thanking them for their work. Send a copy of the questionnaire results to Jim Baldree, president of Student Government, and Kim Anderson, director of your state's Humanities Council, each of whom was helpful in providing financial support for the conference. In an accompanying memo, thank them for their support.

8. As administrator of University Hospital, you wish to inform the staff about a new employee educational tuition reimbursement plan. According to its provisions, employees are eligible if they have worked full-time for at least one year and have satisfactory performance and attendance records. In addition, they must have completed thirty hours with at least a C average in related work programs at a college or technical school. To obtain the reimbursement, employees have to attend class on their own time, pass with a grade of at least C, and agree to work for at least one year at University Hospital after receiving the tuition reimbursement. If they terminate their employment earlier, they will be liable to pay a pro-rated amount of the reimbursement grant, which will be decided by the tuition reimbursement committee. Employees will be reimbursed for only one three-hour course a semester and must present evidence of their grade and payment for it. First, however, employees must file an application form available in room 2019, the office of Mr. William Grant, Associate Administrator and chairman of the tuition reimbursement committee. This committee will approve applications based on the criteria announced and the funds available. It will also be responsible for distribution of tuition reimbursements.

Write a memo to the 1,000 employees of the hospital, informing them of this new tuition reimbursement plan.

NOTES

[1] Don Shoemaker, "What This Country Needs Is More Memowriters," *The Lexington (Kentucky) Herald*, September 5, 1980, p. A-12.

[2] For a thorough analysis of memorandum format, see Jo Ann Hennington, "Memorandums—An Effective Communication Tool for Management," *The ABCA Bulletin*, 41 (September 1978), pp. 10–14. Much of the following discussion is based on this source.

[3] Martha H. Radar and Alan P. Wunsch, "A Survey of Communication Practices of Business School Graduates by Job Category and Undergraduate Major," *The Journal of Business Communication*, 17 (Summer 1980), p. 39.

[4] George H. Douglas, "What to Do About Cobblestone Writing," *The Technical Writing Teacher*, 5 (Fall 1977), pp. 18–21.

[5] William Strunk, Jr., and E. B. White, *The Elements of Style*, 2nd ed. (New York: Macmillan, 1972), p. x.

The Short Report

Objectives

After reading this chapter, you should be able to:

- Explain several meanings of the word *report*
- Identify the purposes and characteristics of reports
- Describe the applications and typical formats of letter reports, progress reports, periodic reports, information reports, analytical reports, recommendation reports, and instructions, directions, and procedure manuals
- Explain the various methods of gathering information for composing reports
- Explain how using first-person pronouns and topic sentences helps you communicate naturally and clearly
- Describe how readability testing improves reports

Plan

Strategy
Report Writing
   Report Functions
   Chief Characteristics of Reports
Short Report Types
   The Letter Report
   The Progress Report
   The Periodic Report
   Information and Analytical Reports
   The Recommendation Report
   Instructions, Directions,
      Procedure Manuals
Report Research
   Observation
   Experimentation
   Survey Research
Technique
Words: The First-Person Pronoun
Sentences: Topic Sentence
Style: Readability
Summary

The only relevant standard by which to judge any straightforward piece of prose is the ease with which it conveys its full intended sense to the readers to whom it is addressed. . . .

ROBERT GRAVES AND ALAN HODGE

STRATEGY

The importance of being able to write effective reports is underscored by the experience of one of our recent students. On graduating with a B.S. in Business Education, this young man took a lucrative job with a national advertising agency as a field representative on an import-car account. Although he was no expert in advertising and no veteran in dealing with people, his hard work and winning personality made his account work satisfactory. But the short weekly and the long quarterly reports he had to write to his national headquarters were excellent. In fact, they were so professional—and so much better than the reports of other field representatives—that in little more than a year he was invited to join the headquarters staff as account supervisor.

Today this young man is a highly paid vice president of the agency—and, we're happy to note, he says he owes his success mainly to being able to write outstanding reports.

Of course, report writing ability alone will not assure you of a meteoric career. But having the ability to write fine reports will certainly improve your chances for success.

REPORT WRITING

In business, the word *report* is used loosely for virtually any communication. It is used to refer to conversations ("I just heard a report from my officemate that the Pirates won."), to prepared speeches ("In her after-dinner talk, she gave a fascinating report on stock futures."), to memos ("I just received a *!#'.*# report from the manager canceling our Memorial Day holiday."), and to 500-page publications ("First-class postage on each copy of the company report will cost $3.50."). It is also used to refer to such nonhuman communications as computer printouts ("According to this ticker-tape report, I've hit the jackpot with the new mining stock.").

Furthermore, written reports can be classified in innumerable ways:

- by content: annual, credit, feasibility, laboratory, proposal reports
- by function: information, analytical, recommendation reports
- by printed forms: absence, accident, trip, petty cash reports

- by format: memo, letter, informal, formal reports
- by time: preliminary, progress, periodic, final reports
- by length: short, long reports

Reports can often be classified more than one way: a credit report might also be a short report or an informal report, or an annual report might also be a long report or a formal report.

Because of the slippery meaning of *report*, you should always find out what your instructors, employers, or colleagues mean when they use the word. (The context will probably make it clear when neither an oral communication nor a computer printout is intended.)

Specifically, if you are asked to prepare a report you will need to know whether what is meant is a two- or three-page informal message in memorandum format or a thirty-page formal report (the subject of chapter 10). Should it deviate from a common format, such as those described in textbooks, in order to conform to school or company policy? Should it appear on a printed form, as might an absence report or accident report? Should it be strictly *informational* and provide only facts, or should it be *analytical* and provide both facts and conclusions?

Often, the person requesting or authorizing the report will specify exactly what is wanted. If not, you must ask.

Report Functions

For at least four reasons, modern businesses depend heavily on reports.

First, reports serve the obvious purposes: they supply reliable information for making decisions, and they provide permanent records.

Second, they help businesses meet deadlines. For example, if on January 1 an engineering company receives an invitation to bid on constructing a six-mile-long bridge, one person will find it virtually impossible single-handedly to determine the costs, compile highly detailed specifications to accompany the bid, and deliver the complete report before a June 1 deadline. The most expedient way to handle this huge task is to assign sections for research and writing to various departments in the company—geology, marine technology, engineering, construction, personnel, and accounting. The person in charge would then compile and edit these short reports into the major sections of the final report and submit the bid in time to meet the deadline.

Third, reports bring together the expertise of many specialists to help solve complex problems. Could an accountant working alone plan all of the details for building a six-mile-long bridge? It's unlikely that such a feat could be managed without the help of a small army of experts from other departments. Yet, as in the previous case of preparing specifications and costs for a vast project, reports enable us to handle complex tasks by uniting knowledge from different fields.

Finally, reports serve as the means (often the *only* ones) for young executives to communicate their ideas to the chief executive officer. So they are excellent tools for encouraging creativity, for bringing new talent to the attention of the "brass," and for evaluating young executives.

COMMUNICATING BY MEMOS AND REPORTS

Chief Characteristics of Reports

No matter what your reasons are for writing them, your reports will be more effective if they accommodate your readers. To do so, they should be:

- attractive—to invite a favorable reading
- clear and methodically organized—to be easily understood
- rounded out with visual aids (see Appendix M)—to make the report more attractive, readable, and clear
- accurate and well documented—to be reliable and credible

Certain features are usually evident in effective reports: these include familiar formats and headings.

FAMILIAR FORMATS   Besides simplifying the writing of reports, standard organizational plans make it easy for readers to find various sections, such as conclusions and recommendations, and to anticipate the placement of each component of the report. Such plans help those reading an entire report as well as those reading only selected portions. Sometimes companies adopt a single organizational format. Examples of prescribed formats for short reports are shown here:

- Statement of Problem
  Discussion of Possible Solutions
  Conclusions

- Statement of Problem
  Proposed Solution
  Advantages
  Disadvantages
  Supporting Documents

- Statement of Problem
  Description of Equipment Used
  Discussion of Procedure
  Statement of Results
  Conclusions
  Recommendations

HEADINGS   The word *report* implies that you will use headings (known also as *captions*) to simplify the task of your reader. Similar to newspaper headlines and subheads, and the headings used in textbooks like this one, these division markers signal a change from one topic to another and also indicate the relationships of the topics.

Although any clear and consistent system of headings will work, writers often follow the form illustrated here:

1. FIRST DEGREE HEADING: All capital letters and centered on page.
2. Second Degree Heading: Initial capital letters on all words and centered on page.

3. <u>Third</u> <u>Degree</u> <u>Heading</u>: Initial capital letters on all words and underlined. Begin at left two spaces above paragraph following.
4. <u>Fourth</u> <u>Degree</u> <u>Heading</u>: Initial capital letters on all words and underlined, followed by period or colon. Begin at left on same line as paragraph opening.
5. <u>Fifth</u> <u>degree</u> <u>heading</u>: Initial capital on first word and all words underlined. Indented four to six character spaces from the left, and on same line as paragraph opening.

The advantages of these headings are that they clarify organization, help with information retrieval, and leave attractive white space on your paper. But what might be overlooked is that they force you to organize your paper carefully. In effect, your headings come directly from your outline; they are the topic headings for different divisions of your paper:

I.   =   first degree

   A.   =   second degree

      1.   =   third degree

         a)   =   fourth degree

           (1)   =   fifth degree

And because reports ordinarily require at least two or three degrees of these division headings, you will generally have to outline your ideas. As a result, your report is easier to read not only because of its headings, but also because of its orderly arrangement.

OTHER FEATURES   In addition to familiar formats and captions, other helpful report features are itemization, visual aids, and documentation. These are examined in detail in other parts of this book.

Short Report Types

We will now look at the seven types of short reports (from one to several pages) used most often in American business and industry. The first of these, the letter report, is a format that can be used for many different functions. The remaining six—the progress report, the periodic report, the information report, the analytical report, the recommendation report, and instructions—appear in memo, letter, or other report formats, but have specific functions. Knowing the formats and principles used in writing these reports will enable you to handle most short report assignments effectively.

The Letter Report

As its name implies, the letter report is a report that appears in letter format. Through the use of such features as a salutation and a complimentary close, the letter format personalizes the reported information. Whereas memo reports are in-house communications, letter reports are typically sent outside an organization for credit, personnel, or summary reports.

Letter reports use all the standard and some of the special parts (for example, reference initials and enclosure notations) of letters. They also use strategies generally associated with reports—careful organization of the message, headings to identify major divisions, itemization of chief points, and sometimes even visual aids (for example, a table showing an installation schedule). Many are only a page or two long, while others may run to four or five pages.

As seen in figure 9–1, the letter report format combines the helpful features of two forms of business writing, the letter and the report. The letter report in figure 9–1 functions as a recommendation report, but the letter format may be used for other purposes.

The Progress Report

The purpose of a progress report, as its name suggests, is to inform supervisors about the status of a project or assignment. Often supervisors will simply be curious about how you are progressing toward the completion of a project. In other cases they may be eager to know if you have finished each phase of an assignment schedule and if you can meet the target date for the job. Sometimes they want an account of how a project is developing in order to know if they should alter or abort it.

The frequency of progress reports depends on the length and complexity of the project and the wishes of your supervisors. For a project that can be completed quickly, a single progress report may be all that is needed before the final report. But for a long project, a weekly or monthly report, or a report after completing each phase of the project, may be necessary. In the latter case, each report in the series ought to follow the same plan.

The contents of progress reports vary. Some go into much detail and provide lengthy statements for each of the following divisions:

1. Background of assignment
2. Purpose, aim, or objective of assignment
3. Schedule
4. Summary of progress
5. Problems or other special observations
6. Forecast about completion

However, for the sake of economy, many progress reports include details only under the following divisions:

1. Summary of progress to date
2. Statement that the project is on schedule, or explanation of why it is not
3. Forecast about the remaining work

Figure 9–1. Letter Report.

Global
Computer
Corporation

120 East First Street   Bismarck, North Dakota 58501   (701) 555–7834

May 16, 19--

Mr. Donald Young
Alpha Equities, Inc.
485 Mina Avenue
Aberdeen, SD 57401

Dear Mr. Young:

Here is the proposal you requested for installing a GCC System/96 at Alpha Equities. Your detailed specifications for the proposal and the time we spent with you at Alpha have given us valuable insight for determining the system and the implementation plan which will best serve the needs of your company.

Software Requirements

Since the total integrated on-line system that Alpha requires would make it difficult to implement an existing software package, the most feasible approach is to develop custom software. Designing and programming such a detailed system to accommodate the specific needs of Alpha can be accomplished in one of two ways: (1) by using an in-house data processing manager/programmer; or (2) by hiring a contract programmer.

As you requested, we are supplying the names of three contract programmers and the names of references for three of their installations. Whether an in-house or contract programmer is chosen, Thomas Leshko and I will work with the individual throughout the implementation process. We have outlined this support in the enclosed proposal.

Implementation Approach

The implementation approach we recommend would satisfy the short- and long-range goals of your company. This approach is to design most of the systems and develop most of the programs prior to the delivery of the hardware.

COMMUNICATING BY MEMOS AND REPORTS

Figure 9–1   (continued).

Mr. Donald Young
Page 2
May 16, 19--

In order for you to utilize your System/96 most effectively, we reiterate how important it is to provide the time required initially for educating personnel and collecting data compatible for computer use. The enclosed "Installation Planning Schedule" proposes a realistic time-frame which, if followed, can implement the total program in ten months. Only by providing employees adequate time for following the schedule closely can the implementation be accomplished in ten months. And only by following the schedule closely can Alpha realize the maximum return on its investment.

Your written approval of our recommendation, Mr. Young, will enable us to begin working toward the installation of a successful system. We look forward to working with you and your personnel during the implementation of this system.

Cordially yours,

Sara Stroud

Sara Stroud
Sales Representative

SS:rb

Enclosures

Or, as one writer has phrased it, the report may touch on these three points:

1. What has been done
2. What is being done
3. What is expected to be done[1]

No matter what pattern of organization you follow, you should neither include unnecessary information nor try to make your project appear to be further along toward completion than it really is. Your report should be accurate and detailed, providing your reader with whatever information is needed for a complete account of the project's current status.

Since most progress reports are in-house communications, the memorandum form is commonly used. But occasionally progress reports are outside communications, and in such cases the letter form is appropriate. In either form, report headings usually label the various divisions of the report, as seen in figure 9–2.

The Periodic Report

Unlike the progress report, which provides information about a single project or assignment, the periodic report describes all the jobs assigned during the reporting period. It includes both projects that have completion dates and continuing programs.

Because most organizations require employees to account for their activities, periodic reports are common communications in business, industry, and government. They are written at stated intervals—for example, weekly, monthly, or annually—and are often referred to by the time-span covered. Some periodic reports are short (less than a page), while others are long (three to six pages) and require the use of visual aids and two or three degrees of headings.

No universally acceptable organization plan exists for periodic reports. Many organizations provide a standard report form that employees can periodically fill out. In other cases, a memo heading is followed by an organizational plan chosen by the writer, as seen in figure 9–3. All formats require that the inclusive date of the reporting period appear prominently in the heading.

A familiar form of periodic report is the annual report of a large company, copies of which are available in most college libraries, placement offices, and broker's offices. Nearly all these reports contain the following: names of officers and directors, letter from the board chairman or CEO, financial highlights, financial statements, statement from the accountant, and comparative financial data (from five to ten years). They may also contain information about products, sales, research, development, physical plant, employees, subsidiaries, future plans, and management. And they often contain many photographs, tables, or other visual aids. Of course, many of these reports are written by communications or public relations specialists and are printed as booklets.[2] But these lavishly budgeted corporate reports, with their colorful artwork and snappy layout, bear little resemblance to their typewritten counterparts.

The contents of periodic reports vary widely, depending on how often they have to be submitted, what type of company they are written for, and what kind of information is needed. Writers usually try to give complete facts and figures (especially

Figure 9–2. Progress Report.

O. Percy Fairchild
Genealogical Record Searcher
1204 Queen Street, NW
Salt Lake City, Utah 84100

2 August 19--

Ms. Kaye Shoulars
6810 Lauman Drive
Nashport, OH 43830

Dear Ms. Shoulars:

SUBJECT: PROGRESS REPORT NO. 2: RESEARCH ON THE PARENTAGE OF PATRICK (R.)
          O'DONNELL

Summary of Progress

     Since my first progress report to you last month, accompanied by a
copy of Patrick O'Donnell's service record in the Lenoir County, N.C.,
Militia during the War of 1812, I have discovered the following additional
information about your great-great-grandfather.

1. Patrick (R.) O'Donnell is _not_ the Dr. Patrick J. O'Donnell who served
    as the first professor of classics at Davidson College and who later
    served as president of Hampden-Sydney College. This Dr. O'Donnell
    was born in 1801 in Lincoln County, N.C., and would not have been old
    enough to have served in the War of 1812.

2. Patrick (R.) O'Donnell appears in the 1820 Census of Lenior County,
    N.C. The entry shows one male under 10; one male 16-25; one female
    under 10; one female 16-25; and one female 45 and over. My assumption
    is that Patrick O'Donnell is the male 16-25; that his wife is the
    female 16-25; that Patrick and his wife have a son and a daughter,
    both under 10; and that the female over 45 is Patrick O'Donnell's
    mother or mother-in-law. If my assumption is correct, Patrick would
    have been born between 1795 and 1804. His service in the War of 1812
    from 1813 until 1815 suggests that he was born around 1795.

3. Patrick O'Donnell may be the P.R. O'Donnell who appears in the 1830
    Census of Chesterfield County, S.C. The entry shows one male under 5;
    one male 30-40; one female 5-10; and one female 20-30. This entry ap-
    pears on p. 264, while an entry for John O'Donnell appears on p. 265.
    The proximity of the two entries suggests a connection between the
    two men.

Figure 9–2 *(continued)*.

Ms. Kaye Shoulars
Page Two
2 August 19--

Schedule

As you know, research into the parentage of early nineteenth century Americans moves slowly. Since the Federal Government collects no family history records per se, researchers have to examine old bibles, cemetery markers, church histories, military records, census reports, emigration lists, etc., and then piece together every little shred of data.

For this reason, I have not made the progress that I had intended toward finding the names of your ancestor's mother and father. Although I had hoped by the end of my second month on this project to have determined if O'Donnell was born in North or South Carolina, I can now see that I will be at least in my third month before I can do so.

In short, the research project is a month behind schedule.

Forecast

I will continue to ferret out details of Patrick O'Donnell's life, including the names of his in-laws and the names of his other children besides your great-grandfather, Isaac (E.) O'Donnell. If I am lucky in determining soon where he was born, I should then be able to ascertain from local records the name of Patrick's father. Whether I am able to provide you with a final report at the end of one year, as we planned, will now depend on how long it takes me to determine his birthplace.

In the meantime, I will continue to report to you about any progress I make. Please inform me of any leads that come to your attention.

Sincerely,

O. Percy Fairchild

Enclosures: 1. Extract of Patrick O'Donnell entry, 1820 Lenoir County, N.C., Census
2. Extract of P.R. O'Donnell entry, 1830 Chester-field County, S.C., Census

Figure 9–3.   Periodic (Annual) Report.

8 September 19--

To: Dr. Robert G. Zuck
            Vice President for Student Life

From: James W. Ingle, Director
            Office of Student Financial Aid

Re: 19-- Annual Report

The Office of Student Financial Aid administers the University's program of financial assistance to students attending the University and the Community Colleges. The office also has the responsibility for collection of student loans.

The stated objectives of the financial aid program are to:

1. Provide financial assistance in the form of scholarships, grants, loans, and work opportunities to students who, without such aid, would be unable to attend the University.

2. Assist in meeting the goal of equality of educational opportunity by providing the financial means for students to attain a university education.

3. Counsel students regarding their financial needs and provide information concerning financial aid to students.

During the past year the Office of Student Financial Aid accomplished the objectives above insofar as available funds and resources would permit. Funds were generally available to provide assistance to those students who had identifiable financial need.

In order to meet the goal of equality of educational opportunity, students were provided a balanced package of financial assistance insofar as available resources would permit. An attempt was made to provide exceptionally needy students with gift assistance equaling at least 50 percent of their need, thereby reducing loans and grants to a reasonable amount. Students having smaller needs primarily received loans.

The amount of aid awarded an individual student ranged from $200 to $3,800. The average aid awarded was approximately $1,200 per student.

In accomplishing the foregoing, the Office of Student Financial Aid has worked closely with the Admissions Office, Talent Search, Office of Development, Vice President for Community Colleges' Office, and other such offices.

Increased costs and inflation continue to increase the demand for financial aid. These factors will require additional funds in the future.

(1)

Figure 9–3 *(continued).*

FINANCIAL AID AWARDS

GIFT AID	19-- to 19-- Number	Amount	19-- to 19-- Number	Amount
Institutional Scholarships	667	$ 296,219	647	$ 335,000
Outside Scholarships	304	167,166	332	189,191
BEOG	6,668	4,667,471	6,800	4,795,000
SEOB	550	301,767	564	344,565
Health Professions Scholarships	55	55,385	17	26,070
Nursing Scholarships	69	33,600	84	38,689
State Grants	1,091	258,175	1,241	324,197
Total Gift Aid	9,404	$ 5,779,783	9,685	$ 6,052,712
BANK				
National Direct Student Loans	1,713	$ 1,100,246	1,745	$ 1,229,939
Health Professions Loans	221	264,397	154	238,032
Nursing Loans	161	85,650	176	97,050
State Institutional Loans	80	16,800	174	26,300
Federally Insured Loans	933	1,250,000	933	1,250,000
Total Loans	3,108	$ 2,717,093	3,182	$ 2,841,321
WORK				
College Work-Study Program	1,582	$ 785,494	1,585	$ 801,372
Student Employment Service	900	800,000	900	800,000
Total Work	2,482	$ 1,585,494	2,485	$ 1,601,372
TOTAL AID	14,994	$10,082,370	15,352	$10,495,405

Estimated Figures--Actual Figures Not Available

Report of Activities

The table above provides a report of the number of awards and dollar volume for the past two years. Total awards increased by 358 and amount of dollars increased by $413,000.

The following table reflects the activity in loans collections:

	Borrowers in Collection Status	Amounts Collected
National Direct Student Loan	5,329	$668,035
Health Profession - Medicine	822	119,231
Health Profession - Dentistry	552	90,901
Health Profession - Pharmacy	229	23,757
Nursing	737	31,409
Institutional Loans	351	31,738
TOTAL	8,020	$965,071

(2)

Figure 9–3 (continued).

Wachovia Services provided billing and data processing for National Direct Student Loans. All other collections were handled manually (2,691).

Delinquencies remained a concern. The office utilized a skip-trace service to locate lost borrowers. By the year's end, 1,538 accounts had been placed with Financial Collection Agency. Delinquencies have not been a problem with Health Profession and Nursing Loans.

Significant Accomplishments

1. The financial needs of all applicants were met, by the provision of balanced packages of financial aid. Some students still had to assume larger than desirable loans.

2. Microfilming of out-of-school records continued.

3. A brochure was published in May to provide information to current and prospective students concerning the University's student financial aid resources.

4. The addition of a professional staff member and a secretary greatly facilitated coordination with the Community Colleges.

5. The administrative expense allowance provided by the Federal Government was increased from 3 percent to 4 percent. This enabled the addition of the staff mentioned in number 4 above, and some additional funds for administrative expenses, including the brochure referred to in item 3 above.

6. The Director and staff have served as consultant to U.S. Office of Education, consultant to College Scholarship Service, member of Executive Committee of College Scholarship Service Council, and author of the "National Direct Student Loan" section of the 19-- Student Financial Aid Handbook.

Projections

1. Total dollars awarded in student financial aid should show a slight increase next year.

2. A handbook will be developed during the coming year for use in the following academic year. This will be for use by students who are awarded financial aid.

3. The need is still great for data processing assistance. As indicated in this report, over 15,000 awards, exceeding 10 million dollars, were processed and records maintained manually. In addition, 2,691 loans were billed and collected manually.

JWI:nft

(3)

if profits and losses are involved), often with comparable data at least for the previous period. Complete information helps readers make the best possible decisions and, usually, creates favorable impressions of the activities. When conclusions, recommendations, or evaluations appear at the report's end, the information presented earlier should prepare the reader for them.

Information and Analytical Reports

Among the short reports you will most likely be asked to write are those classified according to their general functions—information, analytical, or recommendation reports. The recommendation report is used so often that we will discuss it at some length. First, however, we want to explain briefly the difference between information and analytical reports. The distinction can be important in helping you know what to include in your reports.

INFORMATION REPORTS   In writing an information (or informational) report, you present data without any interpretation or evaluation. Preparing such a report entails thorough research and clear presentation of your findings (as seen in figure 9–4). In turn, your readers examine the facts you present, analyze them, and arrive at whatever conclusions they wish. So an information report would not include a section entitled "Analysis of the Facts" or "Conclusions." As an old saying puts it, the information report provides the evidence and the reader renders the verdict.

Information reports can take many forms—credit reports, laboratory reports, library research reports, annual reports, absence reports, progress reports, and the like. If the person authorizing a report does not specify whether you should provide facts only or facts accompanied by interpretation, you should ask.

ANALYTICAL REPORTS   In an analytical report, you go a step further: you not only provide facts but you also interpret them. In other words, the writer's responsibility here is to compile, present, and analyze the facts. This analysis usually appears in a section labeled "Conclusions." Readers base their decisions on these conclusions.

The following conclusion appeared in "Sexism in *Contemporary Business Writing*," a report submitted by a student committee in "Writing for Business and Industry" at the University of Iowa:

Conclusions

While <u>Contemporary Business Writing</u> is a helpful and interesting book on the methods of business writing, the sexist comments and innuendos are offensive to the reader. Remarks such as ''a paper's length should be like a girl's skirt: short enough to be attractive but long enough to cover what is important'' are not only inappropriate for a time when the awareness and acceptance of changing sex roles is prominent, but also are insulting to the female audience.

Numerous examples of varying types and degrees of sexism have been cited in this report along with the reasons given as to how and why they are offensive. The sexism seems to emerge in three basic manners: portrayal of women as sex objects, portrayal of women as nagging housewives and other stereotypical roles, and finally, portrayal of the male business student as a flamboyant, girl-crazy, sports fan. In the book the highest position a woman holds is a secretary. She also cries at silly soap operas and complains about the coffee. The men hold all the jobs, play all the sports and embody the role of the ''all-American'' male. The narrow audience scope excludes the female audience as well as a great portion of the male audience who cannot identify with the author's presuppositions. The reactions from both the female and male students show they feel that the sexist comments lag behind the times and detract from the subject matter.[3]

Note that the conclusion section does not merely summarize the facts presented earlier in the report. Instead, it alludes to those facts as it interprets them for the reader.

While an analytical report interprets facts, it does not propose a course of action based on the interpretation. A report that goes one step further than the analytical report by proposing action is often called a *recommendation report*.

The Recommendation Report

The recommendation report describes a problem and proposes a solution. Because it offers a proposal and then justifies it, it is sometimes called a proposal or a justification report. (The word *proposal* often implies a request for project funding.) Its length and organizational plan vary; most reports are from one to several pages. Many follow this plan:

1. Problem
2. Recommendation
3. Rationale
4. Rejected Alternatives
5. Limitations

In the "Problem" (or "Background") section, you establish the context of the recommendation and show readers the need for it. If the problem is obvious, your description of it may be brief (see figure 9-5).

In the "Recommendation" (or "Proposal") section, you provide a solution to the problem or a way to improve the situation. If this section includes more than one recommendation, you may itemize them. When the report goes to someone familiar with the problem, you may open with the recommendation, omitting the problem section.

Figure 9–4. Information Report.

McDonald's Corp. 1447K

NYSE Symbol MCD Put & Call Options on CBOE

Price	Range	P-E Ratio	Dividend	Yield	S&P Ranking
Sep. 3'82	1982				
84½	85⅜-58	12	[3]1.32	[3]1.6%	A−

Summary

Aggressive expansion and creative merchandising over the years have enabled McDonald's to maintain its position as the dominant force in the fast-food industry. Continuation of these programs should permit the company to extend its impressive record of long-term earnings growth in 1982, although at a more moderate pace than in the past. A 3-for-2 stock split is pending.

Current Outlook

Earnings for 1982 should increase to about $7.60 a share from 1981's $6.54, unadjusted for the 3-for-2 split payable October 6, 1982.

The quarterly dividend has been raised 10%, to the equivalent of $0.33 on present shares, from $0.30.

The long-term uptrend in sales should continue in 1982, aided by further expansion in the U.S. and abroad, as well as by menu diversification. Margins should narrow slightly as the company attempts to maintain its competitive edge through fewer price increases, despite industry projections of a rise in the cost of beef. However, this should be more than outweighed by gains garnered from MCD's long-term expansion program.

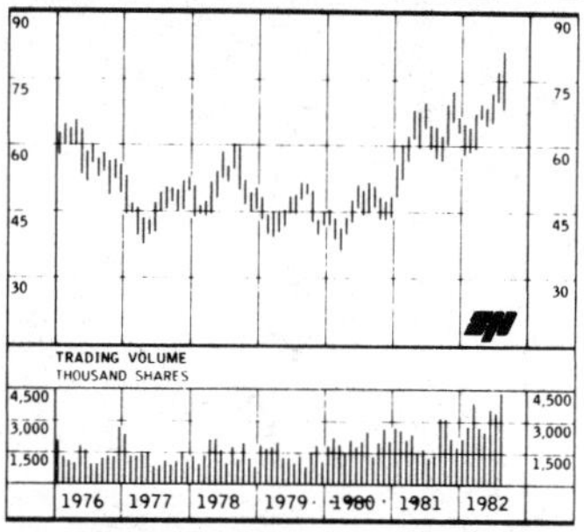

Total Revenues (Million $)

Quarter:	1982	1981	1980	1979
Mar.	617	562	493	419
Jun.	725	650	563	489
Sep.		668	589	520
Dec.		636	570	510
		2,516	2,215	1,938

Revenues for the six months ended June 30, 1982 advanced 11%, year to year. Net income advanced 14%, to $3.62 a share from $3.16.

Common Share Earnings ($)

Quarter:	1982	1981	1980	1979
Mar.	1.46	1.28	1.06	0.90
Jun.	2.16	1.88	1.54	1.32
Sep.		1.87	1.59	1.37
Dec.		1.52	1.30	1.10
		6.54	5.49	4.68

Important Developments

Aug. '82—MCD sold publicly $160 million ($40 million due 1988 and $120 million due 1994) or zero coupon notes priced to bear an equivalent yield to maturity of 12.3% and 12.6%, respectively. Proceeds of $47.5 million were applied toward the partial repayment of outstanding commercial paper.

Jul. '82—In the first half of 1982, MCD added 166 restaurants to its system and had 6,905 units worldwide at June 30, including 1,243 internationally, compared with 6,418 and 1,085, respectively, a year earlier. Also as of that date, there were 199 units under construction, including 62 outside the U.S. Chicken McNuggets were in 4,700 U.S. restaurants, with domestic rollout completion expected by year-end.

Next earnings report due in late October.

Per Share Data ($)

Yr. End Dec. 31	1981	1980	1979	1978	1977	[1]1976	[2]1975	[2]1974	[1]1973	[1]1972
Book Value	**32.05**	26.66	21.95	18.58	14.85	12.14	9.59	7.63	5.94	4.51
Earnings	**6.54**	5.49	4.68	4.00	3.37	2.72	2.17	1.70	1.31	0.94
Dividends	**0.95**	0.74	0.51	0.32	0.17½	0.07½	Nil	Nil	Nil	Nil
Payout Ratio	**14%**	13%	11%	8%	5%	3%	Nil	Nil	Nil	Nil
Prices—High	**72⅞**	52	51⅞	60½	53⅜	66	60½	63¼	76⅞	77⅜
Low	**48⅜**	36¼	39¼	43⅞	37¾	48¾	26¾	21¼	44⅛	37
P/E Ratio—	**11-7**	9-7	11-8	15-11	16-11	24-18	28-12	37-13	59-34	82-39

Data as orig. reptd. Adj. for stk. div(s). of 100% Jun. 1972. **1.** Reflects merger or acquisition. **2.** Reflects merger or acquisition and accounting change. **3.** Based on initial quarterly payment aft. 3-for-2 split.

Standard NYSE Stock Reports
Vol. 49/No. 176/Sec. 21

September 13, 1982

Standard & Poor's Corp.
25 Broadway, NY, NY 10004

Figure 9–4 (continued).

1447K   McDonald's Corporation

Income Data (Million $)

Year Ended Dec. 31	Revs.	Oper. Inc.	% Oper. Inc. of Revs.	Cap. Exp.	Depr.	Int. Exp.	Net Bef. Taxes	Eff. Tax Rate	Net Inc.	% Net Inc. of Revs.
1981	2,477	667	26.9%	427	133	104	482	45.0%	265	10.7%
1980	2,184	575	26.3%	410	113	102	403	45.1%	221	10.1%
1979	1,912	483	25.2%	459	92	83	345	45.3%	189	9.9%
1978	1,644	423	25.7%	357	75	69	313	48.0%	163	9.9%
1977	1,384	363	26.2%	309	62	59	267	48.8%	137	9.9%
¹1976	1,156	283	24.5%	231	46	42	217	49.3%	110	9.5%
²1975	926	229	24.7%	225	37	38	172	49.5%	87	9.4%
²1974	715	170	23.7%	237	26	26	135	50.2%	67	9.4%
¹1973	583	122	21.0%	180	19	11	101	48.7%	52	8.9%
¹1972	380	82	21.6%	114	12	6	69	47.8%	36	9.5%

Balance Sheet Data (Million $)

Dec. 31	Cash	Current Assets	Current Liab.	Ratio	Total Assets	Ret. on Assets	Long Term Debt	Common Equity	Total Cap.	% LT Debt of Cap.	Ret. on Equity
1981	40	176	353	0.5	2,899	9.5%	926	1,371	2,483	37.3%	21.1%
1980	113	234	333	0.7	2,643	8.8%	970	1,141	2,251	43.1%	21.1%
1979	141	247	274	0.9	2,354	8.8%	966	952	2,025	47.7%	21.6%
1978	157	243	252	1.0	1,953	9.0%	783	796	1,651	47.4%	22.6%
1977	132	208	215	1.0	1,645	9.3%	688	643	1,385	49.7%	23.4%
1976	116	176	171	1.0	1,284	9.3%	497	525	1,073	46.3%	23.3%
1975	101	154	136	1.1	1,069	9.0%	444	414	897	49.5%	23.2%
1974	82	124	112	1.1	853	9.1%	354	331	709	49.8%	22.7%
1973	77	110	87	1.3	624	9.8%	235	261	510	46.0%	22.4%
1972	59	81	71	1.1	422	9.6%	117	199	327	35.7%	21.4%

Data as orig. reptd. 1. Reflects merger or acquisition. 2. Reflects merger or acquisition and accounting change.

Business Summary

McDonald's Corp. operates, licenses and services the world's largest chain of fast-food restaurants. At 1981 year-end, there were 5,554 units in 50 states and Washington, D.C., plus 1,185 abroad, including 389 in Canada, 302 in Japan, 155 in Germany, 123 in Australia and 216 in 25 other countries or territories.

1981	Revs.	Profits
United States	80%	85%
Canada	11%	9%
Other	9%	6%

Units in operation at year end were:

Operated by—	1981	1980	1979	1978
Company	1,746	1,608	1,547	1,406
Franchisees	4,580	4,302	3,927	3,573
Affiliates	413	353	273	206
Total	6,739	6,263	5,747	5,185

The restaurants offer a substantially uniform menu featuring hamburgers, fries, fish sandwiches, beverages and desserts; most also serve breakfast. Average revenue per unit was roughly $1,050,000 in 1981. Under current agreements, franchise fees paid to McDonald's generally amount to 11.5% of sales.

Dividend Data

Dividends were initiated in 1976.

Amt. of Divd. $	Date Decl.	Ex-divd. Date	Stock of Record	Payment Date
0.25	Feb. 1	Feb. 5	Feb. 11	Mar. 2'82
0.30	May 13	May 24	May 28	Jun. 7'82
0.30	Jul. 19	Jul. 20	Jul. 26	Aug. 11'82
3-for-2	Aug. 31	---	Sep. 14	Oct. 6'82
0.22	Aug. 31	Oct. 15	Oct. 21	Nov. 4'82

Finances

In 1981 funds generated from operations (some $447 million) were 107% of expenditures for property and equipment, compared with 92% in 1980 and 71% in 1979. At December 31, 1981 $234,429,000 had been taken down under or supported by $275 million of bank credit lines with interest at prime.

Capitalization

Long Term Debt: $1,052,000,000, incl. some $80,704,000 of capital-lease obligations.

Common Stock: 40,215,389 shs. (no par).
About 12% owned by R. A. Kroc.
Institutions hold some 69%.
Shareholders: 22,717.

Office—McDonald's Plaza, Oak Brook, Ill. 60521 Tel—(312) 887-3200. Chrmn & CEO—F. L. Turner. Pres—E. H. Schmitt. VP-Secy—D. P. Horwitz. VP-Treas—R. B. Ryan. Investor Contact—S. Vuinovich. Dirs—R. J. Boylan, J. M. Greenberg, D. P. Horwitz, R. A. Kroc, D. G. Lubin, G. Newman, M. R. Quinlan, E. H. Schmitt, A. P. Stults, R. N. Thurston, F. L. Turner, D. B. Wallerstein. Transfer Agent—American National Bank & Trust Co., Chicago. Registrar—Northern Trust Co., Chicago. Incorporated in Delaware in 1965.

Information has been obtained from sources believed to be reliable, but its accuracy and completeness are not guaranteed.   R.S. Natale

(SOURCE: Standard and Poor's. Stock Reports)

The "Rationale" (or "Support," "Defense," or "Justification") section explains the benefits of the recommended action. Whenever helpful, they may be itemized (see figure 9–5).

Under the heading "Rejected Alternatives," you point out the comparative disadvantages of other possible solutions. Sometimes, instead of appearing under a separate heading, the rejected alternatives are mentioned in the rationale section.

The "Limitations" (or "Precautions") section, which is omitted in some reports, explains any qualifications to your recommendation. As one authority has written, "This section includes a statement of conditions under which you would change your recommendation, any lack of information which might result in your recommendation's being incorrect, precautions to be taken in carrying out your recommendation, and the like."[4] A statement of limitations is illustrated in figure 9–5.

Instructions, Directions, Procedure Manuals

Instructions, directions, and procedure manuals deal not only with physical objects, such as machinery to be assembled, repaired, or dismounted, but also with the steps for processing applications, following legal procedures, and the like. If instructions are not written simply and clearly, readers will misunderstand them and fail to execute them correctly. The result can be costly.

Writing instructions consists mainly of:

- analyzing your audience thoroughly
- understanding the process completely
- writing simply and clearly
- testing the final draft carefully

ANALYZING YOUR AUDIENCE   Analyzing the reader is essential. The first step for the writer is to consider who the readers are and how much they already know about the process. For example, a credit union should define *credit* and *debit* in providing deposit and withdrawal instructions for the average factory worker, but these definitions would be unnecessary for bookkeepers. Furthermore, fuller information should be furnished to readers unfamiliar with a process than to those partially familiar with it. Consequently, how complete the instructions need to be, how carefully words must be defined, and whether explanations should be provided depend on the reader.

UNDERSTANDING THE PROCESS   It is difficult to write well about anything you do not understand well. Before sitting down to write about a process, you should watch it or work through it several times, studying each step. Sometimes, as in instructing others about how to clean and check a lawn mower, you may find the process tedious. Nevertheless you should actually run through such jobs instead of merely visualizing them.

Figure 9–5. Recommendation Report.

North American Glass Panes, Inc.

5830 Seaview Boulevard   Atlantic, Maine 04608   (207) 555–3600

21 July 19--

OFFICE OF THE PERSONNEL DIRECTOR

CONFIDENTIAL

TO: Mr. Charles P. Quinn
           Personnel Director

FROM: Melissa Orr   *(M.Orr)*
           Deputy Personnel Director

SUBJECT: Recommended Procedure for Monthly Meetings Between Personnel
           Staff and Production Line Foremen

Problem

Obviously, we have a problem with those foremen who view the
monthly meetings as unruly grievance sessions instead of convocations for
sharing information and planning constructive actions. By requiring each
foreman to speak up, our current round-robin procedure seems to call
forth unproductive griping which in turn stifles the progress of the
meetings.

Recommendation

To improve this situation, I recommend that, beginning next month,
we impose a more formal structure on the meetings.

The structure I recommend is the traditional parliamentary one, as
follows:

    I.   Call to Order
   II.   Approval of Minutes
 III.   Announcements (from Personnel Director)
  IV.   Old Business
      A.
      B.
      C. etc.
   V.   New Business
      A.
      B.
      C. etc.
  VI.   Adjournment

I propose also that a tentative agenda be distributed at least a
week in advance of each meeting.

Figure 9–5 (continued).

Mr. Charles P. Quinn
Page Two
21 July 19--

Rationale

      Implementing this procedure should improve the effectiveness of the meetings for several reasons:

- It will permit the personnel staff, rather than the foremen on the floor, to control direction and timing.

- It will discourage the one-division-only issues that now often crop up in the round robins.

- It will impose an orderly progression of events.

- It will call for parliamentary activity, which will make the foremen take firm public stands on personnel and company issues and thus be responsible and accountable for their statements and actions.

- Since it will be clear that any parliamentary actions will only advise the Personnel Director, all bickering about issues will be among the foremen, not between the foremen and the personnel staff.

- It will allow the foremen to discuss issues beforehand with their line workers and thus to bring representative views to the meetings.

- If the personnel staff will pack the agenda time allotted for the meeting, it will encourage a brisk pace and prevent the meeting from bogging down on unproductive issues.

Rejected Alternatives

      Our options are to continue the present procedure, to impose a gag rule on the foremen, or to discontinue the meetings.

      I rejected these options because the first is a proven loser, the second would stir morale problems, and the third is out of the

Figure 9–5   (continued).

Mr. Charles P. Quinn
Page Three
21 July 19--

question because the meetings are necessary for disseminating information
and for detecting the pulsebeat of our employees.

Limitations

    Of course, parliamentary procedure will not work miracles and
transform the meetings into models of propriety and efficiency overnight.
Following a packed agenda will at first seem strange to everyone. And
the formality will give the meetings a stiff, wooden quality.

    But since we're dealing with educated, civilized, rational people,
the more formal procedure ought to lend the meetings a simple, flexible
orderliness that will discourage emotional outbursts while encouraging
reasonable participation.

MD:wg

WRITING SIMPLY AND CLEARLY Writing instructions, directions, or procedures consists chiefly of making certain that the various steps are arranged in chronological order, that the sentences are short, and that the language is simple enough for the average reader to understand. If certain tools are necessary, if the weather or other outside conditions are important, if specific skills are required, or if preliminary preparations have to be made, then these should be stated at the outset. The imperative should generally be used, sentences should be complete, and telegraphic style avoided. Because each step should be numbered and the instructions presented in outline form, transitions are usually not needed.

Any special warning or advice should be printed in a second color, underlined, italicized, or treated in some other way to make it stand out. It is best placed at the beginning or end, rather than buried in the middle.

TESTING THE FINAL DRAFT You would be wise to try your written instructions, directions, or procedures on several people before finally completing them. It is surprising how often questions will arise in such field trials—as in the case of a nurse reading the following on a label: "This vaccine may contain rabies." While she hoped it would *restrain* or *limit* rabies, she was concerned about its having the potential to *give* this dreaded disease. So it is best to have instructions checked by several individuals—preferably with backgrounds similar to those of the people for whom the instructions are intended.

Good instructions, directions, and procedures—like those to Homelite Chain Saw owners in figure 9–6—are surprisingly difficult to write. On the other hand, bad ones are simple to dash off. So do not underestimate the assignment. You can be confident of doing a good job only if you go through the four-step process: analyzing your audience thoroughly, understanding the process completely, writing simply and clearly, and testing the final draft carefully.

REPORT RESEARCH

The word *research* has a formidable ring to it, conjuring up visions of scientists in chemistry or electronic laboratories, scholars in library carrels, or field workers on archaeological trips. But research is also conducted by nonspecialists on much more common subjects. You yourself may have engaged in research in shopping for an expensive consumer item, such as a car. In this process, you may have read several magazine articles pricing and evaluating cars. Then you might have visited some dealers to see what models were available and at what prices. Probably you sought advice from friends and relatives. You also test-drove a few cars. Finally, you selected one. In this way, you engaged in library research, survey research, observation, and experimentation.

Research is conducted along similar lines in the worlds of business, industry, government, and the professions. Let's say you have been asked to write a report for your company about whether a sales incentive award program should be instituted, and if so, how to establish one. Your first step would be to read about the subject.

Figure 9–6.   Sample Instructions.

HOW TO START THE SAW CORRECTLY

1. Flip the ignition switch to "ON."
2. Push CHOKE LEVER all the way up to choke the cold engine fully.

— FULL CHOKE
— HALF CHOKE
— OPEN CHOKE

3. Hold the saw down firmly on a level surface with the bar and chain in the clear. Never lean across the saw or straddle the guide bar.

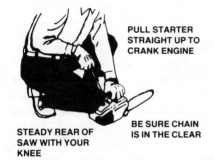

PULL STARTER
STRAIGHT UP TO
CRANK ENGINE

STEADY REAR OF
SAW WITH YOUR
KNEE

BE SURE CHAIN
IS IN THE CLEAR

4. When cranking, place your knee over the rear of the throttle control handle to help steady the saw. Hold down the throttle control handle with one hand and depress the throttle trigger with one finger (see cranking illustration). Use your other hand for pulling the starter cord.
5. Pull STARTER GRIP out a short way until you feel the starter dogs engage. Then pull cord briskly to give a fast cranking spin to the engine. (Do not pull to the very end or you may damage the starter.) Hold onto the grip to let the cord rewind smoothly. Do not let it snap back.
6. CRANK UNTIL ENGINE FIRES.   Normally, an engine that has just been fueled will require three to five cranks to prime with fuel. In cold weather, additional cranking may be required for initial prime. On the other hand, a recently run engine will usually start up on the first pull.
7. When the engine fires, it may not keep running. If this occurs, push the CHOKE LEVER halfway down and continue with cranking. When the engine starts and runs, keep it running at half choke long enough to warm it up (10-30 seconds), then flip the CHOKE LEVER *down* to the open position.

NOTE: **Any engine which has fired several times at full choke will start at half choke.**

8. Normally, a hot engine needs no choking to be restarted, and an engine which has cooled only a little should be started at half choke. Also, if the engine is warm enough, you may not have to depress the trigger to restart it.

(SOURCE: *Owner's Manual for XL Chain Saw with Automatic Chain Oiler* [Charlotte, North Carolina: Homelite Division of Textron Inc., 1976], p. 5.)

Then you might survey other companies to find out what their experience has been. Finally, you might visit with a few of their managers and employees. On the basis of this research, you would write your report.

In these two examples—buying a car and investigating a sales incentive program—you would start with library research, to inform yourself thoroughly about the subject. For example, although you might be writing only about a sales incentive award program, you would do well to read about the entire field of sales inducements: business gifts, customer coupons, suggestion awards, prizes to customers for prompt payments. Then, if you recommended establishing a plan, you would investigate the various companies specializing in consulting about or planning an incentive program.

Library research, therefore, is the usual first step. Whether selecting a career, vacationing at home or abroad, deciding on an insurance policy, choosing a graduate school, or recommending a product, program, or policy at work, you would be wise to read as much as you can about it.

How to go about library research is the subject of Appendix L, "Documentation and Library Sources." In this chapter we shall focus on the other forms of research—observation, experimentation, and surveying—that you probably did not study in your earlier writing courses. What follows, then, is an attempt to help you compile reliable information for your reports by means other than library research.

Observation

Observation is a technique of the sciences that is also applied in business and related fields. This research method is not restricted to people watching people, as in time and motion studies, traffic counts, or customer behavior. It also includes the observation or study of statistical data, such as financial reports and population figures. You would use observation, for example, to determine the ten most commonly misspelled words in your class—going through all the written papers, noting the misspellings, and running a tally on them.

Experimentation

Another methodology generally associated with the sciences but also used in business-related fields is experimentation. In business it might involve a comparison between a current product or operating plan and a proposed new one, or between two groups of people, one the regular or control group; the other, the group experimented on (the experimental group). This technique could be used to determine whether freshmen will improve their writing more in small classes or in large ones. In such an experiment, small and large classes of comparable students would be taught by comparable instructors using the same textbook and following the same curriculum. An evaluation of pre-semester and post-semester writing samples would indicate whether the small or the large classes were more successful.

But experimentation with humans is fraught with problems. For instance, in our example, it would be difficult to select comparable students and comparable instructors. If the groups were dissimilar in any way other than class size, those variables could affect the results. Another problem with human experiments is that people tend to overachieve or react uncharacteristically if they know they are being studied. As a result, subjects in medical experiments are not informed whether they are given new drugs or harmless, unmedicated placebos because of possible psychological reactions that might affect physical health.

Experimentation is frequently used in test-marketing new products in various communities around the country. But the locales for the studies must be selected carefully: what might sell well in one geographical area might not in another.

Survey Research

Business, industry, government, and the professions frequently make use of surveys to determine consumer attitudes, voter preference, and public opinion. The largest survey is conducted by the U.S. Census Bureau; among the best known of other surveys are the Gallup, Roper, Harris, and Nielsen polls.

Surveys may be conducted by mail, telephone, or personal interview. Each has its advantages and disadvantages. Mail surveys are the least expensive and can cover the widest geographical area. They are effective in eliciting responses because they are convenient and because people often do not mind providing private information anonymously. Among their drawbacks is the possibility of skewed results due to misleading replies given by annoyed or indifferent individuals. Another is the likelihood of distorted findings, answers being provided only by interested people.

Personal interviews are expensive both because they are time-consuming and because the interviewers must be trained. But a person-to-person encounter can provide detailed information that is more apt to be accurate than information obtained in other ways.

Telephone interviews are relatively inexpensive and can be effective in obtaining brief information. Usually people are willing to answer a few questions on the telephone. The main difficulty arises in reaching people. Often they are out, busy, inaccessible, or sometimes so annoyed with telephone solicitors that they will not talk to any stranger.

Regardless of the method used, the effectiveness of a survey depends on the validity of the sample and of the questions used. Ideally, the best sample is one that consists of the entire *population*, meaning all the people about whom information is desired. The U.S. census comes closest to achieving this objective. In contrast, the Nielsen ratings are based on the television habits of about 1,200 out of 74 million households. Yet the fate of television programs and the investment of millions of advertising dollars are determined by this sample.

The Nielsen survey is an example of stratified random sampling, the most complex type; other forms are random sampling and systematic random sampling. Let us begin with the simplest.

RANDOM SAMPLING   Random sampling is similar to drawing names out of a hat. But everyone in the population must be represented in the sample. For example, the telephone directory should not be used in an accurate community survey because it excludes people without phones. Similarly, in a campus study of student attitudes about the library, selecting students at random in the library would result in a faulty study because students who were not in the library could not express their opinions.

SYSTEMATIC RANDOM SAMPLING   It is easy to draw a few names at random. When many are involved, a definite procedure is desirable. In systematic random sampling, a plan is established for selecting names, but the actual selection is made by numerical chance. For example, a campus survey of students might be conducted by choosing names from a college directory, but a number might be drawn to determine whether every third, seventh, or fifteenth name should be selected from every page.

STRATIFIED RANDOM SAMPLING   The most complicated and accurate of all, this method is used by professional pollsters. It consists of determining the percentage of pertinent subgroups (blue-collar workers, rural people, college graduates, and so on) in the population and then constructing a sample identical to the larger group.

The Gallup Poll, for example, selects a sample of about 1,500 people according to such characteristics as age, income, sex, race, location, and education.[5]

Although professional surveys such as the Gallup and Harris polls are highly scientific and considered valid, there may be a decisive margin of error when people indicate future plans or actions. In the case of the Edsel automobile, for example, extensive and highly professional marketing surveys indicated that people liked it. But when it rolled off the Detroit production lines months later, people did not buy it. Why do such things happen? For one thing, we do not always buy what we say we like. For another, the final product and its trade name may not have public appeal. Or the economic climate changes. And pollsters also know they must allow for the fact that, after reading the results of polls, people may change their minds.

THE NUMBER TO BE SURVEYED   In addition to determining how to conduct a survey, you must decide on the number of people needed for the random or random systematic methods to be valid. A course in statistics or advice from a survey expert would be helpful. In their absence, you might plan to obtain responses from about 25 percent of the population. If that percentage is impractical, survey the highest percentage you can and then use the split-sample test. Arbitrarily split the total replies you have been able to obtain into two or more groups. If the replies from the partial samples are comparable, then the total sample is generally considered to be valid.

THE QUESTIONNAIRE   Whether your survey is conducted by mail, phone, or personal interview, the questions must be constructed carefully. This is especially true of the mailed questionnaire; it must be attractive enough to entice responses and clear enough to be self-explanatory. Here we shall be concerned only with the mailed questionnaire, but much that applies to it applies to other kinds of surveys.

ENCOURAGING A REPLY   The questionnaire (also known as *survey instrument*) should be accompanied by a letter requesting a reply and a stamped, return-address envelope. Like all request letters, it should be courteous. In addition, as we pointed out in chapter 3, it should include statements about why the questionnaire is being sent, how the responses will be used, how respondents will benefit, and when the replies are needed. If possible, sign each letter or add a personal note or postscript. This friendly touch usually increases the number of responses.

The questionnaire should be designed attractively, with a great deal of white space so that it looks easy and quick to complete. Obviously it should be as short as possible, containing only essential questions. In revising your first draft, keep asking yourself, "Is this question necessary? Why?"

ARRANGEMENT OF QUESTIONS   Although questions should follow a logical arrangement, you should make every effort to begin with general questions that people find easy to answer. Then, when the respondents reach more specific, complicated questions, they will usually complete them as well. (See figure 9–7.) Personal

Figure 9–7. An Easy-to-Answer, Clearly Worded, Impartial Question.

"AND FINALLY, WHAT IS YOUR OPINION
OF OUR QUESTIONNAIRE?"

(SOURCE: Drawing by Chon Day. © *Changing Times*)

questions, such as name, age, sex, and marital status, should be placed either first or last. With sensitive questions, such as age or income, it is usually more productive to ask for information within ranges, as exemplified here:

Income: Below $10,000 _____ $10,000–20,000 _____ $20,000–30,000 _____
Over $30,000 _____

TYPE OF QUESTIONS The writing of questions looks easy. But it is anything but easy to construct a questionnaire that is clear, attractive, and reliable. Here are some guiding principles:

- *Easy-to-answer questions:* Avoid questions requiring detailed information that is not recent or easily recalled.
- *Specifically worded questions:* Be careful of using general words that may have different meanings for different people. The question "Do you go to the movies frequently?" is faulty because *frequently* can be interpreted in various ways.

- *Clear-purpose questions:* The purpose of each question should be clear. For instance, if you wish to know what particular stylistic feature caused customers to select a certain shirt, avoid asking, "Why did you buy this shirt?" An answer of "It was on sale" fails to provide specific information—about the appeal of the style, fabric, or workmanship, for example.
- *Nonleading questions:* Avoid questions that assume certain existing conditions: "Before biting your nails, what was your bad habit?" "Why don't you stop beating your wife?" "Why don't you like the food at the student cafeteria?"
- *Easy-to-tabulate questions:* In constructing a questionnaire, look ahead to the problem of evaluating the responses. While a few questions may be open-ended to allow for lengthy and individual comments (see the second question in figure 9–8), most should allow answers that can be easily tabulated and interpreted.
- *Questions of fact, not opinion:* Whenever possible, try to obtain factual information instead of opinions. Note in the section on "Concerning Our Delivery Service" in figure 9–8 that instead of asking whether customers like the delivery service, the questionnaire seeks factual responses.
- *Single-topic questions:* Questions combining two topics may provide misinformation. For example: "Would you attend concerts if they were held at noon in the Student Center?" A negative answer would not distinguish among students who would never attend concerts, those who would not go to the Student Center, and those who do not favor the noon hour.
- *Questions that allow for all possible answers:* When asking people to select from among numerous answers, you should furnish them with all available possibilities. If you cannot anticipate all possible answers, then leave space for "other" as in figure 9–8, third question.
- *Space for open-end questions:* Be certain to allow sufficient space for people to write comments or suggestions. Note again how this is handled in the second question in figure 9–8.

Test your questionnaires on a few associates to get the bugs out. You'd be surprised how questions that seem perfectly clear to you can be interpreted differently by someone else. It would be far better to have associates point out a weakness than to have your survey spoiled by a faulty question or two.

TECHNIQUE

Having compiled your information, you must next write it up in report format. Following are three writing techniques for communicating research naturally, clearly, and understandably. These techniques involve using first-person pronouns and topic sentences and adjusting your style to your audience's reading level.

Figure 9–8.   Mail Questionnaire.

A MAIL QUESTIONNAIRE

Which of the following newspapers do you read?

	Regularly	Sometimes	Not At All
Lizella Free Press	☐	☐	☐
Macon Times	☐	☐	☐
Bibb County News	☐	☐	☐
Monroe Weekly	☐	☐	☐

Generally speaking, are you happy with ROSE's? Do you have any suggestions so that we might do a better job of serving you?

_____

_____

_____

_____

Would you please place a check mark (✔) under the Macon store where you usually shop for the following types of merchandise: (If the store you shop at most often is *not* shown, please write in the name of that store.)

	Rose's	Church's	Penney's	Monroe's	Tucker's	Other
Women's Clothing	☐	☐	☐	☐	☐	_____ (Name)
Men's Clothing	☐	☐	☐	☐	☐	_____ (Name)
Children's Clothing	☐	☐	☐	☐	☐	_____ (Name)
Furniture	☐	☐	☐	☐	☐	_____ (Name)
Other Home Furnishings	☐	☐	☐	☐	☐	_____ (Name)

Zip Code <u>28501</u>   _____
                                                                  Name (Not Required)

Occupation of Chief Wage Earner_____

Please return this questionnaire in the enclosed, prepaid business-reply envelope.

Figure 9–8 (continued).

	GOOD	AVERAGE		POOR		NO Experience
	5	4	3	2	1	NE

CONCERNING OUR DELIVERY SERVICE:

Packages

Is merchandise delivered when promised?	5	4	3	2	1	NE
Does the package arrive in good condition? . . .	5	4	3	2	1	NE
Are the drivers courteous? . . .	5	4	3	2	1	NE
When you give special instructions for delivery, are they followed? . . .	5	4	3	2	1	NE
How does our delivery service compare with that of other stores? . . .	5	4	3	2	1	NE

Large Merchandise (Furniture, Appliances, etc.)

Does this large merchandise (Furniture, Appliances, etc.) arrive in good condition? . . .	5	4	3	2	1	NE
Are the drivers courteous? . . .	5	4	3	2	1	NE

WHEN TELEPHONING THE NANCY HARPER ORDER BOARD TO PLACE AN ORDER FOR AN ITEM IN OUR CATALOG OR NEWSPAPER:

Are your calls answered promptly? . . .	5	4	3	2	1	NE
Do those taking your orders know their merchandise? . . .	5	4	3	2	1	NE
Are your orders taken courteously? . . .	5	4	3	2	1	NE
Do you receive the merchandise as ordered? . . .	5	4	3	2	1	NE

WHEN TELEPHONING ORDERS DIRECTLY TO SELLING DEPARTMENTS:

Are your calls answered promptly? . . .	5	4	3	2	1	NE
Do those taking your orders know their merchandise? . . .	5	4	3	2	1	NE
Are your orders taken courteously? . . .	5	4	3	2	1	NE
Do you receive the merchandise as ordered? . . .	5	4	3	2	1	NE
When necessary, are your calls transferred properly? . . .	5	4	3	2	1	NE

CONCERNING OUR ADVERTISING:

When shopping for merchandise we have advertised, do you generally find an adequate supply? . . .	5	4	3	2	1	NE
Do you feel our sales people are generally well informed about an item we have advertised? . . .	5	4	3	2	1	NE
Does our advertising sufficiently describe merchandise for mail or phone ordering? . . .	5	4	3	2	1	NE

Do you receive our sale booklets? . . . Yes ☐   No ☐

By what means are they delivered? . . . Mail ☐   Door Hung ☐   Don't Know ☐

WORDS: THE FIRST-PERSON PRONOUN

As you've read the letters, memos, and reports (for example, figure 9–1) in this book, you may have wondered what happened to the old-time taboo about using *I* or *we* in your writing. But today nothing is taboo in business writing if it is appropriate for audience, purpose, and occasion. Nowadays, *I* and *we* usually are appropriate except in formal scientific or academic reports.

The use of *I* or *we* in an article, letter, or report makes your communication seem more personal and sincere. Even in objective writing, personal pronouns are often preferable to passive constructions or other evasions. In less objective writing, *I* or *we* should always be used instead of such monsters as *this writer, the undersigned,* or *your correspondent.*

It is true that years ago people refrained on grounds of modesty or objectivity from using *I* or *we.* But styles change. Our written language has moved closer to conversation, often becoming quite chatty. The aim in business and industry is to please the reader, and therefore, in weighing alternatives in writing, we should choose the one that will sound more natural and straightforward. Nothing can create this effect better than the direct, person-to-person *I* or *we.*

In many corporations, stockholders' reports are dreary, impersonal, ponderous communications written by computers—or so it seems. Here, however, is a welcome change in excerpts from a quarterly report from Peter Peterson, when he was Chairman of the Board of Bell & Howell:

> I also want you to know that . . .
> We have concluded that . . .
> I will now attempt to explain . . .
> Now, I'd like to review some of the background . . .
> Frankly, we at Bell & Howell think this is a proper concern . . .
> I want to re-emphasize that . . .
> I would personally welcome . . .

Here is the way that Merrill Lynch might have written copy for a report years ago:

> *Why Do Business With Merrill Lynch?*
> Year in and year out, Merrill Lynch holds rank as one of the biggest underwriters and distributors of municipal bonds. It is active in both the primary and secondary markets. As investment brokers, Merrill Lynch bids on issues that its specialists regard as top quality and offers them for sale to the general public. It is also active in the secondary market, trading in seasoned issues of all kinds.

Here is how they actually wrote this paragraph recently (italics added):

> *Why Do Business With Merrill Lynch?*
> Year in and year out, Merrill Lynch holds rank as one of the biggest underwriters and distributors of municipal bonds. *We* are active in both the primary and secondary markets. As investment brokers, *we* bid on issues that our specialists regard as top quality and offer them for sale to the general public. *We* are also active in the secondary market, trading in seasoned issues of all kinds.

The actual copy transforms Merrill Lynch from a giant corporation into a group of human beings, while losing nothing in modesty. The old notion that using *I* or *we* injects a note of egotism by calling attention to the writer is just not true. Of course, our current reaction is conditioned by the common use today of first-person pronouns; they no longer startle us. Therefore, writers should use *I* and *we* whenever directness, friendliness, warmth, sincerity, and naturalness are desirable. And they usually are in business writing.

Of course, first-person pronouns will not by themselves guarantee your reader's goodwill. But writers often overlook their effectiveness in creating a favorable image in the reader's mind.

Sentences: Topic Sentences

Paragraphs are small units packaged within larger ones. They focus on a central idea and follow certain patterns—time, space, cause and effect, analysis, problem and solution, comparison and contrast, or enumeration. No matter what the pattern, nearly all paragraphs—particularly in business writing—move from a general assertion to more specific ideas that amplify, develop, or illustrate. The general assertion, called a topic sentence, announces the topic or thesis of a paragraph.

Although occasionally the topic sentence may be placed in the middle or at the end of a paragraph, or may even be implied rather than expressed, writers most often begin with it. Just as drivers would prefer to see the names of communities posted as they enter them, instead of as they reach the business districts, so readers appreciate an initial statement announcing what will follow. Note that while the following passage provides information, it forces you to figure out its purpose:

> Although interest rates have already fallen sharply, the still higher inflation rate could prove to be more nearly intractable than is generally expected. If inflation remains high while interest rates continue to decline, the United States dollar could be subjected to renewed pressures. Moreover, no one could foresee what steps Washington might take . . . if the recession turns out to be more severe than now seems likely and if unemployment rises sharply. The stock market would probably not take kindly to stimulative economic measures that would only rekindle inflationary pressures. Finally, no one can foretell what might develop in an already tense international situation, and surprises could certainly unsettle financial markets.

You could help readers of this passage by adding a topic sentence. A statement at the end would do the trick: *So any number of unpredictable events could cause stock prices to give way.* But unless there is some reason for an inductive approach, such as the desire for a climactic effect, it would be better to lead off with this sentence:

> Any number of unpredictable events could cause stock prices to give way.

As you can observe, placing the topic sentence at the beginning of the paragraph helps readers to see where the writer is going and to know what to expect. For variety, you may wish to imply rather than express your topic sentence or insert it later in a paragraph. But be certain you have a solid reason for doing so.

STYLE: READABILITY

Readability refers to whether a written passage is suited to the audience's reading level. Revising your report drafts to ensure their readability helps readers comprehend your communication. As the quotation at the opening of this chapter points out, the ease with which your reports convey their messages is the chief stylistic factor by which your communications will be judged.

Among specialists recently attaining prominence are readability experts. They have established clinics, conducted workshops, set up laboratories, and even patented a measuring device. Their readability formulas have been successfully used by government and industry. Best known of these experts are Rudolph Flesch, whose *Art of Plain Talk*[6] has long been a best seller, and Robert Gunning, whose "Fog Index"[7] is widely used. Gunning's Fog Index is illustrated here because of its simplicity.

The Gunning yardstick may be applied to any sample passage of about one hundred words. Here is all you need to measure writing for clarity:

1. Select a representative passage. Count out 100 words. If you are in the middle of a sentence, end the sample with the sentence bringing your total nearest to 100. For example, in the passage preceding this numbered instruction, there are 97 words.
2. Find the average words in a sentence by dividing the number of sentences into the number of words. Count each independent clause as a separate sentence.
   Example: 7 sentences, 97 words. Average words in a sentence = 13.9.
3. Count the number of difficult words (words with three or more syllables). Exclude:
   a. Capitalized words
   b. Simple compounds (bookkeeper, butterfly)
   c. Verbs whose third syllable is *-ed* or *-es*
   Example: Difficult words = 16
4. Add the average words in a sentence to the difficult words.
   Example: 13.9 + 16   Total = 29.9
5. Multiply the total by .4.
   Example: 29.9 × .4 = 11.96

This score means that a reader will need 12 years of schooling to understand the passage easily. According to these calculations, *T.V. Guide* averages about 6, *Time* and *Newsweek* 11. Anything much higher would be heavy going for average readers.

Although unfamiliar two-syllable words like *arrant, flaccid, effete, nadir,* and *vapid* can invalidate the measurement, the Gunning formula (as well as the Flesch formula) does provide an objective, impartial method of testing any piece of writing to determine its approximate readability. For instance, if a memo to custodians about waste disposal has a score of 13, the writer should review the work carefully to simplify it for these employees, who probably have at most a high school education.

Do not feel restricted while you write, but use the formula during revision. You need not turn statistician to clarify your sentences; just be aware that uncommon words and long sentences make reading more difficult. So you should avoid trying to impress the reader with your command of language.

As you revise, remember the significant impact that sentence length has on reader comprehension. Research indicates that for college-educated audiences you should review sentences exceeding thirty words or three typed lines; for high school audiences, those exceeding twenty words or two typed lines. Naturally these rules are not rigid because the structure of a sentence has much to do with clarity and readability.

For example, someone should have spotted the following fifty-four-word monster in recent Federal Income Tax Instructions:

> The amount of loss to be deducted is measured by the fair market value of the property just before the casualty less its fair market value immediately after the casualty (but not more than the cost or other adjusted basis of the property); reduced by any insurance or compensation received and the $100 limitation.

The rewritten version, with five short sentences instead of one long one, is easier to understand:

> Here is how to calculate the amount of the loss. Take the fair market value of the property before the casualty. Subtract the fair market value after the casualty. The result cannot be more than the cost or other adjusted basis. Then subtract any insurance or compensation received, and also the $100 limitation.

A word of caution about the other extreme—sentences that are too short. Studies have shown that sixth-graders average twelve words per sentence, high school seniors twenty, and college seniors twenty-two. Of course, you don't want to try to make the length of every sentence conform to any of these averages. In fact, varying sentence lengths contributes to the interest of a report, memo, or other form of communication. So while you should review your drafts to see that they have a good mix of sentence lengths, you should be careful that the final draft does not include sentences that are too long to be readable.

SUMMARY

The word *report* is used to refer to many kinds of communication—spoken and written, short and long, informal and formal. No matter what they are called or how they are classified, written reports serve many useful purposes: gathering data, supplying reliable information, providing permanent records, meeting deadlines, combining expertise, communicating ideas, and encouraging creativity. An effective report is attractive, clear, and reliable, and uses a familiar format and headings.

Among the reports most common in business and industry are the letter report, the progress report, the periodic report, the information report, the analytical report, the recommendation report, and instructions. Most of these reports range in length from one to several pages. Knowing how to write them will help you compose most other short reports.

Report research may be conducted by reading printed works such as the books and periodicals found in libraries. It may also be conducted by less bookish means—by observation, which involves watching, investigating, and studying; by experimentation, which involves comparisons and tests; and by surveying, which involves using mail or telephone questionnaires or personal interviews. However, you should be careful that your observations are accurate and fully explained, that your experimentation takes variables into account, and that your surveys use valid samples and reliable questions.

As you compose your findings in report format, using first-person pronouns and topic sentences will help you communicate your research naturally and clearly. And revising your drafts to suit your reader's capabilities will ensure the readability of your final report.

Since writing reports will be such an important responsibility for you as your career develops, the points covered in this chapter may be crucial to your success.

EXERCISES

Discussion Questions

1. Explain why the word *report* is often confusing to those who hear or read it.
2. Cite the basic functions of reports.
3. Describe at least five ways reports can be made more readable.
4. What kinds of short reports do specialists in your professional field have to write? Is report-writing ability a criterion for success in the profession you've chosen? Explain.
5. Describe the purpose of letter reports, progress reports, periodic reports, information reports, analytical reports, and recommendation reports.
6. Describe the contents of progress and periodic reports—the points covered by each. In what ways are the two types of reports different?
7. What are the steps involved in composing effective instructions or directions?
8. Someone has sarcastically referred to questionnaires as "instruments that allow you to avoid accepting responsibility for what you write." Explain why this criticism has been leveled at surveys as a way of gathering information.
9. What are the advantages of using first-person pronouns in business writing? Disadvantages?
10. What are the functions of a topic sentence? Within a paragraph, where does such a sentence usually appear? Do all paragraphs have topic sentences? Explain.
11. Explain how the Gunning Fog Index can help you accommodate your readers. What are some limitations in using the Gunning formula?

In-Class Applications

1. Visit or write several businesses and industries in your area and obtain copies of their short reports. Do they conform to the report guidelines that are given in this chapter? Be able to lead a discussion in class about the similarities and differences. Be prepared to defend your preference for one practice over the other.

2. Interview specialists in the field you plan to enter and ask them about the reports they write. Compile a list of the various types of reports they mention. In class discussion, compare your list with those of your classmates and note whether report types vary from one field to another.

3. Analyze an article in a recent magazine to discover at least two paragraphs using topic sentences. In class, show whether the topic sentences appear at the opening of the paragraphs, whether they appear later in the paragraphs, or whether they do not appear at all and are only implied. Write a paragraph imitating the use of topic sentences as found in your models.

4. Examine this report preface, noting its use of the first person:

> In our study of career advising for students enrolled in premedical and predental programs at other institutions, we have talked with advisors at over twenty colleges and universities. Since we found that most advisors faced the same problems we are faced with, we believe our discussions have helped us identify ways of improving our committee's advising system at East Carolina University.
>
> In this report, we will explain our prehealth career advising problems at East Carolina and then propose solutions for them. The problems are as follows:
> 1. Failure of our advising system to reach all students who are majoring in prehealth fields.
> 2. The heavy workload on the advising committee chair.
> 3. The large volume of committee work presently handled by the committee chair's departmental secretary.
> 4. The need for official summer operations.
>
> After explaining these problems and proposing solutions for them, we will recommend a plan for implementing the solutions.
>
> If you need additional data on any item or on the report as a whole, we will be glad to elaborate.

What effect does the first person have on the reader? Rewrite the passage using only impersonal language. Then compare the difference in effect.

5. Write down the steps for sharpening a pencil with a manual pencil sharpener. Use commands for each step. To test the clarity of your instructions, read the step-by-step procedures aloud while a classmate follows them.

Writing Assignments

1. The downtown area in your home or college community is dying. In other communities, the following suggestions have helped to reverse this decline:
   a. Additional parking space
   b. Improved appearance
   c. Increased bus service

d. Promotional programs

e. Wider sidewalks

f. Improved traffic flow

g. Public benches and rest rooms

h. A greater variety of stores

Write a letter report for the chamber of commerce urging any of these suggestions or others that you would like to offer.

2. Because the company that you are working for as a summer intern has done poorly in recruiting college graduates in the last few years, the president has asked you to write a letter report suggesting ways to improve the program. From a study entitled "M.B.A. Recruitment," you have read about the following practices that have proved successful for other companies:

a. Sending candidates a month's subscription to a local newspaper.

b. Using phone calls to follow up on candidates.

c. Inviting candidates' spouses to accompany them to visit the company. Helping spouses to find jobs.

d. Promptly reimbursing candidates for travel expenses.

e. Bringing people in to meet candidates instead of having them walk around to many different offices.

f. Meeting candidates at the airport and later returning them there.

Write a letter report using any of these suggestions, or adding others that you can think of or learn from seniors or graduate students.

3. After having chosen one of the letter or recommendation report projects in this section, and after doing the preliminary research and planning a schedule for completing the report, write a report to your instructor about your progress on the assignment.

4. Write a term report in which you describe your progress during the previous or current term toward the completion of your degree. Assume that the report will be one of a series of such reports, each describing your progress during one academic term.

5. As assistant to the Director of Admissions, you have been asked to suggest ways to attract better high school students from your state. Write a recommendation report indicating what you could do with a budget of $5,000.

6. Write a report for the president of student government presenting ideas about improving any one of the following:

orientation program	residence halls
advisory system	lecture series
student-faculty relationships	fraternity or sorority rush
voting by students	athletic ticket distribution

7. Competition among motels in your community has become intense. You have been employed by one of them to suggest ways that it might attract more guests. After surveying several motels in other communities, talking to numerous travelers, and thinking about the program, you have jotted down the following recommendations: establishing get-togethers similar to those at resort hotels; providing lockers where sales representatives and other regular guests could store some of their belongings; stocking small refrigerators with snacks and drinks, and

charging for whatever is used; serving buffet-style breakfasts; furnishing typewriters without charge to business travelers; and having a less rigid policy on checkout time for people waiting for late-afternoon planes. Write a report incorporating several or all of these suggestions.

8. Numerous campus problems have been the focus of attention in recent years. Review the policy of your institution in any one of the following areas or any other, and prepare a report for student government recommending a change:

excessive drinking	approval of student organizations
off-campus misconduct	controversial speakers
premarital pregnancy	control of student publications
visitation hours in dorms	open admission
black studies	drugs in the dorms
cheating	parking

9. As an assistant to the Dean of Students, you have been asked to formulate a new policy for renting university apartments, which are highly desirable because of their location, attractiveness, and relatively low cost. Your task is to establish and justify a priority system for different categories of students, and possibly for faculty members. In proposing your plan, be certain to answer the following questions:

   a. Should the apartments be restricted only to married students?

   b. Because of the university's desire to play a more important role in graduate education, should all or a large proportion of the apartments be reserved for graduate students?

   c. Should in-state students be given a higher priority than out-of-state students?

   d. Should students now living in the apartments be evicted at the end of their one-year lease if they would not qualify for an apartment under the new system?

   e. What should be done about students whose names have been on the waiting list for a year or more but who would now receive a low priority?

   Write a recommendation report proposing the new policy.

10. Write directions for campus visitors who are trying to find their way from your classroom building to a neighboring restaurant.

NOTES

1 Herman M. Weisman, *Basic Technical Writing* (Columbus: Charles E. Merrill, 1980), p. 343.

2 For over forty years *Financial World* has sponsored the *Financial World* Annual Report Awards, with winners usually announced in mid-October. *FW* awards Silver Medals to eleven finalists and a Gold Award for the best report of the year. The awards are highly coveted by the professional writers and artists who prepare these spectacular documents. Many of these writers and artists are members of selective professional societies such as the New York Financial Writers Association and the American Institute of Graphic Arts.

COMMUNICATING BY MEMOS AND REPORTS

[3] Robin Willadsen Anderson, "Conclusion" to "Sexism in *Contemporary Business Writing*" (a group report submitted to Professor Deborah H. Pickering in partial fulfillment of the requirements for English 8W113, University of Iowa, Iowa City, Iowa, May 1, 1979), p. 6. Reprinted with permission of Professor Pickering.

[4] Homer L. Cox, "If At First You Don't Succeed, Try Another Tack," *The ABCA Bulletin*, 42 (June 1979), p. 2.

[5] "Opinion Polls Are ( ) Accurate, ( ) Slanted, ( ) Don't Know," *Changing Times*, 34 (March 1980), p. 65.

[6] Rudolph Flesch, *Art of Plain Talk* (New York: Harper & Brothers, 1946).

[7] Robert Gunning, *The Technique of Clear Writing* (New York: McGraw-Hill Book Company, 1968).

10 The Long Report

OBJECTIVES

After reading this chapter, you should be able to:

- Prepare the preliminaries, body, and supplements in long reports
- Streamline long reports
- Apply standard organizational patterns in drafting reports
- Choose words that sound human and natural
- Enliven reports by eliminating clichés and jargon
- Use transitions to make your reports flow smoothly and clearly
- Use visual aids to illustrate your reports

PLAN

Strategy
Divisions of Long Reports
   Preliminaries
   Body
   Supplements
Streamlined Long Reports
Organizational Patterns
   Time
   Space
   Cause and Effect
   Analysis
   Problem and Solution
   Comparison and Contrast
   Enumerative Order
   Combined Patterns
Technique
Words: Naturalness
   Personal Style
   Vividness
Sentences: Transitions
   Directional Transitions
   Natural Transitions
   Paragraph and Division
      Transitions
Style: Visual Aids
   Purposes
   Guidelines
Summary

We have never received a report that
was too clear.[1]

STRATEGY

Although most business and industrial reports are short, like those discussed in chapter 9, occasionally you may be responsible for writing a long report. Long reports, which range in length from eight or ten to hundreds of pages, are sometimes called *formal reports*—because such formalities as covers, title pages, tables of contents, lists of figures, preliminary summaries, and appendixes are commonly used. In this chapter, however, we will refer to the reports using these formalities as *long reports*.

DIVISIONS OF LONG REPORTS

Like short reports, long reports vary in format from organization to organization and from company to company. So, the following guidelines for preparing a long report are only suggestions. Determine whether they are acceptable in your class, company, or organization before following them slavishly. In the absence of other guidelines, you should find these helpful.

Long reports usually have three major parts—the *preliminaries*, the *body*, and the *supplements*:

Preliminaries	Body	Supplements
Letter of Authorization	Introduction	Documentation
Letter of Transmittal	Background (Statement	Appendixes
Cover	of Problem)	
Title Page	Purpose	
Table of Contents	Method	
List of Figures	Scope and Limitations	
Summary	Definitions	
	Plan	
	Discussion	
	Conclusions	
	Recommendations	

In the following discussion, we will examine each of these divisions and refer to excerpts from a sample recommendation report illustrating most divisions.

Preliminaries

The more report preliminaries, the more formal the report. The preliminary parts dress up the report and offer much incidental information—who authorized the report, its title, who prepared it, the date, the job number, a list of its divisions and subdivisions, a list of its visual aids, and even a condensed version of its contents. Whether you include some or all of the preliminary parts will depend on your audience, purpose, and occasion.

LETTER OF AUTHORIZATION   The letter of authorization is usually a follow-up of a discussion during which you were asked to write a report. This letter instructs you to research a topic and prepare the findings in report form. It carefully explains the assignment, states the purpose the report will serve, and gives a deadline for delivery. As the letter of authorization in figure 10–1 illustrates, the person requesting the report will often make suggestions about sources, methods, and procedures and will specify a budget.

Often, a copy of the letter of authorization is included near the front of the report. The letter explains the circumstances that led to the report. It can be helpful when you discuss such matters as limitations, research methods, and plan of organization.

Although the other report divisions are usually double-spaced, preliminary letters such as the letter of authorization are single-spaced like regular business letters.

LETTER OF TRANSMITTAL   The letter of transmittal may appear together with the letter of authorization either before or after the title page. It serves a number of functions, as seen in figure 10–2. It adds a personal touch to what is usually an impersonal report and explains to readers why the report was written. The writer usually begins the letter by saying in effect, "Here's what you requested."

Occasionally, the transmittal letter will summarize the report, thus eliminating the need for a separate summary. In some cases, it may state a recommendation or express a need for future study. It often includes statements about problems incurred, expressions of gratitude for assistance, matters of special interest, and suggestions for further research, none of which could conveniently appear in the report itself. And, in closing, it usually expresses willingness to provide additional information.

COVER   For professional appearance and for storage, reports are usually enclosed in attractive, durable covers. Companies often provide employees with standard covers, or you may buy commercially prepared ones from bookstores or office supply stores.

The cover typically contains the title, the contract or order number, and the delivery date.

TITLE PAGE   The title page (see figure 10–3) includes vital information—the title of the report, the names and positions of its authors, the names of the persons the report was written for, and the delivery date. If necessary, the contract or order number should also appear. No single design is standard for the title page, but clarity and attractiveness are essential.

Figure 10–1. Sample Letter of Authorization.

INVERSHIEL MICROELECTRONICS, LTD.

Steeplechase Road   Southern Pines, North Carolina 28387

Office of the Plant Manager
(919) 555–4200   Ext. 301

October 30, 19--

Mr. Ramon Davis
Supervisor
Research and Development

Dear Ramon:

I would like you and Pam Casale, Joyce Evans, Chris Farren, and Kim Fleetwood to prepare a report about the accessibility of Invershiel buildings for employees who are confined to wheelchairs. The buildings I wish you to research are the Accounting Office, Administrative Complex, Construction Shop, Data Processing Center, Employee Recreation Lounge, Payroll Office, Research and Development Building, Security and Information, Shipping Office, and Warehouse.

Specifically, I would like to know if wheelchair-bound employees encounter architectural (i.e. structural, design, or equipment) barriers to the functions or services housed in these buildings. If the functions or services are not accessible or convenient, how might the situations be corrected?

I intend to bring the findings, conclusions, and recommendations of your report to the attention of C. P. Rowe, Director of Employee Services. As you are aware, C. P. has asked for suggestions about how services might be further improved at Invershiel for our handicapped colleagues. The focus of your report should thus be to identify any accessibility problems for disabled employees and to recommend how C. P.'s office might solve these problems.

As we agreed in our discussion this morning, you are to use whatever research tools you deem appropriate, including legal documents such as building regulations if they prove helpful. Any bills incurred in researching, writing, and preparing the report should be forwarded to me for approval.

Please submit the report to me by November 16, 19--. You may call on me at any time in my office for further clarification of your duties or for assistance.

Sincerely,

John Fordham

John Fordham

er

Figure 10–2.   Sample Letter of Transmittal.

INVERSHIEL MICROELECTRONICS, LTD.

Steeplechase Road   Southern Pines, North Carolina 28387

Research and Development

(919) 555–4200   Ext. 308

16 November 19--

Mr. John Fordham
Plant Manager

Dear Mr. Fordham:

Here is the report you authorized on handicapped employees' accessibility to
the main buildings at Invershiel Microelectronics, Ltd.

As you suggested, we limited our investigation to those handicapped persons
who are confined to wheelchairs but have use of their upper bodies, and to
those main buildings specified in your letter.

As you will see in the findings of the report, the main Invershiel buildings
present few accessibility problems for our colleagues confined to wheelchairs
thanks to the progress of C. P. Rowe and his staff. In those cases where
problems do exist, the report recommends specific corrections.

Please call on me if our committee can offer additional assistance with the
accessibility problem. We will be glad to conduct further research on this
topic for you.

Sincerely,

Ramon Davis, Chair
Accessibility Report Committee

fz

Enclosure

Figure 10–3.   Sample Title Page.

```
                    The Accessibility of Main Buildings

                    at Invershiel Microelectronics, Ltd.

                    for Physically Disabled Employees




                                    for

                            Mr. John Fordham

                             Plant Manager




                                    by

                    Ramon Davis, Pam Casale, Joyce Evans,

                      Chris Farren, and Kim Fleetwood

                      Research and Development Office




                             16 November 19--

                    Invershiel Microelectronics, Ltd.

                      Southern Pines, North Carolina
```

TABLE OF CONTENTS A report of considerable length includes a table of contents to help the reader locate the various sections. The table of contents usually consists of the report's chapter headings and the headings of major subdivisions. Each main division may be labeled with the appropriate Roman numeral and the sub-divisions denoted only by indentation, as shown in figure 10–4.[2] Page numbers appear in a column on the right.

LIST OF FIGURES The list of figures, also known as a *table of graphics*, indexes each visual aid by number, descriptive title, and page number. In reports containing just a few tables and illustrations, the list of figures is omitted.

SUMMARY Often called an *abstract, synopsis, epitome*, or *précis*, the summary is a miniature report—a condensation of the introduction, text, conclusions, and recommendations. In other words, the summary (see figure 10–5) should be complete in itself so that the reader can obtain an overview of the entire report. It is often placed in an information retrieval system, such as a card catalog or microfiche index.

Whether summarizing your own work or another's, you should select the important ideas in each section, omitting minor points and all examples, illustrations, and supporting data. Next, you should write your first draft, then hack away until what remains is about five percent of the original, or one typed page for every twenty. Don't underestimate the difficulty of this work; it's tough!

The summary should preserve the organization of the report, indicate the relative importance of its ideas, but not repeat its exact words. Its sentences should flow as smoothly as the plot summaries in a student guide.

People often find it difficult to write effective summaries because they fail to distinguish between descriptive and informative statements. Descriptive statements tell what something is about—for example, "This report discusses the advantages and disadvantages of establishing a junior department in the stores located in college communities." This statement tells the reader what the report deals with but fails to provide information. You should remember the purpose of the summary: to enable the reader to learn the important points of the report without having to read it. Thus an informative summary might be:

> Visits to our stores in twenty college communities reveal a demand for a junior department. Although renovation costs would be high and some valuable space would be lost, the resulting increased volume of sales indicates that junior departments should be established in these stores.

By remembering the function of a summary—namely, that it must serve as a condensed report—you can best avoid writing a description, an interpretation, or a commentary.

Figure 10–4. Sample Table of Contents.

TABLE OF CONTENTS

ii

Figure 10–5. Sample Summary.

SUMMARY

This report presents the results of a study about the accessibility of
Invershiel Microelectronics buildings for physically handicapped employees.
Library research, interviews, and experimentation indicate that, in spite of
advances in accommodating these employees, those confined to wheelchairs still
encounter a few accessibility problems that should not exist.

These accessibility problems could be corrected by installing in the
Accounting Office a telephone that is not enclosed by a booth; relocating the
trash can in the Administrative Complex men's restroom; installing a special
turnstile accommodating wheelchairs at the Construction Shop and marking as
such the lanes designed for this purpose; installing ramps at entrances to the
Shipping Office and the Employee Recreation Lounge; removing or lowering the
granite sill on the main entrance of the Shipping Office; installing a level
area between the ramp and the door at the Warehouse; continuing the special
arrangements that permit employees to obtain services on the upper floors of
all buildings; equipping water fountains in all buildings with paper cups and
dispensers; and installing tilted or angled mirrors in bathrooms in all
buildings.

Body

Following the preliminaries is the body, the most important part of the report. Besides introducing the subject, the body presents your research findings and, if appropriate, states your judgments and proposes action. There are usually four separate sections in the body: introduction, discussion, conclusions, and recommendations.

INTRODUCTION The introduction may consist of two or three prefatory paragraphs, or it may discuss the background, purpose, method, scope and limitations, definitions, and plan of organization of the report (see figure 10–6). Whether you touch on just a few introductory subjects in a few paragraphs or devote a separate division to each subject will depend on your audience, occasion, and purpose. In either case, using these standard introductory subjects as touchstones will simplify your chore.

Background The introduction may contain a concise statement or history of the problem to be investigated and mention how the report was initiated, by whom, and when—for the benefit of people who may be unfamiliar with the background of the situation. In short, this section explains *why* the report was written.

Purpose As clearly and precisely as possible, the introduction should announce the purpose of the report—often to propose a solution to a problem or present the findings of a study. In other words, this section states *what* the report is about. It may be only one sentence, "The purpose of this report is to . . . ." Sometimes *purpose* appears before *background*.

Method Unless readers are convinced that the research procedure is sound, they may doubt your facts and conclusions. You should clearly explain the method or methods you used in securing the data—that is, tell *how* you obtained your information. If an explanation of the methodology is highly technical and tedious, details or samples (questionnaires, tests) may be provided in an appendix. Remember, however, that unless you take pains to show that your data is reliable, you may damage your report's credibility.

Scope and Limitations *Scope* is a positive statement about what is within the report. It clarifies for readers what they can expect from the report by explaining how dependable, thorough, and far-reaching it is. A careful statement about scope explains the extent of your investigation.

On the other hand, *limitations* are negative statements about what is *not* within the report. Usually reports are restricted in several ways: in the purpose for conducting the investigation, in the resources supporting the investigation, in the area of investigation, in the period covered by the investigation, and in the research methods employed. These limitations should be explicitly stated to show the boundaries of the report, or you may be held responsible for matters beyond the limits of the paper.

Figure 10–6. Sample Introduction.

INTRODUCTION

Background

The most recent example of the effort in North Carolina to make all
man-made environments available to physically handicapped people was the
addition in 19-- of a section to the State Building Code entitled "Making
Buildings and Facilities Accessible to and Usable by the Physically
Handicapped." At Invershiel Microelectronics, Ltd., the process of
making buildings accessible to the disabled was begun in 19-- and still
continues. On October 30, 19--, the writers of this report were authorized
by Mr. John Fordham, Plant Manager, to investigate the main buildings of
the Invershiel plant. This report is the result of that investigation.

Purpose

The purpose of this report is to investigate the accessibility to
physically disabled employees of certain buildings at Invershiel Microelectronics, Ltd. Specifically, ten buildings are examined to determine if
they present any barriers to the mobility of individuals in wheelchairs.

Method

Three methods were used to collect information for this report.
First, library research yielded North Carolina laws concerning the

1

Figure 10–6   *(continued).*

handicapped (see Appendix A), a relevant vocabulary, and background
information (see Appendix B). Second, interviews were conducted with
various handicapped employees at Invershiel as well as with administrative
personnel: Mr. C. P. Rowe, Director of Employee Services; and Mr. Rick
Ferris, Associate Chair of The Affirmative Action Committee. Third, an
experiment was performed on the accessibility of specified service
buildings by a wheelchair-confined individual. This handicapped employee
visited all ten buildings named in this report to determine if architectural
barriers were present.

Scope and Limitations

The ten main buildings investigated for barriers were the Accounting
Office, Administrative Complex, Construction Shop, Data Processing Center,
Employee Recreation Lounge, Payroll Office, Research and Development
Building, Security and Information Building, Shipping Office, and Warehouse.

The investigation was confined to the Invershiel main plant area between
Steeplechase Road and Tufts Lane. Only the ten main buildings were investigated;
no buildings at auxilliary sites, such as the one at Pinebluff, were included.
The study was conducted to determine barriers only to a person confined to a
wheelchair; no other type of handicapped person was considered. Although the
handicapped employee did not use the lower half of his body, he used the upper
half to assist himself in various activities. In all likelihood, the results
would have been different if more severely handicapped individuals had been
considered.

Moreover, only accessibility features of the buildings were examined;
the inaccessibility of functions or services was not included when caused
by mere distance.

2

Figure 10–6 (continued).

Definitions

Definitions appear below of key terms used throughout this report.

accessible	(adj.) Applies to any building which allows a disabled individual to enter, and move from place to place within, that building.
barrier	(n.) Any object, or arrangement of objects, which obstructs the path of a physically disabled person.
paraplegic	(n.) An individual who has lost complete, or nearly complete, use of the lower appendages while retaining the use of his upper appendages.
physically disabled	(adj.) Applies to any paraplegic who is confined to a wheelchair.
ramp	(n.) A sloping walkway which is attached to a building as a means of moving from one floor elevation to another without encountering any obstructions. Ramps are above normal level.
main building	(n.) Any building, other than auxilliary facilities, that provides a vital function or service requiring employees to be present.
water closet	(n.) The toilet and adjacent stall.

Plan of Organization

The text of the report is divided into ten main headings: each of the ten main buildings investigated is represented by one heading. The secondary headings are: ramps, entrances, upper floors, restrooms, other facilities, and special problems. Conclusions and recommendations follow the discussion.

3

Figure 10–7. Even Everyday Terms Need Defining.

*"My opponent has called me a liar and a cheat.
I think he ought to define his terms."*

(SOURCE: Drawing by Peter Steiner. © *Changing Times*)

Definitions One of the stickiest sections of the introduction is the definition of key terms as the cartoon in figure 10–7 suggests. Even simple words like *poor* can cause tremendous problems. Exactly who, for example, is to be considered poor? Young married students with little income but high future potential? Farm families who require less food, rent, and clothing than ghetto dwellers on the same income? Retired people who earn little but own their homes? All these and many other questions must be answered before writing a report on the poor. And, once you have answered them, you must take a paragraph—or several, if necessary—to show readers how the word *poor* has been used in the paper.

Underestimating the importance of definition can damage the clarity of your writing. For this reason, you should be careful to examine all your key terms to determine whether any are ambiguous. Remember, it is always safer to define a term than to assume it is understood. Pay particular attention to apparently simple words. At one school, a committee spent hours trying to define what appeared to be an obvious word, *faculty*, in order to determine eligibility for a faculty senate.

Definitions take three forms: the *synonym*, the *sentence*, and the *extension*. The synonym form appears in statements like the following:

Conglomerates, or multi-industry corporations, are regaining their appeal for investors.
conglomerates = multi-industry corporations
term = synonym

The following is an example of the sentence definition:

A conglomerate is a large corporation consisting of a number of companies in different unrelated businesses.

$$\text{conglomerate} = \text{corporation} + \text{number of companies in unrelated businesses}$$
$$\textit{term} = \textit{category} + \textit{distinguishing characteristics}$$

Here, *conglomerate* is the term, *corporation* the category, and the rest of the sentence distinguishes a conglomerate from other kinds of corporations.

For most readers, however, these definitions of conglomerates would be inadequate. An extension of the definition would explain the meaning of *different, unrelated businesses*; furnish illustrations by discussing the empires of ITT or Litton; compare and contrast these corporations with a multi-industry corporation like American Tobacco; perhaps provide an analogy by likening a conglomerate to a vast university with heterogeneous students, and contrasting it with a selective private college with homogeneous students; indicate what a conglomerate is not; explain the etymology of the word; and mention the shortcomings of other definitions.

These techniques may be helpful in writing an extended definition. Of course, not all reports will require exhaustive treatments of terms, or even need any definitions at all; but you must be careful because, as we explained in chapter 2, words are far more complicated than they appear to be at first glance.

In your introduction, therefore, define any terms your readers might not be familiar with or might misconstrue. If you use so many difficult terms that defining all of them in your introduction is not feasible, then you can define them in a glossary at the end of the report. However, if you use a glossary, you should refer your readers to it, perhaps using a brief introductory definitions section for this purpose, before they begin reading the discussion section of your report.

Plan of Organization The sections of the introduction may appear in whatever order is logical and helpful, but the report's plan of organization should always be stated at the end of the introduction, to show readers what is to follow. In effect, the plan serves as a map, showing the main divisions of the report and their order. Sometimes the plan is stated in a separate paragraph, sometimes only in a sentence, such as: "The following discussion is divided into three parts: (1) an analysis of the price of similar products; (2) an analysis of our product; and (3) a recommended price for our product." The organizational patterns discussed in this chapter help you choose a plan suitable for your report.

DISCUSSION The discussion section of a large report presents the findings of your research or investigation, with headings indicating each major division and subdivision (see figure 10–8). Like the text of an article or other piece of writing, the discussion section is organized according to the nature of the material. Yet one strategy popular among experienced writers may help you plan its structure: you may present uninterpreted facts in the discussion section and defer interpreting them until the sections

Figure 10–8.   Sample Portion of a Report Discussion.

FINDINGS OF THE INVESTIGATION

Administrative Complex

Entry Ramp

The Administrative Complex was equipped with a concrete ramp, with handrails, which led to the main entrance. The employee in the wheelchair encountered no difficulties ascending the ramp.

Door Entrance

The entrance was comprised of a single wooden door. This door presented no barrier to the employee.

Upper Floors

The absence of elevators in the complex rendered the upper floors inaccessible to the employee. It should be remembered, however, that services located on upper floors have been made obtainable through the Employee Services Office.

Restrooms

The following information applies to both male and female restrooms in the Administrative Complex.

Mirrors. The single mirror was neither lowered nor angled, and the handicapped employee was unable to use it.

Sinks. The sinks were low enough to facilitate their unhindered use for the handicapped employee.

Water Closets. One water closet was equipped with a wide stall, handrails, and a raised toilet. The disabled employee was able to maneuver his wheelchair without difficulty.

4

Figure 10–8   (continued).

Other Facilities

    Water Fountains. At the height of 34 inches from the rim of the basin to the floor, the fountain was entirely within state limits.

Despite this fact, the handicapped person was unable to drink normally; water dripped from his chin and onto his shirt. After several attempts, the employee could drink comfortably only with assistance, as is shown in Figure 6.

Figure 6. The handicapped employee was able to drink only with assistance.

    Telephones. There were no public telephones in this building.

    Turnstiles. The Administrative Complex contained no turnstiles.

Special Problems

    A heavy trash can was located inside the entrance of the male restroom, as shown in Figure 7. The subject was unable to maneuver past this barrier without calling for assistance.

A—Corridor
B—Walls
C—Door
D—Metal Partition
E—Trash Can

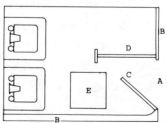

Figure 7.   Location of the trash can in the male restroom of the Administrative Complex.

5

COMMUNICATING BY MEMOS AND REPORTS

for conclusions and recommendations. The separation of data from interpretations can be viewed this way:

Discussion | Conclusion
uninterpreted data ----> interpretation of data

The discussion might present only partial conclusions. For example, you might report that Cadillacs require less maintenance and have higher resale value than Lincolns, but that Lincolns cost less initially. Yet the discussion section would not announce the verdict that all the evidence might point to—that Cadillacs would be better long-range buys than Lincolns. This verdict would be deferred until the concluding sections of the report.

The partial-conclusion strategy has much to recommend it. Because interpretive statements appear only in the conclusions and recommendations, the report uses fewer words. Also, the writer appears to readers as impartial and, therefore, reliable. Skeptical readers do not have an opportunity to quarrel with the writer's interpretations until they have read through the cumulative evidence; they are thus more likely to be convinced.

The presentation of facts in the discussion section usually follows one of the patterns discussed on pages 323–328 of this chapter.

CONCLUSIONS As we explained in chapter 9, in an information report you present no conclusions or recommendations; you merely state your research findings and allow readers to draw conclusions and make their own recommendations.

However, in an analytical, or interpretive, report, the discussion is followed by a section entitled "Conclusions," in which you present your judgments. Even if these judgments have already been implied or stated, they are usually repeated for people who may read only this section of the report.

Veteran report writers sometimes itemize each conclusion in a separate statement or short paragraph, as in figure 10–9, rather than grouping them in longer paragraphs. The reason for this practice? Each conclusion can stand on its own merits, not on its connection with neighboring statements. Writers using this strategy might thus succeed in convincing readers of at least some conclusions.

RECOMMENDATIONS The section with recommendations is optional. It may contain a definite proposal for action, a series of proposals, or a series of alternatives. Recommendations should be clearly based on the preceding conclusions. For example, you might set forth a specific plan, stemming from your earlier conclusions, to solve the community's recreational needs; recommend a three- or five-year plan showing exactly how the community should appropriate money each year to meet its immediate and long-term needs; or propose a series of alternatives contingent on available revenues. Generally, recommendations should be brief and to the point. As figure 10–10 illustrates, recommendations, like conclusions, may be itemized in separate statements, for the same reasons that each conclusion may be.

Figure 10–9. Sample Conclusions.

CONCLUSIONS

Of the ten main buildings investigated, only two did not have ramps.

Of the six buildings which had upper floors, five did not have elevators.

Of the nine buildings containing public restrooms, two were not equipped with water closets accommodating the handicapped person. However, only two of the many restrooms had lowered or angled mirrors.

All of the water fountains presented a problem because they were not equipped with paper cups.

All telephones in the buildings were accessible except the one enclosed in a booth in the Accounting Office.

Of the three turnstiles found in various buildings, only the one in the Construction Shop presented a barrier to the handicapped employee.

Two buildings, the Shipping Office and the Data Processing Center, contained vertical drops greater than one-half inch. These drops proved to be a hindrance to the disabled employee's mobility. This same problem was caused by multiple floor levels inside the Employee Recreation Lounge.

Of the nine buildings which had public restrooms, only the male restroom in the Administrative Complex, which had a heavy trash can blocking the door from opening completely, proved to be a barrier to the disabled employee.

Of the two buildings with check-out lanes, the lanes of one, in the Construction Shop, were too narrow for a wheelchair. In the same shop, one check-out lane did accommodate the wheelchair. But there were no signs indicating which lane would or would not allow entrance by wheelchair.

18

Figure 10–10.   Sample Recommendations.

RECOMMENDATIONS

1. In the Accounting Office, a telephone that is not enclosed in a booth should be installed.

2. In the Administrative Complex, the trash can in the men's restroom should be relocated.

3. In the Construction Shop, a special turnstile accommodating wheelchairs should be installed. Check-out lanes designed to accommodate wheelchairs should be labeled accordingly.

4. In the Data Processing Center, vertical drops and inconsistencies in floor levels should be eliminated.

5. In the Employee Recreation Lounge, vertical drops and inconsistencies in floor levels should be eliminated.

6. In the Shipping Office, ramps should be installed at one entrance, and the granite sill at that entrance should be lowered or removed. Also, vertical drops and inconsistencies in floor levels should be eliminated.

7. At the Warehouse, ramps should be installed at the main entrance, and a level area ought to be fabricated between the ramps and the door.

8. In general, special arrangements allowing disabled employees to obtain services located on upper floors should be continued. Tilted or angled mirrors should be installed in restrooms where they are lacking. And all water fountains should be equipped with paper cups and dispensers.

19

Supplements

Although the body of a report can usually stand alone, you can add to its usefulness and credibility by making helpful or marginal information easily available to readers. A handy way of offering this optional material is in supplements—sections added at the end of the report.

DOCUMENTATION Having completed the body, report writers often wish to indicate their indebtedness or to lend authority to their statements by citing printed sources. They do so by documenting with endnotes, a bibliography, or both. Sources may be presented in an appendix or in a supplementary section called "Notes," "Bibliography," or "Documentation." Forms of documentation are discussed in Appendix L, "Documentation and Library Sources." A sample bibliography appears in figure 10–11.

APPENDIXES The appendixes (or *appendices*) of the report contain detailed and complicated material that may not interest most people, but should be included for special and technical readers. Other material that might be included in appendixes would be information and visuals useful to readers, but not sufficiently vital for inclusion in the body. In addition, appendixes may contain a glossary of terms, statistics, tables or illustrations, sample questionnaires, primary data (for example, computer print-outs), working papers, a bibliography, specifications, and items too large or bulky to be included conveniently in the body of the report.

The criterion for the placement of such materials is the audience. Depending on readers' needs and interests, a particular chart might appear either in the body or in an appendix.

Each appendix should be labeled as Appendix A, B, C, and so on, and then by descriptive title (for example, "North Carolina Building Code Regulations for the Physically Handicapped") as seen in figure 10–12. Appendixes are more cogent and relevant if you refer to them in your discussion.

STREAMLINED LONG REPORTS

Except in circumstances when virtually every formality is required, many companies nowadays prefer shorter, less formal reports. The reason for this preference is that a condensed report reduces production time, costs, and reading time.

If your audience is familiar with the background, research methodology, and organizational plan, you can streamline long reports by excluding several preliminary and supplementary divisions, such as the letter of authorization, the title page, the list of figures, and the summary. A streamlined report might have relatively few divisions:

- Transmittal Letter
- Introduction
- Discussion
- Conclusion (optional)
- Recommendations (optional)

Figure 10–11.   Sample Bibliography.

BIBLIOGRAPHY

Bartholomew, Robert. <u>Planning Considerations in Designing Facilities for</u>
    <u>the Physically Handicapped</u>. Monticello, Illinois: Council of
    Libraries, 1976.

Battle, James K. "Current EEO and Handicapped Employee Developments,"
    <u>The Business Lawyer</u>, 36 (March 1981), 711-720.

Copland, Keith. <u>Aids for the Severely Handicapped</u>. New York: Grune and
    Stratton, 1974.

Harkness, Sarah P., and James N. Groona. <u>Building Without Barriers for</u>
    <u>the Disabled</u>. New York: Watson-Suystill, 1976.

Hull, Stephen B. "Accommodating Disabled Employees," <u>American Business</u>,
    17 (August 24, 1979), 17-21.

Mace, Ronald L. <u>Accessibility Modifications</u>. N.P.: Barrier Free
    Environments, Inc., 1976.

Mace, Ronald L., and Betsy Laslett. <u>An Illustrated Handbook of the</u>
    <u>Handicapped Section of the North Carolina State Building Code</u>.
    Springfield, Illinois, 1974.

20

Figure 10–12. Sample Appendix.

APPENDIXES

APPENDIX A

North Carolina Building Code Regulations for
the Physically Handicapped

The following are excerpts taken from the North Carolina Building Code,
Volume 1, Section (XII), "Making Buildings and Facilities Accessible to and
Usable by the Physically Handicapped."

Water Fountains

In buildings where Section (XII) 1.1 applies and where water fountains
are provided, such water fountains shall comply with the following
requirements:

a. Water fountains or coolers shall have upfront spouts and controls.
b. Water fountains or coolers shall be hand-operated or hand- and
    foot-operated.
c. Where provided, at least one-per-floor conventional wall- or
    floor-mounted water cooler shall have a small fountain mounted
    on the side of the cooler, with the edge of the small fountain
    basin no higher than 30 inches above the floor. Wall-mounted,
    hand-operated coolers serve the able-bodied and the physically
    disabled when the cooler is mounted with the edge of the basin
    36 inches from the floor.

Public Telephones

All "banks" of public telephones should have at least one telephone
which can be used by the physically disabled, including those in wheelchairs
and those with hearing and sight disabilities.

The following are minimum requirements:
a. The dial and headset shall be placed no more than 4 feet above
    the floor.
b. The telephone shall be equipped for those with hearing disabilities
    with an adjustable volume control for the headset with instructions
    for use.
c. The telephone shall be equipped for those with sight disabilities
    with visual and tactile instructions for use. Large tactile
    letters shall be used for instructions.
d. On every floor where telephones are installed, at least one
    should be placed so that the dial and headset are no more than
    4 feet above the floor, and equipped for those with hearing and
    sight disabilities and so identified with visual and tactile
    instructions for use.

21

These divisions may be adjusted to provide all the necessary information. For example, the title page information may be condensed and placed at the top of the first page of the report. Or a brief summary may be included in the transmittal letter.

But be certain to include every division needed for credibility, completeness, and clarity. Trying to reduce production time by cutting out essential divisions can make your report less authoritative and force your readers to ask for additional information and clarification of certain portions. So reduce the formality of your reports judiciously, keeping in mind the practices of your company and the needs or expectations of your readers.

Organizational Patterns

The most widely known organizational patterns are time, space, cause and effect, analysis, problem and solution, comparison and contrast, and enumeration. To choose among them, decide which is most appropriate for your purpose.

Time

Most popular and simplest of all organizational plans is chronological order. Many writing assignments lend themselves readily to the first-things-come-first approach. A report about changes in social security benefits might follow this plan. So might historical accounts, descriptions of processes, and instructions on how to assemble something. Nearly all of these may be organized according to one of the following three time options:

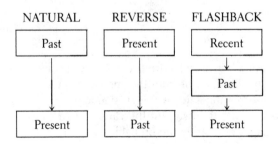

For example, an article describing the growth of the Xerox Corporation might begin with an account of the work done in a small Rochester garage by its founders and proceed through time to the present; commence with a description of the company's current success and move back to its past; or start with a picture of the company today, flash back to its beginnings, and then portray its growth since then.

Because of its simplicity, time order should be selected whenever possible. But a writer should realize its two possible drawbacks—monotony and lack of emphasis— and compensate for them.

Space

Equally easy for reader and writer but not as frequently applicable as time order is spatial order—for example, east to west, top to bottom, close to far, inside to outside, left to right:

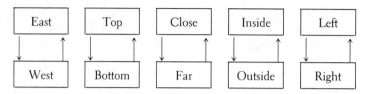

A survey of FM broadcasting stations across the country, for example, might start in the East and move to the West. Other types of assignments lending themselves to spatial order include studies of parking facilities, plant layouts, or zoning, and descriptions of machines, factories, or sites.

Like time arrangement, organization by space may be monotonous and may fail to emphasize important information.

Cause and Effect

The thirst for knowledge about the future and for understanding of the past results in frequent questions. The writer is faced with infinite queries, from the child's "Why does it rain?" to the entrepreneur's "Will it be profitable?" In answering such questions, you as a writer should decide upon one of these two cause-effect patterns:

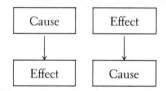

Generally you move from the known to the unknown: from the known cause to the probable effect, or from the known effect to the probable cause. For example, a study of decreasing sales would first document the effect by citing figures on sales and profits and then suggest the causes. The cause-to-effect design would be followed in a paper estimating the probable outcome of a tax increase, or a decrease in corporate capital spending.

A variant of this pattern might occur when an immediate effect would differ significantly from a long-range effect. The initial impact of a tariff on foreign cars, for example, might have to be described before discussing the long-range effect.

The causal approach, unfortunately, has many pitfalls. Most dangerous of these is the logical fallacy known by its Latin name of *post hoc, ergo propter hoc*, meaning, "After this, therefore because of this." In other words, we must be careful about mistaking a time sequence for a causal one. Several years ago, consumers boycotted numerous grocery chains after noting an increase in food prices when various sales-incentive games were introduced. It was later shown, however, that these increases were primarily caused by supply and demand, not by the games.

Another common error in the causal pattern results from failure to distinguish among primary (main), contributing (incidental), and immediate (most recent) causes. The immediate cause for a television retailer's going into bankruptcy may have been a poor season; but the primary cause may have been fiscal mismanagement and the contributing cause, the competition from a new discount appliance store.

Analysis

Analysis involves the division of a subject into its parts. For example, if you are studying subjects such as automobiles, fire extinguishers, or NOW checking accounts, then your initial task is to organize your material. You might break it down into such categories as cost, weight, size, function, structure, or services. You may further divide and subdivide the resulting groups. The writer of a report on NOW checking accounts, for example, might break the topic into an outline and use the divisions and subdivisions as headings, as follows:

> Balance Required
>   Minimum
>   Average
> Interest Calculation Method
>   Interest Rate
>   Interest Compounding Method
> Penalty Charges
>   Interest Loss
>   Service Charge
>   Check Fee

Be wary of two traps in using analysis. Any time you divide a subject into its parts, you must be certain that the parts add up to the whole. To be complete, a study of American automobiles, for example, would have to include *all* American makes, and not omit such cars as the Excalibur. Also, a paper on student expenses would have to include such incidental and easily overlooked matters as newspapers, toothpaste, stationery, stamps, magazines, check charges, haircuts, and dry cleaning. Therefore, you should decide at the outset what your study will include, and so specify in your introduction. For example, you might state in your scope and limitations section that you are limiting your study of American cars to Chevrolets, Fords, and Plymouths.

Another pitfall in analysis results from overlapping. Categories must be clearly established so that each item belongs only to one category. If cars are classified according to their price, for instance, you must define your basis of analysis carefully; otherwise many luxury models of inexpensive cars will have to be grouped with the regular models of more expensive cars.

In summary, watch out for gaps and overlaps.

Problem and Solution

Many reports are written to propose a change or to solve a problem. For example, you may want to recommend the purchase of word processing equipment either because it will handle your paperwork better or because it will solve your problem of continually having to update form letters. In such instances, the following formula may be used:

1. Statement of situation or problem
2. Description of solution
3. Unbiased discussion of solution's advantages and disadvantages
4. Evidence of why proposed solution is better than other solutions

When the problem or need is evident, the first step is not important. But often in reports suggesting a change, the reasons why the change is needed constitute the most crucial part of the paper. Generally people are satisfied with the status quo; they fear the uncertainties produced by change. Therefore, a writer must convince them, for example, of the serious shortcomings of present accounting procedure, filing system, or billing policy before introducing a new plan. Otherwise, readers will not even consider the proposal.

Comparison and Contrast

Comparison may be useful to explain something complex or unfamiliar, or to recommend a change. Thus, to help readers understand theories or mechanisms, scientists and engineers frequently compare them to similar household items.

In writing about business policies and procedures, comparison is likewise useful. For example, a convincing argument for using a particular plan in a business situation is to demonstrate that it was effective in a similar situation.

Contrast is especially useful in evaluating alternatives. People in business and industry must frequently decide what site, machine, policy, or person would be best for their companies. If they examine all possibilities and contrast their advantages and disadvantages, they are most apt to select wisely. Consumer organizations use these methods to evaluate such products as automobiles, television sets, and cameras.

Comparisons and contrasts may be organized in two ways, as in this illustration:

Subject Pattern	Characteristic Pattern
Item A: Cadillac	*Point 1:* Cost
Point 1: Cost	Item A: Cadillac
Point 2: Upkeep	Item B: Lincoln
Point 3: Resale	Item C: Mercedes-Benz
Item B: Lincoln	*Point 2:* Upkeep
Point 1: Cost	Item A: Cadillac
Point 2: Upkeep	Item B: Lincoln
Point 3: Resale	Item C: Mercedes-Benz

Item C: Mercedes-Benz	*Point* 3: Resale
Point 1: Cost	Item A: Cadillac
Point 2: Upkeep	Item B: Lincoln
Point 3: Resale	Item C: Mercedes-Benz

Subject pattern is effective when only information is requested; in a sense it says to the reader: "Here are the facts—you decide." Characteristic pattern is effective in emphasizing specific differences or similarities. In both patterns, the facts prepare readers for any recommendations being made.

A final word about comparisons and contrasts: whenever possible, use tables. With the cost, upkeep, and resale of three brands of cars, for example, most of the material can be presented clearly and succinctly in a table with a column for each item or point.

Enumerative Order

In setting forth a series of ideas, facts, examples, or opinions, you can follow certain traditional arrangements. Depending upon your subject, audience, and purpose, you might organize the material according to importance, generality, complexity, or persuasion.

IMPORTANCE   Because the most emphatic positions are first and last, many writers place their important points in these positions and the lesser points in between. Opening with a key point stirs readers' interest, and closing with another helps to maintain it. And, since the most vital points receive the most emphasis, they are most apt to be remembered.

GENERALITY   Although people enjoy occasional surprises, usually they prefer to know where they are going and what is happening. So most writers begin with a general proposition and then provide details, examples, or illustrations. The opposite approach, from particular to general, may be effective in a relatively short report because, like a detective story, it keeps readers in suspense. But while reader patience may not wear thin in trying to solve a murder, it may give out in trying to get to the point of a lengthy report. Particularly in business, readers favor knowing at the outset the general point or purpose of the report.

COMPLEXITY   For psychological reasons, a writer usually moves from the simple to the more difficult and complex. A reversal of this pattern could prove disastrous— readers failing to comprehend the beginning of the report may not bother to finish it.

PERSUASION   In advancing arguments for proposals, opinions, or decisions, writers should begin with the ideas they wish to discredit and end with those they advocate. In other words, first strike down what you oppose, then advocate what you favor. As a result, you gain a psychological advantage. Because readers are best prepared for what comes last, they are more likely to concur with the final points. Arguments, like battles, usually go to those who have saved their strength until the end.

Combined Patterns

Although the organizational patterns have been described individually, they may be used in combination. Main divisions may be arranged in one sequence (for example, time), major subdivisions in another (for example, cause and effect), and minor subdivisions in a third (for example, enumeration). A writer should always be flexible, ready to shift from one strategy to another to help the reader. Remember: It's not what is easiest to write that is important, but what is easiest to read.

TECHNIQUE

Familiar formats (discussed in chapter 9), conventional divisions, and customary organizational patterns will help your reader decode the information you are reporting. In addition, three writing techniques—natural and vivid words, transitional sentences, and visual aids—will further relieve your audience of their difficulties with decoding. Diminishing these difficulties makes your reports not only more effective and memorable but also more pleasant to read.

WORDS: NATURALNESS

To lend an impartial and authoritative tone to their reports, and bolster their credibility and persuasiveness, many writers try to create an air of formality. Of course, because of their important functions and their prescribed divisions, reports must be less personal and more formal than letters and memos. And sometimes audience, occasion, and purpose will call for a detached, lofty, dry tone. Yet without sacrificing either credibility or persuasiveness, you can achieve a natural tone by choosing words that sound human and natural. And you can enliven your writing by avoiding worn-out expressions and by suiting your expertise to your readers' abilities.

Personal Style

Some writers feel that if readers are aware of a person's being involved in researching and writing a report, they may not believe the contents: humans, after all, are fallible. So these writers try to make their reports sound as impersonal as possible. Too often the result is a lifeless, awkwardly stated document with little added credibility.

Personal pronouns—"I," "you," "he" or "she," "we," "you," "they"—call attention to people. So proponents of an impersonal style favor noun substitutes, as in these cases:

Personal Pronouns	Noun Substitutes
I	the writer
you	the reader
he, she	the subject
we	the writers
you	the readers
they	the subjects

Whether you choose these noun substitutes, which depersonalize writing, making it colorless and antiseptic, will depend on your audience, occasion, and purpose. But you should remember that your choice may be a swap—the gain of credibility at the loss of liveliness.

Don't let audience, occasion, and purpose take second place to the impulse to impress others with language. Unless you are writing for a highly educated audience under formal circumstances, such as a report for a learned society, select the natural instead of the learned word. And you should usually avoid the other extreme, the colloquial word. For example:

> *Learned:* The controller made several sagacious recommendations.
> *Natural:* The controller made several intelligent recommendations.
> *Colloquial:* The controller made several smart recommendations.

In these sentences, *sagacious* smacks of the dictionary, *intelligent* of polite conversation, and *smart* of campus chatter.

Be constantly aware that some words are formal and should therefore be reserved for formal occasions. Note the following contrasts:

Formal	Informal	Formal	Informal
accommodations	rooms	obtain	get
accompany	go with	possessed	had
activate	start	prior	before
cease	stop	proceeded	went
commence	begin	purchase	buy
compensation	pay	render assistance	help
concur	agree	require	need
donation	gift	reside	live
endeavor	try	secure	get
expedite	hasten	similar to	like
initiate	begin	terminate	end
inquire	ask	transpire	occur

In this age of plain talk and simple statements, you should favor the words in the right-hand column. We enjoy informality—in dress, in manners, in people, and in words. If you strive to impress others with fancy words and picturesque phrases, you will sound pompous and insecure.

Of course, there are occasions for impersonal, dignified language, but they are few. In most situations, choose the word that sounds human and natural rather than the one that sounds lofty and affected.

Vividness

Language can be dull and dreary or vibrant and pungent. Words can snap, crackle, and pop, or they can sag, sink, and plop—depending on your ability to use them effectively. You can deaden your writing with clichés and jargon.

CLICHÉS Trite, stereotyped, and colorless, clichés *bore you to tears*. They are *a dime a dozen* and *as old as the hills*. They are expressions that have lost their original freshness and have, *in the final analysis, slowly but surely*, come to *a bitter end* in the hands of poor writers. It is true that once they may have been *good as gold*, but now they are *as weak as water* and make you feel *as uncomfortable as a turkey at Thanksgiving*. If you want to stay *abreast of the times* in using words, then avoid clichés *like the plague*.

JARGON Shoptalk, the specialized language of a trade or profession, appears in three forms: (1) technical terms and acronyms; (2) all-too-familiar phrases; and (3) Bizlish, or pretentious, polysyllabic language intended to impress or confuse readers. Jargon appears frequently in business, industry, and government reports because people in organizations tend to do and write everything in the customary way. So young executives striving for high positions copy the ways and words of their bosses—who, of course, have copied the words and ways of their own bosses.

Figure 10–13. How Acronyms Can Confuse.

Bountiful In Acronyms

KNOXVILLE, Tenn. (AP)—The Tennessee Valley Authority is changing the name and the acronym—held in so much favor by government officials—of its Office of Community Development.

TVA's directors informally have approved changing the name to Office of Economic and Community Development to promote its new image as an industrial recruiter as opposed to a social worker.

But a couple of officials commented that the change and the new acronym, OECD, may create some temporary confusion along with the problem of memorandums occasionally going to the wrong place.

There is not much difference between OECD and OEDC, the Office of Engineering Design and Construction responsible for building TVA's dams and nuclear plants.

A tongue-tied bureaucrat, or one having trouble with his bifocals, also could send a memo intended for OECD or OEDC to OACD, the Office of Agriculture and Chemical Development where the fertilizers are made.

(SOURCE: Reprinted by permission of Associated Press.)

COMMUNICATING BY MEMOS AND REPORTS

The problem with technical terms like *metacommunications, floppy disks, hereinabove, standard deviation, oxymoron, depth of field, wow,* and *flutter* is that they may baffle nonspecialists. Especially confusing to laymen are acronyms, or names formed from the initial letters of words—*SOAP* (Subcommission on Academic Programs), *NASA* (National Aeronautics and Space Administration), *SALT* (Strategic Arms Limitation Talks), *COBOL* (Common Business Oriented Language), *GIGO* (garbage *in,* garbage *out*), and so forth. (See figure 10–13.) Although these specialized terms may damage the style of a communication, they do provide a convenient, compressed, and colorful means of communicating ideas among insiders—people of the same occupation—just as medical terminology expedites communication among health professionals. When you analyze your audience, remember that specialized language confuses outsiders and stirs their resentment.

Overworked phrases are usually intelligible to specialists and nonspecialists alike, but like clichés they are trite—*earliest convenience, enclosed herewith, yours of the ninth instant, thanking you in advance, acknowledge receipt of, please do not hesitate, the bottom line, pursuant, touch base, at this point in time, with respect to,* and so forth. Such shopworn language bores readers and implies the writer has not provided them with the courtesy of an individualized communication (see figure 10–14).

The third type of jargon, Bizlish, is puffed-up, highfalutin, often wordy language: "With all due respect I beg to inform you that the absence of your esteemed approbation is a source of deep and undeviating concern and discomfort to one who has long held for you the deepest and most genuine affection"—or, in other words, "I'm troubled that you don't like me." Of course, such incredible pomposity is akin

Figure 10–14. Shopworn Phrases Can Offend.

"People don't 'touch base' with me, sir—they either call me or come in to see me!"

(SOURCE: From *The Wall Street Journal,* Permission-Cartoon Features Syndicate)

to the "learned" diction we discussed earlier. Whether it is intended to impress the reader or disguise the message, it produces the unwanted effect of portraying the writer as a contemptible stuffed shirt.[3]

While overworked phrases and Bizlish generally detract from the vividness of your letters and reports, specialized language should not be so easily dismissed. As suggested earlier, technical words used judiciously can help you transmit information concisely and even naturally to fellow specialists. For example, jargon would be perfectly appropriate in a technical report prepared by an accountant for an audience of fellow accountants.

But what of a report whose audience includes people with a variety of backgrounds—specialists, semispecialists, and novices? Chris Morgan, editor of the computer journal *BYTE*, has cleverly pointed out the difficulty of accommodating technical language to such a mixed group:

> Imagine your readers to be sitting at . . . intervals along a large seesaw. At one end are the most technically astute members of your audience; at the other, the interested novices. In the middle are people with varying degrees of knowledge in the subject you are writing about. Your job is to keep the seesaw as level as possible by attending to the various groups in proportion. If there are many novices involved, you must "hold up" their side by providing them with a lot of introductory material. But if you go too far in this direction, the experts will get bored, dismount, and leave you. . . .

Suiting your specialized terminology to the abilities of a mixed audience is clearly not easy, and Morgan adds that "some seesaws can't be balanced despite the best intentions of writers."[4]

If you must use technical jargon in long reports for a mixed group, you may find it helpful to design certain sections chiefly for nonspecialists and other sections chiefly for specialists. For example, the summary, introduction, conclusions, and recommendations may be designed for general readers, such as the corporate officers who will decide whether to adopt your recommendations. And the text, visual aids, documentation, and appendixes may be designed mainly for fellow specialists—say, the accountants who must verify your figures before the corporate officers make their decisions. Or you could suit the language of your preliminaries and text for general readers and use technical jargon only in your supplements.

In general, however, you should remember that language is most effective when it is simple, direct, and natural. So your writing should usually sound conversational—not the conversation of the college locker room but of the executive boardroom. The voice should be that of a person, not a machine. Because the unnatural and mechanized language that typifies so much business, industrial, and government writing can sap forcefulness and obscure clarity, you should be wary about using it.[5]

Sentences: Transitions

Clear report writing flows from sentence to sentence and from paragraph to paragraph; each unit of thought is connected and related to the previous one. The links, or *transitions*, come in all sizes and shapes: captions, words, phrases, subordinate clauses, complete sentences, and short paragraphs. As helpful to readers as a scoreboard to football fans, transitions are not difficult to master.

Think of each sentence as an island that must be connected to the preceding one by some bridge. This bridge or transition (etymologically, "a crossing") should also prepare the reader for any change of direction. Failure to provide the bridge and sometimes the signpost will make the reader's journey through your ideas a vexing and tedious one.

Directional Transitions

Transitions that both bridge the gap and signal the way might be termed *directional transitions*. Pictorially they might be represented like this:

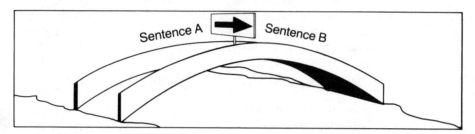

The selection of a particular directional transition in a sentence depends upon the relationship between the statement and the one that preceded it. The following list indicates some possible relationships and their corresponding transitions:

Relationship	Directional Transitions
For sentences adding similar information	also, and, furthermore, moreover, next, and numbers (first, second, etc.)
For sentences adding conflicting or contrasting information	but, however, nevertheless, on the contrary, on the other hand, yet
For sentences adding illustrative information	for example, for instance, in other words, likewise, similarly, specifically
For sentences adding information involving space, time, or degree	above, around, earlier, formerly, later, more, to the left (right, east, etc.), then
For sentences adding information involving cause or effect	as a result, because, consequently, hence, since, so, therefore, thus, for this reason
For sentences signaling a conclusion	after all, at last, finally, in conclusion, last, to conclude, to sum up

Your task is not only to post a sign for the reader, but to select the specific one that accurately indicates the correct route. For example:

> Instead of moving all his stock to the new store, he decided to clear out many small items. Nevertheless,

The sign, *nevertheless*, has indicated that what follows will conflict or contrast with what has preceded. When the remainder of the sentence fails to satisfy this expectation, the reader is disconcerted:

> Nevertheless, he worked at night to select and mark down the items for sale.

An accurate signal would have clarified what followed:

> Therefore, he worked at night to select and mark down the items for sale.

Natural Transitions

Although highly effective, directional transitions can easily be overused. A page filled with *however*'s, *therefore*'s, and *yet*'s is as distracting as a highway crammed with signs. For a while, they are welcome; soon they become annoying.

A more subtle way of linking sentences is to use what might be called *natural transitions*. These transitions consist of devices we normally use in talking—demonstratives (*this*, *these*), synonyms, and repetitions. Note how the natural and directional transitions signal relationships in the following paragraph:

Demonstrative adjective and repetition	A company should benefit from establishing a suggestion system in its plants. *This system* would allow employees below the management level to submit ideas for improving machinery, procedures, and plant conditions.
Synonyms	*Workers* contributing acceptable suggestions would be rewarded with a cash prize or a fixed percentage of the savings
Repetition	effected during the first year. If *the savings* are difficult to evaluate, as they might be if they improved safety conditions, then a management committee would decide upon a reasonable valuation. Employees submitting acceptable
Directional transition	suggestions should *also* receive recognition. The company organ and the local newspapers should carry stories with
Pronoun	*their* names, *their* awards, and *their* suggestions.

The natural transitions function like a coupling link by hooking on to some part of the preceding sentence and attaching it to the one following. Watch how it works:

> A company would benefit from a suggestion system. It would. . . .

The same sort of linking effect may also be created by parallel structure. Observe how this device functions in the remainder of the preceding paragraph:

Demonstrative and synonym; repetition; directional transition	Naturally the company as well as the employees would benefit from this favorable publicity. But the company would profit in other ways. By providing a means for exchanging ideas between employment and management, the suggestion system would foster a spirit of cooperation. By
parallel	directing attention toward increased efficiency, it would promote desirable attitudes and objectives. And by eliciting

parallel   suggestions from the employees who perform the various jobs, it would stimulate ideas from the people most familiar with faults, weaknesses, or inadequacies.

Although the last two sentences contain the natural transition *it*, the primary link is the parallel structure:

1. By providing, . . . the suggestion system would. . . .
2. By directing, . . . it would. . . .
3. And by eliciting information, . . . it would. . . .

Paragraph and Division Transitions

Parallelism is also highly effective in linking paragraphs. Here are the initial sentences in five consecutive paragraphs:

1. We would gain certain advantages by locating in the suburbs.
2. We would gain certain advantages by locating in a small town.
3. We would gain certain advantages by locating in a city.
4. We would gain certain advantages by locating on a superhighway.
5. But we would gain the most advantages by locating in an industrial park.

A caption, a sentence, or a short paragraph may also help link paragraphs or divisions of a report. Usually, the sentence or paragraph summarizes and foreshadows. For example:

1. Having examined the causes and effects of price support, now let us consider how we may use this knowledge to avoid or reduce future recessions.
2. You have seen how air freight volume has increased greatly since 19––. You have also observed how the rate of gain by air cargo has increased faster than that of the railroads and trucks. Now you may wish to look ahead to note why many people are confident that the future for air freight is indeed bright.

Nearly everything you write will consist of a chain of paragraphs, each of which must be linked to the preceding one. And within these paragraphs are smaller chains composed of sentences that also must be linked. If a link is missing, readers must replace it. If a link is faulty, readers must correct it.

Placing these burdens on readers increases their work, decreases the clarity of your report, and reduces its effectiveness. Therefore—use transitions.

STYLE: VISUAL AIDS

Visual aids are known by many names: *visuals, graphic devices, graphics, figures, exhibits, charts, pictorials, illustrations,* and the like. But no matter what they are called, visual aids, like headings, are trademarks of an effective report writing style. Appendix M explains how to prepare visual aids and provides numerous examples of them. Here we will explain their purposes and some general guidelines for using them.

Purposes

Visual aids serve a number of purposes in reports. In the first place, they supplement words. In describing the differences between Doric and Corinthian architecture, for example, you would help readers visualize them more clearly with a careful drawing or a clear photograph than with words alone. Nevertheless, most professional writers would insist that visuals serve only as a backup for the verbal description. Pictures reinforce words, but seldom replace them.

Visuals can also simplify data. For instance, if you wanted to compile the dollar amounts and percentages of a person's pay raises over a five-year period, writing all the figures in a long paragraph might lead to confusion. But summarizing the dollar and percentage increases in a short paragraph and presenting the complete data in short tabular form or a graph would condense and simplify the presentation.

Also, in many cases visuals can communicate ideas or data more clearly than words. A tabular presentation can give a clearer, more condensed view of mathematical relationships than can words alone. Graphs also show trends more vividly than words. Maps and charts can make an audience comprehend space and time relationships when words sometimes fail. And drawings and pictures convey shapes and colors far better than words.

By condensing, simplifying, and clarifying concepts and information, and by making a vivid impression on readers, visuals also emphasize important points. A line graph showing a steady increase in house construction from 1976–78, a marked drop during 1979–81, and an upsurge from 1982–84 would portray the facts dramatically, as you can imagine. Or, as Madison Avenue advertising experts are keenly aware, a simple photograph of a suffering person can drive a point straight into a viewer's heart.

Finally, a visual aid enlivens the page. A simple table or a clever drawing breaks up the monotony of black type on white paper and gives readers welcome eye relief.

The ultimate purpose of visual aids may be summed up in two familiar sayings:

- *A picture is worth a thousand words.*—Chinese proverb
- *Don't tell me. Show me.*—Missouri adage

Of course, you should be careful that your visuals do not distort the facts, as the speaker has done in the cartoon in figure 10–15. But, certainly, whenever visuals may clarify material by saving time and space, emphasizing details, comparing numbers, and showing rates and degrees of change, you should use them.

Guidelines

When you realize that a concept or body of information can be communicated effectively by a visual, decide whether a table or illustration is more suitable. Sometimes you have to experiment with both types before deciding. If you have a choice, remember that several different kinds of visuals help make an interesting paper.

Use visual aids only when they are appropriate—never when their subjects are not clearly related to your discussion and never merely to pad the length of your report.

Figure 10–15. Visual Aids Should Not Distort Facts.

"Take your pick, gentlemen. We've got figures to fit any of 'em."

(SOURCE: Reprinted by permission of Tribune Company Syndicate, Inc.)

Since visual aids ordinarily follow the paragraphs they are related to, you usually have this sequence: *related paragraph, visual aid, new paragraph.* To help readers see the relevance of the visual, refer to it from the appropriate point in the related paragraph, using such instructions as these:

> As table 14 shows, the cost of a 1.5 liter bottle of Paul Masson Chablis varies from a high of $3.79 at Harrison's to a low of $3.19 at Kroger's.
>
> The purchase price for the same model has risen 110 percent over the last four years, as the graph in figure 3 shows.
>
> As the map in Appendix C (p. 13) points out, you will bypass forty-two towns in your drive to Charleston.

Note that these instructions avoid vague phrases like "the previous figure" or "the following illustration." And they interpret the contents or state the significance of the visual aid, thereby ensuring that readers do not miss the point.

In some cases, the visual aid must appear on a different page than the reference to it. This situation occurs when you refer to a visual near the bottom of a page and do not have adequate space for inserting it until the next page; when you relegate a figure to an appendix; or when you refer to an earlier visual that you have already cited in another context. To make such figures easy to find, refer your reader not only to the table, but also to the page or appendix where it appears:

This trend is evident in exhibit 2–1 on p. 83.

A breakdown of the employees' responses is given in figure 10 in Appendix A.

Since readers are reluctant to turn to figures in appendixes, place them there only when necessary. But oversized visuals, visuals that are mentioned in numerous places, and visuals that are pertinent only to a small percentage of your readers may have to appear in appendixes.

SUMMARY

Paying close attention to the guidelines for writing long reports will enable you to cover virtually every point you need to communicate to your readers. By using standard divisions (instead of devising a new approach every time you prepare a report), you will also present your readers with a familiar format and thus ease the transfer of information.

A special feature of the long report is that it generally forces writers to organize their material carefully: the sections of a topic outline become the sections of the report, and the phrases of the outline become the captions in the body. Following standard organizational patterns as you devise your outline and draft your text will assist you in encoding your material in the most logical, readable manner.

Using natural words, effective transitions, and visual aids will go a long way towards easing your readers' task. These strategies will help to portray you as a thoughtful, competent writer whose reports are a pleasure, rather than a dread, to read.

For inexperienced writers, the long report with its many (and occasionally overlapping) divisions can at first seem perplexing and frustrating. But for seasoned writers who know the difficulty of communicating clearly and of satisfying the needs of a variety of readers, its clear and orderly transmission of information and ideas makes a well-written long report an example of fine craftsmanship.

EXERCISES

Discussion Questions

1. Name the three major parts of long reports and their divisions.
2. What is the purpose of a letter of transmittal?
3. Explain why an informative summary is more helpful to a reader than a descriptive one.
4. Why is it important for a report writer to explain special or unfamiliar terms in the introduction?

COMMUNICATING BY MEMOS AND REPORTS

5. What is the difference between conclusions and recommendations?
6. How should a writer determine whether something like a chart showing the breakdown of the sales dollar should be placed in the body or in an appendix of a report?
7. What are the eight organizational patterns for reports? Cite a writing situation that might be organized according to each.
8. What are the advantages and disadvantages of the time and space patterns?
9. Explain the *post hoc, ergo propter hoc* fallacy.
10. In what two ways may a comparison-contrast report be organized? Explain the advantages and disadvantages.
11. Name the different types of order to be considered when enumerating a series of ideas, facts, examples, or opinions.
12. Why do many report writers adopt an impersonal style? What are some of the tactics they resort to in order to depersonalize their writing?
13. With your classmates and instructor, discuss the lists of formal and informal words presented in this chapter. Are the informal words always synonymous with the formal ones? In general, which list do your classmates prefer?
14. Why are transitions important?
15. Distinguish between natural and directional transitions. When should each be used?
16. Define *cliché*. Distinguish between *clichés* and *idiomatic expressions*. Cite several examples of *clichés*.
17. Explain why *clichés* can be offensive to readers.
18. What three types of jargon are there? Provide an example of each.
19. Exactly what is wrong with jargon? Can its use ever be justified?
20. Explain why jargon and clichés have been referred to as "mechanized language." Why might mechanized language detract from your writing style?
21. What other names are visual aids known by?
22. Explain the purposes of visual aids.
23. Discuss at least three guidelines for keying visual aids to the related discussion.
24. Why do writers interpret visual aids in their discussions?
25. Under what circumstances might a visual aid appear on a different page than the one on which the related text appears?

In-Class Applications

1. Write an informative summary of a short article provided by your instructor.
2. Find a magazine or journal article that uses headings. Prepare an outline showing each heading. Note whether the subdivisions are clearly evident in the headings.
3. What organizational patterns would you use in the following contexts?
   a. An article for the *Wall Street Journal* advancing five reasons why there will be a major change in the economy next year.
   b. A company report recommending one plant site over two others on the basis of nine criteria.
   c. A proposal written for *Fortune* about correcting an unfavorable trade balance.

d. A business letter reviewing the merger plans between two companies.

e. A speech to a men's luncheon club showing how most states have increased taxes in the past two years.

f. An essay for *Time* illustrating the numerous ways that Americans are taxed and showing how our total rate is lower than that of most countries.

g. A company memorandum stating the procedure to be followed in applying for a transfer to another department or plant.

h. A memorandum to the company president reviewing the qualifications of three candidates for promotion and recommending one of them.

4. Turn to any page in this book and analyze how the paragraphs are linked.

5. In a paper advocating closer communication between business and education, you have just completed a section revealing how business has failed to work closely with the universities. Now you plan to point out that the universities have not stayed in touch with business. Devise five transitions to link and signal the new section.

6. Translate the following telephone message into simple, direct language:

> My dear spouse, I regret very much to inform you that the termination of my day's responsibilities will be delayed to a certain extent. A reduction in the available secretarial staff has resulted in an unavoidable escalation of dictation for my secretary, who therefore has been unable to process my inter-office communication as per the schedule. Will you please convey my sincerest regards to the youngest member of our organization and tell him that I hope to be informed that he transfers to bed with a minimum of disturbance. I also hope to receive word upon my return to the effect that our oldest offspring has been upgraded in her educational institution. And furthermore and finally, it would give me great jubilation to be informed that you have been successful in replenishing the diminished supply of petroleum in the family vehicle.

7. Translate the following into Bizlish, just the opposite of what you were instructed to do in question 6:

a. Jack and Jill went up the hill to fetch a pail of water. Jack fell down and broke his crown and Jill came tumbling after.

b. Good guys finish last.

c. A fool and his money are soon parted.

d. There is no business like show business.

e. You can take Salem out of the country but you can't take the "country" out of Salem.

f. We try harder.

g. Sighted sub. Sank same.

h. Make love—not war.

Writing Assignments: Research Reports

1. Research one of the following subjects, restrict its scope if necessary, and write a report based on your findings. Ask your instructor whether you should write an information, analytical, or recommendation report and what documentation form you should follow:

Tax Reform	Developments in Homebuilding
Voluntary Bankruptcy for Individuals	Computers for the Home
Developments in the Electric Car	Future of Electronic Games
Recent Changes in Retailing	Future of Cable TV
Job Discrimination (Blacks, Women)	Future Telephone Services
Minimum Income Plan	Mass Transportation
The National Debt	Burglar Alarms
Computer-based Services	Classic Cars as Investments
Services for Handicapped People	Ethics in Advertising
Franchising	Antitrust Action

2. It is usually challenging and fascinating to speculate about the future. Select one of the following subjects and indicate what changes can be expected in the next thirty years. Prepare your findings as a long report. In a conference with your instructor, decide whether you should write an information, analytical, or recommendation report:

Food	Energy
Automobiles	Medicine
Housing	Electronics
Computers	Weapons
Television	Cameras
Space Launches	Audio Equipment
Leisure	Home Heating and Cooling
Education	

Committee Reports

To provide you with the experience of working with a group in writing a report, divide the class into several committees. Each committee should then elect a chairperson, who should divide the project into parts (research, organizing findings, drafting, typing) and assign them to subgroups of two or three students. After the report has been written, also submit a report evaluating the performance of each of your fellow committee members.

The following projects are suggested:
1. An evaluation of the placement office and its services, and recommendations to improve them.
2. A comparison of local bookstores, their prices for new and used textbooks and for miscellaneous items, and the prices they pay students for used textbooks.
3. A comparison of laundry and drycleaning establishments near campus.
4. A study of student preference for teaching fellows or professors as instructors.
5. A survey of off-campus housing that would include prices, services provided, and restrictions imposed.
6. A study of the dating habits of students.

7. A survey of freshman church attendance and participation in religious activities.
8. A comparison of food prices at several supermarkets.
9. A study of the job market for students on campus, in the local community, or both.
10. A study of racial discrimination in housing near the campus.
11. A comparison of checking charges at local banks, or prices at record stores, service stations, and barber shops or beauty salons.
12. A survey of pawnshops to determine which will loan or pay the highest amounts for several selected items.

Writing Assignments: Information Reports

1. The dean of students has asked you to write a report about expenses for one school year. The dean wants this information to advise new freshmen inquiring about how much money they will need. In addition to stating the total sum, provide a breakdown of expenses and also include information about fraternity or sorority costs if you wish.
2. Shortly after graduating from high school, you won a four-year college scholarship awarded by a local company. Mr. Mizell of their personnel division has just written you requesting a progress report about your current class standing, academic average, courses completed, honors, extracurricular activities, and any other pertinent information. Reply with an appropriate report.
3. The dean of your college has requested you to write a report comparing your major program with those of three other comparable institutions. Consult their catalogs and write the report.
4. The director of personnel has asked you to obtain information about the various returns that employees could receive by putting their money in banks, savings and loan associations, treasury notes, money-market funds, credit unions, government bonds, or high-grade corporate bonds. Write a report giving the information and providing the specific names of the various institutions or investments.
5. The president of student government is disappointed with the lack of service from the off-campus housing office and has asked you to provide a report on off-campus living, including such information as how to look for housing, price ranges, typical leases, and anything else that might be helpful to students.
6. In the form of an information report, write an extended definition of one of the following terms in order to clarify it for a general audience:

A credit crunch	Saving certificates
Balance of payments	Major medical insurance
Econometric model	Analog, hybrid, digital computers
Discount store	Paid-up insurance additions
Input-output analysis	Selling short
Small-business company	Snowmobiles
Annuity	A sports car
Consumer credit	Wind turbine generators
High-definition television	

COMMUNICATING BY MEMOS AND REPORTS

7. Review the "Franchise Facts" column in recent issues of *Venture* and select a new franchise business that you might wish to operate. Obtain information about the company from the national franchise office (address given in the *Venture* column) and supplement this information by consulting some of the following sources*:

The International Franchise Association
1025 Connecticut Avenue, N.W.
Suite 1005
Washington, DC 20036

Franchise Opportunities Handbook ($9.50)
Superintendent of Documents
Washington, DC 20402

The National Franchise Association Coalition
P. O. Box 366
Fox Lake, IL 60020

The Better Business Bureau in the franchisor's city

A Dun & Bradstreet report on the company

The chamber of commerce in the franchisor's home city

Other franchisees. Names may be listed on the disclosure statement accompanying the information that the franchisor sends you. If not, request the names.

Other franchisors in the same industry.

The Association of Canadian Franchisors
88 University Avenue
Suite 1005
Toronto, Ontario, Canada M5J 1T9

The Small Business Administration
Washington, DC 20036

Compile the findings of your research as an informational report that you can share with an acquaintance who might be interested in a partnership with you.

8. Read the article "TV Seeks New Look," *High Technology* (September/October, 1981), pp. 22, 26, 27. As you read the article, note the history and explanation of high-definition (HD) television. Prepare a report based on additional research in which you inform your classmates in simple terms about HD television and about its current or future availability for American consumers.

---

* The source for this list is *Venture* (September 1981), p. 67.

Analytical Reports

1. If you are interested in world travel and international business, read Claire Makin Green's article "The 50 Leading Exporters," *Fortune* (August 24, 1981), pp. 84–85. Select a company that you might wish to work for and obtain information from that company's personnel office about the qualifications you need to be hired in a position of your choice. Write an analytical report to a friend who might wish to join you in working for the company. Conclude with a means for acquiring the qualifications (for example, through college courses or part-time work experience) and a timetable for becoming fully qualified.

2. Read the article "Harvesting the Wind" in *Venture* (September 1981), pp. 70–72, and then investigate the profitability of owning a wind turbine generator in your area. Write an analytical report explaining the results of your investigation to your classmates.

3. Read the articles "International Robotics" in *World Business* (September 14, 1981), p. 21, and "How Smart Robots Are Becoming Smarter" in *High Technology* (September/October 1981), pp. 32–40. From other sources, investigate recent developments about robots as they relate to your major or vocation. Prepare an analytical report for someone else in your major field, concluding with a section on how these developments will affect your field.

4. Read the articles "Loyal Clientele: Morland's Cemetery Chain," *Fortune* (September 7, 1981), p. 8, and "Executive Car Wash Guided by an MBA," *Venture* (September 1981), p. 8, and note how an enterprising person can launch a profitable business without much capital. Research and write an analytical report about a business you might launch with limited funds. In addition to start-up costs, consider other pertinent factors including annual operating costs, market demand for the products or services, competition, expansion prospects, and amortization of debts. Address the report to a banker you might apply to for credit.

5. Select two major corporations from a field that you might like to work in—for example, Boeing and McDonnell in aircraft, Philip Morris and R. J. Reynolds Industries in tobacco products, du Pont and Union Carbide in chemicals and plastics, Digital Equipment and Sperry in computer systems and equipment. Obtain information from both companies about job prospects for a person with your credentials. Ask about starting salaries, fringe benefits, promotion expectations, and any other factors you deem important. Write an analytical report comparing the findings of your research. Conclude with an assessment of which company offers better employment opportunities. Address the report to an acquaintance who might have the same career aspirations as you.

6. Locate and study recent demographic data about the American population—for example, the population increase since 1950, the most current ratio of males to females, the ratio of rural to urban residents, educational levels, birth rates, life expectancy, and income averages for different types of employment. (Many figures from the 1980 census can be found in "Latest Profile of America's People," *U. S. News & World Report* [September 14, 1981], pp. 26–28.) Select data about one facet of our population, such as divorce rates or life expectancy; analyze the data; and write a report to your classmates, concluding with some major social, political, economic, or business changes that the data suggest.

7. Many companies have recently opened manufacturing facilities in the Sun Belt. In a related move, many administrative offices are now making moves from metropolitan areas to smaller cities—as explained in Charles F. Harding's article "Why Administrative Offices Are Moving to Smaller Cities," *Administrative Management* (September 1981), pp. 40–43. After researching the reasons for this move, write a report to the chamber of commerce of a small city you are acquainted with, pointing out the town features that should help to attract administrative offices. Explain that the chamber can use this information to lure administrative offices to town and thereby strengthen the local economy.

Recommendation Reports

1. Numerous campus problems have been the focus of attention in recent years. Review the policy of your institution in any one of the following areas and prepare a report for Student Government recommending a change:

Visiting in dorms	Pornographic movies
Excessive drinking	Controversial speakers
Off-campus misconduct	Control of student newspapers
Pass-fail grades	Open admission
College athletics	Distribution of tickets to athletic events
Black studies	

2. Read A. F. Ehrbar's article "It May Be Time to Rent" in *Fortune* (August 24, 1981), pp. 57–59, which suggests that, because of a projected decline in house prices during the 1980s, anyone thinking of buying a house ought to consider renting. For your classmates, prepare a recommendation report about the financial advantages of renting an apartment or, depending on the findings of your research and analysis, buying a home. Base your report on current economic forecasts for your region.

3. President Joseph Gardner of your company, which employs 1,500 people, has asked you to propose ways of dealing with the absentee problem. After investigating, you have discovered that other companies handle absenteeism in these various ways:
   a. An official visits a sick worker's bedside to express interest in the employee's welfare and hope for a quick recovery.
   b. A foreman phones to inquire about a tool, part, or some other matter to see whether the worker is at home.
   c. Employees with good attendance records are given small gifts or trading stamps.
   d. The absent worker is required to furnish a doctor's note.
   e. A company nurse is sent to visit the absent worker.
   Decide upon the best way of handling the problem and write the report.

4. Two-thirds of the students on your campus have indicated in a poll that they received little useful career guidance, selected majors before knowing what they wanted to do, and decided on careers too early. The Faculty Committee on Student Affairs has asked you to write a report for them that would suggest ways to improve this situation.

NOTES

[1] Paraphrased from Thomas O. Richards and Ralph A. Richardson, *Technical Writing*, (Detroit: General Motors Corporation, 1941), p. 4.

[2] Gordon H. Mills and John A. Walter, *Technical Writing*, 4th ed. (New York: Holt, Rinehart and Winston, 1978), pp. 376–78.

[3] The classic article on Bizlish and pompous language in general is Stuart Chase's "Gobbledygook" from *Power of Words* (New York: Harcourt Brace and World, 1954), reprinted in *The Practical Craft: Readings for Business and Technical Writers*, ed. W. Keats Sparrow and Donald C. Cunningham (Boston: Houghton Mifflin, 1978), pp. 62–70.

[4] Chris Morgan, "What's Wrong With Technical Writing Today?" *BYTE* (December 1980), pp. 7–8.

[5] *Simply Stated*, the monthly newsletter of the Document Design Center, offers helpful tips for writing about complicated subjects in a clear, vivid, nontechnical manner. For information about receiving the newsletter, write to the Document Design Center, American Institutes for Research, 1055 Thomas Jefferson Street, NW, Washington, DC 20007.

Part V
ORAL
COMMUNICATIONS

 # Oral Presentation

OBJECTIVES

After reading this chapter, you should be able to:

- Explain six ways to cope with stage fright
- Describe four ways to improve your voice quality
- Point out four ways to use body language in making a talk more effective
- Explain the advantages and disadvantages of reading a paper, memorizing a talk, or using notes
- Discuss four considerations affecting the selection of a subject
- State the three objectives of the introduction
- Discuss four problems in using visual aids

PLAN

Performance
   Stage Fright
   Eye Contact
   Voice
   Body Language
Method of Presentation
   Reading
   Memorizing
   Speaking From Notes
   The Advantage of Performing
Content
   Subject Selection
   Planning the Presentation
Summary

My father gave me these hints on speech-making: "Be sincere . . . be brief . . . be seated."

JAMES ROOSEVELT

You've been talking all your life. By now, you're an expert. You have mastered even such specialized forms of oral communication as small talk, double talk, pep talk, smart talk, and heart-to-heart talk. You can talk big, talk back, talk over, talk up, talk down, and even talk turkey. But if you had to *give* a talk—well, that's another matter. And you're not alone. It's been reported that Americans fear speaking in public more than they fear heights, bugs, or death.[1]

But your inability to speak effectively may be the death of your career. Once on the job, you may not have numerous opportunities to address others, but when you do, it will be important. You may be involved in meetings, discussions, conferences, and interviews for the purpose of presenting your ideas or selling your product or services to customers, managers, supervisors, clients, associates, assistants, or co-workers. You may also find yourself a member of job-related organizations, professional or trade, that meet regularly and hold annual conventions, where you may chair sessions, read papers, moderate panels, or discuss issues. And then, of course, various speaking opportunities may arise in your outside activities. If you belong to a church group, PTA organization, Young Democrat or Republican party, Junior Chamber of Commerce, alumni organization, or a sports, neighborhood, or other group, you'll be involved in numerous speaking situations.

At work, the more responsible your position the more often you will have to express your ideas orally and the more important it will be for you to do so effectively. Thus if you aspire to managerial or leadership positions in business, industry, government, or the professions, you should learn how to speak effectively in various routine situations.

Perhaps you already possess competent speaking skills. You may have engaged in debate, had a speech course in high school, or held a class office that required you to talk before people. But even if you are adept at communicating orally, you should strive to improve. This part of the course will provide you with an opportunity to do that by offering information, practice, and criticism—the three learning components we mentioned previously in our discussion of writing.

If you do not possess competent speaking skills, you are like the majority of your classmates. You may be apprehensive about talking aloud from your seat. Or, you may be able to speak from there but would panic when standing in front of the class, or at best, would hem and haw your way through a boring presentation. If you have

349

Figure 11–1.   From Failure to Fame in Four Easy Lessons.

(SOURCE: © 1982 by The New York Times Company. Reprinted by permission.)

these problems, then here is a wonderful opportunity for you to learn an invaluable skill—how to speak effectively.

We use the word *learn* deliberately because talking before others is not a simple, natural activity like breathing. It may be easy to speak before family and friends, but it is another matter to address a group of new employees, request scholarship contributions from a local alumni group, or instruct entering college students about registration procedures. You can prepare for such occasions by learning certain basic principles, applying them in classroom speeches, and benefiting from the advice and suggestions of your classmates and instructor. But don't expect miracles. Despite what some people suggest (see figure 11–1), improvement takes time, just as it does on the golf course or tennis court.

In the following pages, we have organized our suggestions for oral presentations into three sections—performance, method of presentation, and content—that deal with the delivery of a talk and its subject matter. Performance and content are much like the offensive and defensive football units: both are important in producing a winner.

After considering the performance and content of oral presentations in this chapter, we shall turn in chapter 12 to help you in conducting interviews, planning and chairing group discussions, and sharpening your listening skills. As you can see, you will be improving your ability in oral communication, whether transmitting or receiving.

PERFORMANCE

A discussion of oral presentations includes a consideration of such matters as stage fright, eye contact, voice, and body communication. We use the word *performance* because speaking before others involves many acting techniques. You play a certain role, project and react to your audience, plan your entrance and exit, and even rehearse just as you would for a play. And, like actors and actresses, you experience stage fright.

ORAL COMMUNICATIONS

Stage Fright

Nearly everyone suffers from stage fright in some form or other—it is a natural expression of anxiety. Talking or performing in front of others involves the risk of making a fool of yourself. No wonder then that amateurs and professionals in sports, concerts, dance recitals, political campaigns, and other public performances experience fear. So, if your hands get moist, your heart pounds, your stomach has butterflies, and your breath is rapid, you are reacting normally. And take comfort from the fact that these physiological signs indicate you are functioning effectively, adrenalin helping your muscles, sugar and insulin preparing your body, and additional blood providing oxygen to alert your mind. As a result, you are stimulated to perform well. But if you are unprepared for this stress and tension, and unable to use it effectively, you can be harmed rather than helped. To prevent you from being harmed, we offer the following advice about ways to control and reduce anxiety:

- *Expect stage fright:* You should accept what we've just told you: stage fright is natural and beneficial. So what you must avoid is fright about stage fright. Accept the tension as a normal reaction just like anxiety before an exam. To paraphrase Franklin Delano Roosevelt: The only thing you need to fear is fear itself.
- *Plan carefully:* Careful planning will make you feel the speech is important and informative, and give you a positive attitude towards it and your audience. If you believe you have something worthwhile and interesting to say and if you know you have prepared thoroughly for saying it, you will worry less. So psych yourself up. Get enthusiastic about your subject. Be eager and talk about it to friends and others, asking for their help and suggestions.
- *Rehearse frequently:* Practice your speech with a cassette recorder, a friend, or several acquaintances. You will gain confidence from knowing that you indeed have something to say and that you have said it previously. Even when you practice alone, be certain to present the talk aloud rather than in your mind because the actual sound of your voice will be reassuring. And, of course, the more you rehearse, the more confident you'll feel.
- *Look attractive:* Being well-dressed and well-groomed may seem unimportant, but paying particular attention to what you wear and how you look will give you a lift, as well as create a favorable impression on the audience. Dress much as you would for an interview (see page 211), making certain that your clothes fit the occasion. And observe the previously mentioned grooming tips about combed hair, shined shoes, clean nails, fresh shave. If you look your best, you'll feel more confident.
- *Prepare the setting:* If possible, familiarize yourself with the place where you're going to talk. Naturally, this is unnecessary for your class presentations. But if you plan to address a group elsewhere, scout the setting and make any needed changes. For example, you should remove any distractions in the background, such as words or sketches on a chalkboard or a distracting picture or poster. Also, if possible, arrange the seats in a semi-circle or fan shape so you can easily see everyone. Shortly before you give your talk, open doors and windows to cool off the room. Hot, stuffy air can put even interested

audiences to sleep. By seeing where you will speak and by making any possible needed changes, you will feel more secure, more in control of the presentation, and more confident in your ability to do well.

- *Start and end strong:* Make your introduction as appealing as you can and your ending as forceful and memorable as possible. If you get started well, the audience will react favorably, easing your stress and tension. And by knowing you can conclude effectively, you will gain confidence as you talk, realizing that you can end on a high note at any proper time. You'd be surprised how much less you will worry if you know that you have an interesting introduction and a strong conclusion.

A final word about this frightening subject. The more often you make oral presentations, the more confident you will be. The first time you stand up before people, you may be terrified by seeing all those eyes staring at you. From then on, it's all downhill, but you will never be completely free of anxiety. Yet practice will make you a better speaker by showing you how you will react, how you can control your nervousness, and how stage fright can get you up for a talk instead of knocking you down.

Eye Contact

Direct eye contact with your listeners enables you to obtain a favorable response from them and to note how they respond to you. In conversations, we prefer people who look us in the eye when they talk. They impress us with their honesty and sincerity; we feel they are interested in us, not in others who may be in the background. Listeners respond the same way, liking a speaker who maintains direct eye contact with them.

This does not mean you should stare at one person or rotate your head like an oscillating fan from one side of the room to the other. It does mean you should look at different members of the audience, stopping at one for a few seconds and then going on to others, particularly those who are smiling or nodding their heads in agreement.

But also be alert for the frowns, the glazed eyes, the whispering, the glances at wrist watches, the stares out the window, and most deadly—the yawns. These signals provide valuable feedback, indicating you are not communicating well, allowing you to adjust your delivery or to clarify, restate, or revitalize your material.

Eye contact, therefore, helps you significantly in numerous ways: in creating a favorable impression, in communicating with each person in the audience, and in obtaining feedback. If you show interest in your audience, it will show interest in you.

Voice

Without study, practice, and coaching, there is not a lot you can do with the quality of your voice. But you can avoid certain pitfalls. Strive for variety in pitch, volume, rate of speed, and emphasis. In this way you can avoid the monotony that puts listeners to sleep and instead achieve the liveliness that keeps them interested.

PITCH Become aware of the pitch of your voice, its highness or lowness. Realize that when it falls, as at the end of a declarative sentence, it signals a completeness of thought, while when it rises for a question or exclamation, it conveys a different message. But too great a drop in pitch, or in pitch and volume, at the end of sentences creates a deadly sing-song effect, much like a first-grader reading. If you have this problem, correct it by working with a cassette recorder.

Also, try to vary your pitch within your sentences, raising and lowering it slightly to avoid monotony. Those who drone on in the same pitch will soon lull an audience to sleep.

VOLUME Another way to achieve variety is by changing the volume of your voice. Usually, you should speak slightly louder to a group than you do in ordinary conversation. Remember: your voice sounds much louder to you than it does to others.

One way to check on whether people can hear you easily is to note whether those in the rear are having difficulty—cupping their hands to their ears or straining forward in their seats. A firm, loud voice sounds energetic and confident to an audience, commands attention, and helps to keep people alert.

A change of volume is also effective when moving from one point to another, or emphasizing some word or idea. Realize, too, that softness can be used for variety to stress a point as well as loudness. But whatever you do, don't mumble. Look up and speak out. Let them hear you in the bleachers.

RATE OF SPEED If you are highly nervous and want to end it all, there is some danger that you may race through your speech. We don't suggest you . . . creep . . . along . . . at . . . a . . . snail's . . . pace, but move deliberately, speaking energetically and enthusiastically. Once again, use variety, much as a pitcher throws an occasional off-speed ball to be effective. Slow down for important ideas or points you want to stress.

And pause every now and then. Pauses are like new paragraphs, places for listeners to rest and refresh themselves—unless you clutter the silence with such distracting sounds and words as "ah," "er," "uhm," "well," and "you know." Become more self-conscious about these vocalized pauses when you rehearse, and deliberately try to avoid them when you speak. Also, remember that pauses are more apparent to you than to others. But for the pause that emphasizes, signals a climax, or indicates thoughtfulness, listen to radio personality Paul Harvey, the pause-master.

Many inexperienced speakers try to race through their oral presentations; it is far better to slow down instead to a walk or a jog. Realize that you must talk more deliberately than in conversation because your words have farther to go and must reach more people.

EMPHASIS In speaking, emphasis or stress can be conveyed by varying volume and rate of speed, as we have already mentioned, but you can also convey emphasis by the intensity of your voice. In a sense, it is like underlining in writing to call attention to words or ideas. Emphasis should be used sparingly, saved for special occasions, but it is one of the ways to accentuate what you say by the way that you say it.

As you can see from our discussion of pitch, volume, rate of speed, and emphasis, you can use your voice effectively. Experiment with these options in rehearsing your speech aloud, and try to see that your voice adds vitality and interest to your speeches.

Body Language

Much of how we feel about what we say is communicated by our bodies. A speaker's posture, movement, gestures, and facial expression all influence audience response. Body language can do much to help or harm a speech by either supporting the points made or distracting the audience from them. In general, the best advice about what to do with your body is to act naturally. But acting naturally in the unnatural situation of addressing a group of people is difficult. How to achieve this unnatural naturalness? Read on.

POSTURE   You should first realize that your speech performance starts not with your first word, but from the moment you stand up to walk to the front of the class. Or, if you are talking at a public gathering, from the moment you are in public view—even though you may be the last speaker on a program. Whether you are walking forward or sitting up front, the audience is sizing you up. Consequently, stride forward with body erect, head high. Or sit tall, intently listening to others talk, then arise when introduced and move to the lectern without stumbling. In speeches, the approach is part of the performance.

MOVEMENT   Once at the lectern, desk, or center of the stage, stop for a moment or two, smile at your audience (if it would be appropriate to do so), get yourself set, and only then begin to talk. Avoid speaking while walking to the front, or before you have settled yourself there.

After beginning, keep your weight evenly balanced, neither leaning, slumping, nor slouching. Any unplanned shifting, shuffling, or pacing will reveal your nervousness, distract listeners, and make them nervous. But deliberate changes are fine: a few steps forward for intimacy or to share a confidence; or a step or two off to one side to signal a transition from one point to another. Except for such meaningful movements, stand your ground and face your audience.

But standing still is not easy. To begin with, what should you do with your hands? Until you talk before an audience, you may never have noticed how awkward hands are. But if you just let them hang by your side, no one will notice them except you. This position may seem uncomfortable at first, but after a few practices and presentations, it will seem almost natural. Keeping your hands at your side will also protect you from lecternitis, a weakened condition characterized by a speaker's need to hang or lean on a lectern.

Such positions as sitting on the edge of a desk or leaning against the blackboard or wall are highly informal, suitable for class instructors but not for formal speech occasions. Also inadvisable are the rigid military parade rest pose with arms locked behind; or the supplicant's posture with both hands clasped in front, waist-high; or any disco stance, rocking, swaying, shifting weight from one foot to another. The simplest is best: stand tall, hands at your side, head high. Thomas M. Sawyer has an interesting suggestion: Think of yourself as suspended from the ceiling by an invisible wire screwed onto the top of your head.[2]

GESTURES   Your hands should remain by your sides throughout the speech except when you gesture to emphasize ideas or to describe something in your presentation. Such gestures not only complement what you say but also indicate to your audience that you are a lively, energetic person, greatly interested in your subject. This positive image can do much to obtain a favorable response from listeners.

Some people carry on animated conversations, using their hands frequently to express ideas. Most seldom do. So you should probably practice some gestures, watching yourself in a mirror until you are comfortable about using them. You might even plan to insert one or two at appropriate points, making sure that they do not appear forced but are natural and spontaneous. After several presentations, you will find that gesturing is easier.

The more popular hand gestures are the pointing index finger to suggest a warning or threat, the use of one or several fingers to number points or items ("the third advantage"), the fist to express strong feelings, the upward palm to implore or to signal "on the one hand . . . and on the other hand" transitions, and the karate slash to emphasize statements. To see how effective speakers gesture skillfully, watch Billy Graham or some of the other popular television clergymen.

These gestures will help you in other ways besides interesting your audience and reinforcing your message. They consume nervous energy, keeping you from such distracting mannerisms as jingling the coins in your pocket, playing with your bracelet or ring, touching the buttons on your dress or shirt, tapping your fingers, or scratching your head. If your hands are by your sides, they can be used for gestures instead of for distracting listeners.

FACIAL EXPRESSION   Just as some movement of the hands and body is helpful, so is movement of the face. A deadpan is deadly. Instead, try to show expression in your face by smiling whenever the occasion allows it, scowling or frowning when appropriate, tilting your head occasionally, and moving your eyes to look at one person and then another. Take a lesson from head-on shots of television speakers in commercials or in talk shows. Notice how they reveal animation in their faces by changing their expressions and moving their heads and eyes. Although television requires a subtle style because of the intimacy of the camera, you can learn much from watching it, not only about the facial expression but also about the movement, posture, and gestures of speakers.

METHOD OF PRESENTATION

Up to this point, we've been talking about performance, discussing the best delivery for oral presentations. But also important is the particular method of presentation: reading a paper, memorizing it, or delivering it from notes.

Reading

Speeches should be read only when absolutely necessary: on important occasions when precision of language is essential; when tradition calls for it, such as at press conferences or conventions; or when time is crucial, such as on radio or television. Otherwise, you would be wise to speak informally, relying on notes, because audiences prefer the live performance with its freshness and spontaneity to the "dead" one of reading from a paper. Also the audience may be distracted by your manuscript, watching you turn the pages and wondering how many more there are.

If you have to read a paper, practice aloud beforehand. You'd be surprised at how you will stumble over certain words and sentences, some of which you may want to rewrite for easier reading. Triple-space your reading text so you will minimize the chance of confusing lines or losing your place. In addition, underline certain words in your text to stress them, and write stage directions for yourself, such as "slow down," "increase volume," "smile," and "pause."

When presenting the paper, remember to maintain eye contact with your audience. This is essential because otherwise you will stare at the pages, concentrating only on the printed words. Also, if you don't look up often, projecting your presentation to your listeners, they will simply turn you off. It's the way of the world: If you aren't interested in them, they won't be interested in you. One way to help you focus on the audience is to know your material so well that you can deliver some parts or sentences by memory, looking at various individuals while you speak.

Memorizing

Speaking entirely from memory has much against it and little for it. If you can deliver a memorized speech as if it were not memorized, then you have a rare talent. Few people can recite sentences as if they had just come to mind. Most talk mechanically, trying to think of what comes next instead of seeking audience feedback. The other danger of a memorized speech is that you may stumble and forget some parts. In some circumstances—speech contests, short formal talks—you may have to memorize. But when it's not necessary—don't.

Speaking from Notes

Speaking from notes requires advance planning of the talk, practice in delivering it, and the use of small note cards in presenting it. With this advance preparation, you should be so familiar with the material that you can deliver it easily and confidently. At the same time, you can maintain close contact with your listeners and adjust to the feedback from them. From their standpoint, they perceive you as giving a live performance, fresh, natural, and spontaneous, almost as if you were conversing individually with them. This form of presentation carries with it the excitement of a live television program, such as a sports event, where anything can go astray—and so people watch it more intently than they do taped programs carefully edited for language and flaws. Obviously, we recommend speaking from notes. Listeners prefer it.

As for the note cards, think of them as insurance, to be used just in case. Often only one will be needed for your main points and a few sub-points or key examples. But type these points in capitals or print them in large letters on one side only. Keep the cards hidden from the audience, either on the lectern or table. The idea is not to distract the audience with the cards or to clutch them in your hands, thus preventing gestures.

Our experience indicates that cards are usually unnecessary for five- or ten-minute talks. Yet it's comforting to have them handy, knowing you can rely on them in a pinch.

The Advantage of Performing

In some respects, speaking is easier than writing because of all the advantages gained from the performance. Your nervous system stimulates you, your eyes enable you to adjust your material to your audience's reactions, your voice gives your words emphasis and meaning, and your body aids communication through facial expression, posture, movement, and gestures. All these are working for you, once you understand how they help and how to employ them skillfully. In time, you will improve through practice and constructive criticism from your instructor and classmates. Successful speakers are made, not born. And successful speakers know not only how to deliver a speech but how to prepare one—which brings us to the subject of content.

CONTENT

In this section we will offer suggestions about selecting a subject and planning an oral presentation, paying particular attention to preparing the statement of purpose, outline, introduction, body, and conclusion. In discussing content, we shall also consider such matters as transitions, rhetorical questions, methods of support, and visual aids. But material covered in previous chapters, such as outlining and transitions, will be mentioned only in passing here.

Subject Selection

You know at this point how to present a speech, but what are you going to talk about? Sometimes you will be furnished with a subject. For example, your high school principal might ask you to speak to the senior class about the differences between college and high school. Or a PTA group might ask you to appear on a panel to discuss how high school students can make wise career choices. But in many situations, you will have to select a subject. In class, you may be given free rein. And in the future, you may be invited by some community group or a local men's or women's club to talk on general subjects, such as what interests or concerns college students today. What do you do then?

YOUR INTERESTS, EXPERIENCES, KNOWLEDGE Your choice of subject depends to a large extent on your own interests, experiences, and knowledge. You can find topics by rummaging around among your hobbies, things you like to do or make or read about, such as purchasing a bicycle, shopping at garage sales, playing soccer, or keeping house plants healthy. The advantage of topics that interest you is that you are more apt to be informed and enthusiastic about them, and can convey that attitude to your listeners. Or you may have had certain experiences that will provide you with an excellent topic. A summer job as a waiter or waitress, a camping trip, or problems in buying a new or used car can all be interesting if you can adapt your speech to the needs and interests of your audience.

If your interests and experiences fail to provide you with material, turn to subjects you have studied or would like to research. You may be informed about careers in law and business, the social security system, new technological breakthroughs or medical advances, or the history of your community or region. Or you may have studied some topic, such as recent tax laws, a Supreme Court decision, or new child-care theories, and want to learn more. You need not be an expert but should know more than your audience and enough to be substantially well-informed and accurate.

AUDIENCE INTEREST, EXPERIENCE, KNOWLEDGE You cannot rely on your own interests, experiences, and knowledge without considering those of your listeners. That means, you should consider what would appeal to them, what they would like to know about a particular subject, what they already know about it, and how much more they want or need to know. To help you in this analysis, you should have some general ideas about their attitudes, values, and abilities and about such specific matters as their age, sex, education, occupation, and their social, economic, and political status. This information will help you select certain subjects and eliminate others. For example, a talk about speculating on commodity futures would probably bore most college students. If your listeners won't feel that your topic will help them to live happier, more fulfilling, rewarding, or interesting lives, then you should select another subject.

OCCASION AND TIME LIMITATION Two other factors have some bearing on subject selection. One is the occasion for the speech. A commencement ceremony, a fund-raising drive, or a July Fourth celebration all call for certain kinds of speeches. It is usually wise to give listeners what they expect. Similarly, time limits influence your choice of subject. You obviously can't discuss the federal budget in five minutes or the drop shot in tennis for an hour.

ASSIGNED SUBJECT This discussion about selecting a subject according to your interests, experiences, and knowledge, and those of your audience, and according to the occasion and time provided, assumes that you are free to determine your own topic. But in the working world, you may have no choice. You may be asked to report on marketing plans for a new product, progress with a particular project, advantages of purchasing a new machine, or reasons for a budgetary allocation. In other situations, you may be asked to give a talk, but the invitation will be extended to you in your career role as a public school administrator, mechanical engineer, tax accountant, style coordinator, estate lawyer, or public health nurse. In those instances, you will be expected to talk about a pertinent subject in your field of work.

Whether or not you are restricted in selecting your topic, keep your listeners' interest in mind. Your purpose is not to deliver a talk mainly to show people how bright *you* are but to help them benefit either directly or indirectly, either immediately or later, from what you have to say. Your audience's interest should be foremost in your mind.

Planning the Presentation

Planning the presentation consists of formulating a statement of purpose, outlining the material, and preparing an introduction, body, and conclusion. Good plans make good speeches.

STATEMENT OF PURPOSE   After selecting a subject, you should restrict your topic by developing a tentative statement of purpose and indicating precisely whether you want to amuse, inform, or persuade your listeners and to what effect. The key to writing an effective purpose statement lies in making it specific and restricted. The following examples are faulty:

> **Not specific:** To inform listeners about used cars
> **Not restricted:** To inform listeners about buying cars

Instead, an outline like the following will prove helpful:

> **Subject area:**   Cars
> **Specific, restricted subject:** Buying used cars
> **Purpose statement:**   To inform listeners when, where, and how to buy used cars

Certainly, the time available influences your purpose statement. A talk about buying both new and used cars would probably be too lengthy for most occasions. How can you tell? A helpful rule of thumb is to allow about a minute for your introduction and conclusion, and four for each main point and each sub-point in your talk. Or, if you want to think in terms of written words, figure that you speak at about 150 words a minute. A three-page, double-spaced typed essay of about 750 words would take five minutes. But it's wise to figure on another minute or two for unplanned delays, additional remarks, unforeseen asides. Normally, it's better that the talk take too little time rather than too much. Few listeners ever complain about being shortchanged while many get annoyed at having to sit overtime.

You should regard the purpose statement as tentative. You may want to change it as you work on your talk. Fine. For instance, you might find so much to say about buying used cars that you'd want to limit the subject to testing them.

OUTLINE   Armed with a purpose statement, you can construct an outline, checking to see that every point on it is related to what you want to amuse, inform, or persuade your listeners about. As we have discussed outlining previously (see pages 263–264), further comment here is unnecessary except to suggest that whenever possible, you should follow the easy-to-remember chronological, enumeration, cause-effect, or problem-solution patterns. For instance, our previous example of buying a used car would lend itself naturally to a chronological outline:

I. When to buy a used car
II. Where to buy a used car
III. How to inspect and select a used car
IV. What to pay for a used car

INTRODUCTION The introduction to a speech should accomplish three objectives: (1) attract the attention and interest of the audience, (2) create a favorable image of the speaker, and (3) state the thesis and organization of the talk. For better or worse, first impressions strongly influence people's attitudes—your audience's reactions to you will be formed largely in the first few minutes of your talk. Consequently, you should work overtime on your introduction, referring to the occasion, the audience, or the significance of the subject to gain the attention of your audience. Note how Paul S. Wise, President of the Alliance of American Insurers, begins by talking favorably about his listeners and their organization:

> This is an important meeting. It is important because this organization which represents much of our industry's leadership is devoting a major portion of its program to the subject of arson.
>
> The Society of Chartered Property and Casualty Underwriters is recognizing that management of the arson problem is critical. But, more than that, the Society is challenging us to re-examine our attitude about arson.
>
> As CPCUs you have demonstrated your commitment to excellence. You have met the highest standards of your profession. These are leadership qualities. It's not surprising that many of you fill senior management positions. Others of you will provide the industry with its leadership in the future.[3]

A similar introductory technique is to link the speaker with the audience. Note how David Rockefeller, former Chairman of Chase Manhattan Bank, establishes this bond with his listeners:

> As always, I feel it is a special honor—even a spiritual homecoming—to address the American Bankers Association. I have been a banker now 35 years, and there is no audience before which I feel so comfortable—and compatible.[4]

Sometimes speakers plunge right into their subject, using anecdotes, startling statements, quotations, surprising statistics, or other attention-getting devices. Jack Valenti, President of the Export Association of America, prods his audience with this beginning:

> The great economic issue of the 1980s will be the capacity of the United States to rise to the challenge of both productivity and export trade.
>
> The war for export trade will be waged without pause by a growing number of nations in all parts of this shrunken planet. Unless we in this land understand that plain fact,

ORAL COMMUNICATIONS

we will—in time and with certainty—slowly, haltingly, sluggishly be counted among the losers in the battle.[5]

Another form of introduction involves the telling of a humorous story or joke. But this beginning is fraught with danger for all except those who have previously demonstrated a knack for making people laugh. Why? Here's how Art Linkletter, television personality and popular speaker, explains it:

> Joke-telling is the riskiest, least understood, and highest paid of the performing arts because jokes require timing, inflection, authority, and native skill that most people don't possess.[6]

If you possess this skill, give your listeners a laugh. If you don't possess it, don't try.

Besides attracting attention, the introduction should establish a favorable image. Remember: listeners react not only to what you say but to what you are, or more precisely, what you seem to be. Plan in your introduction to convey a sense of your credibility, your objectivity, and your sincerity. Try also to show how you share certain interests, values, and experiences with listeners. These qualities are vital to an audience trying to size you up as you start to speak. People have certain questions in their minds about you:

- What qualifies you to talk on this subject?
- Are you impartial or biased about the subject?
- Are you like them or able to understand their viewpoint?
- Are you honest and trustworthy?

Usually, you can directly or indirectly answer all these questions except the last. Your honesty and trustworthiness will become apparent during your speech not only from your statements but from your eye contact, gestures, posture, and other visual and vocal characteristics.

Once you have attracted the audience's attention and created a favorable image, you should turn to your subject, stating your thesis and announcing the main divisions and their order. The best advice about organizing speeches is presented in the old chestnut: Tell 'em what you're going to tell 'em, tell 'em, and then tell 'em what you've told 'em. Note how Professor Leonard L. Berry, Chairman of the Marketing Department of Georgia State University, illustrates this technique in an address to the American Association of Advertising Agencies:

> I would like to sketch five forces for change in America—some more familiar than others—that have very significant implications for marketing in the years immediately ahead.
>
> These forces for change are:
> 1. The New Demographics
> 2. The Rising Level of Education
> 3. The New Values
> 4. The New Economic Realities
> 5. The Growing Poverty of Time
>
> After reviewing these forces for change, I will then suggest several increasingly important consumer orientations that are emerging as a result.[7]

The statement of the main ideas and the order of these ideas prepare listeners for what is to follow, just like a map shows people where they are going.

BODY   A discussion of the body of the speech includes a variety of matters. Although the main part of a talk is structured like a report, some matters such as visual aids are peculiar to speeches, and others like transitions and rhetorical questions need to be emphasized.

Transitions   Transitions, particularly those directional ones of the word, sentence, or paragraph variety, should be old hat to you because we discussed them in chapter 10. But they are crucial in speeches because listeners more than readers need to know where you are going and where you have been. Readers can stop to reread what you have written, and they are not as subject to distractions as listeners are. Any sound or movement in the room while you are talking can disconcert the audience, and often, by association, even a word in your speech will send their minds miles away. You would be wise to assume that your audience is listening only about two-thirds of the time; thus you should frequently restate what you have said, indicate when you move from one point to another, and summarize several times, particularly in speeches over ten minutes long. Note how transitions help to do many of these things:

> Let's look now at the increasing interest in hypnosis in recent years . . .
>
> Having looked at the increased interest in hypnosis, we might note its use in relieving anxiety, treating asthma, stopping smoking, and controlling pain . . .
>
> Hypnosis is used effectively in relieving anxiety, treating asthma, stopping smoking, and controlling pain, but people vary greatly in their receptivity to it . . .
>
> Just as the ability to be hypnotized is limited to certain people, so the power a hypnotist exerts on subjects is limited . . .

Often it is helpful to enumerate points in a talk (first, . . . second, . . . third).

Rhetorical Questions   Another effective device is the rhetorical question, which can reach out to grab not only readers but listeners. A rhetorical question calls for no vocal answer from the audience but arouses curiosity, causing people to check whether the answer they formulated in their minds is the same as the one you will provide. You can understand, therefore, the psychological impact of a rhetorical question, can't you?

Although rhetorical questions should be used sparingly, evidence that supports your points should be used abundantly. To a great extent, the body of the speech should consist of a number of points with a clear explanation and proof or support of each.

For example, if you're writing about the underground economy, you should first define the term: the economy activity conducted in cash that is unreported to the Internal Revenue Service or any government agency. Then you should offer proof of its existence, either from your own personal examples—let us say of people paid in cash for cleaning, painting, repairing; child and nursing care; small-appliance repair; and the like—or from what others have told you, or you have read. Other supporting material might include a quotation from an authority on this subject, facts or statistics about the various estimates of cash not reported, and explanations of why people are engaged in such activities. All these supporting materials—examples, quotations, facts, statistics, reasons—add significance and credibility to your talk.

Visual Aids   To make this evidence easier to understand and remember, you may want to present some of it visually. Visual aids—objects, chalkboards, slides, graphs, flip charts, and overhead projectors—all add variety to your speech by providing your audience with something to look at and focus on, thereby making the subject more interesting and vivid. In addition, they greatly increase the audience's ability to recall the illustrated points. According to one study, sales representatives who heard an oral presentation remembered only 10% of the material three days later. But they recalled 67% of the material presented in a similar talk using visual aids.[8] Yet a visual aid is a two-edged weapon: it will work against you if you are not prepared for certain problems.

1. *The visual aid may distract the audience:* If the visual aid is displayed before you talk about it, listeners will be attracted by it, and may tune you out. Therefore, depending on the size and shape of the aid, and the nature of the room and lectern, table, or stand, keep it out of sight, draped, or with a blank side facing the audience. Also, remove it when you have finished because otherwise it will continue to distract listeners.

2. *The visual aid may distract you:* A visual aid is seductive, attracting not only the audience but also the speaker. If you aren't careful, you're apt to keep looking at it instead of at your listeners. Of course, you'll need to glance at it occasionally, but you should mainly focus on people's faces, noting whether they understand and accept what you are saying or whether you will have to repeat, clarify, or expand on some ideas. Practice with the visual aid ahead of time, figuring out how you can best position your body in displaying or writing on it, which hand you should use to explain it, and how to refer to it without losing eye contact or turning your back to your audience. Unless you anticipate all these problems, you can block your audience's view, lose their attention, and fail in your presentation.

3. *The visual aid may not be visible:* A visual aid not large and clear enough to be seen and understood is far worse than no visual aid at all. Nothing is as exasperating and frustrating to listeners as to be unable to follow references to a visual aid because it is too small, or the writing is indistinct, or the speaker is blocking it. If possible, test your visual aid beforehand by standing in the rear of the room you will be speaking in.

   By keeping the information on a graph, chart, or sign simple, you can make the letters and figures larger and clearer. The same cautions apply to writing or drawing on a chalkboard or sketchpad. Be certain that the diagram or sketch is quick and easy to construct. Beforehand, you may lightly pencil straight lines, circles, or anything else difficult to draw. Check to see that chalk, an eraser, or watercolor markers are available if you will need them, and consider the advantages and disadvantages of erasing the board during your talk, that is, the time and trouble versus the possible distraction. And if you're using slides, be certain they're in the proper order and right side up.

4. *The visual aid may not work:* Gremlins or other elves are busy sabotaging speakers everywhere, blowing out fuses, jamming slide projectors, wearing out bulbs, and snarling cassette recorders. If you depend on some powered visual aid, check and double-check everything involved in working it, such as the location of the electrical outlet, the switch for it, and the machine itself. Just remember that Murphy's law applies: If anything can go wrong, it will.

Our calling these four hazards to your attention is not designed to scare you away from using visual aids. Forewarned is forearmed. As we have said, a visual aid is a two-edged weapon: it can give your speech a fine edge or cut into your audience's attention. And to hone that fine edge, consult appendix M, which provides other helpful hints on visual aids.

CONCLUSION   In mentioning the "tell 'em what you've told 'em" ending previously, we've already suggested that a conclusion might take the form of a summary. Especially if the talk is at all involved or lengthy, you need to pull the parts together. Nearly all listeners will daydream or let their minds wander from time to time during your talk. Few speakers are so electrifying that people hang on their every word. A summary, therefore, puts the pieces together so that the audience will not puzzle over any part.

You may end with the summary or with an appropriate quotation, serious or humorous anecdote, or—in persuasive speeches—plan of action, challenging appeal, or inspirational words.

A quotation is used effectively by J. Paul Sticht, President of R. J. Reynolds Industries, in ending his talk to students at the University of Pittsburgh:

> You'll find yourself faced with tough choices. Sometimes they may confront your sense of integrity, decency, and honor with the easy option of accepting things that outrage all three by "just going along." If you face such choices, I hope you follow Mark Twain's advice, which in closing I pass along as my own: "Always do right. This will gratify some people, and astonish the rest."[9]

Another type of conclusion involves a call for specific action. Listeners might be urged, for example, to write to their congressional representative, contribute money, or buy a product or service. Be careful that you tell people not only to act but exactly how to do so. For instance, furnish the names and addresses of congressional representatives.

The most eloquent example in recent history of a challenging, inspirational appeal is Reverend Martin Luther King, Jr.'s stirring conclusion to his "I Have a Dream" speech to a civil rights rally in Washington:

> When we let freedom ring, when we let it ring from every village and hamlet, from every state and every city, we will be able to speed up that day when all God's children,

black men and white men, Jews and Gentiles, Protestants and Catholics, will be able to join hands and sing in the words of the old Negro spiritual "Free at last! free at last! thank God almighty, we are free at last!"[10]

Word your conclusions so as to signal your audience that you are ending your talk. Whether or not you use such signals as "finally," your conclusion should let your audience know that this is the finale, that you have covered certain key ideas they should remember, and that you are a person they should respect. Perhaps that adds up to a paraphrase of an old song: "Give them something to remember and something to remember you by."

The conclusion is important, providing an opportunity for a favorable last impression on listeners. Make it short—perhaps three or four sentences—and memorize it. In this fashion, you will gain confidence from knowing that you can conclude succinctly and gracefully, without fumbling and without turning the end into a lingering farewell that lovers may enjoy but that will annoy your audience.

SUMMARY

In some respects, speaking is easier than writing because of the ways in which your performance and method of presentation enhance communication. Your nervous system stimulates you, your eyes enable you to adjust your material to your audience's reactions, your voice gives your words emphasis and meaning, and your facial expression, posture, movement, and gestures aid communication. All these can work for you, once you understand how they can help and how to employ them skillfully. In time, with practice and with constructive criticism from your instructor and classmates, you can improve your speaking skills. Successful speakers are made, not born. And successful speakers know not only how to deliver a speech but how to prepare one.

Preparing the content of a speech involves selecting the subject and planning the speech. Subject selection is obviously unnecessary when you are assigned a topic. But when you are not, you should consider your own interests, experiences, and knowledge, and those of your audience, with some recognition of the occasion and time limitation. Once you have decided on the subject, you should set about planning the speech by writing a statement of purpose, preparing an introduction and conclusion, and outlining the material. Try to use visual aids to support ideas in the body of your talk, but anticipate the problems involved with them.

In working on your speech, keep in mind the importance of interesting listeners. You would also be wise to remember an old adage: never overestimate your audience's knowledge nor underestimate its intelligence.

EXERCISES

Discussion Questions

1. Which of the suggested ways to reduce stage fright do you think will be most helpful? Why?

2. From your own speaking experience, describe some of the problems in maintaining direct eye contact with an audience.
3. Which suggestion about using your voice more effectively seems most helpful? Explain.
4. Choose a political figure, TV or film star, athlete, clergyman, or some person on your campus, and analyze why he or she is an effective speaker.
5. Why is speaking from notes usually more effective than reading a paper?
6. Why is establishing a bond or link with an audience helpful in the introduction of a talk?
7. Explain why transitions are more important in oral communication than in written.
8. What problems have you observed in the use of visual aids by instructors or others?

In-Class Applications

1. In pantomime, describe an object to the class.
2. Select a subject for a talk that you think would interest each of the following and explain your choices:
   a. Teachers at your former high school
   b. Elderly patients in a nursing home
   c. A local business group
   d. A fraternal organization
   e. A group of touring college students from another region
3. Write two introductions for one of these talks. Ask your classmates to determine which one is the better.
4. Write two conclusions and ask your classmates to select the better one.
5. Where is the best place for a visiting speaker to give a talk on your campus? Why? Would you like to change the facilities there in any way? Where is the worst place? Why? How could it be improved?
6. Describe an instructor who uses body language effectively. Illustrate.
7. Analyze the introduction and conclusion of a speech in *Vital Speeches* or *Representative American Speeches* and report to the class how interest was established, a link implied or stated, and the subject introduced; and how a note of finality, a summary, or some other closing device was used.
8. Report to your class on the performance of some visiting speaker on campus.

Speaking Assignments

1. Make a copy of a speech you like in *Vital Speeches* or *Representative American Speeches*. Introduce it with information about the speaker and the occasion. In order to save class time, summarize the body of the speech except for certain passages you feel are memorable, and then read the conclusion.
2. Give a 5- to 7-minute talk about why a new business or business expansion in your home or college community will do well or not.

3. Present a 5- to 7-minute report on a company, based on its annual report or other material. Use at least one visual aid.
4. Assume you are talking to a group of travel agents visiting your college. Try to persuade them to visit an interesting, historic, or scenic location in the community.
5. Give a 5- to 7-minute talk to your class, defining and explaining a business term that you were not familiar with last year.
6. Give a 10- to 12-minute talk, refuting an argument about a business subject in a previous speech, editorial, or letter to the editor. You might look through copies of *The Wall Street Journal, Business Week, Fortune, U.S. News and World Report, Forbes*, or some other business publication.
7. Give a 10- to 12-minute talk about some new development in accounting, advertising, marketing, selling, word processing, or other aspect of business.

NOTES

[1] Irving Wallace, David Wallechinsky, and Amy Wallace, *The Book of Lists* (New York: Bantam Books, 1978), p. 469.

[2] "Preparing and Delivering an Oral Presentation," *Technical Communication*, 26, no. 1 (1979), p. 7.

[3] "The Arson Profit Business," *Vital Speeches*, 45, no. 2 (November 1, 1978), p. 61.

[4] "Facing Up to the Hard Facts of Inflation," *Vital Speeches*, 47, no. 3 (November 15, 1980), p. 74.

[5] "Webb Pomerene," *Vital Speeches*, 47, no. 1 (October 15, 1980), p. 26.

[6] Art Linkletter, *Public Speaking for Private People* (Indianapolis: Bobbs-Merrill Co., 1980), p. 51.

[7] "Forces for Change and the New Consumer," *Vital Speeches*, 44, no. 16 (June 1, 1978), p. 489.

[8] Mentioned by Chester K. Guth and Stanley S. Shaw, *How to Put on Dynamic Meetings* (Reston, Va.: Reston Publishing Co., 1980), p. 47.

[9] "Public Leadership: A Challenge to New Executives," *Vital Speeches*, 44 (September 15, 1978), p. 719.

[10] *Representative American Speeches 1963–64*, Lester Thonssen, ed. (New York: H. H. Wilson Company, 1964), p. 48.

12 Interviews, Meetings, and Listening

OBJECTIVES

After reading this chapter, you should be able to:

- Describe the four-part structure of the interview
- Know how to conduct effective interviews
- Point out four ways to plan for meetings
- Explain four ways to chair meetings effectively
- Discuss how best to deal with six types of problem people at meetings
- Describe three special meeting procedures: brainstorming, nominal grouping, and the interaction method
- Explain five barriers to effective listening
- State six ways to improve listening skills

PLAN

We are a meeting society.

MICHAEL DOYLE AND DAVID STRAUS

From the moment they begin their day with a "hello" until they depart with a "good-bye," people at work are engaged in forms of oral communication other than presentations. In addition to telephone and face-to-face conversations, they conduct interviews, participate in meetings, and occasionally attend conferences. We'd like to help you communicate well in two of these settings—interviews and meetings—and suggest ways you can engage effectively in them. And we'll also talk about the art of listening, because it too is a crucial part of oral communication.

INTERVIEWS

In chapter 6, we discussed interviews from the viewpoint of the person seeking a job. Now we will examine them from the other side of the desk. Interviews serve as a management tool for providing and obtaining information, improving working relationships, solving problems, building goodwill, and of course employing, transferring, and promoting people.

Managers use interviews to communicate with employees in various ways. For example, the *appraisal* interview is held at least yearly to evaluate employees and to let them know what they are doing well and how they might improve their work. *Counseling* interviews are held to advise and assist employers with personal or professional difficulties. *Disciplinary* interviews are conducted to alert employees to their shortcomings and, if they are to be penalized, to see they understand why. *Problem-solving* interviews serve to acquaint employees with issues, such as poor quality control, production delays, or petty theft, and to seek solutions. *Persuasive* interviews promote new ideas, programs, or goals. And *exit* interviews provide an opportunity for expressing appreciation, for promoting a positive attitude toward the organization, and for discussing the reasons for a resignation.

All of these interviews involve a one-on-one relationship; all require the interviewer to take charge. And all generally follow a basic pattern consisting of four stages: (1) planning; (2) welcoming; (3) questioning; and (4) concluding.

Planning

Too often interviews occur on the spur of the moment or are conducted haphazardly even though they have been scheduled. Someone arrives for the interview; the interviewer, who has forgotten the appointment, drops everything else, mumbles "Oh yes, I'm glad to see you," ushers the person in, and fumbles around formulating questions.

Instead, interviews should be carefully planned. First, consider *purpose:* What do you hope to achieve? Why hold the interview? Then, think about *place:* Where should you hold it? Are you apt to be interrupted in your office? Would a conference room or place for lunch be more conducive to communication? Where should you both sit? Do you want to create a barrier by being behind a desk or not? Then there is the matter of *information:* Should you have sales, production, or other figures handy? Financial records? Personnel folder? What might you need? And finally, you should formulate the important *questions.* Rather than hoping they will spring to mind, you'd be wise to jot down several, phrasing them carefully.

As you can see, planning an interview involves thinking out these four major aspects ahead of time. Usually, the better the plans, the better the results.

Welcoming

As you may recall from our discussion of interviews, the first portion is normally devoted to the greetings and pleasantries that help put interviewees at ease. In any superior-subordinate relationship, the tension can be eased by friendly remarks or an explanation of the purpose and plan of the meeting. For example, you might open a problem-solving interview in this way:

> I've asked you here, Ruth, to help me with the problem of the lunch break. People are leaving early and returning late. First, let me suggest some ways we might handle this. Then I'd like you to react to these ideas.

Other ways to reduce the interviewee's nervousness include questions about mutual acquaintances and interests, or recent events. Much of the success of an interview may depend on your starting it on a friendly, positive note.

Questioning

The actual interview consists mainly of your questioning the interviewee and listening critically to the replies, although you may also have to respond to some questions. Good interviewers are skilled listeners who can accurately observe and evaluate what interviewees say, how they say it, and why they say it.

Interview questions may take any of several forms. You can select the most advantageous for your purpose.

THE DIRECT QUESTION Also called the *close-ended* question, this type permits little freedom of response. It seeks specific, usually factual, information and eliminates misinterpretation. Example: *What was your college G.P.A.?* But intensive direct questioning can be threatening, sounding like a police or courtroom grilling.

THE OPEN-ENDED QUESTION   This kind of question provides interviewees with great freedom in replying. Open-ended questions serve mainly to allow people to reveal their attitudes. Example: *How might the company help its employees improve production?* However, while open-ended questions may disclose the quality of a person's mind, they allow for digression and can be time-consuming.

THE CLARIFICATION QUESTION   When an interviewer wants clarification, amplification, or qualification of a response, it is a good technique to ask a follow–up question seeking additional useful information. You might ask for clarification in any of several ways: *Could you tell me a little more about that? Would you give me an example of it? Exactly what did you mean by that?*

Instead of repeating clarification questions, you may obtain additional information by other means. Sometimes silence creates a tension that may compel the interviewee to continue talking. Other ways to elicit more information consist of uttering neutral encouraging phrases, such as "yes," "sure," "go on," and "uh-huh," and from time to time interjecting summaries like the following:

> I think you've thoroughly explained the problem our sales reps have in laying out cash in advance for travel expenses, Bill. Now I wish you'd discuss further why the travel allowance is inadequate.

THE HYPOTHETICAL QUESTION   To test how an interviewee would handle some situation, you might pose an imaginary example, allowing the person to assume some new role. Example: *If you were manager of this division, what would you do to improve morale that would not require much money?*

A mixture of all these questions can be particularly useful.[1] You could start with several direct and easy-to-answer questions, allowing the other person to relax. Then you might move to open-ended questions, keeping an eye on the time. One or two hypothetical questions at the close could provide a stimulating end to the interview. And throughout, where needed, you would use clarification questions.

Concluding

When the time allotted for an interview has ended, or when you feel that you can neither provide nor obtain more information, you should conclude the meeting. In doing so, summarize the agreements or key points, mention any future meeting or follow-up action, and express appreciation. If the interviewee fails to understand, stand up, shake hands, and move toward the door.

MEETINGS

At various times in college, you may have to lead meetings in student committees, panels, symposiums, or other small groups. In future years, you will probably find yourself chairing study groups, task forces, project teams, working parties, or boards. Such meetings are often highly productive, bringing people together to share ideas and stimulate one another for the purpose of arriving at better decisions than they would by acting individually.

An interesting experiment validating this conclusion is the NASA Moon Survival Task, designed by Jay Hall, a social psychologist (see table 12–1). He found that when the members' individual responses before entering the group were compared with the subsequent group decision, it was almost always superior, and often it was better than even the best individual response.[2]

TABLE 12–1. NASA Moon Survival Task

You are in a space crew originally scheduled to rendezvous with a mother ship on the lighted surface of the moon. Mechanical difficulties, however, have forced your ship to crash land at a spot some 200 miles from the rendezvous point. The rough landing damaged much of the equipment aboard. Since survival depends on reaching the mother ship, the most critical items available must be chosen for the 200 mile trip. Below are listed the 15 items left intact after the landing. Your task is to rank them in terms of their importance to your crew in its attempt to reach the rendezvous point. Place number 1 by the most important item, number 2 by the second most important item and so on through number 15, the least important.*

_____ Box of matches	_____ Life raft
_____ Food concentrate	_____ Magnetic compass
_____ 50 feet of nylon rope	_____ 5 gallons of water
_____ Parachute silk	_____ Signal flares
_____ Portable heating unit	_____ First-aid kit containing injection
_____ Two .45 calibre pistols	needles
_____ One case of dehydrated milk	_____ Solar-powered FM receiver-
_____ Two 100-pound tanks of oxygen	transmitter
_____ Stellar map of moon's constellation	

* For the answer by NASA's Crew Research Department, see p. 388.

Meetings also usually increase people's understanding of an organization and their commitment to it. As they exchange ideas they learn from one another, and as they work toward a general consensus that each contributes to, they come to believe in and feel a part of it.

Because group discussions have great potential for circulating information, management relies on them heavily. Regularly scheduled staff meetings can be an important forum where progress reports, reviews of projects, personnel changes, and department plans are reported. More common are the special problem-solving meetings, where individuals representing various interested units or areas meet to deal with personnel, production, sales, financial issues and the like.

An estimated 11 million meetings are held every day in the United States.[3] In fact, it is not uncommon for some people to feel they could get their business done if only they did not have to attend so many meetings. This resentment often results from the poor planning and conducting of many meetings. Their fate is in the hands of the chairperson. And because you may be in that position—either in college or in business—it is important for you to understand how to run a meeting effectively.

Planning Meetings

Planning meetings usually involves determining the size of the group, arranging the room, preparing the agenda and other documents, and formulating introductory remarks and key questions.

DETERMINING GROUP SIZE   You may have no choice in determining group size. Members may be appointed by someone else or may be selected because they are representatives of various sections or divisions. If you have any voice in the matter, try to restrict the members to 6–8 people, 12 at the most. Larger groups can be cumbersome and their size often inhibits people from participating.

ARRANGING THE ROOM   To a surprising extent, the climate at a meeting is determined by the arrangement of chairs and tables. Here are some possibilities:[4]

Classroom Style   This arrangement fails to promote discussion because the chairman is established as an authoritative figure and some people can see only the back of others' heads.

Boardroom Style   This arrangement also encourages an authoritarian atmosphere because the chairperson dominates the seating arrangement. While appropriate for information meetings, it is not ideal for discussions because people tend to exchange ideas with others across the table but not with those sitting on their left or right.

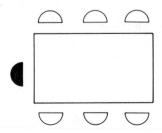

U or Semicircular Style   Although there is still an authority figure in this arrangement, the participants can relate to the chairperson and one another easily, so they feel involved.

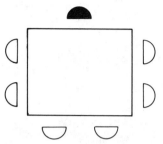

The Closed or Circle Style   This arrangement, suggesting the equality of all members including the chairperson, seems to be most conducive for a free-flowing discussion.

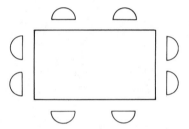

When planning seating, place the group so that individuals arriving late or departing early will not disrupt the members. Also consider other distractions, such as the view from a window.

Obviously, enough chairs should be provided. Pens and pads might be furnished, coffee made available, and any helpful visual aids (chalkboard, sketchpad, etc.) should be on hand.

PREPARING THE AGENDA AND OTHER DOCUMENTS   Members should be furnished with an agenda at least a day in advance or further ahead of time if possible. Each item to be discussed should be listed along with the starting time, the place, and the ending time. Along with the agenda, send any background papers, reports, or documents that will be discussed. Any pertinent material requiring more than several minutes to read should be distributed well in advance of the meeting.

FORMULATING OPENING REMARKS AND KEY QUESTIONS   Instead of waiting for a last-minute inspiration, plan your opening remarks, which should state the exact purpose of the meeting and what is expected of the group's members. It would also be wise to have some initial and key questions prepared to stimulate the discussion.

Conducting Meetings

There are few hard-and-fast rules for chairing a meeting, because of the differences in personalities, purposes, and participants. But a few general guidelines may be suggested. We'll examine them in a discussion of four distinct leadership functions: (1) opening the meeting; (2) running the meeting; (3) dealing with problem people; and (4) making decisions.

OPENING THE MEETING   You should open the meeting promptly by welcoming the members, introducing them to one another, and reviewing the purpose of the meeting. You might wish to break the ice by having the members identify themselves and their departments, thus giving each an opportunity to say a few words. After you have concluded all necessary explanatory remarks, begin with the first of the key questions you had previously prepared.

Let's consider an example. Your student committee has met to review a faculty proposal for a *relative grade transcript*. This is a graduation record showing not only a student's grades but the number of students in each class, the average grades in each, and the other grades given. The advantage cited for the relative grade transcript is that it would give graduate and professional schools and prospective employers a way to interpret grades by revealing how competitive and difficult courses were. After explaining the relative grade transcript to your group and pointing out that it would be voluntary for students, you might begin with these questions:

- Is there a need for a relative grade transcript?
- What are the advantages of the relative grade transcript?
- What are its disadvantages?
- The relative grade transcript is an answer to grade inflation. Are there easier, less expensive, or more practical answers?

However you start, avoid directing a question at a specific person or asking a difficult question that might stump the group.

RUNNING THE MEETING   Once the discussion has begun, encourage it to flow freely, avoiding whatever might stifle participation. Allow the group free rein, permitting people to interrupt each other occasionally. When conflict develops between members, encourage it as long as pertinent ideas are being exchanged, but discourage personal remarks about individuals' characters or reputations.

One of the most difficult leadership functions is to keep the discussion on the subject. Speakers quite often digress, sometimes talking at length about a personal experience or interest only remotely associated with the subject. At such times, you must direct the group's attention back to the subject, either by mentioning the point at issue, or by summarizing some of the points previously made. Here's how:

John:	(*Long digression about the grades in his accounting class, and his personal problem with the instructor.*)
Chairperson:	John's main point is that as a nonmajor in a class with accounting majors, his grades suffered. But, let's consider whether the relative transcript would help or hurt him.

or

> *Chairperson:* We've discussed how the relative transcript system might affect nonmajors, as John just indicated, and how it might cause students to appear below average if they attend classes with bright students. Let's see now if there are any other disadvantages to relative transcripts.

In addition to coping with digressors, you should encourage the quiet, bolster the timid, stimulate the uninterested, and mediate between combatants. And from time to time, you should summarize what has been agreed on and point out what else needs to be considered. Above all, be careful not to talk too much. View your role as that of a coach, trying to get the best performance out of your team. You should guide people, not dominate them. Although you may sometimes have to assert your authority to limit discussion, you should serve primarily as a moderator—clarifying, stimulating, interpreting, summarizing, and directing the talk to keep it moving ahead on course.

DEALING WITH PROBLEM PEOPLE   Certain personality types can create difficulties for chairpeople who do not expect them or know how to handle them. Here are a few:

The Persister: This person keeps repeating the same idea over and over again. After a second or third repetition, you might try asking, "Is there anyone here who does not understand what Bill has said? Does anyone want to ask Bill any questions? If not, I would assume, Bill, that everyone gets your point so you need not repeat it again."

The No-er: This negative individual throws cold water over every idea, pointing out why it won't work or won't be practical. One remedy is to ask that the group withhold criticism of an idea until everyone has had an opportunity to contribute ideas and to consider their merits.

The Silent: This person may be naturally quiet but still should be coaxed to contribute once or twice. To avoid embarrassing him or her, ask a simple question of someone else. Then direct the same question to the silent person, who will have had a few minutes to think. During a break, discuss the importance of participation with this individual.

The Dominator: There's always at least one person who talks too much. First, try gentle persuasion by saying something like, "We've heard from you several times already, Bill. I'd like to find out now what Joe and Mary think." If this doesn't work, you might explain during a break, or even in the meeting, that for a while you will only allow others to talk, so that all may have an equal opportunity to state their views.

The Wise Guy: Like the dominator, the wise guy will try to take over the meeting, not in monopolizing the discussion but in using education, experience, rank, or seniority to impose ideas. This person can best be handled by pointing out the need for the group to formulate an opinion that reflects all their views after they have listened to all ideas. And also, you might point out the need for new people unfamiliar with the old ways to contribute fresh ideas.

The Interrupter: This person constantly breaks in when others are speaking. If you tolerate this rudeness, you will upset the people trying to state their ideas. So you must be firm with interrupters, telling them to let the speaker finish talking.

These are only a few of the many types of problem people you will encounter. For a more complete roster, see Michael Doyle and David Straus's *How to Make Meetings Work.*[5]

MAKING DECISIONS   The purpose of meeting as a group is usually to arrive at some agreement about a decision. But how do you actually arrive at a final decision, which may consist of numerous minor decisons that must be agreed on? Here are some of the common methods:

> *Consensus:* When there appears to be general agreement on some subject that has been sufficiently discussed, you might ask, "Is it generally agreed, then, that we should recommend this?"
>
> *Vote:* Whenever there is disagreement about a subject that has been hotly argued for some time, you might bring it up for a vote. This technique should be a last resort, however, because it causes some members to win and others to lose, leaving bad feelings. It would be far better to seek an alternate solution or a compromise, but sometimes a vote must be taken.
>
> *Steamroller:* Although the technique is not recommended, many chairpeople resort to strong-arm tactics to reach a decision. After an extensive discussion that results in a deadlock, you might say: "In view of the time we've devoted to this issue and the little time left today, if no one objects strongly, I'd like to suggest we do this and move on to the next item."
>
> *Leader's Favor:* This technique is similar to the steamroller but gentler. Employed by chairpeople who are liked and respected by the group, it might take this form, "I'd appreciate it if you let me work out the details of this decision so that we may move along to consider the next subject."
>
> *Listing:* Some subjects lend themselves to the listing technique, which, as its name suggests, consists of placing all the solutions on a board, sketchpad, or some other visual aid. Then go through a series of votes, eliminating the least popular solutions until a favorite is clear.
>
> *Appeasement:* Although not often imposed deliberately, this technique results from the desire of the chairperson or the group to soothe the feelings of a member whose views have been defeated on a previous issue. There is a tendency to allow this person at least a minor victory on some other issue.

Of all these techniques, the consensus is the most desirable, because it involves and satisfies all members of the group.

CONCLUDING THE GROUP DISCUSSION   Near the end of the period scheduled for a meeting, call attention to the time limit. If all aspects of the problem or subject have not been explored, notify the group in this manner:

> In the fifteen remaining minutes, we should consider the point that the relative transcript is a voluntary plan. Only students wanting one would get one. What's your reaction to that?

Finally, save a few minutes to summarize what has been accomplished, to thank everyone, and to decide on the next meeting time and place if one is necessary.

Such an ending gives people a sense of achievement, makes them feel appreciated, and conveys the idea that their time was well spent. Settling arrangements for the next meeting then and there can accomplish in minutes what it might take secretaries or members many telephone hours to decide on later.

WRITING THE MINUTES OF A GROUP DISCUSSION In small meetings, the chairperson is often responsible for taking notes and getting out the minutes. Although there may be a temptation to do without them, they are a valuable record of what was discussed and agreed upon. Also, if someone will be responsible for providing information or is given some other assignment for the next meeting, the minutes will serve as a reminder.

Minutes usually follow a standard form, presenting the following information:

- Meeting date, time, and place
- Names of chairperson and others attending
- Agenda items discussed, decisions reached, and action decided on. (Sometimes these are listed separately.)
- Names of persons making proposals and given assignments
- Closing time
- Date, time, and place of next meeting

Note in the sample minutes provided (see figure 12–1) that the first two items appear at the beginning and the last two at the end, and that the minutes are signed, which is obligatory for meetings of large groups but not small ones.

Special Methods for Meetings

Often, routine meetings fail to produce fresh, creative ideas, especially in business, where the unusual or novel is usually discouraged. To foster the flow of innovative thinking, several relatively new techniques for meetings have proven successful. Among these are *brainstorming*, the *Nominal Group Technique*, and the *Interaction Method*.

BRAINSTORMING This technique, first mentioned by Alex Osborn, requires that a group abide by four guidelines to promote a free flow of ideas:

1. No idea should be criticized during the session.
2. Wild or unorthodox ideas are encouraged.
3. The quantity of ideas is the objective: the more, the better.
4. Building or piggybacking on other ideas is encouraged.[6]

Ideally, brainstorming should be used with specific problems having concrete solutions, such as, "How can we decrease our overhead expenses by 10 percent?"

Brainstorming meetings are usually small, with five to ten participants who have been notified previously about the problem and may bring written solutions to the meetings. They should be seated in a circle, semicircle, or square so they can see

Figure 12–1.   Minutes of a Small Group Meeting.

Committee for Re-Organization of the Senate

March 7, 19--

The Committee met at 2:00 p.m. in 245 Patterson Office Tower with Chair-person Kent presiding and the following members present: Falcone, Kent, Collins, Tong, Ogilvy and Samuels.

Minutes of the last meeting were approved.

Bernard Samuels presented a plan for reducing the student members of the Senate to 15. Some Committee members expressed concern that the reduction might be too great in the College of Arts and Sciences, but otherwise thought it was excellent. He is to take the proposal back to the Student Association for its modifications or approval and then return it to the Committee at the next meeting.

It was agreed to recommend that the ex-officio members of the Senate would remain the same but that they would become nonvoting members.

As a result of a discussion about the status of the computer record of Senate decisions and rule changes, Ogilvy agreed to check with the Senate Council office.

Falcone raised the question of the length of term of Senators, the lapse between terms, and the possibility of shorter terms or longer lapses in order to involve more faculty in the Senate. After some discussion, it was agreed not to recommend a change in the present rules.

Collins suggested that committee chairpersons should have the privilege of requesting replacement of committee members for those who fail to attend. After discussion, it was agreed that nothing in the present rules prevents a chairperson from asking the President of the Senate Council to add additional members to the committee. Therefore no action was taken.

Falcone is to prepare a draft of the recommended Senate rules and have them ready for discussion at our next meeting.

The next meeting date was set for Wednesday, March 25, at 2:00 p.m. in Room 245 of the Patterson Office Tower.

The meeting was adjourned at 3:34 p.m.

Respectfully submitted,

James Kent

James D. Kent

and talk to one another. The chairperson begins the meeting by explaining the topic and reviewing the four brainstorming guidelines. During the meeting, the chairperson discourages interruptions or negative reactions, stimulates the group, and writes the ideas on a sketchpad or blackboard.

Sometimes brainstorming is conducted in a stop-and-go fashion, with people suggesting ideas for several minutes, thinking quietly for several more, and continuing to alternate in this manner. Or, the chairperson may call on one person after another for ideas, allowing anyone to skip a turn and offer ideas later. With larger groups, *buzz sessions* can be used by dividing participants into subgroups. Each subgroup searches for ideas and then reports its best ones at a meeting of the larger group.

After all brainstorming ideas are recorded, a separate decison-making committee or members of the brainstorming group itself may rate them and determine the most feasible. But the main function of the brainstorming method is to generate new and different ideas, rather than to make final decisions.

Brainstorming is a highly effective method that has achieved great success. But it does have some disadvantages. Among those are its failure to reward or recognize individual employees, its ineffectiveness with complex problems, its time limits on the incubation of ideas, its time-consuming and therefore costly nature, and its lack of success where trial and error rather than judgment is needed.

NOMINAL GROUPING TECHNIQUE (NGT) Developed by Andre L. Delbecq and Andrew Van de Ven, NGT consists of a five-step process:

1. At the beginning of the meeting, each participant compiles a list of ideas about the subject.
2. Each member is called upon in turn to suggest one idea, which is written for all the others to see. This process continues until all ideas have been listed.
3. After a brief discussion to explain or clarify the ideas, a vote is taken to determine the best five ideas.
4. The top five ideas are debated. The group may combine, modify, eliminate, or otherwise change the ideas.
5. The members vote to determine which of the highest-scoring ideas to recommend.[7]

The main advantage of the NGT method is that the group has the opportunity to think about and thoroughly discuss the ideas.

THE INTERACTION METHOD Recently devised by Michael Doyle and David Straus,[8] this method calls for the chairperson to become a member of the group rather than run the meeting. Instead, a *facilitator* acts as an impartial group leader, who skillfully conducts the meeting but cannot contribute to the discussion or evaluation of ideas. Another person, a *recorder*, writes down the ideas on large sheets of paper that are prominently displayed before the group and referred to as the "group memory."

ORAL COMMUNICATIONS

The facilitator is in charge but may be overruled by the group or directed to run the meeting properly. The chairperson is responsible only for calling the meeting, setting the agenda, and making all final decisions.

The advantage of The Interaction Method is its modification of the conventional structure of business meetings in several important ways. It assigns a new role to the chairperson to prevent him or her from dominating the meeting through superior rank. Two other new roles are created by introducing the facilitator and the recorder. Each is entrusted with a single responsibility: the facilitator must conduct the meeting efficiently and impartially, and the recorder must write down all ideas. Consequently, the members may participate as equals, freed from their customary roles within the corporate hierarchy and their concerns about the fairness of procedures.

LISTENING

In a series of full-page ads in leading newspapers and magazines, Sperry Corporation recently pointed out the importance of listening in the work of its executives. Here is an excerpt from one of those ads:

> It starts the moment you walk through the door.
> The phone rings. You pick it up and listen.
> An associate comes in your office with a problem. And you listen.
> You rush off to one meeting after another. And listen.
> The fact is executives spend more time listening than they do anything else.
> But unfortunately, much of this time is wasted.
> Research studies show that on the average we listen at a 25% level of efficiency.
> A statistic that is not only surprisingly low, but terribly costly.
> When executives don't listen effectively, communication breaks down.
> Ideas and information get distorted by as much as 80% as they travel through an organization.
> Yet as critical as listening is, it's one skill we're never really trained to do.
> Well, as one of the world's largest corporations, we at Sperry are making sure our executives are as qualified at listening as they are at everything else.
> We have special listening programs that Sperry employees worldwide can attend.[9]

Most people are surprised to learn that they listen poorly and can be taught to improve. But many corporations like Sperry have found that it pays to institute special in-house seminars and workshops to improve employee listening.[10]

Why do we need instruction in listening? Why don't we listen well? You can understand why we listen at a 25 percent rate of efficiency if you realize the barriers to effective listening.

Barriers To Effective Listening

Effective listening involves more than hearing. Nearly all of us hear well. But we often fail to understand, interpret, evaluate, remember, and respond to what we hear. (See figure 12–2.) Good listening consists of all these. It is an active process requiring interest, attention, and effort. Instead, most of us think of listening as a passive activity occurring as we sit back, relax, and absorb what enters our ears. In

Figure 12–2. Anyone Listening?

(SOURCE: Courtesy Sperry Corporation.)

this way, we may hear a speaker's message, but fail to register it in our minds because of several barriers.

BRAIN SPEED One barrier results from the fact that our brain works four times faster than we speak.[11] We can hear and comprehend what is being said and still have time left over to think about numerous other matters. That's why listeners often interrupt speakers to fill in the rest of a sentence or to answer a question before it has been completely stated. And that's why, as you sit in lecture classes, your mind often races ahead, creating a barrier to effective listening.

SUBJECTS Often, we fail to listen well because we decide beforehand that we can't understand or aren't interested in a subject. Some people, for instance, block out discussions about mathematical, statistical, or financial matters because of "math anxiety." Other people are deaf to other subjects: some to literature, some to science, some to politics, some to economics. Different barriers exist for different people.

PEOPLE We also tune out certain people. Sometimes they are individuals we dislike. Other times, they are people with faces, complexions, clothes, bodies, voices, hair styles, beards, manners, or mannerisms that we don't care for. Whatever our prejudice, it can create a barrier to the speaker's message.

IDEAS Just as we are prejudiced toward some people, so we are towards some ideas. We might be so emotionally involved about a subject like abortion, prayer in the public schools, forced busing, gun control, or the death penalty that we cannot listen carefully to ideas contrary to our own. Our ears are open, but our minds are closed. We hear but do not listen.

DISTRACTIONS The ideal place for listening would be a soundproof, empty room with no windows, where two people could sit face-to-face, undistracted by sounds,

ORAL COMMUNICATIONS

movements, odors, or anything else. But we do not meet in such cells for presentations, discussions, or conferences.

Instead, we are usually surrounded by distractions. As you sit in class, you can hear the scratching of pens, the shuffling of feet, the turning of pages, and the coughing, breathing, and whispering inside the lecture hall, and the cars, trucks, buses, planes, birds, and people outside. And there is much to look at—other students listening, writing, talking, dozing, day-dreaming, slouching, flirting, reading, and squirming. And, of course, there are windows, ceilings, lights, shades, pictures, chairs, lecterns, desks, and floors to look at and think about. If our attention is not diverted by sounds, people, or objects around us, then we can always poke around in our minds. There's the weekend, the game, the date, the party, or the job to think about, or money problems, roommate difficulties, family quarrels, health worries, love-life obstacles, or concerns about exams or papers. With so much to distract us, who can listen?

Lessons on Listening

What can you do? How can you listen more effectively?

LESSON #1: CONCENTRATE   Just by being aware of all the barriers to effective listening, you can improve. And by realizing that listening is a difficult process, you can force yourself to concentrate, actively engaging in the process instead of sitting back passively, hoping to absorb what is said. You must focus your mind on the speaker's message, ignoring everything else around you and anything else that pops into your mind.

LESSON #2: GENERATE SELF-INTEREST   Your chances of listening effectively will be increased if you are eager to hear what is said. The trick then is to psych yourself up for the occasion; convince yourself how important it is to catch every word and understand every idea. Try to find some way to benefit personally from the message or to help someone else. Imagining uses for information or developing simple curiosity will help you to listen more effectively.

LESSON #3: BLOCK OUT THE BLOCKS   You know yourself better than others do, and you ought to be aware of your prejudices about people, subjects, and ideas. If you let these biases interfere with your listening, you will receive a distorted account of what is being said. So you must bend over backward to avoid becoming emotionally involved. Keep your cool. Tell yourself, "I don't care for this subject (or those ideas, or this person), but I'm going to make a special effort on that account to understand the message."

LESSON #4: WORK YOUR BRAIN   To keep that fast brain of yours from straying off the course, give it extra assignments. During the talk, ask yourself the following questions: "What is the speaker's central idea? Supporting ideas? Main evidence? How is this point related to the ones discussed previously? What might come next?" Such questions keep you focused on the talk and help you understand the speaker's main point, key ideas, and organizational structure.

LESSON #5: EXERCISE YOUR CRITICAL FACULTIES Listen not only to understand, but to evaluate as well. To be a critical listener, William S. Tracey suggests that you become "a healthy doubter."[12] By this he does not mean that you should doubt everything, but that you should question what a speaker says. Among the questions you might ask yourself are some of the following:

- How important is the main idea? The other ideas?
- How valid and reliable is the evidence? Is it current?
- Has anything important been overlooked?
- Why should there be some change?
- What other alternatives are there? Are any better than the proposed solution?
- Is the solution practical? How can it be implemented?

These and similar questions help you to evaluate a presentation, providing you with a way to discover and discern its strengths and weaknesses. As a result, you will be better able to respond to the speaker's message.

LESSON #6: STORE IN MEMORY According to the Sperry Corporation, tests have shown that immediately after a ten-minute talk, an average listener retains only half of what was said. And within 48 hours, that drops to 25 percent.[13] You can do better. One way is to take notes, not writing at length, but trying to outline the main points and evidence. Then check these notes with the speaker's concluding summary.

But often in meetings, interviews, and on other occasions, you cannot take notes. What then? Listen intently for the central and main supporting ideas, and review them constantly during and at the conclusion of the talk. Also, as you leave, repeat to yourself the gist of the message. And to cement it in your mind, mention it to someone shortly afterwards. Saying it aloud to another person helps to store the information in your computer-like brain for later retrieval.

Rewards of Effective Listening

We read more than we write, we talk more than we read, and we listen more than we talk. Yet, although we are taught how to write, read, and talk, few of us learn how to listen. It is not a communication skill that should be taken for granted. Indeed, in schools and companies where listening programs have been adopted, comprehension has increased significantly. So you owe it to yourself to be aware of the barriers to good listening and to heed the lessons on listening. But it's up to you to use your ears to full advantage!

SUMMARY

In this chapter, we focused on interviews and meetings, particularly on how to plan and conduct them. And because listening is so important in both these communication situations, we have pointed out its significance, described the obstacles to effective listening, and suggested ways to improve listening skills.

Interviewers should plan carefully for interviews by considering their purpose, arranging for conducive surroundings, collecting pertinent data, and preparing key questions. Once the interview begins, the interviewer should welcome the interviewee cordially, ask different types of questions to obtain a variety of responses, and conclude the session promptly.

Meetings provide an excellent opportunity for a group to obtain information, exchange ideas, and work more effectively on problem-solving than they could as individuals. Preparations for meetings consist of determining the group size, arranging the chairs and tables in keeping with the meeting's purpose, and sending out an agenda and other pertinent materials for group members to study beforehand.

After opening a meeting promptly and graciously, the chairperson should explain any necessary matters and then initiate discussion by asking a key question or two. During the main part of the meeting, the chairperson should keep interruptions to a minimum, limit digressions, but encourage disagreements except when they become personal. Certain types of problem people should be dealt with tactfully but firmly. In general, the chairperson should moderate the discussion, entering it occasionally, not dominating it.

The group should arrive at its decisions through general agreement, but sometimes a vote may have to be taken or other techniques used to arrive at a conclusion. Near the end of the allocated time for the meeting, the chairperson should notify the group that it's getting late and raise any remaining issues. He or she should decide on another meeting time and place, if necessary, before summarizing the discussion and thanking people for attending. If a secretary is not responsible for writing the minutes, the chairperson should attend to this as soon as possible.

Among the techniques developed to produce more effective meetings are brainstorming, nominal grouping, and the interaction method. The first is specifically designed to stimulate creative thinking, the second to take advantage of brainstorming but to allow for thorough discussion, and the third to provide more effective management of meetings so that no ideas will be overlooked and high-ranking members will not dominate discussions.

In the last section of the chapter, we explained the importance of improved listening skills, those concerned with hearing, understanding, interpreting, evaluating, responding to, and remembering what is said. Tests have shown that most people do not listen well, usually retaining only 25 percent of a message.

This failure is understandable when we recognize the barriers to effective listening. Often we do not pay close attention to speakers because we dislike their subject, ideas, appearance, or personality. In addition, we are distracted by many sounds and sights around us, and because our brain works so much faster than people talk, we have time to think about other matters.

To overcome these barriers to effective listening, we should determine to concentrate on the message; generate interest in it; block out our prejudices against the subject, speaker, or ideas; occupy our minds with questions about the talk; and involve our critical faculties in evaluating its central and key ideas. Finally, we need to review the important points in the speech, perhaps repeating them to others in order to remember them.

Being able to listen skillfully, hold successful interviews, and conduct meetings effectively are important business skills that will prove valuable to you. Try to apply the suggestions in this chapter in your classroom or college activities. And in future years, review the suggestions as you become more successful in your business career.

EXERCISES

Discussion Questions

1. As head of production, you have decided to interview several factory supervisors to find out why productivity has decreased. What plans should you make for these interviews?
2. Provide examples of direct, open-end, clarification, and hypothetical questions that you might ask in these interviews.
3. How have room arrangements in your high school or college classes detracted from or been more conducive to free discussion? Discuss the settings and their influence on the exchange of ideas.
4. To prevent time from being wasted at meetings, some executives have scheduled them at 11 a.m. or 4 p.m. so that group members will be anxious to leave in an hour. What do you think of this idea?
5. In his study of meetings, Jay Hall found that the groups showing the most improvement in decision-making were those that "actively sought out the points of disagreement, and thus provoked conflicts, especially in the early stages." How would you account for this finding?
6. Name the six types of problem people. Have you ever had any of them in your classes? How do your teachers deal with them?
7. Name six methods that chairpersons may use to enable groups to arrive at decisions. In the high school, college, or other committees that you have served on, how have the chairpersons determined what the group wanted to do or recommend?
8. Speculate on the reasons for the four brainstorming guidelines.
9. Rank the five barriers to effective listening in order of the most-to-least distracting to you.
10. Name the six suggestions for improving listening skills and discuss which one is most apt to help you.

In-Class Applications

The instructor will divide the class into groups of 6 to 8 students, select a chairperson for each group, or request the group to select its own. Then, the instructor will either assign one of the following problems to the chairperson, or the group will choose one:

1. Individual members should first work on the Moon Survival Task problem presented in this chapter. Then the group should decide on a solution. Finally, each group member should evaluate to what extent the group was more effective than the individual members, as Hall concluded.

2. As manager of the accounting department, you are concerned about the excessive time that your employees are spending in restroom breaks. Although you are well aware that nature's call must be heeded, you know that some employees are going to the restroom to style their hair, read the newspaper, chat and lounge, and sleep. You call a meeting of employee representatives to decide what to do about this problem.

3. As director of personnel, you have become aware that certain employees in your division are receiving an excessive number of personal phone calls. Lines are tied up and work is interrupted. You meet with some key personnel to decide what to do.

4. As the plant manager, you are concerned about the mess around certain employee work stations. This poor housekeeping contributes to a loss of efficiency in numerous ways: time wasted looking for missing tools or equipment, poor safety records, high machine downtime, and excessive supply costs. Meet with employee representatives to see what can be done to improve housekeeping habits.

5. You are head of a university disciplinary committee that has been asked to review the case of a graduating senior who plagiarized a term paper in history. The student's instructor has decided to give the student an *E* in the course. The student has the right to come before your committee to protest the severity of the penalty. She does so, explaining that the plagiarism resulted from her forgetting to footnote several passages. Your committee should review the case and advise the instructor whether the penalty is excessive or not.

6. An instructor has appealed to you as head of a student policy committee to pass a rule barring students from selling copies of her lecture notes, which were taken down in shorthand, typed, duplicated, and sold for five dollars. With your committee, decide how this problem should be handled.

7. As head of a student committee on academic affairs, you have been asked to formulate a policy on class attendance. Should students be required to attend classes, be given a certain number of unexcused absences before being penalized, or be free to attend whenever they wish? Should the policy differ from class to class, or should it apply equally to everyone, freshmen as well as seniors? Decide with your committee.

8. Some students in your business communications course feel that they should be graded on improvement, others on effort, and yet others on achievement. Decide with your committee how students should be evaluated.

NOTES

[1] S. Bernard Rosenblatt, T. Richard Cheatham, and James T. Watt, *Communication in Business* (Englewood Cliffs, N.J.: Prentice Hall, 1977), pp. 211–214.

[2] Jay Hall, "Decisions, Decisions, Decisions," *Psychology Today*, Nov. 1971, p. 51.

[3] Anthony Jay, "How to Run a Meeting," *Harvard Business Review*, 54 (March-April, 1976), p. 45.

[4] For a more complete discussion of seating arrangements, see Martin Jones, *How to Organize Meetings* (New York: Beaufort Press, 1981), pp. 86–89.

[5] Michael Doyle and David Straus, *How to Make Meetings Work* (Chicago: Playboy Press, 1976), pp. 107–117.

[6] Alex Osborn, *Applied Imagination* (New York: Scribner's, 1953), pp. 298–301.

[7] Andre L. Delbecq and Andrew Van de Ven, *Group Techniques for Program Planning* (Glenville, Ill.: Scott Foresman, 1975).

[8] Doyle and Straus, pp. 83–87.

[9] *The Wall Street Journal*, 29 January 1980, p. 9.

[10] J. Donald Weinrauch and John R. Swanda, Jr., "Examining the Significance of Listening," *Journal of Business Communication*, 13, no. 1 (Fall 1975), p. 26.

[11] Ralph Nichols, "Now Hear This," *Nation's Business*, August 1966, p. 79.

[12] *Business and Professional Speaking*, 2nd ed. (Dubuque, Iowa: Wm. C. Brown, 1975), p. 144.

[13] "Your Personal Listening Profile," Sperry Corporation, n.d., n.p.

TABLE 12–1 (continued).   Solution to the *NASA Moon Survival Task*.

Don't peek until you have attempted it!

Scoring Key

15	Box of matches has little or no use on moon.
4	Food concentrate can supply daily food required.
6	50 feet of nylon rope is useful to help in climbing.
8	Parachute silk can shelter against sun's rays.
13	Portable heating unit is useful only if party had landed on the moon's dark side.
11	Two .45 calibre pistols: self-propulsion devices could be made from them.
12	One case dehydrated milk provides nutrition if mixed with water for drinking.
1	Two 100-pound tanks of oxygen fill respiration requirement.
3	Stellar map of moon's constellation is a principal means of finding directions.
9	Life raft and CO_2 bottle for self-propulsion across chasms.
14	Magnetic compass: probably no magnetic pole; thus useless.
2	5 gallons of water: replenishes water loss.
10	Signal flares: distress call.
7	First-aid kit containing injection needles: oral pills or injection medicine valuable.
5	Solar-powered FM receiver-transmitter: distress-signal transmitter, possible communication with mother ship.

APPENDIXES

 # Business Terminology

accounts payable A bookkeeping term indicating the money owed by one company to another.

accounts receivable A bookkeeping term indicating the money due from a company's customers.

agent Someone who legally acts on behalf of or represents another person or a company. *Example:* an insurance agent.

amortization The reduction of a debt by regular payments of principal and interest over a period of time. *Example:* Amortization of a mortgage.

arbitration The settlement of a dispute, usually between labor and management, by involving the services of an impartial professional person.

bankruptcy A legal condition in which people unable to pay their debts have most of their assets allocated to their creditors by an administrator. As a result, the debtors are not responsible for additional payments.

beneficiary The person named to receive the benefits of a will or insurance policy.

bequest Gift of property or money in a will.

bill of lading A list of goods for shipment and their destinations; given by the transporter to the shipper.

bond A promissory note issued by a company or government acknowledging money loaned to it and agreeing to repay the money at a designated maturity date and to pay a specified rate of interest a year until that time.

boycott A protest that takes the form of refusing to do business with some company.

capital gain (or loss) Profit (or loss) on any capital asset including stocks and bonds.

carrying charge The charge paid to a store for the privilege of goods or services purchased and possessed but not paid for.

cartel A group of corporations, usually international, who regulate the price, production, and marketing of a product. *Example:* OPEC is often called an oil cartel.

cashier's check Bank-guaranteed check written by a bank on its account, which can be obtained by paying the bank the full amount of the check and a small fee. It is widely used to transfer large sums of money from one place to another, because it is readily accepted.

caveat emptor A Latin phrase meaning "let the buyer beware," implying that people buy at their own risk.

certificate of deposit An interest-bearing note from a commercial or savings and loan bank, usually insured by the U.S. government.

certified check A regular check certified by a bank to show that the amount has been deducted from the bearer's account and to guarantee that the check is good. A small fee is charged.

charge account A credit arrangement that allows a customer to buy goods in return for the promise to pay for them, usually within thirty days of purchase.

closed shop A company closed to everyone except union members. All employees have to join the union.

codicil A legal addition to a will.

collateral Anything of value pledged as security against borrowed money. Failure to repay the loan results in the loss of the item put up as collateral.

commercial paper Short-term promissory notes issued by corporations to raise cash for less than a year.

condemnation Legal action by federal, state, or local government to take land for public use.

condominium Usually an individually owned dwelling in a multi-unit complex with the owner having a proportionate interest in common facilities and areas.

conglomerate A corporation consisting of several unrelated corporations in different industries.

convertible bond A bond that may be converted into common stock according to certain specified terms.

creditor A person or company to whom a debt is owed.

credit union A co-operative association of employees, professionals, union members, and so on, who become shareholders in a group that accepts savings, makes loans, and may provide other services. Most credit unions are insured by the National Credit Union Association (NCUA) in Washington.

current assets Cash and those assets that will be turned into cash usually within a year—for example, marketable securities, accounts receivable, inventories.

debt service Required payments of interest and principal at specified times toward the retirement of a debt.

debtor A person or company who owes a debt to another.

default Failure to pay either principal or interest when due.

delinquent A past-due credit account.

depletion allowance A tax reduction that uses up or exhausts the value of an asset that cannot be renewed, such as an oil well.

depreciation An accounting term to indicate the decline in value of a fixed asset due to wear and tear or the passage of time.

dividend A share of a corporation's profits distributed to stockholders usually four times a year in the form of cash.

earnest money A deposit that a buyer gives to a seller of real estate to indicate serious interest in the property.

equity In real estate, the owner's value of the mortgaged property, which usually amounts to the principal paid but does not include the interest.

escalator clauses A clause in a contract calling for increases or decreases according to sales, profits, the cost of living, or some other index.

escrow A legal agreement involving a third party who maintains custody of a bond, deed, or other item until the two parties to the agreement have fulfilled certain conditions.

estate The total worth of a person including money, property, possessions, insurance, etc. Usually calculated at bankruptcy or death.

executor Person or institution named in a will to administer an estate during its probation and to distribute the property.

fixed assets Assets not intended for sale, usually consisting of property, plant, and equipment.

franchise An authorization usually by a company—McDonald's or Chevrolet, for example—to sell its product in a particular area.

fringe benefit Compensation in addition to wages or salary, such as group insurance, paid vacations and holidays, educational benefits, and health insurance.

garnishment A court order obtained by a creditor instructing an employer to withhold a portion of an employee's pay until the debt is repaid.

gross national product (GNP) The total monetary value of goods and services produced in a country, usually in one year.

inflation A financial condition occurring when prices increase and the purchasing value of money decreases.

intestate A person who dies without a will.

inventory All goods, supplies, or stock on hand; or a detailed list of such items.

invoice A bill itemizing quantities, prices, shipment date, and other pertinent information about goods shipped.

jobber A middleman, who buys from manufacturers and sells to retailers.

letter of credit A letter authorizing credit to the bearer that is guaranteed by the signer. Often issued by banks.

lien A claim against property (house, car, and so on) that usually represents security for a debt.

line position A job in a company that involves work on whatever product or service the company produces. *See* staff position.

liquidation The selling of the assets of a business usually to raise cash for bankruptcy.

macroeconomics Economic study of a large market area, such as a nation's economy.

microeconomics Economic study of a particular people and companies in a small market area.

margin Normally the difference between the cost and the selling price; often called the profit margin.

monopoly Sufficient control of a product by one company or several so as to establish its price.

mortgage A pledge of property to a creditor as security against a loan.

mutual fund A company that invests shareholders' pooled funds in various types of securities.

net sales Total sales less any returns.

option A contract usually giving someone the right to buy property at some future time at a stipulated price.

outstanding Term applied to the unpaid balance of an account or a loan.

per capita A Latin word meaning "by the individual or person." *Example:* The per capita income in California is relatively high.

perquisite Usually referred to as *perk*, a privilege, such as the use of a company car or membership in a country club, given in addition to salary and normal fringe benefits.

petty cash Small amounts of cash kept for minor expenses like postage stamps.

portfolio The securities held by an individual or company.

power of attorney A legal document authorizing one person to act for another in certain business transactions, such as signing checks, and buying stock.

preferred stock Stock that gives its owners preferred claims in case a company is dissolved. Preferred stock usually has a fixed dividend rate that must be paid before common stockholders receive any dividend.

prepayment privilege The privilege written in a loan or mortgage contract that allows the borrower to pay part or all of the loan in advance of the due date, either with or without an interest penalty.

prime rate The preferential interest rate that banks charge their best customers.

pro rata Proportionally. *Example*: If you leave before the end of the month, you will have to pay only the pro rata cost of the utilities.

proxy A person authorized to act for another or a document authorizing this.

rebate A refund of part of an amount paid.

receivership A legal action in which a court-appointed person acts as custodian of the business or property of a party in a lawsuit.

repossession The taking back of the goods purchased on an installment sales contract because payments have not been made as specified.

retainer The fee paid to engage a lawyer, consultant, or some other professional person.

revolving charge account A credit arrangement by which a maximum limit is placed by a store on the amount a customer may owe. The customer agrees to pay a stated sum on the balance every month plus interest on the unpaid balance.

right-to-work laws Laws prohibiting a closed or union shop.

royalties Normally payments to an author, composer, inventor, or owner of oil properties for the proceeds of sales.

secondary boycott A refusal to have dealings with a business that is only indirectly involved in a labor dispute. *Example*: A secondary boycott against a trucking company to stop them from delivering appliances from a company that is the object of the main boycott.

securities Stocks, bonds, and other certificates of value.

seniority A system of establishing preference by the length of service on the job or with the company.

solvent Condition of a company that has sufficient money to pay its debts and liabilities.

staff position A position whose holder works in a support capacity for someone directly in the line positions of management, production, or marketing.

stock A share of ownership in a corporation. A stockholder owns a certain percent of a company according to the number of shares owned in proportion to the total shares authorized.

subcontract A contract between the main contractor and someone else to do a portion of the work.

subsidiary A company that is mainly owned by another company.

subsidy Financial support usually given by the government to an individual or company.

tariff A duty or tax usually paid on imports, sometimes exports.

title A document giving legal ownership, usually of property.

traveler's checks Checks purchased in amounts of $10, $20, $50, $100, and more from banks and travel agencies for the face value of the checks plus a small fee. The purchaser's identity is established by signing the checks when they are bought and again when cashed. Money for lost uncashed checks is refunded if the loss is reported promptly.

vendee The buyer of something.

vendor The seller.

warranty A written statement promising that a product is as it is represented and specifying what the manufacturer will do if it fails to perform properly. A warranty may also be unwritten, being implied in the sale.

wildcat strike A sudden or unofficial strike, usually not called by the union.

B Letter Parts and Layout Style *

Business letters usually consist of six standard parts and sometimes also include up to seven special parts. The placement of these parts on the stationery depends on the layout style or format of the letter.

These standard and special parts of letters and three popular layout styles are discussed and, in most cases, illustrated below.

STANDARD PARTS

The six standard parts of business letters are (1) heading, (2) inside address, (3) salutation, (4) body, (5) complimentary close, and (6) signature section.

Heading

The heading consists of (a) the return address and (b) the date. Most business letters appear on letterhead stationery, as seen in figure B–1, so that you need add only the date.

If you do not have a letterhead, you need to include a return address, using the appropriate state abbreviation (see Appendix C) and ZIP code. Place the date, with the month spelled out, on the line following the city, state abbreviation, and ZIP code.

Inside Address

Typically, the inside address contains (a) a courtesy title (for example, Mr., Mrs., Miss, Ms., Dr.); (b) the name of the person to whom the letter is being sent; (c) the official title of the person (for example, President, Comptroller, Chief Accountant, Executive Secretary); and (d) the complete address with appropriate state abbreviation and ZIP code.

As shown in figures B–1, B–2, B–3, the official title can appear just after the name or on a separate line below the name.

---

* Portions of this appendix were based on the following article: Scot Ober, "The Physical Format of Business Letters," *Business Education World*, 62 (September–October, 1981), 8, 11, 22.

Figure B–1. Full-Block Letter Style.

Nelson Real Estate

207 North Herritage Street
P.O. Box 1095
Columbia, South Carolina 29202

May 6, 19--

Mr. Otto Nischan, Trust Officer
Citizens Union Bank
1898 Southwood Drive
Jacksonville, FL 32211

Dear Mr. Nischan:

SUBJECT: REPAIR OF LEE HARPER PROPERTY, COLUMBIA, SOUTH CAROLINA

The Lee Harper rental house at 323 E. Caswell Street, Columbia, South
Carolina, which I manage for you, now needs a new roof. The shingles
currently on the house have been damaged by strong winds. The damage is
so extensive that during heavy rains, water leaks into the attic and then
seeps into the rooms below. The internal damage at this time is minimal
and requires no repairs.

When I was informed of this problem by the lessee, Mrs. Angelou Rodriguez,
and had personally inspected the premises, I called three local roofing
contractors and obtained bids on replacing the roof with asphalt shingles.
For your records, I am enclosing copies of the job specifications and of
the three bids.

As soon as I receive authorization, I will approve one of the bids and
see to it that the job is completed according to specs and without delay.
To prevent any further water seepage, I urge you to act at once.

Sincerely yours,

John D. Nelson, Sr.

JDN/eb

Enclosures 4

Figure B–2.   Semiblock Letter Style.

Nelson Real Estate

207 North Herritage Street
P.O. Box 1095
Columbia, South Carolina 29202

May 6, 19--

Mr. Otto Nischan
Trust Officer
Citizens Union Bank
1898 Southwood Drive
Jacksonville, FL 32211

Dear Mr. Nischan:

   SUBJECT: REPAIR OF LEE HARPER PROPERTY, COLUMBIA, SOUTH CAROLINA

   The Lee Harper rental house at 323 E. Caswell Street, Columbia,
South Carolina, which I manage for you, now needs a new roof. The
shingles currently on the house have been damaged by strong winds. The
damage is so extensive that during heavy rains, water leaks into the
attic and then seeps into the rooms below. The internal damage at this
time is minimal and requires no repairs.

   When I was informed of this problem by the lessee, Mrs. Angelou
Rodriguez, and had personally inspected the premises, I called three
local roofing contractors and obtained bids on replacing the roof with
asphalt shingles. For your records, I am enclosing copies of the job
specifications and of the three bids.

   As soon as I receive authorization, I will approve one of the bids
and see to it that the job is completed according to specs and without
delay. To prevent any further water seepage, I urge you to act at once.

                         Sincerely yours,

                         John D. Nelson

                         John D. Nelson, Sr.

JDN/eb

Enclosures 4

Figure B–3. Simplified Letter Style.

Nelson Real Estate

207 North Herritage Street
P.O. Box 1095
Columbia, South Carolina 29202

May 6, 19--

Mr. Otto Nischan
Trust Officer
Citizens Union Bank
1898 Southwood Drive
Jacksonville, FL 32211

REPAIR OF LEE HARPER PROPERTY, COLUMBIA, SOUTH CAROLINA

The Lee Harper rental house at 323 E. Caswell Street, Columbia, South
Carolina, which I manage for you, now needs a new roof. The shingles
currently on the house have been damaged by strong winds. The damage is
so extensive that during heavy rains, water leaks into the attic and then
seeps into the rooms below. The internal damage at this time is minimal
and requires no repairs.

When I was informed of this problem by the lessee, Mrs. Angelou Rodriguez,
and had personally inspected the premises, I called three local roofing
contractors and obtained bids on replacing the roof with asphalt shingles.
For your records, I am enclosing copies of the job specifications and of
the three bids.

As soon as I receive authorization, I will approve one of the bids and
see to it that the job is completed according to specs and without delay.
To prevent any further water seepage, I urge you to act at once.

JOHN D. NELSON, SR.

eb

Enclosures 4

Salutation

The salutation or greeting should accord with the first line of the inside address. If that line is addressed to Miss Lottie Lanier, the salutation should be "Dear Miss Lanier"; but if it is addressed to Axelrod Industries, Inc., the salutation should be "Ladies and Gentlemen." The salutation does *not* correspond to the attention line (discussed below under "Special Parts").

The use of *Dear* in the salutation is diminishing. Some writers think it is old-fashioned and insincere; certainly in an unfriendly letter, it is hypocritical. You may avoid its use altogether by using the simplified letter format (discussed below under "Letter Styles"), which includes no salutation.

The formality of the salutation should match that of the complimentary close:

<u>Personal</u>:	Dear Jack	Best wishes
	Jack	Cordially
<u>Informal</u>:	Dear Jack	Cordially yours
	Jack	Sincerely
	Dear Mr. Leggett	
	Mr. Leggett	
<u>Formal</u>:	Dear Mr. Leggett	Sincerely yours
	Mr. Leggett	Yours truly
	My dear Mr. Leggett	Respectfully yours
	Sir (or Madam)	

Commonly used forms of salutation are given in Appendix E.

Body

The body or message of a letter begins one blank line after the salutation. The body is single-spaced with double-spacing between paragraphs, as seen in figures B–1, B–2, and B–3. To enhance readability, avoid paragraphs of excessive length.

Complimentary Close

The complimentary close is typed two blank lines below the last line of the body. We discussed the most common forms previously, under "Salutations"; old-fashioned forms—*I have the honor to remain; I remain; I am, kind Sir* (or *Madam*); and *Your faithful servant*—should be avoided. Note that only the first letter of the first word is capitalized.

Signature Section

If the company name appears in the letterhead or inside address, you need not use it again in the signature section. But if it is necessary to include the company name, type it in all capitals one blank line below the complimentary close, as in the following example:

```
Sincerely yours,

MEGACOUSTICS CORPORATION


(Ms.) Pat Anderson, Director
Customer Relations
```

Your typed name appears three blank lines below the complimentary close, with or without the company name, thus leaving ample room for your signature. Your title may appear on the line with your typed name, separated by a comma; or it may appear on the line below.

```
Cordially yours,



Don D. Kintz
Director of Personnel
```

Women often indicate the appropriate courtesy title before their typed name: *Miss*, *Mrs.*, or *Ms.* If you are unsure about a woman correspondent's preference, use *Ms.*

SPECIAL PARTS

Seven special parts of business letters are (1) attention line, (2) subject line, (3) reference initials, (4) enclosure notation, (5) copy notation, (6) postscript, and (7) second-page caption. Use one or more of these parts only as needed.

Attention Line

In a letter addressed to a company, you can use an attention line to direct the letter to a certain department or person. If you do not know the person's name, you may use an official title—for example, Vice President or Director of Personnel.

The attention line may appear on the second line of the inside address (as seen in the first address example of Appendix B) or between the inside address and salutation:

```
Fordham, Outlaw, and Rouse, Attorneys
12003 Hancock Drive
Jacksonville, FL  32211

Attention Mr. J.E. Rouse, Jr.

Gentlemen:
```

Note that the salutation corresponds with the first line of the inside address, not with the attention line.

Subject Line

Like the subject line in a memo, the subject line in a letter announces your topic and refers your reader to the appropriate records. It usually appears, either on the left margin or centered, two blank lines below the salutation and two above the body (see figures B–1 and B–2).

Typically, the subject line opens with SUBJECT, SUBJ, IN RE (In regard to), or RE (Regarding) and is followed by a colon and short description of the subject. For emphasis, the entire line may be capitalized, underscored, or both.

Reference Initials

The initials of your typist, or those of you and your typist, appear at the left margin two blank lines below the signature section (see figures B–1 and B–2). If your name is typed in the signature section, your initials can be omitted (see figure B–3). If your initials are used, they usually precede those of the typist, as in these examples:

```
JRS/cd

ENS:jad

BEF/PCE
```

Enclosure Notation

If you include one or more enclosures, the words *Enclosure* or *Attachment* or the abbreviation *Enc.* may appear at the left margin one blank line below the reference initials. This notation may be followed by a number indicating the number of items attached (see figure B–1) or by a colon and an itemized list of the attachments:

```
Enclosures 2    Enclosures:  1.  Check No. 1466 ($2,500)
                             2.  Check No. 1467 ($2,750)
```

In the body of the letter, refer your reader to the enclosures.

Copy Notation

This notation tells the person to whom you are addressing the letter that copies are being sent to others. The initials *cc* (carbon copy) appear at the left margin, one blank line below the reference initials or enclosure notation, whichever comes last. The names of the people receiving copies are listed afterwards, either alphabetically or by rank:

```
cc   Mr. Charles Quinn

cc   Dr. Maier, Vice Chancellor
     Mrs. Cain, Assistant Vice Chancellor
```

The initials *pc* are generally used when copies are made by other means (e.g., photocopying).

In some cases, you may not wish the person to whom the letter is addressed to know that copies are being sent to others. If so, use a *bc* (blind copy) notation to inform the typist: *bc Janet Blackstock*. The notation will appear on the blind copies and on your file copy, but not on the original.

Postscript

A brief postscript can lend an air of spontaneity to a business letter, express an afterthought, or emphasize a key point. Begin this special part (always the last item on the page) at the left margin two lines below the preceding notation. The abbreviation *P.S.* is often omitted since the position of the message indicates that it is a postscript.

Second-Page Caption

Instead of letterhead stationery, plain stationery is used for second and subsequent pages of long letters. A caption should appear on these pages six blank lines from the top and should include the name of the person to whom the letter is addressed, the page number, and the date. Either of these styles is acceptable:

```
Dr. Carrie Nunn              2              March 12, 19--

or:

Dr. Carrie Nunn
Page 2
March 12, 19--
```

Resume the body of the letter three blank lines below the heading.

Layout styles

The three layout styles described below—full-block, semiblock, and simplified—are popular and widely accepted. Departures from these formats may be necessary or on occasion even desirable. However, adhering to one of the familiar formats ensures attractive letter placement, creates a favorable impression, minimizes reader distraction, and indicates your familiarity with conventional business practices.

Full-Block

Nearly one-fourth of all business letters appear in full-block style. As shown in figure B–1, this style uses no indentions; each line begins at the left margin. Its advantage is that it is relatively quick and easy to type; its disadvantage, that it seems to lean toward the left.

Semiblock

The semiblock style is the one most often used for business letters, accounting for approximately three-fourths of the total. In this style (figure B–2), the date, complimentary close, and signature section begin at the center, or to the right of center, of the page. Also, the first line of each paragraph may be indented five spaces. Except for the subject line, which is often centered, all other lines begin at the left margin. The advantages of semiblock style include balanced layout and painstakingly careful appearance—an almost personal touch; the disadvantage, time-consuming indenting.

Simplified

Although widely discussed, the simplified style is rarely used; it accounts for fewer than 3 percent of all business letters. As in full-block, in the simplified style (figure B–3) all lines begin at the left margin. Neither a salutation nor a complimentary close is included. An all-cap subject line and all-cap signature section are always used. The advantages of this streamlined format include easy typing and economical layout, as well as the avoidance of unnecessary salutations and complimentary closes; the disadvantages, left-heavy appearance, the absence of a personal touch, and the danger of the unconventional.

Official Two-Letter State, District, and Province Abbreviations*

Alabama	AL	Montana	MT
Alaska	AK	Nebraska	NE
Arizona	AZ	Nevada	NV
Arkansas	AR	New Hampshire	NH
California	CA	New Jersey	NJ
Colorado	CO	New Mexico	NM
Connecticut	CT	New York	NY
Delaware	DE	North Carolina	NC
District of Columbia	DC	North Dakota	ND
Florida	FL	Ohio	OH
Georgia	GA	Oklahoma	OK
Guam	GU	Oregon	OR
Hawaii	HI	Pennsylvania	PA
Idaho	ID	Puerto Rico	PR
Illinois	IL	Rhode Island	RI
Indiana	IN	South Carolina	SC
Iowa	IA	South Dakota	SD
Kansas	KS	Tennessee	TN
Kentucky	KY	Texas	TX
Louisiana	LA	Utah	UT
Maine	ME	Vermont	VT
Maryland	MD	Virginia	VA
Massachusetts	MA	Virgin Islands	VI
Michigan	MI	Washington	WA
Minnesota	MN	West Virginia	WV
Mississippi	MS	Wisconsin	WI
Missouri	MO	Wyoming	WY

* The Caroline, Mariana, Marshall, Samoan, and Wake Islands have no two-letter abbreviations.

D Common Abbreviations Used in Addresses

Association, ASSN
Avenue, AVE
Boulevard, BLVD
Bypass, BYP
Circle, CIR
Company, CO
Corporation, CORP
Drive, DR
East, E
Expressway, EXPY
Freeway, FWY
Heights, HTS
Highway, HWY
Hospital, HOSP
Incorporated, INC
Institute, INST
Lake, LK
Lakes, LKS
Lane, LN
Limited, LTD
Manager, MGR
North, N
Northeast, NE
Northwest, NW
Office, OFC

Palms, PLMS
Park, PK
Parkway, PKY
Place, PL
Plaza, PLZ
President, PRES
River, RIV
Road, RD
Route, RT
Rural, R
Secretary, SECY
Shore, SH
South, S
Southeast, SE
Southwest, SW
Square, SQ
Station, STA
Terrace, TER
Treasurer, TREAS
Turnpike, TPKE
Union, UN
Vice President, VP
View, VW
Village, VLG
West, W

E Addresses, Salutations, and Closings to Public Officials*

The following forms have been established by usage. Accordingly, they are familiar and widely accepted. By no means are they the only correct or acceptable forms. Other forms that are polite and tasteful would serve as well.

Title	Address	Salutation	Closing
The President	The President The White House Washington, DC 20500	Mr. President Dear Mr. President Madam President Dear Madam President	Yours faithfully
The Vice President	The Vice President United States Senate Washington, DC 20510	Dear Mr. Vice President Sir Dear Madam Vice President Madam	Yours faithfully
The Chief Justice	The Chief Justice of the United States Washington, DC 20543	Dear Mr. Chief Justice Sir Dear Madam Chief Justice Madam	Yours respectfully
Cabinet Member	The Honorable (Name) Secretary of (Department) Washington, DC ZIP	Dear Mr. Secretary Sir Dear Madam Secretary Madam	Yours very truly
Ambassador	His (Her) Excellency The American Ambassador Address	Dear Mr. Ambassador Dear Madam Ambassador Your Excellency	Yours very truly Yours faithfully

* Portions of this appendix were based on William A. Sabin, "Forms of Address," *The Gregg Reference Manual*, 5th ed. (New York: McGraw-Hill, 1977), pp. 296–299.

U.S. Senator	The Honorable
	    (Name)
	United States Senate
	Washington, DC
	    20510
		Dear Sir
		Sir
		Dear Madam
		Madam
			Yours very truly
			Yours faithfully

U.S. Representative	The Honorable
	    (Name)
	House of
	    Representatives
	Washington, DC
	    20515
		Dear Sir
		Sir
		Dear Madam
		Madam
			Yours very truly
			Yours faithfully

Governor	His (Her) Excellency the
	    Governor of
	    (State)
	State Capital, State ZIP
	
	or:
	
	The Honorable
	    (Name)
	Governor of (State)
	State Capital, State ZIP
		Dear Governor
		    (Surname)
		Sir
		Madam
			Yours faithfully

State Senator or
Representative
	The Honorable
	    (Name)
	General (or State)
	    Assembly
	State Capital, State ZIP
		Dear Senator
		    (Surname)
		Dear Representative
		    (Surname)
		Sir
		Madam
			Yours very truly
			Yours faithfully

Mayor	The Honorable (Name) Mayor of (City) City, State ZIP	Dear Mayor (Surname)	Very truly yours Yours faithfully

Other High
Officials:
Federal, State,
Local
	The Honorable
	    (Name)
	Office
	Address
		Dear Mr. (Surname)
		Dear Madam
		    (Surname)
		Dear Sir
		Dear Madam
			Yours sincerely
			Yours very truly

College or
University
President
	Dr. (or Mr. or Ms.)
	    (Name) , President
	College or University
	City, State ZIP
		Dear President
		    (Surname)
			Yours sincerely
			Yours very truly

Title	Address	Salutation	Closing
Professor	Professor __(Name)__ Department of _____ College or University City, State ZIP	Dear Professor __(Surname)__	Yours sincerely Yours very truly
School Principal	Mr., Ms., or Dr. __(Name)__ , Principal School Address	Dear Mr., Ms., or Dr. __(Surname)__	Sincerely yours Very truly yours
Teacher	Mr. or Ms. __(Name)__ School Address	Dear Mr. or Ms. __(Surname)__	Sincerely yours Very truly yours
Military Officers	Rank + Name, Branch Initials (Rear Admiral Pat Ray, USN) Address	Dear Rank __(Surname)__ (Dear Admiral Ray) Dear Sir Dear Madam	Very truly yours Yours faithfully

Postal Mailing Information

The U.S. Postal Service has installed automated Optical Character Readers (OCRs) to help process the growing volume of mail. An OCR reads the address and sorts a piece of mail according to its ZIP Code. By reading the various ZIP digits, the OCR routes the piece to one of nine regions of the country, to a regional distribution center, to a specific post office, to a particular block, and even to a certain building.

To ensure that this OCR equipment operates efficiently, the Postal Service has established guidelines and requirements for selecting and addressing envelopes. By following these guidelines and regulations, you can help reduce errors and delays in delivery and postage costs.

SIZE STANDARDS FOR ENVELOPES

Regular business envelopes should be rectangular. To qualify for mailing, they must be at least 3 1/2 inches high and 5 inches long. To avoid a surcharge, they should be no larger than 6 1/8 × 11 1/2 inches. With enclosures they should be between .007 (postal card thickness) and .25 of an inch thick.

The three envelope sizes most often used in business writing easily conform to these regulations: All-Purpose (3 5/8 × 6 1/2 inches), Executive (3 7/8 × 7 1/2 inches), and Standard (4 1/8 × 9 1/2 inches). For larger, thicker documents, standard manila envelopes are generally used: 6 1/2 × 9 1/2 inches, 9 × 12 inches, and 11 1/2 × 14 5/8 inches. Nonstandard envelopes are subject to a surcharge.

ENVELOPE ADDRESSES

As shown in figure F–1, the return address should appear in block format near the upper left-hand corner of the envelope. It should contain complete return information, including the ZIP Code.

The delivery address should appear centered on the front of a standard envelope in an imaginary rectangle.

Dr. Solomon Michelak
Mind and Quill
Department of English
Prentice College
Weston, Vermont 05161

HOLD FOR ARRIVAL

PROFESSOR DIANE D'AMICO
DEPARTMENT OF ENGLISH
HELEN C WHITE HALL
UNIVERSITY OF WISCONSIN
MADISON WI 53706-0127

The address should be in block format and contain complete delivery information:

- Top line—name of recipient
- Next—information/attention line
- Line above last—delivery address (including, if necessary, the P.O. Box, apartment, or suite number)
- Last line—post office (town or city), two-letter state abbreviation (see Appendix C), and ZIP Code

The Postal Service prefers all upper-case letters and standard typefaces (pica or elite), as well as the avoidance of punctuation marks. Addresses should be single-spaced.

EXAMPLES: BETTER EQUIPMENT INC
ATTN MR ROBERT HOSKINS
1225 N MAIN ST
HARRISBURG VA 22801- 0127

APEX CAMERAS LTD
16 N LARK ST
PO BOX 1968   ←—— delivery
CLEVELAND OH 44135-1473   address

APEX CAMERAS LTD
16 N LARK ST
PO BOX 1968   ←—— delivery
CLEVELAND OH 44135-1473   address

```
MISS RENE GISGARD
PUBLICITY DEPT
PANDY CORP SUITE 16
WATERLOO IA 50703-3482


DR W W ORR
2001 42D BLVD APT J7
CHEYENNE WY 82001-1028


MME FRANCOIS BILODEAUX
290 RUE TOULOUSE
OTTAWA ONTARIO K3P0C4


CANADA              ←——— foreign
                         country name,
                         two spaces
                         below the city
                         line
```

SPECIAL NOTATIONS

Special mailing notations such as REGISTERED or SPECIAL DELIVERY should appear capitalized below the postage stamp, as shown in figure F–1. Receipt notations such as PERSONAL, CONFIDENTIAL, HOLD FOR ARRIVAL, and PLEASE FORWARD should appear capitalized below the return address.

CLASSES OF MAIL SERVICE

First class Preferential handling by the Post Office for standard-size envelopes weighing twelve ounces or less.

Priority mail First Class mail weighing over twelve ounces.

Second class Periodical publications of the same size and weight with a minimum of 200 pieces. A special permit and fund account must be established with the Post Office prior to the mailing.

Third class Printed matter or merchandise parcels weighing less than sixteen ounces. There are two types:

single piece: used only for pieces weighing more than four ounces; anything below four ounces is charged the same as first class.

bulk: the most economical of all classes if the pieces number over 200 and are identical in size and weight for each mailing.

Fourth class Bound printed matter, library materials, or books weighing at least one pound but not exceeding ten pounds.

SPECIAL POST OFFICE SERVICES

Special delivery Provides hand delivery to the address on the same day of arrival at the destination post office, but does not necessarily speed delivery to the destination post office. Requires additional charge.

Certified mail Provides a receipt of delivery to be held for two years by the post office where the item was mailed. Requires additional charge. For an additional fee, a return receipt will be mailed to the sender showing the date delivered and the signature of the person who received the item. Sending material by Certified Mail can delay delivery if no one is at the address to sign the receipt.

Registered mail Furnishes receipt, protection, and insurance up to $25,000 for valuable materials sent by mail. Requires additional charge.

Word Processing *

The term *word processing* refers to an office system centered around sophisticated equipment on which written communications can be typed, edited, printed, reproduced, and even distributed. Word processing equipment consists of several components—an electric typewriter with a display screen (also referred to as a Cathode Ray Tube or CRT), a memory, and a printer.

As you type on the keyboard, the letters appear on the screen and are recorded on "floppy disks" (thin plastic storage devices) or magnetic tapes. Since the text is recorded, it is available whenever you need it. By simply touching appropriate keys, you can correct misspellings, add or delete words, or rearrange whole blocks of type both on the screen and in the memory. Once you have made all the corrections and changes needed to perfect the draft, you give another command and the printer automatically types, at speeds up to 600 words per minute, as many copies of the finished document as you want.

Because of its memory, a word processor can store paragraphs, messages, or entire documents. This capability greatly increases office efficiency. For example, you might dictate only a short paragraph for a letter. The word processor might then retrieve the remainder of the message from its memory and add the new paragraph at the appropriate place, thus reducing dictating and transcribing time and costs.

The versatility of word processors seems unlimited. Some machines can identify misspelled words, and at least one can identify misspellings in six languages. Some are even capable of checking grammar (e.g., subject and verb agreement). Many are linked to data processors, creating national or international communications networks. A communications network enables you to send messages instantly to a mainframe computer, another terminal, a phototypesetter, or a copying machine. You can also provide instant electronic mail to distant locations by telephone wire or satellite.

Other versatile features often found in word processors include:

---

* Portions of this appendix were based on the following articles: John W. Meroney, "Word Processing—What Skills Should an Entry-Level Applicant Have?" *Century 21 Reporter* (Fall 1979), pp. 5–6; George Kontos, "Merging Word Processing and Data Processing Will Lead to Better Information Management," *The Balance Sheet* (February 1981), pp. 207–209; and "The Word Processing Boom," *Newsweek* (April 6, 1981), p. 75; and "Word Processors on a Budget," *What to Buy for Business* (June 1981), pp. 3–9.

Search and replacement The ability to find and replace any word or phrase with another anywhere in a document.

Automatic pagination The capability of dividing a long document into pages and assigning the appropriate page number to each page.

Document creation The ability to create complete documents from memory by selecting and merging stored blocks of text, paragraphs, phrases, and the like.

Presentation The capability of inserting captions, justifying margins, printing boldface, or laying out in standard formats.

Records processing The ability to follow criteria and select certain entries from lists or retrieve special information from records.

Calculation The power to add, subtract, multiply, and divide figures.

Even though the initial cost of automated equipment is high, word processing offers many advantages to the modern office:

- It permits the specialization and improved supervision of office personnel, with: (a) administrative secretaries answering calls, routing traffic, making travel arrangements, and attending to other nontyping duties; and (b) word processing operators typing and editing documents and overseeing their reproduction and distribution.
- It reduces paperwork and filing space.
- It shortens the time spent on typing and editing.
- It eliminates traces of corrections on the final document.
- It expedites the retrieval and use of stock passages.
- It simplifies the revision of documents.
- It expedites the production of multiple copies.
- It can distribute messages efficiently and quickly, often eliminating the need for postal services and telephone calls.

Since these automated office systems are rapidly becoming commonplace in business, industry, government, the professions, and even modern homes, you would be wise to read articles and books on the subject and enroll in seminars on the uses of word processing equipment.

H Dictation*

To save time and paperwork, executives often dictate the letters, memos, and reports they want to have typed. Sometimes they dictate directly to a stenographer who takes down the message in shorthand. In other cases, they dictate to a tape recorder and then give the recording to a stenographer for transcribing. Recordings are especially useful for traveling executives who send cassettes to their secretaries and have their dictation transcribed while they are still away. They are also useful for those who wish to dictate messages by telephone to the automated switchboards of a word processing center at any time of day.

Dictation involves three steps: (1) preparing for dictation, (2) dictating the correspondence, and (3) checking and signing the completed work. These steps represent important management skills that you can master by careful practice.

PREPARING FOR DICTATION

Many executives schedule regular dictation sessions. They choose times when their concentration abilities are keenest—often in early or mid-morning. These regular sessions help stenographers prepare for taking the dictation and planning the rest of their workday. Also, receptionists will know to prevent interruptions from callers or visitors during dictation scheduled sessions.

Before the session begins, you would be wise to gather and review the material related to the dictation—letters, memos, reports, and the like. Also, you can save time by checking to see that the recorder functions properly and that you have the correct names and addresses of the persons to whom you are writing.

The most important preparation is organizing your thoughts. Of course, you should not compose the entire communication; instead, you should identify its purpose, list the main points by paragraph, choose key words and phrases, and develop a tone that will win the goodwill of your readers. As in all business communication, keeping your readers in mind at all times and aiming for a clear and courteous message will help you write effectively.

* Portions of this appendix were based on Jo Ann Hennington, "Teaching the Dictator to Dictate," *Business Education World*, 61 (November-December, 1980), pp. 21–22; and on Edith E. Ennis, Marilyn E. Price, and Sheila K. Vedder, *The Transcription Specialist: A Text-Workbook* (New York: Harcourt Brace Jovanovich, 1981), p. 32.

Dictating

Adopt a conversational tone and a regular pace. Speak as clearly as you can, distinctly enunciating each word and number, and spelling unfamiliar words or names. Avoid mumbling, smoking, and chewing. Do not rattle papers. If dictating through a recorder or phone, speak directly into the mouthpiece or microphone.

If necessary, begin by giving any special information and instructions. For example, if calling a word processing center, you may need to identify yourself by giving your name, title, department, and phone number. Give the date and identify the type of document you are going to dictate (letter, memo, short report). Mention any special letter style or report format. Help the stenographer prepare the document by specifying the number of copies required and any special mailing instructions.

As you begin dictating, provide all necessary information—the inside address and salutation for a letter, or the *TO, FROM,* and *SUBJECT* lines for a memo. Indicate when you have completed a paragraph and call attention to any unusual punctuation, underscoring, quotation marks, captions, and itemizations. Provide a complimentary close suited to the salutation. Dictate the enclosures, the complete copy distribution instructions (including names and addresses), and any other special notations.

Close by indicating that the dictation is complete, specifying any rush items, and thanking the stenographer or keyboard operator.

Checking and Signing the Completed Work

When you have received the transcribed document for signing, you should examine it carefully for accuracy and appearance. Remember that your signature on a letter or initials on a memo indicate that you have accepted final responsibility for the document. Be sure it is completely error-free and presentable before endorsing it, even if a second typing is required. A compliment to the person who transcribed the document is always appreciated and can pave the way for the satisfactory completion of future work you dictate.

For many, dictating will at first be terrifying, seeming to be as impossible as learning to ride a two-wheeler when your father or mother first held you on. Dictating will become easier as you become accustomed to the process. Finally, you may even enjoy it, finding that it's as natural as talking to another person in the room. As well as saving time, dictating may give a light, natural swing to your writing.

# Consumer Protection Agencies

ALABAMA
Attorney General
State Administration Building
Montgomery, AL 36104

President
Alabama Consumer Association
Department of Economics
Birmingham Southern College
Birmingham, AL 35204

ALASKA
Attorney General
Pouch "K", State Capitol
Juneau, AK 99801

Alaska Consumer Council
833 Thirteenth Ave., W.
Anchorage, AK 99501

ARIZONA
Attorney General
159 State Capitol Bldg.
Phoenix, AZ 85007

President
Arizona Consumers Council
6840 Camino DeMichael Street
Tucson, AZ 85718

ARKANSAS
Attorney General
Justice Building
Little Rock, AR 72201

CALIFORNIA
Attorney General
Room 500, Wells Fargo Bank
    Building
Fifth Street and Capitol Mall
Sacramento, CA 95814

President
Association of California Consumers
% University of California
Institute of Industrial Relations
2521 Channing Way
Berkeley, CA 94704

Director
Consumer Affairs Agency
The Capitol
Sacramento, CA 94814

COLORADO
Attorney General
104 State Capitol
Denver, CO 80203

President
Colorado Consumers Association, Inc.
PO Box 989
Boulder, CO 80203

CONNECTICUT
Attorney General
Capitol Annex
30 Trinity Place
Hartford, CT 06115

Commissioner
Department of Consumer Protection
State Office Building
Hartford, CT 06115

President
Connecticut Consumers Association, Inc.
250 West Rock Avenue
New Haven, CT 06515

DELAWARE
Attorney General
The Court House
Wilmington, DE 19801

DISTRICT OF COLUMBIA
Chairperson
Consumer Association of DC
912 Massachusetts Avenue, NE
Washington, DC 20002

President
DC Citywide Consumer Council
4547 Lee Street, NE
Washington, DC 20019

FLORIDA
Commissioner of Agriculture
State Capitol
Tallahassee, FL 32304

President
Florida Consumers Association, Inc.
PO Box 3552
Tallahassee, FL 32303

for Dade County:

Director
Trade Standards Office
1114 Courthouse
Miami, FL 33130

GEORGIA
Attorney General
132 State Judicial Building
Atlanta, GA 30334

President
Georgia Consumer Council
PO Box 311
Morris Brown College
Atlanta, GA 30314

HAWAII
Attorney General
Honolulu, HI 96813

IDAHO
Attorney General
The Capitol
Boise, ID 83702

ILLINOIS
Attorney General
Supreme Court Building
Springfield, IL 62706

President
Illinois Federation of Consumers
% Illinois Rural Electric Assoc.
PO Box 1180
Springfield, IL 62705

for Chicago:

Commissioner
Department of Consumer Sales and
    Weights and Measures
320 N. Clark St., Room 302
Chicago, IL 60610

President
Consumer Association of Indiana, Inc.
910 N. Delaware Street
Indianapolis, IN 46202

IOWA
Attorney General
State House
Des Moines, IA 50319

President
Iowa Consumers League
PO Box 1076
Des Moines, IA 50311

KANSAS
Attorney General
State House
Topeka, KS 66612

KENTUCKY
Attorney General
State Capitol
Frankfort, KY 40601

President
Consumer Association of Kentucky, Inc.
706 E. Broadway
Louisville, KY 40202

Chairperson
Kentucky Consumer Affairs
  Commission
Office of the Governor
State Capitol
Frankfort, KY 40601

LOUISIANA
Attorney General
The Capitol
Baton Rouge, LA 80804

President
Louisiana Consumer League
PO Box 1332
Baton Rouge, LA 70821

MAINE
Attorney General
State House
Augusta, ME 04330

MARYLAND
Attorney General
1200 One Charles Center
Baltimore, MD 21201

President
Maryland Consumers Assn., Inc.
PO Box 143
Annapolis, MD 21404

MASSACHUSETTS
Attorney General
State House
Boston, MA 02133

President
Massachusetts Consumer Assn.
69 Readville Street
Hyde Park, MA 02136

Executive Secretary
Massachusetts Consumers' Council
State Office Building, Government
  Center
100 Cambridge Street
Boston, MA 02202

MICHIGAN
Attorney General
The Capitol
Lansing, MI 48933

Executive Director
Michigan Consumer Council
525 Hollister Building
Lansing, MI 48933

for Detroit:

Chairperson
Consumer Research Advisory Council
16596 Normandy
Detroit, MI 48221

MINNESOTA
Attorney General
102 State Capitol
St. Paul, MN 55101

President
Minnesota Consumers League
1671 S. Victoria Road
St. Paul, MN 55118

MISSISSIPPI
Attorney General
The Capitol
Jackson, MS 39201

MISSOURI
Attorney General
Supreme Court Building
Jefferson City, MO 65101

President
Missouri Association of Consumers
   % Teachers' Credit Union
1221 Oak Street
Kansas City, MO 64106

for St. Louis:

President
St. Louis Consumer Federation
6321 Darlow Drive
St. Louis, MO 63123

MONTANA
Attorney General
The Capitol
Helena, MT 59601

NEBRASKA
Attorney General
The Capitol
Lincoln, NB 68509

NEW HAMPSHIRE
Attorney General
State House Annex
Concord, NH 03301

NEW JERSEY
Attorney General
State House Annex
Trenton, NJ 08625

Executive Director
Office of Consumer Protection
1100 Raymond Blvd.
Newark, NJ 07102

President
Consumers League of New Jersey
20 Church Street
Montclair, NJ 07042

NEW MEXICO
Attorney General
Box 2246, Supreme Court Building
Santa Fe, NM 87501

NEW YORK
Attorney General
State Capitol
Albany, NY 12225

for New York City:

Commissioner
Metropolitan New York Consumer
   Council
1710 Broadway
New York, NY 10019

Executive Secretary
Consumer Assembly of Greater NY
% United Housing Foundation
465 Grand Street
New York, NY 10002

for Nassau County:

Commissioner
Office of Consumer Affairs
160 Old Country Road
Mineola, NY 11501

Director—Consumer Affairs
City Hall
Long Beach, NY 11561

NORTH CAROLINA
Attorney General
Department of Justice Building
PO Box 629
Raleigh, NC 27602

President
North Carolina Consumers Council
108 E. Jefferson Street
Monroe, NC 28110

NORTH DAKOTA
Attorney General
State Capitol
Bismarck, ND 58501

President
Bismarck-Mandan Consumers League
1105 Sunset Drive
Mandan, ND 58554

OHIO
Attorney General
State House
Columbus, OH 43215

Executive Secretary
Consumers League of Ohio
940 Engineers Building
Cleveland, OH 44114

Secretary
Ohio Consumers Assn.
PO Box 1559
Columbus, OH 43216

City Sealer of Weights and Measures
City Hall
Columbus, OH 43215

for Cincinnati:
President
Consumer Conference of Greater
  Cincinnati
318 Terrace Avenue
Cincinnati, OH 45220

OKLAHOMA
Attorney General
112 State Capitol
Oklahoma City, OK 73105

OREGON
Oregon Consumers League
1837 NE Thirteenth Avenue
Portland, OR 97212

PENNSYLVANIA
Attorney General
238 Capitol Building
Harrisburg, PA 17120

Director
Bureau of Consumer Protection
Pennsylvania Department of Justice
2–4 N. Market Square
Harrisburg, PA 17101

Executive Chairman
Pennsylvania League for Consumer
  Protection
PO Box 948
Harrisburg, PA 17108

RHODE ISLAND
Attorney General
Providence County Court House
Providence, RI 02902

President
Rhode Island Consumers' League
Two Progress Avenue
East Providence, RI 09214

Executive Director
Rhode Island Consumers' Council
365 Broadway
Providence, RI 02909

SOUTH CAROLINA
Attorney General
Hampton Office Building
Columbia, SC 29201

SOUTH DAKOTA
Attorney General
State Capitol
Pierre, SD 57501

Executive Director
South Dakota Consumers League
PO Box 106
Madison, SD 57042

TENNESSEE
Attorney General
Supreme Court Building
Nashville, TN 37219

Executive Director
Tennessee Advisory Commission on
    Consumer Protection
State of Tennessee
Nashville, TN 37219

TEXAS
Attorney General
Supreme Court Building
Austin, TX 78711

Commissioner of Consumer Credit
10111 San Jacinto
PO Drawer WW, Capitol Station
Austin, TX 78711

President
Texas Consumer Assn.
2633 Greenland
Mesquite, TX 75149

UTAH
Attorney General
The Capitol
Salt Lake City, UT 84114

President of Utah Consumer
180 E. First South
Salt Lake City, UT 84111

VERMONT
Attorney General
State Library Building
Montpelier, VT 05602

Assistant Attorney in Charge
Consumer Protection Bureau
PO Box 981
Burlington, VT 05401

President
Vermont Consumers' Assn.
72 Lakewood Parkway
Burlington, VT 05401

VIRGINIA
Attorney General
Supreme Court-Library Building
Richmond, VA 23219

President
Virginia Citizens Consumer Council
3408 Cameron Mills Road
Alexandria, VA 22305

President
Peninsula Consumer League, Inc.
648 Bellwood Road
Newport News, VA 23605

WASHINGTON
Attorney General
Temple of Justice
Olympia, WA 98501

Deputy Attorney General and Chief
Consumer Protection and Antitrust Div.
Seattle, WA 98104

President
Washington Committee on Consumer
    Interests
815 36th Ave., E.
Seattle, WA 98102

WEST VIRGINIA
Attorney General
State Capitol
Charleston, WV 25305

President
West Virginia Consumer Assn.
410 Twelfth Ave.
Huntington, WV 25701

WISCONSIN
Attorney General
State Capitol
Madison, WI 53702

President
Wisconsin Consumer League
PO Box 1531
Madison, WI 53702

NATIONAL ORGANIZATIONS
Executive Director
Consumer Federation of America
1012 Fourteenth St., NW
Washington, DC 20005

General Secretary
National Consumers League
1029 Vermont Ave., NW
Room 203
Washington, DC 20005

President
American Council on Consumer Interests
141 Home Economics Building
University of Wisconsin
Madison, WI 53706

Grammar

In this section, you will find a brief review of grammatical terms, the parts of speech, the types of sentences, and sentence elements.

Parts of speech

Adjectives

An adjective is a word that modifies a noun or pronoun by describing or qualifying it. Adjectives can usually be recognized as words that appear before nouns and that can be inflected by the addition of *-er* or *-est*:

> *Bright young* executives demand *fast* rewards.
> adj.   adj.   adj.

In addition, adjectives may occur after nouns and after linking verbs, such as *be, feel, look, appear,* and *become*:

> In the northeast, many employees, particularly *unskilled* and *semi-skilled*, seem *worried*
>   adj.   adj.   adj.
> about layoffs.

Generally, short adjectives of one and two syllables form the comparative and superlative by adding *-er* and *-est*. Longer adjectives use *more* or *most*:

> A *more exhaustive* check of job references should result in a *lower* rate of turnover.

A few adjectives have irregular forms of comparison:

good	better	best
bad	worse	worst

The comparative form is used to compare two people or things; the superlative, three. However, when special emphasis is desired or when the number being compared is unknown, the superlative may be used except in formal writing:

Of the two products, ours is the *stronger.* It is the *best* in Peoria.

Some words function sometimes as adjectives, sometimes as pronouns:

Both interviews by *both* of them were highly favorable.
adj.   *pronoun*

Among other common words appearing both as adjectives and pronouns are the following: *all, any, each, either, some, this, what,* and *which.*

Adverbs

Adverbs commonly modify, qualify, or describe verbs, adjectives, other adverbs, or whole sentences. Usually, adverbs can be recognized by their *-ly* endings. They generally indicate time, manner, or place by answering such questions as: when? how? where?

She interviewed the applicant *briefly* but *thoroughly.*
(Modifies the verb *interviewed,* tells manner.)

He wrote an *exceptionally* fine letter *shortly* after the interview. (*Exceptionally* is an adverb of manner modifying the adjective *fine; shortly* is an adverb of time, modifying the verb *wrote.*)

Fortunately, he felt *amazingly* well *yesterday.* (*Fortunately* is an adverb of manner modifying the sentence; *amazingly* is an adverb of manner modifying the adverb *well;* and *yesterday,* generally a noun, is an adverb of time.)

Adverbs can be confusing because (1) not all words ending in *-ly* are adverbs, (2) some not ending in *-ly* are adverbs, and (3) some have two forms. Pay attention to how the word functions in the sentence:

She is a *lovely* person but *little* experienced in marketing.
      adj.   *adverb*
When you turn into the company road, drive *slowly* (or *slow*).

In the latter sentence you are safer using *slowly;* in other adverbial situations rely on *surely* for *sure, really* for *real, badly* for *bad,* and *well* for *good.* But for a causal or conversational effect, you might choose the adjective form:

Accepted: He surely talked well in the meeting.
Informal: He sure talked good in the meeting.

Conjunctions

Conjunctions link sentence elements or sentences together. They come in two forms: coordinate (*and, but, or, nor, yet*), which join equal elements; and subordinate (*because, while, when, after, if, where,* and so on), which join subordinate clauses to main clauses:

> Most large *and* small companies would benefit by reducing turnover
>   *coordinate*
> *because* high turnover raises hiring and training costs and unemployment tax expenses.
> *subordinate*

Nouns

A noun names. *Proper nouns* name particular persons, places, or things, such as *Bill, San Francisco, Coke. Common nouns* name general persons, places, or things, such as *student, team,* or *stock.* Nouns can also be classified as *concrete,* those that can be perceived by the senses (*cash register, shipping ticket, buzz*); or *abstract,* those that cannot (*arbitration, experience, motivation*).

Most nouns have singular and plural forms (*invoice, invoices; memorandum, memorandums, memoranda; memo, memos; criterion, criteria*). These nouns are called *count nouns;* nouns that do not have separate forms are called *mass nouns* (*scissors, bread, furniture*). *Collective nouns* refer to a group (*company, committee, team*). And *compound nouns* are nouns composed of two or more words: *credit card, income tax, savings and loan bank.*

Prepositions

Prepositions link nouns and pronouns (their objects) to other sentence elements. The *preposition* and its *object* is called a prepositional phrase:

> The secretary drove the van *into the warehouse.*
>   *preposition   object*
>   └─────────────┘
>   *prepositional phrase*

One way to identify prepositions is to determine whether they can fill prepositional slots:

> The driver steered the van _____ the warehouse.

Such common prepositions as *across, at, by, in, near, on, over, through,* and *under* would pass this particular test. Other common ones like *for, between, like, of, until,* and *with* would fit in different sentences.

Sometimes you may have trouble knowing what preposition to use with a particular verb. For example, do you compare something *with* or *to* something else? When in doubt, check your dictionary.

Pronouns

Pronouns substitute for nouns; indeed *they* do. But unlike nouns, they change form according to their use in the sentence, as we illustrated on pages 328 and 425.

Pronouns are classified according to form, meaning, or use. As a result, the same pronoun may be found in different groups. The *personal pronouns* consist of *I, you, he, she, we, they,* and their various other forms. The *reflexive pronouns* are formed by combining certain personal pronouns with *-self* and *-selves.* They are used as an object after a verb or preposition to refer to the subject, or after a noun or pronoun to emphasize it:

> *Object:*   He wrote *himself* a note.
> *Emphatic:* She *herself* set the high sales goals.

Relative pronouns (*who, whose, whom, which,* and *that*) introduce subordinate clauses by referring to a noun or pronoun in the main clause:

> Successful sales managers are individuals *who* realize the importance of informing and inspiring their sales force.

Some of the same words (*who, whose, whom, which,* and *what*) are *interrogative pronouns. What* do they do? As just indicated, they precede verbs in direct questions. They also introduce indirect questions in subordinate clauses:

> I did not know *what* managerial abilities he had.

Demonstrative pronouns (*this, that, these, those*) point out some person, thing, place, or idea. *That* should be easy to understand. When they modify nouns, they are called *demonstrative adjectives:*

> *This* sentence illustrates *that* point.

Indefinite pronouns usually refer to people but do not designate specific ones. Here is a list of some common ones:

all	each	many	one
any	either	most	several
anyone	everyone	nobody	some
both	few	none	such

Verbs

Verbs are usually defined as words that express action or state of being, but this definition can be confusing. It may be easier to understand verbs by thinking of them as words that say something about the subject and have *tenses*—that is, they indicate time by changes in their form. Verbs that form the past tense by adding *-d* or *-ed* are called *regular verbs;* those that form it in other ways are called *irregular verbs.*

Transitive verbs are those that transfer the action from a subject to an object; *intransitive verbs* do not. *Linking verbs* mainly join the subject to a noun, pronoun, or adjective that says something about it:

Transitive verb: He *mailed* the order. (transfers action)
Intransitive verb: She *smiled* at the request. (no transfer)
Linking verb: He *was* the plant manager. (verb merely shows time, joins *he* and *plant manager*)

Among the more common linking verbs besides the various forms of *be* (*am, is, are, was, were, be, being, been*) and verbs referring to some particular sense (*smell, taste, feel*) are the following:

appear	grow	remain
become	look	seem

Sometimes words that function ordinarily as linking verbs are used to convey action. When this occurs, they require an adverb:

He felt strong after the operation. (*felt = was =* linking)
He felt strongly about it. (*felt = reacted =* not linking)

Although the expression "I feel badly" is now generally accepted, the use of adverbs in similar constructions ("I feel angrily," "it looks badly") should be avoided.

Verbs can create problems when they are used to express time other than simple past, present, and future. Note the six tense forms:

Present tense: The committee decides.
Past: The committee decided.
Future: The committee will decide.
Present perfect: The committee has decided.
Past perfect: The committee had decided.
Future perfect: The committee will have decided.

The present tense is used to express not only present action but also habitual and future action, timeless truths, and action in literature:

Today Bill drives. He is late. (present action, present tense)
Employees receive ten paid holidays. (habitual action, present tense)
The new contract starts tomorrow. (future action, present tense)
They realized hard work pays. (timeless "truth," present tense)
Huck respects Jim. (Past action in literature, present tense)

The past and future tenses are used to express action before and after the present:

He received vacation pay for two weeks. (past action, past tense)
He will receive overtime pay for Saturday. (future action, future tense)

The present perfect is used mainly to express action occurring in the past and continuing in the present. It is formed by using *has* or *have* (present tense of *have*) with the past participle:

> He has worked here six years. (He *still works* here. Past action continuing in the present = present perfect tense)

The past perfect tense is used to express an action that occurred in the past before some other past action. It is formed by using *had* (past form of *have*) with the past participle:

> He had worked here for six years before he left. (*He had worked* = past perfect tense to indicate action before *he left*)

The future perfect tense is somewhat similar, being used to express action that will occur in the future before some other future action. It is formed by using *will* or *shall* with *have*:

> When he returns from that job, he will have accumulated three weeks' pay. (*will have accumulated* = future perfect tense to express action before *he returns*)

Further complicating the tense problem is the fact that many verbs are irregular, not forming the past tense or past participle with *-d* or *-ed*. So not only do you have to know the tense to use but also, in many instances, the proper verb form. The following list contains many common irregular verbs. For the forms of others, consult your dictionary.

Present	*Past*	*Past Participle* (have)
beat	beat	beaten or beat
begin	began	begun
bit	bit	bitten
break	broke	broken
bring	brought	brought
broadcast	broadcasted, or broadcast	broadcasted, broadcast
burst	burst	burst
catch	caught	caught
creep	crept	crept
choose	chose	chosen
dive	dived, dove	dived
drink	drank	drunk
drive	drove	driven
feel	felt	felt
fly	flew	flown
freeze	froze	frozen
get	got	got or gotten

Present	Past	Past Participle (have)
go	went	gone
hide	hid	hidden, hid
know	knew	known
lead	led	led
lose	lost	lost
mean	meant	meant
ring	rang	rung
prove	proved	proven, proved
see	saw	seen
shine	shone, shined	shone, shined
sing	sang, sung	sung
show	showed	shown, showed
swing	swung	swung
take	took	taken
tear	tore	torn
think	thought	thought
wear	wore	worn
write	wrote	written

Sentences and Sentence Elements

The following section deals with sentences and their parts. It defines and illustrates phrases; clauses (dependent and independent); simple, compound, complex, and compound-complex sentences; sentence fragments; and run-on sentences.

Phrases

A phrase, a group of related words without a subject and verb, is classified according to the beginning word, the use of the phrase, or the key word in it. We will be concerned with the following: noun phrase, prepositional phrase, participial phrase, gerund phrase, and infinitive phrase:

Noun phrase: A *number of American and foreign automobile companies* are experimenting with electric cars.

Prepositional phrase: The production *of electric cars* will begin soon.

Participial phrase: *Using batteries with polyacetylene*, these cars will have a range of about 400 miles.

Gerund phrase: They may be better at *accelerating and climbing* due to the high rate of electrical discharge.

Infinitive phrase: Mass production will enable companies *to decrease costs*.

If you have had any previous experience with grammar in high school or college, you should not have trouble with phrases except for perhaps confusing the participial and the gerund phrases. In the previous examples, both *using* (the participle) and *accelerating* and *climbing* (the gerunds) have similar *-ing* forms. What is distinctive about them is their function: a participle is used as an adjective, a gerund as a noun.

Dependent (or Subordinate) Clause

A dependent clause is a group of related words that has both a subject and verb, but does not express a complete thought. That is why it is called dependent: it depends for its complete meaning on a main or independent clause. For example, *when you write* contains a subject and verb but leaves you hanging in midair as far as its meaning is concerned.

When you write a dependent clause, you begin with a relative pronoun (*that, which, who, whoever,* etc.) or a subordinate conjunction (*after, although, as, because, if, since, unless, when, while,* etc.). If you doubt that statement, just look at the last sentence or this one. Then you will observe that dependent clauses are often introduced by these subordinators.

Independent (or Main) Clause

An independent clause is a related group of words with a subject and verb. In addition, unlike a subordinate clause, it expresses a thought that is sufficiently complete to make sense independent of anything else. It is referred to as a main or independent clause only when it appears in a sentence with another clause. When it stands alone, it is called a simple sentence:

Your casualty loss deduction must be reduced by any insurance reimbursements. (simple sentence)

Unless you use the damaged property for business, you cannot deduct the first $100 of each loss. (dependent clause + independent clause)

Simple Sentence

A simple sentence contains one clause, which has a subject (S) and a verb (V) and usually a complement (C) such as an object, adjective, or adverb. Sometimes the subject or verb or both may be compound. Here are some examples of simple sentences:

Corporations are reacting. (S + V)

Corporate taxes and depreciation methods are changing. (S + S + V)

In view of the inability to recoup long-term investments quickly, corporate managers are concentrating on short-term projects. (Phrase + S + V + C)

Compound Sentence

A compound sentence is formed by joining two simple sentences with a semicolon or a coordinating conjunction (*and, but, or, nor, yet*) as shown on the next page.

Secretaries are trained to take dictation, but few managers are taught how to dictate. (SVC + SVC)

Many managers dictate letters and memos; some dictate reports. (SVC + SVC)

Our students learn to dictate over the phone, and they also practice dictating to machines. (SVC + SVC; note that *students* and *they* are considered different subjects)

Observe that a comma is used between the independent clauses.

Complex Sentence

A complex sentence is a combination of one main clause and at least one subordinate clause:

When you interview applicants, your first objective is to make them relax. (dependent + independent clause)

Rapport should be established immediately if it is to be achieved at all. (independent + dependent clause)

You should try to make applicants believe that they are acceptable to you. (independent + dependent clause serving as the complement of *believe*)

Applicants who are tense might be put at ease with a cup of coffee, a cigarette, or a joke. (dependent clause, *who are tense,* appears between the subject and verb of the independent clause)

Compound-Complex Sentence

A compound-complex sentence is just what it sounds like, a compound sentence (at least two independent clauses) and a dependent clause:

You should not talk much during the first part of the interview unless the applicant is quiet, but you should evaluate the person's skills and abilities against your job requirements. (independent + dependent + independent)

Sentence Fragments

Sentence fragments are incomplete sentences, usually omitting a subject or verb, or consisting of just a dependent clause:

Fragment: Being the dollar value of what stockholders own. (lacks subject and main verb)
Fragment: Because it shows how much money the company made last year. (dependent clause)

While fragments appear quite frequently in advertisements and in sales letters in order to convey an informal, conversational tone, they should normally be avoided in more formal writing. But they may be used after questions. Why? To avoid unnecessary words.

Run-on Sentences

Run-on sentences are just the opposite of sentence fragments, being more than a sentence instead of less. Run-ons occur when two sentences are joined without a conjunction or appropriate punctuation. If the punctuation mark is a comma instead of a period or semicolon, the resulting error is called a *comma splice*:

> You should restrict your conversations, reading, and coffee breaks they can deprive you of what little time you have for thinking and planning. (run-on, no conjunction or punctuation after *breaks*)

> A reminder file or pocket calendar can help you, enter the deadline and a warning date to alert you when to start on the assignment. (run-on or comma splice because a comma is inadequate, either a period or semicolon being needed after the first *you*)

USAGE

As we have discussed previously, language is a social convention just like those involving dress and manners. What to wear is determined by the occasion (a wedding), your purpose (the impression you wish to create), and the audience (the others attending). Whether to eat chicken with your fingers or with a knife and fork also depends upon the occasion, your purpose, and the people you are with. The same is true in writing. For example, it wouldn't be advisable to write *ain't* in most business letters, but you certainly might use this word in a humorous or clever way in some situations, particularly with people you know.

How then should we treat words in a glossary when these three variables—occasion, purpose, audience—should be considered? We can either throw up our hands in helplessness or establish some general guidelines to be helpful. We have chosen the latter course. In doing so, we've decided to set up three categories: *formal* and *general* to suggest classifications of appropriate usage, and *casual* to designate a usage that may be acceptable in conversation but may be embarrassing to you in writing. Here's a more detailed idea of these terms:

Formal

Audience: Highly specialized, consisting mainly of professionals.
Occasion: Formal public addresses and lectures; scholarly, scientific, and legal articles, and others appearing in professional journals; formal social notes; reference books, dissertations, most textbooks and business reports, legal notices.
Purpose: Usually to inform in a serious, dignified, reserved manner.

General

Audience: People not personally known to the writer.
Occasion: Public speaking on radio and television; talks to a general audience; business conferences and interviews; classroom lectures. All writing in print excluding dialogue and formal English. Usually the language of business letters,

memos, newspaper articles and editorials, magazine articles, book reviews, advertisements, brochures, catalogs, and newsletters.

Purpose: To inform or persuade, usually in a friendly, natural manner.

Casual for Business

Audience: People familiar to the writer: family, friends, close acquaintances.

Occasion: Mainly spoken, usually in conversations among peers. Except in written dialogue imitating speech, these usages are seldom found in print but some may appear in personal letters and diaries.

Purpose: Varied.

Obviously, these generalities are sometimes vague, inexact, and inaccurate because social approval or disapproval changes quickly. Read and consult them but check with your Instructor or the latest edition of a reputable dictionary whenever possible.

GLOSSARY

all right, alright If you want to be right *all* of the time, use *all right.*

all together, altogether When you refer to *all* members of a group, use *all together.* When you use an adverb meaning *entirely*, select *altogether.*

> It was *altogether* unfortunate that the managers decided to sit *all together* at the meeting.

almost, most Only in casual writing may *most* substitute for almost.

> *Casual:* He *most* always gave a bonus to *most* all of the agents.
> *General, formal:* He *almost* always gave a bonus to *almost* all the agents.

among, between *Among* is always used with more than two, *between* is usually used with two. But *between* may be used for more than two when each is to be considered individually rather than collectively.

> He divided the commission *among* the *three* agents.
> He divided the commission *between* the *two* agents.
> He divided the commission *between* the *three* agents. (emphasis on each one)

amount, number *Amount* is used with things that can be measured in pounds, gallons, tons, etc. *Number* is used with things that can be counted.

> On the desk were a large *number* of empty glasses and a small *amount* of wine in a bottle.

bank on use *depend on*, in formal usage.

> *Formal:* We can *depend on* his doing the work.
> *General:* You can *bank on* his doing the job.

contact You should know that some people object to the use of *contact*, meaning *to get in touch with*. Although it would be more precise to use *visit, write*, or *telephone, contact* is accepted nearly everywhere in business today.

deal This word is used generally as a synonym for *business transaction*. In formal writing, use *agreement, arrangement, sale, plan*, or *transaction*.

bust Except for the phrases *boom or bust*, or a term with specific meaning such as *block-busting*, avoid this word used in the sense of *break* or *burst*.

buy When used as a noun meaning a *purchase*, this word is appropriate in all but the most formal writing.

> Those housecoats are an excellent *buy*.

criterion, criteria Despite what you may hear in spoken English, the word *criterion* is singular. *Criteria* is plural although *criterions* may eventually replace it.

> We evaluated the sales assistant by one *criterion*: results.

data Although this word is the plural of the Latin *datum*, it is used in both singular and plural forms except in scientific and technical writing where *datum* is the regular singular form.

> *Business:* This *data* has been verified.
> *Scientific:* This *datum* has been verified.

different from, different than These are used interchangeably in general writing. In formal writing, use *different from* except when it is awkward.

> *Formal:* The invoice was *different from* the estimate.
> *Formal:* The amount of the payment was *different than* he had indicated.

due to Formerly frowned upon in formal writing, *due to* is now used for *because of* and *owing to* in almost all writing.

etc. An abbreviation of the Latin *et cetera*, meaning "and others," "and so forth." To avoid saying *and and others*, don't use "and etc.," merely use *etc.*

> The seminar will consider Theory X, Y, and Z, Planning Systems, Job Enrichment, MBO, PERT/CPM, Positive Reinforcement, *etc.*

farther, further In formal writing, use *farther* to denote distance (remember *far*) and *further* for time or degree.

> The woman who has parked *farther away* from the office has progressed *further* up the company ladder than the one who has parked next door.

hardly, only, scarcely Because these words mean *not quite,* they should not be used with another negative in a sentence because a double negative would result.

> *Casual:* On the job, he doesn't *hardly* (or *scarcely*) have time to eat.
> *General:* On the job, he *hardly* (or *scarcely*) has time to eat.

hopefully Although acceptable as a sentence adverbial in nearly all writing, this usage irks a few linguistic conservatives. Be aware!

> *Hopefully,* you will realize that this usage may be unacceptable in some 5 to 10 percent of formal writing situations.

imply, infer Well-educated speakers have trouble with this pair, but in writing you *infer* from what someone else has stated, you *imply* in your own statements.

> My tone *implied* my feelings.
> I *inferred* from her remarks that she would ask for a raise soon.

irregardless Acceptable only in casual speech and writing. *Regardless* will suffice.

its, it's These are probably the most troublesome pair in the language. Think before you select one; remember that *it's* is a contraction of *it is. Its* is a personal pronoun.

> *It's* unfortunate that *its* warranty has expired.

like, as In informal writing, *like* is often used for as (He talked *like* a manager should). But in formal situations, realize that many readers may be distracted by your use of the preposition *like* for the conjunction *as* to introduce a clause.

> *Formal:* He acted *as* if he had never received the memo.
> *General:* He acted *like* he had never read the memo.

Don't get so uptight about this construction that you worry yourself into using *as* for *like.*

> *As* a good manager, he praised his subordinates when praise was due.

perfect, unique, round In formal writing, certain absolute adjectives like *perfect, unique,* and *round* should not be used in a comparative or superlative sense. But in general writing, this logical convention may be ignored.

> This is the most unique can opener on the market.

plus This word is frequently substituted for *and* in compound sentences, but the usage should be avoided in formal writing.

> *Informal:* In the department, six people worked full-time *plus* three worked part-time.
> *Formal:* In the department, six people worked full-time *and* three worked part-time.

real This popular intensifying adverb may be used in real informal writing but *very* or *much* should replace it in formal writing.

reason is because, reason is that In nearly all writing situations, *the reason is because* is considered acceptable although it is repetitious (*reason* is implied in *because*). In all situations, you may substitute *the reason is that*; in a few formal ones, readers will prefer this construction.

> *General:* *The reason* he was not hired *is because* he had little experience.
> *Highly formal:* *The reason* he was not hired *is that* he had little experience.

respectfully, respectively These similar words can be confusing. End the minutes of meetings and other formal communications with *respectfully*. *Respectively* means *in the order mentioned*.

> Bill, Jane, and Mitchell spoke for 10, 17, and 9 minutes *respectively*.
> *Respectfully submitted,*

sure and, try and Except in speech and some informal writing, you should be *sure to* change the *and* to *to*.

> *Dangerous:* *Try and* see him before the meeting.
> *Appropriate:* *Try to* see him before the meeting.

these, those kind or sort Use plurals with plurals (*these kinds, those sorts*) or singulars with singulars (*this kind, that sort*).

where In all but highly informal situations, use *that* for *where* in sentences like "He noticed on the bulletin board *that* (not *where*) the meeting was changed to 3 p.m."

Mechanics

The word *mechanics* as used here does not refer to the people who work on cars or to the scientific study of motion and forces. It refers instead to the processes used in writing: abbreviation, capitalization, numbers, punctuation, underlining (italics), and spelling.

ABBREVIATION

Avoid abbreviations unless you are certain they are normally accepted. A form of shortcut, they indicate your feeling that the complete word is unnecessary; so you risk being discourteous to readers. Stay on the safe side by using abbreviations only in the following conventional situations:

1. For common titles

   Mr. William North   Ms. Clark   Dr. Lavelle

2. For family, academic, or religious designations following names

   Milton May, Jr.   Joseph Morgan, Ph.D.   Sister Teresa, O.S.M.

3. For dates and times

   541 B.C.   8:23 a.m. (sometimes A.M.)

4. For certain businesses, organizations, countries

   IBM   YMCA   TV   USSR   WHAS-TV   U.N.

5. For acronyms (words made from the initial letters of long titles)

   NOW (National Organization of Women)   OPEC   SALT

6. Scientific terms

   45 mph   375 rpm   3000 kwh

7. Certain Latin terms

   e.g. (*exempli gratia* = for example)   i.e. (*id est* = that is)
   et al. (*et alii* = and other people)   etc. (*et cetera* = and others, and so forth)

   viz. (*videlicet* = namely)   vs. (*versus* = against)

If you have any doubts about the spelling, capitalization, or punctuation or abbreviations (periods or not?), consult your dictionary.

In sentences, abbreviations should be avoided in the following instances:

- Names of persons, places, months, days, and units of measure:
  On Thursday, May 2, she weighed 112 pounds on the scale at Boulder, Colorado.
- Words such as *street, avenue, boulevard,* and *company* that are used like proper nouns:
  He took the bus on Madison Avenue to the Whitson Company.
- United States should be abbreviated only when used as an adjective:
  People outside the United States are concerned about the U.S. economy.

CAPITALIZATION

Capitals confer distinction. So in an age when there may appear to be relatively few people deserving of distinction and in a country where relatively few distinctions among people are observed, capitals are somewhat rare. In addition to their obvious use as sentence openers and for proper nouns, days, holidays, months, countries, and religious names and terms, use capitals for the following:

1. The complete names of particular companies, organizations, geographical places, and the like: Warner Communications, National Council of Teachers of English, Cumberland River, the Hyatt Hotel, University of Illinois.
2. Names of people, races, religions, languages: the French, Caucasian, Baptists, Latin. Usually the word *black* is not capitalized (black leaders) although it may be when used with another capitalized word (Black English).
3. Historical periods, documents, events: World War II, the Age of Enlightenment, the Declaration of Independence.
4. Adjectives formed from proper nouns: Texas businessman, Jewish leader, Mideastern oil, American exports.
5. Titles of people with their names, but not their offices alone: the speaker of the House is referred to as Speaker O'Neill. The president of the University of Kentucky is President Singletary. However, when referring to the President of the United States or some other cabinet member, use capitals: The President met yesterday with his Secretary of State. Within individual companies, often titles and offices are capitalized: He was the Manager.
6. Regions: the Southwest, the North; but not directions, such as drive north. Capitals are being used less frequently when adjectives are formed from the names of regions: southern fried chicken, western coal.
7. Titles of books, articles, films, television programs, reports, and the like are capitalized except for articles (*a, an, the*), prepositions, and conjunctions. But these should be capitalized if they come first or last, or if they exceed five letters: *Economics Through the Years in Plain English,* "All You Wanted to Know about Wall Street and Were Afraid to Ask," "A Way to Get By."

8. Abstract nouns when personified, particularly for emphasis: Big Business looked to Accelerated Depreciation for help.
9. After a colon only if what follows is a complete sentence that should be emphasized.

> The sales figures were astonishing: over three hundred units a day.
> He remembered the prediction: "Bond yields will reach 21 percent before decreasing."
> The first-quarter loss was devastating: Sales dropped 83 percent.

Avoid unnecessarily capitalizing the seasons (winter, spring), and *the* in the name of newspapers, magazines, and reference works (the St. Louis *Post-Dispatch*).
Once again, when in doubt, consult your dictionary.

Numbers

In business writing, figures speak louder than words. You can understand this readily by realizing that the number 17, for example, stands out in this sentence because it looks different from the words around it. And because numbers are so important in business, figures are used to emphasize them and to enable readers to locate them easily on a page. The standard practice is to follow newspaper style: spell out the first nine. But from then on, everything is so complicated that it would be best for you to check this section:

1. At the beginning of a sentence, always spell out numbers. Sometimes you may wish to revise the sentence to avoid beginning with a number.
   Fifty-four women reported for work last week.
   Last week 54 women reported for work.

2. In writing numbers over a million, generally apply the spell-out-below-10 rule.
   six million   10 billion

3. Percentages and sums of money are usually expressed in figures.
   6 percent   5 cents $6
   Sums in the millions and billions take the hybrid form.
   $9 million $5.2 billion

4. Dates, times, measurements, pages, chapters, decimals, and stock and bond prices are expressed in figures.
   5 May 1981   6:10 p.m.   p. 6   chapter 9   .2 inches
   US Steel gained 2 points.   a 6-foot desk

5. For fractions, use the spell-out-under-10 rule or the hybrid form when the fraction cannot be spelled out in two words.
   three-quarters of an inch   39½ years
   one-twentieth   15 two-hundredths

6. Be consistent by presenting several numbers and figures all as figures.
   Original: He bought two reams, 16 pens, and five pads.
   Revised: He bought 2 reams, 16 pens, and 5 pads.

7. In writing about two kinds of quantities, express one in words and one in figures for clarity.
   He ordered 30 three-quarter-inch tapes.
   He bought six packages of 3″ × 5″ cards.

8. For addresses, use figures unless it is customary to spell out a word.
   116 West 9th Street   17 Fifth Avenue

9. Except in legal documents, ye olde practice of repeating numbers in words is extinct.
   Obsolete: We shipped you 60 (sixty) gross.

10. Spell out ordinal numbers of one or two words. Use *-st, -nd, -rd,* or *-th* with other numbers and dates.
    fifth package   3rd of May   151st item   twenty-first floor

In punctuating large numbers, set off groups of three from the right with commas (23,951) except in such obvious instances as years, streets, telephone numbers, serial numbers, zip codes, and so forth.

Punctuation

End punctuation communicates a meaning to readers about the sentence—complete or fragmentary—that they have just read. Obviously? No, not so obviously. But, somewhat obviously! Let's look quickly at these three marks of end punctuation: periods, question marks, and exclamation marks.

Periods

You should have little trouble with remembering to use a period at the end of a sentence or after most abbreviations: *We shipped the package C.O.D.* (Note that only one terminal period is used.) But you may be uncertain about using periods after indirect questions and requests:

> He wondered how I would ship the package. (indirect question)
> Will you please try to attend. (request, not a question despite question form)

Question Marks

Obviously, question marks come after questions. But not quite so obvious is the use of a question mark to indicate uncertainty about factual information. Also puzzling to some are the ways to punctuate with question marks in special situations:

On May 15 (?), 19--, the recoverable coal reserves were estimated at 117 billion tons.

"How will the merger affect us?" I was asked. (no comma is used with the question mark)

"The sales increase—or should we call it *surge?*—was caused by the special rebate program." (question within a sentence)

Exclamation Marks

Use exclamation marks sparingly, saving them for interjections, commands, and strong statements:

Oh! We forgot to mention our guarantee. (interjection)
And it won't cost you a penny! (strong statement)
Be certain to lock the door when you leave! (command)

Note the different effect created by the three marks of end punctuation:

Will you finish the report by May 3. (request)
Will you finish the report by May 3? (question)
Will you finish the report by May 3! (command)

Overuse of exclamation marks is like too much yelling; both decrease in effectiveness. So, use these punctuation marks with restraint!

The Comma

Of all punctuation marks, the most difficult to master is the comma. The reasons are many. Sometimes writers must decide whether inserting a comma will help readers or not. Sometimes conventions about commas change: these punctuation marks, for example, are now used less often than they were years ago. And sometimes, we must admit, the conventions are confusing, requiring some study and thought, a commitment many writers are unwilling to make about punctuation.

You can master the comma if you realize that it essentially performs three functions: to introduce, to separate, and to enclose. But you need to know what it introduces, separates, and encloses.

COMMA TO INTRODUCE Commas help readers by separating introductory clauses, phrases, transitions, and interjections from the main sentence elements. Read the following sentences word for word and note how the absence or presence of a comma can change the meaning:

After the first job he had . . .
After the first job, he had . . .

The comma transmits signals to your mind, preparing you for what follows:

After the first job he had, he decided to return to college.
After the first job, he had to change his résumé.

But some authorities allow discretion with the introductory comma. If the phrase or clause is short and the meaning would be clear without a comma, they advise omitting it. But what is *short?* No one ever states. We think it's easier and more consistent to use commas after all introductory elements:

If you have not filed a W-4 Form, you must do so. (clause)
In this way, we can withhold your federal tax. (phrase)
In addition, you must file a state K-4 form. (transition)
Oh, you must submit new forms if you have a child. (interjection)

Note in the last example (and in this sentence) that no comma is normally used when a clause appears at the end of the sentence.

COMMA TO SEPARATE   Commas are used to separate (1) words, phrases, and clauses in a series; (2) the clauses in a compound sentence; (3) contrasted elements; and (4) individual items in dates and addresses. Although these four uses of the comma may sound complex, most are simple.

1. To separate words, phrases, and clauses in a series of three or more

About the only trouble you will have with this convention (*which is stated in a form that illustrates the practice*) is whether to insert the comma before the final *and.* Although usage varies, we recommend doing so because this comma signals the definite pause we make in speaking, and also may clarify a possible ambiguity:

The committee had to nominate a president, vice president, secretary, and treasurer. (four people)

The committee had to nominate a president, vice president, secretary and treasurer. (three people)

A special problem arises with an adjective series. If each adjective individually describes the noun, use commas to separate them. On the other hand, if they modify one another, omit the commas:

The bright red cotton skirts sold quickly. (They were a bright red.)
The bright, red, cotton skirts sold quickly. (They were bright, red and also cotton.)

Look at another set of examples:

They employed an active little old lady for the older customers.
They employed an experienced, intelligent, attractive student for the college shop.

You may apply two tests to determine whether to use commas. If you can sensibly insert *and* between the adjectives (*experienced and intelligent and attractive,* but not *active* and *little* and *old*), use commas. Or, if you can easily reverse the adjectives and have them still sound right (*attractive, intelligent, experienced,* but not *old, little, active*), insert commas. As you can see, you must use some common sense in punctuating an adjective series. But otherwise, a series of three or more words, phrases, and clauses should not trouble you—as this sentence illustrates.

2. *To separate clauses in a compound sentence*

Although you may omit the comma when combining short independent clauses with *and, but, or, nor, yet,* you should use it with longer ones. Here's why:

> He forwarded the recommendation to the supervisor and the foreman . . .

At this point, the sentence may logically proceed in either one of two directions, but the absence of a comma suggests that both the supervisor and the foreman received the recommendation. If not, use a comma:

> He forwarded the recommendation to the supervisor, and the foreman . . .

Here are the complete sentences:

> He forwarded the recommendation to the supervisor and the foreman of the shop. (simple sentence)

> He forwarded the recommendation to the supervisor, and the foreman was never notified. (compound sentence; use comma to separate clauses)

If you have trouble with this separating comma, try to visualize this diagram:

independent clause	+	,and ,but ,or ,nor ,yet	+	independent clause

3. *To separate contrasted elements*

Commas are supposed to help writers, not make writing more difficult. This statement illustrates how a comma separates and contrasts two ideas. Interested college students, not uninterested ones, will particularly note this use of the comma.

4. *To separate geographical names, dates, and addresses*

> The new general hospital in St. Petersburg, Florida, will open June 15, 1982. The mailing address will be 1100 Park Street, N., St. Petersburg, FL 33710. (no commas with the zip code)

Some editors omit the comma after *Florida* in the first line. You may follow our preference or your instructor's.

COMMA TO ENCLOSE   Commas are used to enclose words, phrases, or clauses that interrupt the sentence flow, such as parenthetical elements, transitional expressions, words in direct addresses, and the like. These interrupters are enclosed in commas, appearing fore and aft. Most difficult of this crew is the use of the comma with adjective clauses and phrases that merely add parenthetical or nonessential information. Known as nonrestrictive elements because they do not restrict your meaning, these clauses and phrases require some analysis:

> Bill Jones, whom he hired, will report next week. (The clause *whom he hired* provides nonessential or parenthetical information about Bill Jones. Note that it may be omitted from the sentence.)

> The man whom he hired will report next week. (The clause *whom he hired* is essential, telling readers what man will report next week. It is not a parenthetical element. Note that it may not be omitted because it provides important information.)

Sometimes, the presence or absence of the comma affects the meaning of the sentence:

> He gave a bonus to all the agents, who drive their own cars. (He gave a bonus to all the agents. They all drive their own cars.)

> He gave a bonus to all the agents who drive their own cars. (He gave a bonus only to those agents who drive their own cars.)

Note in the first example that the second comma to enclose the nonrestrictive clause becomes a period. And note also that you cannot guess whether to use a comma or not; you must analyze the meaning of the sentence to determine how to punctuate it.

Here are other examples of the enclosing comma:

> The gains, however, were largely attributable to acquisitions. (transition)

> The third quarter, January–March, is usually our slowest. (nonrestrictive appositive; actually a shortened adjective clause identifying something previously named)

> If you don't mind, Bill, I'd appreciate your tackling it. (name in direct address)

> Both revenues and profits, all things considered, were surprisingly high for the period. (absolute construction)

Alas, we must mention one tricky situation that seems to call for enclosing commas but should not have them:

> Drucker's book *Management* is a classic.

No commas should be used to enclose *Management* because it is a restrictive appositive, informing readers which of Drucker's books is a classic. If omitted from the sentence, it would suggest he had not written other books.

If you're still slightly confused about the comma, the most difficult punctuation mark to master, perhaps this capsule review will help you. Use commas to:

Introduce: Beginning clauses and phrases
Beginning transitions and interjections

Separate: Words, phrases, and clauses in a series
Independent clauses in compound sentences
Geographical names, dates, and addresses

Enclose: Nonrestrictive, nonessential adjective clauses and phrases
Transitional expressions
Nonrestrictive, nonessential appositives
Names in direct address

In addition, use commas whenever and wherever it will help readers better understand what you have written. Remember that it's available to help, not hinder you.

The Colon Family

Colons and semicolons baffle many writers. Yet these punctuation marks are simple to master if you understand how they affect readers. The semicolon halts them; it stops them like a traffic light. The colon, somewhat like a stop sign, merely causes readers to brake momentarily, then move forward again to something ahead: a list, an explanation, or another idea. Here's how they work:

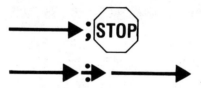

THE SEMICOLON   Generally, the semicolon substitutes for a period to separate short, related sentences:

On Tuesday, Bill White was fired; on Thursday, Tom Snyder was hired.

He could not report for work immediately; however, he started to draw his salary. (Remember that transitional adverbs like *however* cannot join independent clauses, but require a period or semicolon.)

The semicolon is especially effective in setting off a contrast and in helping to shorten a parallel construction by allowing the omission of an otherwise repeated verb:

Software piracy was insignificant five years ago; today it is a major problem. (semicolon for contrast)

Two years ago, our annual dividend payout totalled 60¢ a share; last year, 70¢. (semicolon allows for omission of parallel elements)

The best piece of advice about the semicolon is to remember that it substitutes for the period. But, as you might expect, there is an exception to this rule. In a construction containing a series with internal modifiers, a semicolon can unravel any confusion caused by the string of commas:

> *The problem:* She invited Dick, the office manager, Bill, Tom, Mike, Ray, the shipping clerk, and Mary Lou to the luncheon. (six people or eight?)

If Dick is the office manager and Ray the shipping clerk, then the semicolon can rescue the writer:

> *The solution:* She invited Dick, the office manager; Bill; Tom; Mike; Ray, the shipping clerk; and Mary Lou to the company luncheon. (Note that semicolons must be used throughout.)

Except for its special use to separate elements not clearly divided by commas, the semicolon should be inserted only where you would use a period.

THE COLON The semicolon stops readers; the colon causes them to pause, anticipating the following: a list, a quotation, an appositive, or an explanatory independent clause. Here are some examples:

> The following fixed-income securities are recommended at this time: U.S. Treasury bonds and notes, U.S. Treasury Bills, commercial paper, short-term corporate bonds, and long-term municipals. (A list is often signaled by some form of the verb *follow*.)

> The words of TRB (Richard Strout) are pertinent: "Every child born in America can hope to grow up to enjoy tax loopholes." (quotation)

> For you, we recommend the one that will produce the greatest tax advantage: the percentage depletion. (an appositive)

> Tax investments are not suitable for all investors: mainly those in the 49 percent tax bracket or higher derive full tax benefits. (explanatory independent clause)

Of course, the colon is also used in such special situations as a biblical source (Psalms 12:2–3), the salutation in a business letter (Dear Mr. Rader:), time reference (6:10 p.m.), and titles and sub-titles (*Persuasive Communication: Keys to Successful Selling*).

Dashes and Parentheses

These two marks of punctuation function like commas to enclose and separate ideas. But the dash (typed as two hyphens --) does so in a striking, showy manner that shrieks for the reader's attention. That may be why—and this is only a speculation—the dash is used mainly in informal writing, where some yelling every now and then may be helpful in gaining and maintaining the reader's attention. But use dashes sparingly because too much shouting is annoying. Save them for special occasions: to pound a point home, to insert an emphatic remark, to spring a surprise.

Another instance of the dash's effective substitution for the comma occurs when an introductory series needs to be set off from the appositive or summary reference that follows:

Tuition, endowment, patient fees, federal and state aid—none of these keeps pace with rising costs.

Except for this special situation, save the dash—hoard it, we might say—for occasions needing a touch of color or a change of pace. Certainly you should use it in informal writing—but sparingly.

Sometimes a whisper is as effective as a shout. Like a whisper, parentheses suggest intimacy, imply something personal, hint at the secretive nature of the statement. You can take the reader into your confidence (only if you wish, of course) by using parentheses occasionally.

In addition, parentheses are used to enclose figures or letters used with a series:

Offices can be made safer in three ways: (1) appoint a safety director, (2) conduct regular safety inspections, and (3) encourage the reporting of safety hazards.

Sometimes only the second half of the parentheses is used: 1) appoint a safety director.

Punctuating sentences with parentheses is not simple. Remember that commas, especially commas (but periods sometimes also), come after the parentheses. (If a complete sentence is enclosed in parentheses, the period belongs inside.)

Quotation Marks

You will probably have little occasion in business writing for quotation marks, but you should know that they are used to enclose dialogue or quotations, titles of short literary and creative works (articles, chapters, short stories, poems, songs, and single television programs), and words that are defined and their definitions:

"Anyone who discriminates against waterbeds is unfair," said a large furniture manufacturer. "People who own waterbeds today," he continued, "aren't the kind of hippie types who owned them ten years ago." He referred to the buyers of today as "quality people." (dialogue)

A chapter well worth reading before working on your tax return is "24 Safe Deductions." (chapter of a book)

An "arbitrator" is defined as "an impartial person chosen to settle a dispute." (*arbitrator* may also be underlined [italicized] as may the definition)

What is also important to note is that commas and periods are ALWAYS placed inside the quotation marks unless you are writing in England. Remember: don't think, place them inside always.

The Apostrophe

The apostrophe is slowly disappearing from the language. But while it lingers, you should master it. Most difficulties with this punctuation mark occur in these five situations:

1. The apostrophe for missing letters or numbers

People have little trouble with contractions like *can't*, *don't*, and *shouldn't*, using an apostrophe to signal missing letters. But three contractions give students fits:

it's = it is   let's = let us   who's = who is

This troublesome trio looks harmless enough here. But they have a habit of transforming themselves into *its*, *lets*, and *whose* in student writing. So *let's* try to remember that *it's* about time to see *who's* going to master this threesome.

Often the apostrophe is used to indicate omitted numbers: the '80s, the Class of '73.

2. The apostrophe with singular and plural possessives

Generally, use an 's with singular nouns and just an apostrophe after plural nouns:

secretary's chair   manager's rule   worker's benefits

But when *s* sounds precede or follow the 's in the singular, the *s* is often dropped:

Kansas' wheatfields   for goodness' sake

Words with plural meanings that do not end with *s* add an 's:

women's movement   men's room   children's rights

Note that these so-called possessives do not always show or indicate ownership. Actually the word *possessive* is used loosely, meaning a relationship that can be expressed in an *of* phrase. When in doubt try the substitution test:

dollar's worth (worth of a dollar)
six months' vacation (vacation of six months)

Compound possessives (*son-in-law's*, *someone else's*) add the 's only to the last word.

3. The apostrophe for plurals

The plurals of letters, numbers, and abbreviations are usually formed with an apostrophe, although this practice is changing:

four C's or Cs   three par 3's or 3s   ABC's or ABCs

4. The apostrophe in proper names

Follow the practice of a particular business or organization in determining whether to use an apostrophe in its title. Some communities have a Merchants' Bank, others a Merchants Bank. Some have a Teachers College that grants masters degrees, others a Teacher's College that grants a master's degree. Yours is not to question why but to follow the established form.

5. The apostrophe with double possessives

There's a strange language construction known as the double possessive or genitive that defies logic but troubles few. It uses both the *of* and the *'s: a friend of the manager's, a client of Bill's.* But hold the line at double possessives; avoid the triples:

> *Poor:*   a friend of the buyer's daughter's
> *Better:* a friend of the buyer's daughter

Hyphen

The little hyphen can cause large headaches. The best way to avoid them is to become acquainted with the following conventions:

1. Use a hyphen to divide a word at the end of a line. But check your dictionary to make certain that you are dividing the word properly and if so, make certain you do not leave only one letter at the end of the line (*e-nough*). Obviously, one-syllable words cannot be hyphenated, and hyphenated words should preferably be divided at the hyphen.
2. Use a hyphen with compound adjectives before a noun but not after: He is a *well-known* executive; He is an executive who is *well known.* But do not place a hyphen after an *ly* adverb: He was a *highly* regarded accountant.
3. Use a hyphen with numbers or with numerical modifiers: They took a *five-day* trip on their *twenty-first* anniversary.
4. Use a hyphen to separate a prefix when the root word is capitalized or when the prefix ends with the same letter that begins the root word: *un-American, anti-Japanese; co-owner, de-emphasize,* but *cooperate.*
5. Use a hyphen with single-letter compounds (*T-shirts*), three-word phrases (*mother-in-law*) and with different words that have similar spellings (*re-cover, recover; co-op, coop*).

Use a dictionary whenever you have the least doubt about whether a word should be hyphenated or not. For example, most people would need help on this one: They held an open house to inform people about their open-end fund and served open-faced sandwiches in an openhanded manner.

If this sentence doesn't open your eyes to the importance of checking on the hyphen in a dictionary, we don't know what will.

Underlining

Because you neither write nor type in italics, this section is headed *underlining* instead of *italics*, the term used in most textbooks.

Underline titles of major works, meaning those that would be listed on a library's card catalog—include books, pamphlets, newspapers, magazines, films, radio and television series—and names of ships and aircraft. When underlining, you may underline the words only or the words and intervening spaces:

> <u>Harvard Business Review</u>   <u>19-- Firestone Annual Report</u>
> <u>Ordinary People</u>   <u>60 Minutes</u>   <u>Queen Mary</u>

Exceptions: sacred writings (the Bible, its books, and parts) and parts of a book (the Preface, the Appendix).

Underline foreign words and phrases that have not become part of our language (check the dictionary):

> <u>laissez faire</u>   <u>cliché</u>   <u>quid pro quo</u>   <u>sine qua non</u>

Underline words when calling attention to them: for emphasis, for definition (optional with quotation marks), for special or unusual instances with words (and also letters and numbers):

> Please let us know by <u>Friday, July 1</u>. (Don't overdo this usage.)
> To <u>sell short</u> is defined as <u>to sell stock you do not now own but plan to own in the future at a lower price.</u>
> She could neither spell nor pronounce <u>Schenectady</u>.
> The typewriter was missing a <u>9</u> and an <u>m</u>.

Spelling

Nothing—but absolutely nothing—can cause you as much trouble and embarrassment in writing as poor spelling. It can cost you a job, promotion, sale, goodwill, favorable reception, customers, clients, admission, high grades—you name it. Why is such undue weight attached to what is generally a perfunctory clerical skill, requiring only a glance at a dictionary? The reason may be that most readers, even the many who spell poorly themselves, can spot misspellings. Also, unlike many other aspects of writing, spelling is obviously either right or wrong. And finally, poor spelling more than any other writing error suggests sloppiness, laziness, indifference—all indicative of an unwillingness to look up a questionable word, learn a few spelling techniques, and master some troublesome words.

Unfair? Yes, decidedly, but who ever said that life or the evaluation of writing was fair? Like it or not, the fact is that if you spell poorly, you had better do something about it.

First realize that one problem is our crazy language. Some words that are spelled the same are pronounced differently: Because he heard the *wind*, he started to *wind* it up. Then there are words that are pronounced alike but spelled differently: *there, their, they're.* Also, some words ought to sound similar but do not. For example, look at the *-ough* family: *bough* (bow), *cough* (kawf), *thorough* (thur-oh), *enough* (enuf) and *through* (throo). George Bernard Shaw's classic joke about English spelling is that his nonsense word *ghoti* should be pronounced *fish.* He explained:

$$
\begin{array}{rl}
gh = & \text{like the gh in cough} = f \\
o = & \text{like the o in women} = i \\
\underline{ti =} & \text{like the ti in nation} = \underline{sh} \\
ghoti = & \qquad\qquad\qquad\qquad\quad \overline{fish}
\end{array}
$$

Yet all the illogicalities and jokes about the spelling of words will change nothing. The language is ours and we're stuck with it. Oh, some modifications are taking place, such as the change from *judgment* to *judgement.* But such shifts are few. So resolve to make the most of a bad deal. First, determine to become a competent speller. Then roll up your sleeves and get started by keeping a written list of the words you misspell. Try to master them by any of the following four techniques:

THE RULES   We'll agree that the rules are difficult and the exceptions numerous. But if your spelling problems stem from one of the following four patterns, then it's easier learning the rule than the correct spelling of numerous words governed by it.

Rule 1. The *ie/ei* pattern

If you have trouble with words like *receive, achieve, yield,* and *brief,* then memorize the simple jingle:

> *I* before *e,*
> Except after *c,*
> Or when sounded like *a*
> In *neighbor* and *weigh.*

i before e	after c	sounded like a
chief	receipt	vein
niece	conceive	freight
yield	deceive	heir

Unfortunately, exceptions abound but you can master most of them by remembering this nonsense sentence:

The *weird foreign financier neither seized* the *ancient sheik* nor made him *forfeit* the *counterfeit* money that he had *leisurely* hidden in the *heights.*

Rule 2. The final silent *e* pattern

If you have trouble knowing what to do about the final *e* before the suffix in such words as *desirable, hoping, sincerely,* and *noticeable,* then learn this rule. Drop the silent *e* when adding a suffix beginning with a vowel. Retain the *e* before a suffix beginning with a consonant:

Suffix with Beginning Vowel	*Suffix with Beginning Consonant*
live + ing = living	live + ly = lively
manage + ing = managing	manage + ment = management
hope + ing = hoping	hope + ful = hopeful

Of course, there are exceptions. Some are words ending in -*ce* and -*ge* (*noticeable, courageous*); others are words that might be confused (*dye* + *ing* = not *dying*, but *dyeing*); and still others are just ornery words that don't like to follow rules (*truly, ninth*). We've packaged most of them in this silly sentence:

The *ninth, awful, outrageous* man was *truly noticeable* cause he was *peaceable* and *courageous* while *duly hoeing* and *dyeing*.

Rule 3. The final *y* pattern

If you have trouble with *y*-ending words like *reply, replies; comply, compliance;* and *attorney, attorneys;* then this rule can help you. It states that when *y* endings are preceded by a consonant, the *y* is changed to *i* before adding any suffix except -*ing*. If it is preceded by a vowel, do not change the *y*. Here are the three situations:

Y *after Vowel*	-*ing Suffix*	Y *after Consonant*
valley, valleys	study, studying	duty, duties
attorney, attorneys	try, trying	try, tries
essay, essays	deny, denying	deny, denies

If you have any trouble with this rule, try to remember the story of the young child who told her mother that she had learned how to make babies in school that day. The apprehensive mother asked, "How do you make babies?" The child replied, "You drop the *y* from *baby* and add *ies*."

Rule 4. The double consonant pattern

If you have difficulty deciding whether to double the final consonant before the suffix in such words as *profit, profited; commit, committed;* and *defer, deferred;* then master this rule. It sounds difficult: When adding a suffix beginning with a vowel to a word accentuated on the last syllable that ends with a single consonant preceded by a single vowel, double the final consonant. But let's break it down into its parts:

1. The word must end in a consonant preceded by a vowel: *jog, run, big.*
2. The word must be accentuated on the last syllable. So all one-syllable words are included.
3. The suffix must begin with a vowel: -*ing, -ed, -er, -est, -able, -y, -ance, -ence, -ess, -ary, -ery.*

Words ending in a single consonant preceded by a single vowel	Accent on last syllable	Suffix	Word
stop	yes	ed	stopped
occur	yes (oc-CUR)	ing	occurring
benefit	no (BEN-e-fit)	ed	benefited
mean	no (double vowel)	meaning	meaning

The rule is difficult but the exceptions are few: two of the most common are *reference* and *preference* because the accent shifts when the suffix is added as it does not in *referred* and *preferred*.

PRONUNCIATION The rules can help in many instances. In others, correct pronunciation can assist you. Check your habitual misspellings in the dictionary to determine whether you are pronouncing the words right. For example, if *familiar* is on your list, the dictionary will point out that it should have two *i*'s by the pronunciation of *fa-mil-yar*. Similarly, you will be able to master such common troublemakers as *sophomore* (pronounced *soph-o-more*) and *disastrous* (pronounced *dis-as-trous*).

Correct pronunciation will help you with many words but not all. For example, few people utter the *a* in *temperament* or the first *r* in *February*. Face the facts: some words are not pronounced as they are spelled. But many are. Learning to pronounce words correctly helps often but not always.

DERIVATIVES AND ETYMOLOGY Knowing the family members of a word may help you master its spelling. If you are stumped between *existence* or *existance*, then discovering that its parent was the Latin *existera* may solve your dilemma forever. Some other family members, or derivatives as they are called, can suggest the proper spelling. You should not be troubled with *proceed* if you relate *proceeding* to it. *Practical* helps you with *practice*, *grammatical* with *grammar*.

MNEMONIC DEVICES The most effective way to memorize the spelling of a troublesome word is to associate the part that puzzles you with something that will suggest the proper choice of letters. Few words stump you completely; usually you know all the letters except whether to use an *a* or an *e*, a single or double *o*, a *c* or an *s*, or the like. Devise some mnemonic device, the sillier the better, that will enable you to remember the key letter. Here are some we suggest to our students:

accommodations Most people wishing accommodations are couples. Remember the two *c*'s and two *m*'s.

embarrass It would be embarrassing not to wear two shoes to class. Remember the two *a*'s, *r*'s, and *s*'s.

loose Loose as a goose.

maintenance Proper maintenance costs *ten* dollars an hour.

separate	This commonly misspelled term is A RAT (sep-*a-rat*-e) of a word.
studying	Studs do little studying.
tragedy	People rage in *trage*dy.
undoubtedly	Undoub*tedly* Ted is right.

Have your own fun and games with words you consistently misspell. You'd be surprised how quickly these mnemonic devices can cure your spelling headaches.

In addition to these four techniques—rules, pronunciation, derivatives and etymology, and mnemonic devices—we will give you two lists of words to study. The first contains homonyms (words sounding the same but spelled differently) and other, words often confused. The second list contains the most commonly misspelled words in the language. If you have spelling problems, you should test yourself repeatedly on these words, preferably by writing several spellings on one side of a card and the correct one on the other. Then go through your pack time and time again, weeding out the ones you know, until you have mastered them all. Only by self-testing in this manner (or by having someone test you) can you know whether you have learned to spell the words correctly.

Homonyms and Confusing Words

accept, except	*Accept* Churchill's statement that democracy is the worst system devised by the wit of man, *except* for all the others.
advice, advise	Let us *advise* you that *advice* rhymes with *ice*.
affect, effect	*Effect* is usually a noun preceded often by *the*: The effect; *Affect* is always a verb. How does the *effect* *affect* you?
allusion, illusion	An *allusion* refers to something that exists; an *illusion*, to something that a person wrongly believes to exist.
brake, break	There was a *break* in the lining of his *brake*.
canvas, canvass	We will *canvass* even the people in the *canvas* tents.
capital, capitol	Use *capitol* for Washington and buildings used by state legislatures; use *capital* for other cities and for wealth.
choose, chose	He will *choose* this one today even though he *chose* that one yesterday.
cite, site	He could not *cite* the report that recommended that *site*.
complement, compliment	*Complement* completes; *compliment* praises.
council, counsel	The faculty *council counseled* her to re-apply.
desert, dessert	There are more *s*'s in *dessert* because we would rather have more desserts than deserts.
eminent, imminent	The *eminent* statesman was due *imminently*.

later, latter	The *later* person is late; the last one mentioned is the *latter*.		

later, latter — The *later* person is late; the last one mentioned is the *latter*.

lead, led — *Led* is the past participle and past tense of *lead*; use *lead* for the metal and the present tense (pronounced *leed*).

loose, lose — You can *lose* a *loose* necklace.

passed, past — We *passed* a marker of the *past* accident. *Past* is used only as a noun or adjective.

personal, personnel — Some of the files in the *Personnel* Department are marked *"Personal."*

principal, principle — *Principal* can be remembered as either the head of a school (your *pal*) or the money owed (to your *pal*, perhaps). *Principle* is a law or doctrine. A fine *principle* is to heed the *principal*.

stationary, stationery — Remember that *stationEry* includes *Envelopes*. *StationAry* refers to being in A fixed place.

their, they're, there — *They're* standing over *there* by *their* house.

weather, whether — *Whether* we will have stormy *weather* today is questionable.

whose, who's — I wonder *who's* kissing her now in *whose* room? Remember that the apostrophe stands for a missing letter (who's = who is).

And here are some words not covered previously that trouble many people. Pay particular attention to the tricky italicized letter(s):

abs*e*nce	cour*t*esy	independ*e*nt	privi*l*ege
accident*ally*	de*cis*ion	interest	*p*sycho*l*ogy
a*c*ross	defi*n*ite	knowle*d*ge	repe*t*ition
add*r*ess	describe	l*ei*sure	recom*m*end
analy*z*e	disa*pp*oint	library	relev*a*nt
anx*i*ous	discipline	marr*i*age	resta*u*r*a*nt
arg*u*ment	divine	mathematics	schedule
bene*fi*cial	empha*size*	michi*evo*us	secre*t*ary
brilli*a*nt	exa*gg*erated	mi*ss*pell	speech
business	excellent	mor*t*gage	suc*c*eed
calend*ar*	fin*a*lly	mus*c*le	sur*p*rise
category	*f*orty	nick*el*	ta*riff*
colu*m*n	fund*a*mental	oc*c*asion	tendency
com*m*ittee	government	optimistic	tru*l*y
compe*t*ent	governor	para*ll*el	unti*l*
cons*c*ience	gu*a*rantee	pecul*i*ar	usua*ll*y
cons*ci*entious	hun*gry*	*per*form	valu*a*ble
conv*e*nience	immed*i*ate	pers*ua*de	vege*t*able

One final matter. When Emerson wrote, "Trust thyself," he was not referring to spelling. In that situation, we would suggest just the opposite, "Never trust yourself." Instead, look up every word whose spelling you would not bet five dollars on. To help you do so, follow our practice of keeping a dictionary or spelling book within reach. If it's in a bookcase across the way or in another room, you'll be apt to gamble. If it's within arm's reach, you will probably use it. And you should use it even if you're that unusual person—a good speller.

Remember—the ten minutes you spend checking words can be the most cost-effective time devoted to your paper because nothing—absolutely nothing—is as costly as misspelling.

L Documentation and Library Sources

DOCUMENTATION

In research reports and other communications, it is important for writers to show the sources of their information, ideas, or quotations. Documentation permits readers to verify this material and to obtain additional information if they wish. Sources include not only books, articles, and other printed matter, but interviews, lectures, letters, and radio and television programs. Remember that copyright laws and basic honesty require you to document any material or ideas that you have obtained from someone else's work.

Documentation takes two main forms: endnotes and bibliography. Endnotes, which are rapidly replacing footnotes in almost all books and periodicals, appear at the end of an article, report, chapter, or book, usually under the heading *Notes*. They consist of numbered references identifying sources referred to in the text. In the text itself, material that requires documentation is designated by a number raised slightly above the end of a passage, sentence, or quotation. This raised number always follows punctuation marks, as illustrated here.[1]

Endnote Form

Unfortunately, no single form for endnotes is standard. Form not only varies in different fields, such as economics, accounting, and marketing, but it varies even in different journals in the same field. So when you write for a publication, company, or editor, you should find out the proper form to follow. We will suggest a widely used form here, but if your instructor or employer prefers another, follow that one. The point to remember is that you cannot guess or copy some form from a reference book. You must find out what is required. And you must follow it exactly, noting meticulously every abbreviation, every punctuation mark, and every capitalization. We suggest that you do not memorize a form but open this book (or any good handbook) and imitate the appropriate example.

The standard first reference for a book contains the following information: author, title, publication facts (city, publisher, date), and page number. For example:

[1] Jacquelyn Peake, <u>Public Relations in Business</u> (New York: Harper and Row, 1980), p. 78.

Please note the following:

- The endnote begins with a raised number, which is indented like a paragraph indentation.
- After a space, the author's name appears, first name first. For several authors, see examples on page 461.
- The author entry is separated from the title by a comma, but no comma follows the title.
- The city where the book was published is followed by a colon, then the name of the publisher, a comma, and the year of publication. If several cities are listed on the title or copyright page, use the first. If this city is not well known, add the state (Englewood Cliffs, N.J.:). And if several publication dates are given, use the latest.
- The second line of the endnote is not indented. Endnotes are single-spaced with double spacing between each numbered entry.
- Endnotes end with a period.

There are special endnote forms for different types of books: co-authored books, edited books, anonymous books, and second-edition books. We have provided examples of the special forms on pages 461 and 462.

The standard first reference for an article from a periodical contains the following information: author's name, title of article, title of periodical, volume number, date, page numbers:

² James C. Bennet, "The Communication Needs of Business Executives," The Journal of Business Communication, 8 (Spring 1971), 5–11.

Much of the same advice about the book entry applies also to the article but please note the following:

- The title of the article is placed within quotation marks; the periodical is underlined. Commas separate and enclose each.
- The volume number appears before the date; the page number(s) after. (When a volume number is used, the abbreviation p. or pp. is not used before the page number.)
- The date appears in parentheses. No comma comes before the parentheses.

One major exception: If the periodical is a nationally popular magazine like *Fortune, Business Week,* or *U.S. News and World Report,* no volume number is used but p. or pp. is. In addition, several other changes are made as you will note:

³ Milton Friedman, "An Open Letter on Grants," Newsweek, 18 May 1981, p. 99. (weekly periodical)

⁴ "How to Ask for the Job and Get It," <u>Changing Times</u>, April 1981, pp. 56–58. (no author given; monthly periodical)

As you can see, the date is not placed in parentheses, the day appears before the month, and the abbreviations *p.* and *pp.* are used to stand for *page* or *pages*.

The previous examples and those on pages 461–463 indicate the prescribed form for the first reference to a source. For second and additional citations, merely use the author's last name, a shortened title if there is no author, or both if there are two authors with the same last name:

⁵ Bennet, p. 9. (another reference to article in note 2)

⁶ "How to Ask for the Job," p. 57. (another reference to article in note 4)

⁷ Friedman, "An Open Letter," p. 99. (Assumes that there have been references to two Friedman works. Use of his name alone would not distinguish the particular source.)

⁸ Jacquelyn Peake, p. 120. (Assumes that two writers named Peake have been mentioned in citations. Use of the first name designates the particular source.)

Notes may also contain comments, explanations, and acknowledgments that are not considered important enough to place in the text. Such material should be used sparingly.

Bibliography Form

Although bibliographies are not always used today, you may be called upon to provide one. Usually, bibliographies contain all the sources you have consulted, both those cited and those not cited in the endnotes. In some instances, a bibliography is provided as a list of all the published information about the subject so that readers can consult other sources. In other instances, a bibliography consists of a selective list of the most important sources on the topic. Occasionally, you may wish to use an annotated bibliography, a list of references that includes an evaluation and summary of each.

Here is a standard bibliographical entry for a book:

Peake, Jacquelyn. <u>Public Relations in Business.</u> New York: Harper and Row, 1980.

Note how this entry differs from the endnote entry on page 458:

- It is not numbered, but placed in alphabetical order by the author's last name. In a lengthy bibliography, the sources may be divided into categories (books, periodicals, etc.) and alphabetized in each category.
- No parentheses enclose the publication information.
- Pages are not listed for books.

The bibliographical entry for an article is similar:

Harris, T.E. "Enhancing Listening Effectiveness." Supervision, 42 (October 1980), 3–4.

Note the use of periods after the author's name, the title of the article, and at the end of the entry. For other bibliographical entries, see pages 462 and 463.

One warning about bibliographies: There is a temptation for writers to pad the list in an attempt to impress teachers and other readers. Don't. It is easy for someone with experience to recognize a padded bibliography.

Additional Examples of Endnotes:

Notes

Two Authors

[1] J. Donald Weinrauch and John R. Swanda, Jr. "Examining the Significance of Listening: An Exploratory Study of Contemporary Management," The Journal of Business Communication, 13 (Fall 1975), 25–32.

Comment: Note first names of authors come first. Also observe the use of colon for subtitle. For more than three authors, use the first and *et al.* or *and others* (J. Donald Weinrauch *et al.*).

Author—Commission, Government Agency, Committee

[2] U.S. Commission on Civil Rights, The Excluded Student, Report III (Washington: U.S. Government Printing Office, 1973), p. 54.

Author Unknown or Anonymous

[3] The 1982 Buying Guide Issue of Consumer Reports (Mt. Vernon, N.Y.: Consumer's Union, 1981), pp. 163–165.

Comment: Note use of state abbreviation.

Edition—for Second and Later Editions of a Book

> [4] Michael E. Adelstein and Jean G. Pival, The Writing Commitment, 2nd ed. (New York: Harcourt Brace Jovanovich, 1980), pp. 438–39.

Comment: Note only case of punctuation mark is used before parentheses.

Editor

> [5] W. Keats Sparrow and Donald H. Cunningham, eds., The Practical Craft: Readings for Business and Technical Writers (Boston: Houghton Mifflin, 1978), p. 4.

Articles in Edited Collection of Articles

> [6] Keith Davis, "Making Constructive Use of the Office Grapevine," in Human Relations in Management, eds. I. L. Heckman, Jr., and S. G. Huneryager (Cincinnati: South-Western Publishing Co., 1960), pp. 334–46.

Newspaper

> [7] "World Bank Approves $724 Million of Loans to Three Countries," Wall Street Journal, 15 May 1981, p. 20, col. 1.

Comment: *col.* is the abbreviation for column.

Newsletter

> [8] "A Guide to Good Balance Sheets," Merrill Lynch Market Letter, 27 April 1981, p. 5.

Report

> [9] Annual Report 1981, Firestone Tire and Rubber Co., 1982.

Additional Examples of Bibliographical Entries:
Bibliography

> Adelstein, Michael E., and Jean G. Pival. The Writing Commitment. 2nd ed. New York: Harcourt Brace Jovanovich, 1980.

Comment: Note names of two authors, second edition.

Annual Report 1981. Firestone Tire and Rubber Co., 1982.

The 1982 Buying Guide of Consumer Reports. Mt. Vernon, N.Y.: Consumer's Union, 1981.

Comment: Note this guide is not alphabetized under *the.*

Davis, Keith. "Making Constructive Use of the Office Grapevine." In Human Relations in Management. Eds. I. L. Heckman, Jr. and S. G. Huneryager. Cincinnati: South-Western Publishing Co., 1960, pp. 334–46.

Comment: Note use of the periods after author, article, book of collected articles, editors, and at the end.

"A Guide to Good Balance Sheets." Merrill Lynch Market Letter, 27 April 1981, p. 5.

Comment: This citation would not be alphabetized under *a.*

Sparrow, W. Keats, and Donald H. Cunningham, eds. The Practical Craft: Readings for Business and Technical Writers. Boston: Houghton Mifflin, 1978.

U.S. Commission on Civil Rights. The Excluded Student, Report III. Washington: U.S. Government Printing Office, 1973.

Weinrauch, J. Donald, and John R. Swanda, Jr. "Examining the Significance of Listening: An Exploratory Study of Contemporary Management." The Journal of Business Communication, 13 (Fall 1975), 25–32.

Comment: Note treatment of volume, date, and pages.

"World Bank Approves $724 Million of Loans to Three Countries." Wall Street Journal, 15 May 1981, p. 20, col. 1.

GENERAL REFERENCE WORKS*

Your college library contains many sources of information that can be invaluable to you if you know about them and use them. What follows is a selective list of such

---

* Some information about these sources of business information was obtained from the *University of Kentucky Libraries Subject Guide to Research* and from Ruth Moyer, Eleanour Stevens, and Ralph Switzer, *The Research and Report Handbook* (New York: John Wiley and Sons, Inc., 1981), pp. 167–249.

books and publications that can help you in your business research. Omitted are general sources of information like encyclopedias, almanacs, and indexes in other fields. Instead, we have tried to list only those sources that would be relevant to you in your major. In addition, we have not duplicated sources mentioned elsewhere, such as the works mentioned in chapter 6 that provided information about companies for job-hunting purposes. The following list is divided into these categories: bibliographies, indexes and abstracts, dictionaries and encyclopedias, handbooks and directories, and government publications. Since the reference works listed here merely direct you to the information you need or provide only basic facts, you would not normally refer to the works in your report or document them in your endnotes. For this reason, complete publication information is not customarily given in annotated bibliographies like the following:

Bibliographies

Encyclopedia of Business Information Sources. Wasserman, Paul, ed. 1980.
Bibliography of sources about a variety of subjects of interest to management personnel. References to encyclopedias, dictionaries, indexes, handbooks, periodicals, and other works.

Management Information Guide. 1963 to date.
A series of volumes of annotated bibliographies about subjects of interest to business and professional personnel. Sources are arranged, listed, and described for each topic covered.

The Marketing Information Guide. 1972 to date.
Annotations of selected marketing books and articles. Indexed annually and semiannually.

Public Administration Series: Bibliography. June 1978 to date.
A series of bibliographies about administrative subjects.

Indexes and Abstracts

Accountant's Index. 1921 to date.
Subject and author indexes about accounting articles, books, and pamphlets. An annual publication with quarterly supplements.

Business Education Index. 1939 to date.
An annual subject and author index to articles about business education.

Business Periodicals Index. 1958 to date.
A subject index to about 170 periodicals in accounting, advertising, banking, economics, finance, management, taxation, and related fields. It is issued monthly, appears in cumulative form quarterly, and is bound annually.

Consumers Index to Product Evaluations and Information Sources. 1973 to date.
A general subject index to articles of interest to consumers, businesspeople, and others.

Funk and Scott Index of Corporations and Industries. 1965 to date.
A subject and company index about company, product, and industry information. Compiles articles from over 750 financial publications, business-oriented newspapers, trade magazines, and special reports.

Index to U.S. Government Periodicals. 1974 to date.
An author and subject index to articles in government agency periodicals, such as Monthly Labor Review, Foreign Economic Trends.

Journal of Economic Literature. 1963 to date.
Contains summaries of economic articles and books, which are indexed by subject. Issued quarterly.

Management Research. 1970 to date.
Contains summaries of articles, books, and reports in administration, human factors, and the environment of management. Issued bi-monthly, it has an author and subject index.

New York Times Index. 1851 to date.
A subject index to news stories, features, editorials, and other information in this excellent newspaper, which covers business, financial, and other news. Issued semi-monthly, bound annually.

Newsbank. Indexes. 1980 to date.
Selective index of local news stories in 120 newspapers in all 50 states. Citations are indexed in 13 binders according to subject matter. Of particular interest are binders entitled "Business and Economic Development" and "Consumer Affairs."

Public Affairs Information Service Bulletin. 1915 to date.
A subject index to pamphlets, yearbooks, society publications, government documents, and new legislation

about economic and social conditions. Issued weekly and bound annually.

Topicator. 1965 to date.
Index to articles in periodicals about advertising, communications, and marketing.

Wall Street Journal Index. 1955 to date.
This Wall Street Journal index is divided into two parts: corporate news and general news. Issued monthly and bound annually.

Work Related Abstracts. 1973 to date.
Abstracts from over 200 publications dealing with research and developments in the fields of labor, management, government, and employee relations.

Dictionaries and Encyclopedias

A Dictionary for Accountants. Kohler, Eric L. 1975.
Explanations and definitions of about 2400 accounting terms.

Dictionary of Business and Management. Rosenberg, Jerry M. 1978.
Definitions and explanations of business terms; other general information, such as acronyms, abbreviations, tables of interest, income, and exchange.

Dictionary of Economics. Sloan, Harold S. and Zurcher, Arnold J. 1971.
Definitions and explanations of terms in economics and related areas.

Encyclopedia of Advertising. Graham, Irvin. 1969.
Short definitions of common terms, topics, and phrases in advertising.

Encyclopedia of Management. Heyel, Carl. 1973.
Explanations of basic techniques and concepts of management.

Encyclopedia of Personnel Management. Torrington, Derek, ed. 1974.
Explanations of terms used in personnel management.

Handbooks and Directories

Business Systems Handbook. Haslett, J. W., ed. 1979.
Discusses strategies for establishing and maintaining administrative control.

Consumer Sourcebook. Wasserman, Paul, ed. 1974.
Lists sources available to the consumer, such as government organizations, associations, media services, company and trademark information, and bibliographic information about consumer topics. Includes agencies for consumer complaints.

Directory of American Firms Operating in Foreign Countries. Angel, Juvenal L., ed. 1979.
Provides information about American corporations doing business outside the United States.

Directory of Corporate Affiliations.
List of major corporations showing "who owns whom." Divided into two sections: a list of parent companies, and a list of divisions, subsidiaries, and affiliates.

Financial Analyst's Handbook. Levine, Sumner N. 1975.
Contains information about the principles and procedures used in portfolio management with an analysis of industries.

Government Publications

Guide to U.S. Government Publications. Andriot, John L., ed. 1973 to date.
An annotated guide to current U.S. government publications. Issued at 18-month intervals.

Index to U.S. Government Periodicals. See p. 465.

Monthly Catalog of United States Publications.

Survey of Current Business. U.S. Department of Commerce.
Provides up-to-date information about leading economic indicators, general business indicators, and selected industries.

U.S. Industrial Outlook. U.S. Department of Commerce.
An annual report about the nation's industries with forecasts of industrial activity and performance during the next five years.

# Preparing Visual Aids

Since highly sophisticated visual aids are usually prepared by specialists in graphic arts departments, only simple types that can be easily prepared by students will be discussed here. If you wish to know more, you may read one of the many excellent books on the subject.[1] The purposes of visual aids and guidelines for using them are discussed in chapter 9.

Visual aids may be divided into two types, tables and illustrations. These two general categories may be subdivided as follows:

Tables	**Illustrations**	
Formal tables	Graphs	Drawings
Informal tables	Charts	Photographs
	Maps	

In the following discussion, we will briefly explain how to prepare each of these types of visuals.

TABLES

As seen in table M–1 below, tables show data in two or more rows or columns. The data in the columns are usually numerical, but they are sometimes verbal. You usually read tables from left to right as well as from top to bottom.

Use ellipsis marks (. . .) or dashes (– –) in spaces lacking data. For clarity, you may separate columns with vertical and horizontal lines.

In trying to decide when to use tables or illustrations, you would do well to recall the advice of David E. Fear: "You should use tables when you want the most concise presentation, when you want to present a large amount of information, and when precision is more important than emphasis."[2]

Formal Tables

Formal tables, which are used for complex data, have ruled borders separating them from the text. They are also clearly labeled with figure numbers and short descriptive titles, as seen in table M–1.

Table M-1. A Formal Table.

The Outlook for Selected Occupations Requiring a College Degree

Occupation	Employment '76	Projected Employment '85	Percent Growth '76 to '85
Transportation	146,000	214,400	47%
Health	2,271,500	3,129,700	38%
Social Science	274,000	346,300	26%
Scientific & Technical	2,347,900	2,958,000	26%
Social Service	530,000	646,900	22%
Office Occupations	4,149,000	5,043,300	22%
Art, Design, & Communication	500,500	599,300	20%
Sales	1,407,000	1,699,000	21%
Education & Related	3,516,000	3,734,000	6%

SOURCE: *Occupational Projections and Training Data*, U.S. Department of Labor, Bureau of Labor Statistics, 1979.

Informal Tables

Unlike their formal counterparts, informal tables usually have no table numbers or descriptive titles to identify them and no ruled borders separating them from the text. Although short and simple, they call attention to special information by slowing the reader's pace, as shown above in the second paragraph of this appendix and in chapter 9. You do not always need to refer readers to an informal table because it is usually a natural part of the paragraph; the absence of ruled lines under the column titles helps to make it seem a continuation of the paragraph.

ILLUSTRATIONS

Illustration or *pictorial* can refer to any kind of visual aid except a table. Illustrations include graphs, charts, maps, drawings, and photographs. As with formal tables, illustrations usually have ruled borders, figure numbers, and descriptive titles. But some are treated informally, as seen in chapter 9.

Graphs

Whereas tables present facts and figures, graphs portray them. They are more artful and emphatic, but often less exact in representing minute details.

As a special art form, graphs require more skill and imagination than tables.[3] But you do not have to be a commercial artist to draw acceptable graphs. With a ruler, a compass, a protractor, graph paper, and a little patience, you can draw simple graphs that will enrich your reports.

Bar graphs are especially good for showing comparisons. Although decimal-point accuracy is hard to achieve in such graphs, the various heights of the bars give the reader a vivid impression of the different quantities involved. For presenting specific information, the actual numbers or other pertinent data often appear on the bars, as in figure M–1, an illustration of a simple bar graph. While the same comparison could be shown with horizontal bars, the vertical ones shown here are more popular.

To prepare a bar graph, draw each bar according to the same scale or units (for example, having each quarter of an inch represent $50,000, as in figure M–1). All bars should be the same width and should be divided from one another by equal spaces.

Line graphs, the most widely used, are especially helpful for showing trends over a period of time. You can form the continuous line by connecting points plotted on graph paper according to a scale—time, dollars, percentages, and the like. (For the final draft of the report, trace the graph onto regular typing paper, eliminating the points and grids of the graph paper.) Two or more separate lines, each clearly differentiated from another, can be used for comparisons. Be sure to label the vertical and horizontal axes so that the trend will appear vertically, as seen in figure M–2.

Circle graphs or *pie charts* show how a whole has been divided. After converting each part of your subject into percentages, use a protractor to measure the corresponding wedges in your circle. (Since the 360° circle represents 100 percent, each 3.6° represents one percent.) Typically, you begin with the largest wedge at 12 o'clock and move clockwise toward the smallest. Label wedges clearly and, if appropriate, state the figure or percentage represented by each wedge. Figure M–3 shows a circle graph.

Figure M–1.   A Bar Graph.

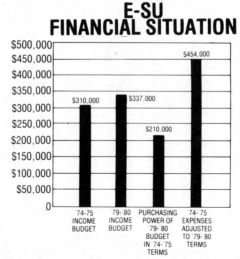

(SOURCE: *The English-Speaking Union News*, 27 [Summer 1980], p. 2.)

Figure M–2. A Line Graph.

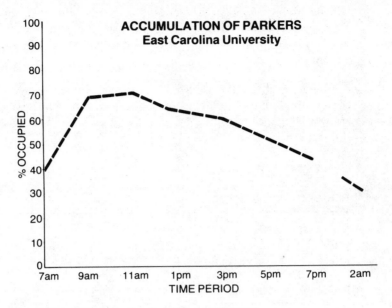

(SOURCE: Chancellor's Office, East Carolina University, 1981.)

Figure M–3. A Circle Graph.

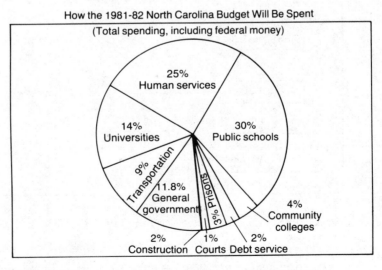

(SOURCE: Reprinted by permission of *The News and Observer* of Raleigh, N.C.)

Charts

Charts are used to diagram a series of movements or organizational structures. They are especially useful in simplifying, clarifying, and condensing the step-by-step procedures of a complicated operation or the ranked relationships in a long chain of command.

Flowcharts illustrate, using boxes or lines connected by arrows, the steps in a complex procedure. Simultaneous steps can be shown by separate boxes and separate arrows. Timing can be noted on or in the boxes or on the arrows. A simple flowchart is illustrated in figure M–4.

Figure M–4. A Flowchart.

REHABILITATION PROCESS

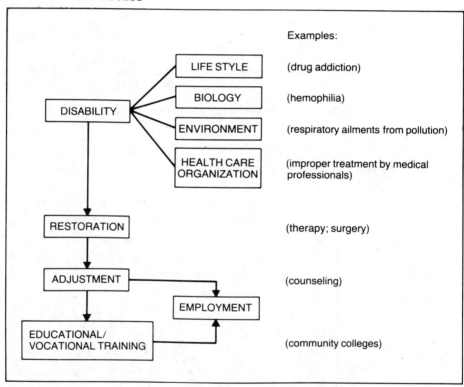

(SOURCE: *Eastern Carolina Health Systems Plan, 1978–83* [Greenville, N.C.: Eastern Carolina Health Systems Agency, 1978], p. 394.)

Organizational charts show the chain of command in an organization and clarify the lines of authority and responsibility. Since no sequence is involved, the names or offices (usually enclosed in boxes) are connected with lines rather than arrows, as shown in figure M–5.

Figure M–5.   An Organizational Chart.

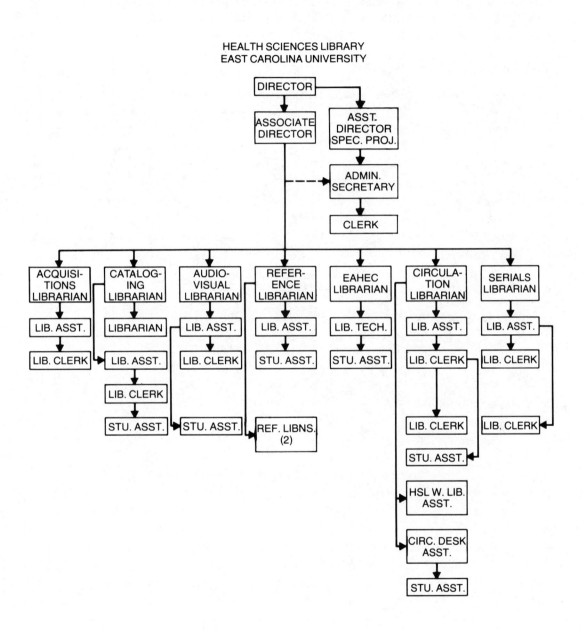

HEALTH SCIENCES LIBRARY
EAST CAROLINA UNIVERSITY

(SOURCE: Reprinted with permission of Jo Ann H. Bell, Director, Health Sciences Library, East Carolina University.)

Maps

Maps show space or conditions related to space. Because they are such familiar illustrations, only a sample will be provided here (figure M–6).

Figure M–6. A Map as a Visual Aid.

MIGRANT HEALTH PROJECT AREAS, HSA VI, 1977

(SOURCE: *Serving Migrant Families*, State Advisory Committee on Services to Migrants, North Carolina, 1977.)

Drawings

Simple drawings, diagrams, and cartoons are usually better than words in helping readers visualize shapes, locations, directions, designs, relationships, concepts, and the like. In drawing such pictures, try to represent proportions accurately and hold details to a minimum. Again, you do not have to be a trained or talented artist to construct basic line drawings. Stick figures and other simple devices will serve the purpose. Note the effective drawing in chapter 10, figure 10–8 ("Location of the trash can in the male restroom of Spilman").

Photographs

Accuracy and dramatic effect are the chief virtues of photographs as visual aids. As seen in chapter 10, figure 10–8, a black-and-white Polaroid photo of a paraplegic trying to drink water from a conventional water fountain can dramatize the need to accommodate handicapped people.

TIPS ON PREPARING VISUAL AIDS

Be consistent with the terminology and numbering you use to label visual aids. As we have done in this book, you may simply use a generic name such as *figure* or *exhibit* to encompass all types of visuals—readers seem satisfied to have no more specific identification. Or, you may differentiate between formal tables and illustrations in identifying each visual according to its type—for example, *table XX* or *Illustration XX*. In longer works, the Arabic numerals used in the identifications are prefixed by the chapter, section, or appendix number (e.g., *figure 9–3*), as has been done in this book. Be consistent in how you position the figure numbers and descriptive titles on your visuals—above, below, or beside the ruled lines.

Prepare your visuals so they will be a credit to your report—simple, clear, neat, attractive, accurate, reliable, and professional. Allow adequate space to prevent crowding. Visuals should be large enough to be easily readable, but not unnecessarily large. Label each column, bar, wedge, or other indicator clearly and accurately. Be sure that all data are in the same units (dollars, pounds, miles, etc.). Use colors, heavy lines, broken lines, shaded areas, or other means to distinguish among different sets of data.

When appropriate, provide keys for abbreviations, codes, symbols, and the like. The key may be provided in a note at the foot of the visual. A slightly raised asterisk [*] or cross [†] may be used to refer the reader to the key.

Cite any sources you used for the data in your visual aid. This citation is usually indicated beneath the visual by the word *Source*, followed by the documentation as shown in table M–1 and in figure M–3.

Notes

¹ The following books provide detailed information about visual aids:

Gibby, J.S. Technical Illustration. 3rd ed. Chicago: American Technical Society, 1969.

Graf, Rudolf F., and George J. Whalen. How It Works Illustrated: Everyday Devices and Mechanisms. New York: Harper & Row, 1974.

Modley, Rudolph, and D. Lowenstein. Pictographs and Graphs—How to Make and Use Them. New York: Harper & Row, 1952.

Philler, Theresa A., Ruth K. Hersch, and Helen V. Carson. An Annotated Bibliography on Technical Writing, Editing, Graphics, and Publishing, 1950–1954. Washington, D.C.: Society of Technical Writers and Publishers; Pittsburgh: Carnegie Library of Pittsburgh, 1966.

Rogers, A.C. Graphic Charts Handbook. Washington, D.C.: Public Affairs Press, 1961.

Turnbull, A.T., and R.N. Baird. The Graphics of Communication. 3rd ed. New York: Holt, Rinehart and Winston, 1975.

² David E. Fear, *Technical Communication* (Glenview, Illinois: Scott, Foresman and Company, 1977), p. 85.

³ To see visual aids transformed into art, note the charts designed for *Time* by Nigel Holmes. The 11 February 1980 (Vol. 115, No. 6) issue highlights Holmes' work on pages 3, 22, 23, 41, and 55.

Copying Machines and Copyright Infringements*

Copying machines have made it easy and inexpensive to reproduce printed works. But copiers have led to a host of abuses—the proliferation of paperwork; the unreasonable distribution of letters, memos, and reports; the sharing of confidential information; the reduction in sales of books, magazines, and journals; widespread plagiarism; and the infringement of copyright laws. As an executive or professional, you should be aware of these abuses and avoid them. Sound judgment in making—and in *not* making—copies is a sign of strong character.

Avoiding one of these abuses—copyright law infringements—requires more than sound judgment: you also need to be familiar with several points of the new copyright law of January 1, 1979. This law, a revision of the original copyright law of 1909, is intended to protect writers and publishers from plagiarism; it gives writers and publishers the right to grant or deny permission to reproduce their work and to require payment for it. If you ignore these rights, you violate the law and are subject to penalties.

The owner of a copyright has five *exclusive rights*, or privileges that *only* the owner can exercise:

1. The right to reproduce the copyrighted work
2. The right to prepare derivative works based upon the copyrighted work
3. The right to distribute copies or phonorecords of the copyrighted work to the public, i.e., printed or recorded material
4. The right to perform the copyrighted work publicly, i.e., musical or choreographic works
5. The right to display the copyrighted work publicly, i.e., works of art

Since these rights are exclusive, they cannot be legally exercised by anyone else unless the copyright owner grants permission. For anyone else to exercise these rights without permission is illegal.

However, the copyright law does recognize a few exceptions. Under its "fair use" provision, it allows you the limited use of copyrighted works for certain purposes, without the permission of the copyright owner. Whether a limited reproduction qualifies as fair use depends on four points.

* Portions of this appendix are based on or quoted from *The New Copyright Law* (Glenview, Illinois: Scott, Foresman and Company, 1979); citations from this work are documented textually by the abbreviation *NCL* and appropriate page numbers.

- The purpose and character of the use, including whether it is for commercial or for nonprofit educational purposes
- The nature of the copyrighted work
- The amount and substantiality of the portion used in relation to the copyrighted work as a whole
- The effect of the use upon the potential market for or value of the copyrighted work

The general language here and the vagueness of the fair use rules mean that there is some latitude in determining fair use. But it is clear that even copies of short passages intended for commercial purposes require permission. And it is very clear that reproduction is forbidden "where the unauthorized copying displaces what realistically might have been a sale, no matter how minor the amount of money involved (NCL, p. 4)."

However, fair use does permit the photocopying of published material under two circumstances: (1) when the copy is used by an individual in private research or study, and (2) when a teacher makes copies for each student in a class (NCL, pp. 4–7).

In at least two instances other than this fair use, the copying of printed works is allowable without the permission of the copyright owner. First, some publications expressly permit free copying; you can usually find this permission stated near the beginning or at the end of a work. Second, U.S. government agency publications can be copied freely. But in neither of these instances should you assume the permission is free unless you see a statement to that effect. You should check to be sure that the permission is clearly stated in the work.

Where the fair use and free copying provisions do not apply, you must obtain written permission before reproducing any extended passage of copyrighted work. The Association of American Publishers, Washington, D.C., suggests that the following information be provided to an author or publisher in your request for permission to copy:

- Title, author and/or editor, and edition of material to be duplicated
- Exact material to be used, giving amount, page numbers, chapters, and, if possible, a photocopy of the material
- Number of copies to be made
- Use to be made of duplicated materials
- Form of distribution (classroom, newsletter, anthology, or the like)
- Whether the material is to be sold
- Type of reprint (ditto, photocopy, offset, typeset, or the like)
- Cost (if any)

Addresses of publishers may be found in *The Literary Marketplace* published by R.R. Bowker Company; a copy of this work may be found in your library.

No matter what form intellectual property appears in—print, film, tape, record, picture, sculpture, or choreography—you should exercise judgment and abide by the law when you use it.

# Writing Your Congressional Representatives

The usefulness of business writing sometimes extends beyond the business world into the political arena. As owner or manager of a small business, or as an employee in a large organization, you may wish to influence representatives and senators about some pending legislation or propose new legislation. Or, as a private citizen, you may wish to express your opinion about such issues as taxes, health care, education, or the environment. If you consider writing to Washington, you might wonder about these matters:

- Should I bother? After all, what difference will one letter make? Do members of Congress read letters? Are they influenced by them?
- What form should such a letter take?
- What strategy is most effective?

Our answers to these questions are based on an article in the *Congressional Record* (123 No. 180, November 3, 1977) by Representative Morris Udall and on information obtained from several administrative assistants of other members of Congress.

The Importance of Congressional Mail

No one can state unequivocally that your letter will make a difference. Members of Congress receive about 150 letters a day, as well as visits from lobbyists, and telephone calls and telegrams from other people. Yet, as Representative Udall writes, "On several occasions a single, thoughtful, factually persuasive letter did change my mind or cause me to initiate a review of a previous judgment."

When you realize that House members and senators may vote on some 500 issues a year, you can understand that they particularly welcome information and opinions about those they know little about. But elected officials are also eager to read mail from home about other matters, especially if the letters are individually written instead of being form letters from lobbying groups. In fact, because of the flood of standardized mail from members of organizations, a thoughtful, well-written, personal letter is a rarity. Most members of Congress read all such letters and may be influenced by them.

The answer to the question—should you write?—is a definite *yes*.

Form

As Appendix *E* illustrates, letters should be addressed like this:
Hon. _____, House of Representatives, Washington, DC 20515;
Senator _____, U.S. Senate, Washington, DC 20510.

If possible, refer to the number of the bill you are writing about; otherwise, describe it by its popular title. Also, if you can, typewrite your letter; if not, be careful to write legibly.

Strategy

Most important is that the letter be brief. Legislators seldom will read more than one page. In this page, you should state the reasons why you favor or oppose a bill, explaining how it will correct some current injustice you suffer from or will impose some unfair burden. Whenever possible, use facts, figures, and examples to inform your readers and to support your opinions.

The tone of your letter should be sincere, courteous, and respectful. Do not threaten, condemn, or engage in name-calling. And avoid any wild claims about your political influence or contributions.

Be certain that you have accurate information about the legislation, and that your letter will arrive while the bill is still in committee or before it reaches the floor for a vote. By writing early, you stand a better chance to influence your representative. But getting an early commitment may be difficult because often bills are amended or modified as new evidence about them comes to light.

By asking specific questions or personalizing your letter in some way, you increase the chances of getting an individual response instead of a form letter.

You vote not only when you cast your ballot in the primaries or the general election, but also when you write to elected officials. On those occasions, you exercise your right to influence our country's decision-makers. Not to do so is to let others determine how your country is run.

Index

Business communications
  defined, 3, 5
  forms of, 16
  importance of, 3–6
  nature of, 2–21
  objectives of, 5
Business terminology, 391–394
Business writing, distinctive characteristics
    of, 13–16
Buzz sessions, 380

C

Campus interviews, 188
Capitalization, 439
Captions, 263
Career objective in résumé, 194
Casual usage for business, 434
Cause and effect approach, 324–325
Channels, 25, 26
  various, advantages and disadvantages of,
    29
Charts, 335, 471
Chronological order, 323
Circle graphs, 470
Claim letters, 133–134, 135
Clarification questions, 371
Clarity of words, 243–244
Classical school, 30
Clauses, types of, 431
Clichés, 330
Close-ended questions, 370–371
Closings, see Complimentary close of letters
Collection letters, 146–156
Collection series
  short, 152–156
  standard, 147–152
  three-letter, 153–156
Collective nouns, 426
Colloquial words, 329
Colon family, 446–447
Colons, 447
Comma splice, 433
Commas, 442–446
  to enclose, 445–446
  to introduce, 442–443
  to separate, 443–444
Common nouns, 426
Communication flow, 31–32

Communication model, 25–26
Communication process, 22–46
  review of, 32–33
Communication situation, 50
Communication theory, application of, 27–33
Communications
  business, see Business communications
  downward, 32
  employment, 192–227
  horizontal, 31–32
  nonverbal, see Nonverbal
    communications
  in operation, 26–27
  price of faulty, 23
  process of, 23–24
  theory of, 25–27
  upward, 32
  written, 29
Company politics, 233–234
Comparison in reports, 326–327
Complex sentences, 120, 432
Complexity, ordering by, 327
Complimentary close of letters, 399
  to public officials, 406–408
Compound-complex sentences, 432
Compound nouns, 426
Compound sentences, 119, 431
Concluding
  group discussions, 377–378
  interviews, 371
  reports, 317, 318
  speeches, 364–365
Conducting meetings, 375–378
Confusing words, 455–456
Congressional representatives, writing, 479–480
Conjunctions, 426
Connotation, 35–36
Consumer protection agencies, 417–423
Contents, table of, 306, 307
Context, word meanings derived from, 36–37
Contrast in reports, 326–327
Convince
  in letters of application, 204
  in sales letters, 99–105
Copy notation in letters, 401
Copying machines, 477
Copyright infringements, 477–478

Personality of writing, 16
Persuasion, ordering by, 327
Persuasive interview, 369
Persuasive letters, 92–131
Peterson, Peter, 291
Photographs, 475
Phrases, 430
 overworked, 331
Pictorials, 335, 469
Pie charts, 470
Pitch of voice, 353
Plan
 of organization of report, 314
 of this textbook, 17
Planning
 for interviews, 370
 for meetings, 373–374
 for writing, 11
Politics, company, 233–234
Poor risks, 147
Position in writing, 162–163
Positive wording, 157
Post office services, special, 412
Postal mailing information, 409–412
Postscripts in letters, 402
Posture in speaking, 354
Précis, 306
Preliminaries, report, 301–306, 307–308
Prepositional phrase, 430
Prepositions, 426
Present perfect tense, 429
Present tense, 428
Presentation, oral, *see* Oral presentations
Problem people, dealing with, 376
Problem-solving interview, 369
Problem statement in reports, 326
Procedure manuals, 278, 282
Progress reports, 265, 268, 269–270
Promotion, qualities important for, 4
Pronoun agreement, 220–221
Pronoun case, 218–220
Pronoun *I, see I*
Pronoun reference, 218
Pronouns, 218–221, 427
 first-person, 291–292
 personal, 218–220, 328–329, 427
Pronunciation, spelling and, 454
Proofreading, 12–13
Proper nouns, 426
Protection agencies, consumer, 417–423

Provinces, official two-letter abbreviations
 for, 404
Public officials, addresses and salutations
 and closings to, 406–408
Publications, government, 467
Published announcements of jobs, 189
Punctuation, 441–450
Purpose
 need to consider the, 27–28
 of report, 309
 for writing, 13–14

Q

Qualities important for promotion, 4
Question marks, 441–442
Questioning interviewees, 370–371
Questionnaires, 286, 289–290
Questions
 arrangement of, 286–287
 clarification, 371
 close-ended, 370–371
 direct, 370–371
 hypothetical, 371
 open-ended, 371
 rhetorical, 361–362
 types of, 387–388
Quick replies, 57, 59
Quick responses, 232–233
Quotation marks, 448

R

Raglan, Lord, 23
Random sampling, 285
 stratified, 285–286
 systematic, 285
Rate of speed of voice, 353
Readability, 293–294
Reader adaptation, 14
Reader-adaptation checklist, 15
Reading speeches, 356
Receiver, 26
 importance of the, 27
Recommendation, letters of, 69–71
Recommendation reports, 275, 278, 279–281
Recommendations of report, 317, *319*

Transitions (*continued*)
  natural, 334–335
  paragraph and division, 335
  sentence, 332–335
Transitive verbs, 428
Transmittal, letters of, 302, 304

U

Ultimatum, 151–152
Underlining, 451
Upward communications, 32
Urgent appeals, 150–151
Usage, 433–434

V

Valenti, Jack, 360
Value cluster, economic development, 4
Van de Ven, Andrew, 380
Verb-noun combinations, avoiding sluggish, 116–117
Verb-subject agreement, 76–78
Verbs, 114–117, 427–430
  selecting lively, 115–116
Visual aids, 335–338
  preparing, 468–475
  in speeches, 363–364
  tips on preparing, 475
Visual devices in writing, 161
Visuals, 335
Vividness of writing, 329–332
Voice
  active, 117–118
  passive, 158–161
Voice in speaking, 352–354
  qualities of, 39
Volume of voice, 353

W

We, using, 291–292
Weaver, Warren, 25

Welcoming to interviews, 370
White, E. B., 250
Who/whom problem, 219–220
Wise, Paul S., 360
Word meanings
  derived from context, 36–37
  in mind of user, 35–36
  no fixed or universal, 34–35
Word processing, 413–414
Wordiness, 246–253
Wording
  courteous, 157
  inoffensive, 156
  positive, 157
  strong, 163–165
Words
  clarity of, 243–244
  colloquial, 329
  confusing, 455–456
  in disagreeable letters, 156–157
  first-person pronouns, 291–292
  formal, 329
  informal, 329
  natural, 71–75
  naturalness in, 328–332
  pronouns, 218–221
  selection of, 71–76
  specific, 75–76
  as symbols, 34
  verbs, 114–117
Work experience in résumé, 194–195
Writing, 7, 11
  business, *see* Business writing
  congressional representatives, 479–480
  economical, 16
  mechanics in, 438–457
  minutes of group discussions, 378
  myths about, 8–13
  reports, 261–264
  significance of, 7
  vividness of, 329–332
Written communication, 29

Y

You attitude, 124–125